ESSAYS
OLD AND NEW

Edited by
ESSIE CHAMBERLAIN
Oak Park and River Forest Township High School
Oak Park, Illinois

REVISED AND ENLARGED

HARCOURT, BRACE AND COMPANY

New York   *Chicago*

3581

CONTENTS

HOW THIS BOOK WAS MADE xiii

A NOTE TO TEACHERS xvi

A WORD TO STUDENTS xix

INTRODUCTION xxi

    I.   THE ESSAY DEFINED xxi

    II.   THE ESSAY FURTHER DEFINED xxii

    III.   CHARACTERISTICS OF THE ESSAY xxiii

    IV.   THE ESSAY RESEMBLES CONVERSATION xxvii

    V.   THE SUBJECT MATTER OF THE ESSAY xxviii

    VI.   HISTORY OF THE ESSAY xxx

    VII.   RELATION OF THE ESSAY TO OTHER LITERARY
           FORMS xxxv

    VIII.   TYPES OF ESSAYS xxxv

AN APOLOGY FOR IDLERS   *Robert Louis Stevenson*   3

AES TRIPLEX   *Robert Louis Stevenson*   15

THE STRENUOUS LIFE   *Theodore Roosevelt*   25

TRAITS OF INDIAN CHARAC-
   TER   *Washington Irving*   33

A DISSERTATION UPON
   ROAST PIG   *Charles Lamb*   46

SAINT JOAN OF ARC   *Mark Twain*   56

ON UNANSWERING LETTERS   *Christopher Morley*   68

WHAT MEN LIVE BY   *Christopher Morley*   73

ON DOORS   *Christopher Morley*   77

A KITTEN   *Agnes Repplier*   80

OXFORD AS I SEE IT   *Stephen Leacock*   91

A, B, AND C — THE HUMAN
   ELEMENT IN MATHE-
   MATICS   *Stephen Leacock*   103

THE NEW FREEDOM	*Woodrow Wilson*	109
EVERY MAN'S NATURAL DESIRE TO BE SOMEBODY ELSE	*Samuel McChord Crothers*	120
INDEPENDENCE	*Rudyard Kipling*	133
THE MAGIC RING	*Kenneth Grahame*	145
BOATING	*Oliver Wendell Holmes*	158
AMERICAN AND BRITON	*John Galsworthy*	166
MY SILENT SERVANTS	*John Kendrick Bangs*	179
WHERE I LIVED AND WHAT I LIVED FOR	*Henry David Thoreau*	189
THE ART OF PROCURING PLEASANT DREAMS	*Benjamin Franklin*	206
MARY WHITE	*William Allen White*	213
SELF-RELIANCE	*Ralph Waldo Emerson*	220
THE GREAT AMERICAN GAME	*William Lyon Phelps*	233
THE MISSISSIPPI	*Lafcadio Hearn*	243
NEW ORLEANS	*Lafcadio Hearn*	247
THE ROMANTIC IN THE RAIN	*G. K. Chesterton*	251
ON RUNNING AFTER ONE'S HAT	*G. K. Chesterton*	255
TRANSLATING LITERATURE INTO LIFE	*Arnold Bennett*	260
POSSESSIONS	*E. V. Lucas*	266
TELEPHONICS	*E. V. Lucas*	270
A MESSAGE TO GARCIA	*Elbert Hubbard*	275
LANDFALLS AND DEPARTURES	*Joseph Conrad*	281
OF RICHES	*Francis Bacon*	292
OF STUDIES	*Francis Bacon*	298
OF FRIENDSHIP	*Francis Bacon*	300
OF TRUTH	*Francis Bacon*	307

CONTENTS

THE FIFTY-FIRST DRAGON	*Heywood Broun*	310
I ENTERTAIN AN AGENT UN- AWARES	*David Grayson*	321
ON MAKING CAMP	*Stewart Edward White*	331
ON CARRYING A CANE	*Robert Cortes Holliday*	343
TO BE READ ONLY BY SERI- OUS STUPID PERSONS	*Charles S. Brooks*	350
THE DEATH OF AN OLD DOG	*William Henry Hudson*	360
THREE DAYS TO SEE	*Helen Adams Keller*	368
ROMANCE	*Simeon Strunsky*	382
MY MOTHER	*Lizette Woodworth Reese*	388
THE JUNGLE SLUGGARD	*William Beebe*	397
EPIGRAMS	*Jonathan Swift*	412
I GET A COLT TO BREAK IN	*Lincoln Steffens*	418
ON WAR	*George Santayana*	429
COLUMN LEFT	*Stuart Chase*	433
DWIGHT W. MORROW	*Walter Lippmann*	444
BOOKS OF ESSAYS FOR WIDER READING		450
ACKNOWLEDGMENTS		460

CHRONOLOGICAL ORDER

For teachers who prefer to teach the essays chronologically, the following order is suggested:

FRANCIS BACON (1561–1626)
Of Riches
Of Studies
Of Friendship
Of Truth

JONATHAN SWIFT (1667–1745)
Epigrams

BENJAMIN FRANKLIN (1706–1790)
The Art of Procuring Pleasant Dreams

CHARLES LAMB (1775–1834)
A Dissertation Upon Roast Pig

WASHINGTON IRVING (1783–1859)
Traits of Indian Character

RALPH WALDO EMERSON (1803–1882)
Self-Reliance

OLIVER WENDELL HOLMES (1809–1894)
Boating

HENRY DAVID THOREAU (1817–1862)
Where I Lived, and What I Lived for

MARK TWAIN (1835–1910)
Saint Joan of Arc

WILLIAM HENRY HUDSON (1841–1922)
The Death of an Old Dog

ROBERT LOUIS STEVENSON (1850–1894)
An Apology for Idlers
Aes Triplex

LAFCADIO HEARN (1850–1904)
The Mississippi
New Orleans

ELBERT HUBBARD (1856–1915)
A Message to Garcia

LIZETTE WOODWORTH REESE (1856–
My Mother

WOODROW WILSON (1856–1924)
The New Freedom

JOSEPH CONRAD (1857–1924)
Landfalls and Departures

SAMUEL McCHORD CROTHERS (1857–1927)
Every Man's Natural Desire To Be Somebody Else

THEODORE ROOSEVELT (1858–1919)
The Strenuous Life

AGNES REPPLIER (1858–
A Kitten

KENNETH GRAHAME (1859–1932)
The Magic Ring

JOHN KENDRICK BANGS (1862–1922)
My Silent Servants

GEORGE SANTAYANA (1863–
On War

RUDYARD KIPLING (1865–
Independence

WILLIAM LYON PHELPS (1865–
The Great American Game

LINCOLN STEFFENS (1866–
I Get a Colt to Break In

JOHN GALSWORTHY (1867–1933)
American and Briton

ARNOLD BENNETT (1867–1931)
Translating Literature into Life

E. V. LUCAS (1868–
Possessions
Telephonics

WILLIAM ALLEN WHITE (1868–
Mary White

STEPHEN LEACOCK (1869–
Oxford As I See It
A, B, and C — The Human Element in Mathematics

DAVID GRAYSON (1870–
I Entertain an Agent Unawares

STEWART EDWARD WHITE (1873–
On Making Camp

G. K. CHESTERTON (1875–
The Romantic in the Rain
On Running After One's Hat

WILLIAM BEEBE (1877–
The Jungle Sluggard

CHARLES S. BROOKS (1878–
To Be Read Only by Serious Stupid Persons

SIMEON STRUNSKY (1879–
Romance

ROBERT CORTES HOLLIDAY (1880–
On Carrying a Cane

HELEN ADAMS KELLER (1880–
Three Days to See

HEYWOOD BROUN (1888–
The Fifty-First Dragon

STUART CHASE (1888–
  Column Left

WALTER LIPPMANN (1889–
  Dwight W. Morrow

CHRISTOPHER MORLEY (1890–
  On Unanswering Letters
  What Men Live By
  On Doors

HOW THIS BOOK WAS MADE

Essays Old and New was first published in 1926, and its wide use and popular appeal have been gratifying to those associated in its preparation. In choosing the additional selections for this 1934 revision, naturally the essential criterion was: Are the new essays as practical, as interesting, and as appealing as those in the original book? If they were, then we could be confident of a happy career for the Revised and Enlarged *Essays Old and New*. Therefore, in fairness to the people who worked on both editions, the story of how the selections were originally chosen in 1926 should be retold.

Many teachers and students helped with the original edition. The puzzling question — *what essays should be included in a book for young people?* — was not answered by relying on the single judgment of the editor, or even on the combined judgment of publisher and editor. The glaring fault of this typical procedure is that it leaves out of consideration the preferences of the very individuals most concerned: those who are to use the book. Instead, the judgment and opinions of hundreds of teachers and students were requested.

This collective judgment was determined by sending a questionnaire to more than two hundred teachers scattered over the country; they were asked to name in order of their preference the writers they wished included in a high school book. It is of more than passing interest to note that Robert Louis Stevenson ranked first with ninety-six teachers. Because of his high ranking Stevenson's name heads the table of contents. The other writers in the original edition follow in order of preference as shown by the questionnaire.

How does this Revised and Enlarged *Essays Old and New* differ from the original book? Every author included in the

1926 edition is retained, and only one selection has been changed. Franklin's "The Art of Procuring Pleasant Dreams" has been substituted for "Poor Richard's Almanac." To this group of forty-one essays have been added eleven new ones, representing both living and classic essayists.

Upon what basis were these new selections made? On the whole, they were chosen to bring the book in content and spirit up to the present. The years between 1926 and 1934 have been stirring and challenging. In the turbulence of economic and social changes many writers have turned to the essay to express their doubts, ideas, and hopes. An extensive search among essays on contemporary civilization uncovered three which have proved interesting to students, easy to understand, and which possess in addition permanent literary value. It is believed that George Santayana's "On War" will stimulate wide reading on this vital subject and that Stuart Chase and Walter Lippmann will stimulate straightforward thinking on problems of contemporary civilization.

Because of Stephen Leacock's growing popularity with students, a second essay of his, "A, B, and C — the Human Element in Mathematics," has been included. His vigorous nonsense will be enjoyed equally by those who find mathematics easy or by those who find it difficult. The selections by William Henry Hudson and Lincoln Steffens present memories of boyhood so vivid and natural that the reader easily recreates life on the pampas of South America or the carefree existence of a lad growing up in California. William Beebe was included because his eye is as all-seeing as that of a camera and his keenness and enthusiasm are typical characteristics of present-day scientists. Both he and Helen Keller will give the reader vicarious experience and make him conscious of the possibility of developing a greater awareness of life.

The routine and poetry of our changing city life shine through "Romance" by Simeon Strunsky. Swift's "Epigrams" will motivate many good discussions on human nature. "My Mother" by Lizette Woodworth Reese will be loved by the thousands who have enjoyed "Mary White."

The first is a daughter's tribute to her mother; the second, a father's memorial to his daughter.

It is hoped that the Revised and Enlarged *Essays Old and New* will serve as a springboard to a new reading habit. The book is filled with reading suggestions, and the student who goes away from this book with a liking for essays will have gained something which can never be taken from him.

To the many teachers and students who helped make this collection go the thanks of the editor. Likewise she extends her gratitude to the publishers who kindly allowed her to reprint copyrighted material.

E. C.

A NOTE TO TEACHERS

Iт is hoped that teachers will find that the fifty-two essays in this volume offer fare sufficiently varied to whet the appetite of all members of any group. It can be taken for granted that few classes will read the entire fifty-two selections, although many individuals may. Having more essays than can be used is a distinct advantage; the teacher can adapt the book to various courses and particular groups and individuals.

The arrangement of essays in the book is *not* recommended as an order to follow in classroom study. The first forty-one selections with Stevenson at the head are arranged in order of their popularity with those teachers and students who cooperated in determining the contents of the original book. The last eleven selections are those added to the 1926 edition to make this new one of 1934.

To help the teacher decide which essays should be read first the editor makes this suggestion: let the maturity and tastes of the class determine the choice. The student's first serious encounter with as slightly known a type of literature as the essay is all important in fixing his subsequent attitude toward it. This is particularly true when he brings to that encounter an armor of prejudice. It is well to begin with simple essays whose subject matter is closely related to the experiences of the student. The teacher alone can know what his students are ready to read and what will ensnare their interests. "The Magic Ring" stimulates happy reminiscences of childhood. "I Get a Colt to Break In" commands whole-hearted attention. "A, B, and C — the Human Element in Mathematics" quickly wins student sympathy. "On Unanswering Letters" touches a common and very human weakness. Other simple essays to start a class on are:

" Mary White "

" A Message to Garcia "

" The Great American Game "

" A Kitten "

" Possessions "

" New Orleans "

" Romance "

" The Strenuous Life "

" A Dissertation upon Roast Pig "

" The Mississippi "

" My Mother "

" Boating "

With guidance the gradual development of the student's ability to read and understand will enable him to take Stevenson, Emerson, Thoreau, Crothers, Galsworthy, Lippmann, Chase, Santayana in his stride and to enjoy them with a sense of growing intellectual power.

The teacher should see that these fifty-two essays are merely the beginning of a new reading experience. It is recommended that simultaneous with the study of this collection students be encouraged to look up other essays written by the same authors. To foster further reading there are lists of additional essays at the end of this volume. The school and city librarians will often cooperate with the teacher by arranging reserve collections on the shelves or by loaning books to the English classroom. The presence of books in the room is always an invitation to reading.

Supplementary reading may center around special subjects. The student may select one essayist with whom he wishes to become better acquainted and make himself a specialist on the works of that author. Or a certain period in English or American literature may provide a reading center for his interests. A successful and highly enjoyable reading plan was developed under the direction of the editor when this book was in preparation. Seventy-five essay volumes were placed in the classroom. The students read lavishly, directed by a real and immediate purpose. Each student was asked to recommend twenty essays for a book to be used for study and discussion. The essays were to possess both interest and merit. Notes were kept of essays read and rejected, as well as of those approved. The written papers were helpful commentaries on student interests.

Young people enjoy estimating and appraising the values of books and their comments often succeed in moving the group when the teacher's invitation does not. Moreover, the student who writes his judgment in carefully chosen and exact words gradually clarifies and raises his own standards. He may be asked to express his estimate of the book in brief notes[1] of three or four sentences which will induce some other student to read it.

The editor strongly recommends reading of contemporary essays. "The child more than the man lives in his own time." Several days may be employed with profit in the discussion of essays contained in current magazines, and if possible copies of at least one periodical should be made available to the students. "The Contributors' Club" of the *Atlantic Monthly* prints brief essays, many of which will interest the high school boy or girl. *Scholastic* (The National High School Weekly) not only includes essays in its own pages but gives "leads" to those appearing in other weekly or monthly magazines. The *Scholastic* Round Table prints student contributions. Teachers will find that *Magazines and Newspapers of Today* by Gladys Campbell and Russell Thomas is invaluable for use in this connection. If it is possible to give class time to the examination of current magazines, the editor recommends that copies of this book be made available to students.

One caution in using *Essays Old and New* seems wise: do not let every reading lesson end with an assignment for original writing on the part of the student. Nothing is calculated to kill appreciation as quickly. The "Subjects for Composition," like all the editorial helps, were included to be used at the discretion of the teacher. For some students the appreciation process is not complete until they have tried their hand at expressing their own kindred ideas.

---

[1] See *Guide to Reading, Annotated by High School Boys and Girls,* Illinois Association of Teachers of English, Urbana, Illinois.

A WORD TO STUDENTS

ESSAYISTS write because they find pleasure in jotting down their opinions on all sorts of subjects. They take the reader into their confidence. They share their beliefs, doubts, loves, hates, prejudices, whims, superstitions, even their ignorance.

Zest! Essays will quicken your reaction to things about you. Try "On Doors" or "Three Days to See."

Wings! How often have you longed for a magic carpet or an airplane to carry you to far places? You have only to start reading "New Orleans" or "The Jungle Sluggard."

Challenge! We are living in a dynamic age. Exciting history is being made daily. It becomes necessary to "think or perish." Stuart Chase, George Santayana, Walter Lippmann are a few of the authors in this book who give expression to the social, economic, and cultural questions confronting us. Contact with minds such as these will sharpen and develop your own.

"'Tis the good reader that makes the good book," says Emerson. You will wish to bring to your reading of these essays all of your interest, all of your knowledge of literature and history. Bring also your sense of the ludicrous and your appreciation of the humorous, for many a laugh lurks in these pages. Become sensitive to the style of the author. Enjoyment in the way a thing is said and pleasure in the beautiful relation between thought and its expression come to those who learn to read essays. The humor may be sly and subtle, and you will need to be alert to discover it.

Suggestive questions have been included to provoke thought, to stimulate discussion, and to relate your new reading with what you have already learned. It is a pleasure to come upon references that are known and understood, "where more is meant than meets the ear." Do not let an occasional unfamiliar word or allusion mar your understanding of the passage; use the dictionary when it is necessary.

One of the greatest pleasures in the enjoyment of a book lies in sharing it with friends. The class discussions will furnish abundant opportunities for this sharing, and you will undoubtedly welcome the privilege of being a contributor to the round table.

Lists of essays for further reading have been placed in the book for your convenience, for once you have enjoyed an essay it is natural to wish to know more of the author and his work. To read widely means to live richly. To love good books is to be certain always of entertainment and companionship. Let the essays in this book be the beginning of a new reading habit.

INTRODUCTION

THE ESSAY DEFINED

THE essay is a form of literature popular with thoughtful readers. It is a short, informal prose discussion upon any subject which, for the moment, appeals to the writer. He may deal with serious problems on civilization or mere fancies. Nothing is too slight, too trivial, too homely or common to engage his interest. Alexander Smith, in *Dreamthorp,* says of this literary form: " The essay writer has no lack of subject matter. He has the day that is passing over his head; and, if unsatisfied with that, he has the world's six thousand years to depasture his gay or serious humor upon. I idle away my time here, and I am finding new subjects every hour. Everything I see or hear is an essay in bud. The world is everywhere whispering essays, and one need only be the world's amanuensis." The essay has been written not only by masters of literature, for all of us have attempted this form in our short informal themes, and in the letters that we write to our friends.

The name comes from the French word *essai,* which means an attempt, an endeavor, a beginning. It has retained in English this original meaning. Irving's *Sketch Book* has this example: " Our first essay in travel to catch fish was along a mountain brook." Tennyson's " Ode to Memory " states: " Thou needs must love thy first essay." Mr. Robert Cortes Holliday's last sentence in " On Carrying a Cane " suggests the same meaning: " This, of course, is the merest essay into this vast and significant subject." The word has been used loosely to cover a wide variety of prose forms and to define its limits is difficult.

The essay is a brief prose composition which treats of one subject in such a way as to give free expression to the personality of the writer. The essayist offers the reader little intellectual excursions in which he opens up the subject but does not complete it. Considering it, Mr. Christopher Morley says: "No matter how personal or trifling the topic may be, there is always a tendency to generalize, to walk around the subject or the experience, and view it from several vantages. . . . So an essay can never be more than an attempt, for it is an excursion into the endless." In the reading of essays, one must not expect completeness. The opportunity, however, of becoming better acquainted with the essayist is more than compensation for the things he neglects to include. In no form of literature with the possible exception of diaries and letters may we come closer to the personality of the writer.

THE ESSAY FURTHER DEFINED

Montaigne, a French gentleman of varied experience and delightful personality, who lived in the sixteenth century, first used the word *essai* to describe a certain form of literary composition. He employed the word in its original meaning: a trial, an attempt, an endeavor, an incomplete beginning. Other writers have used the term variously. Bacon, the first English essayist, states in his preface: "To write just treatises requireth leisure in the writer and leisure in the reader, . . . which is the cause that hath made me choose to write certain brief notes, set down rather significantly than curiously, which I have called essays."

The maker of the first English dictionary, Dr. Johnson, gave this definition: "A loose sally of the mind; an irregular, undigested piece; not a regular and orderly performance." Montaigne's idea of incompleteness of treatment is repeated in Johnson's statement. *Webster's New International Dictionary* describes the essay as "a literary composition, analytical or interpretative in nature, dealing with its subject from a more or less limited or personal standpoint, and with one phase of the subject rather than covering the entire scope of the field."

The modern conception of the essay is expressed by Mr.

Edmund Gosse, in his treatment of this form in the *Encyclopædia Britannica* when he states: "As a form of literature, the essay is a composition of moderate length, usually in prose, which deals in an easy, cursory way with the external conditions of a subject, and, in strictness, with that subject only as it affects the writer." The personality of the writer is here emphasized as in the preceding definition. Further, it suggests charm and naturalness of style, a quality not stressed in the earlier definitions. These statements, ranging from Montaigne and Bacon in the sixteenth century, to the more recent treatment of the essay, suggest its growth and evolution. The form has changed since first the term was used, but the material of the essay is still as much enjoyed as it was in Montaigne's day.

CHARACTERISTICS OF THE ESSAY

Certain characteristics common to the essay are suggested by these definitions. First, it is a *prose* treatment. Sometimes a work in poetic form is given the name, as Pope's "Essay on Criticism" and his "Essay on Man." As used in this book, however, its common meaning is understood. It is a prose form.

A second characteristic common in the essay is its *brevity*. The essayist gives a short treatment of his subject. It demands power of attention for a single sitting. Years ago the term was sometimes used to describe long and systematic treatments of a subject, as Locke's "Essay Concerning Human Understanding." But today, like the short story, the essay is comparatively brief. Sometimes it is a mere fragment.

A third distinguishing mark of the essay is its *incomplete treatment* of the subject. It is not an exhaustive study; rather is it an experiment, a tentative consideration. It pretends neither to system nor completeness. A subject may be chosen, and only one phase of it be considered. The object of the essay is "merely to open questions, to indicate points, to suggest cases, to sketch outlines." Miss Repplier announces "A

Kitten" for the title of an essay. One might, under this general topic, jot down a thousand and one phases of the subject. Miss Repplier gives us no laborious or scientific treatment. Instead, she introduces us to a charming cat family sojourning for a time in her closet, and no one who loves cats can fail to cherish Nero and Agrippina, for they are delightful personalities. Mr. Kenneth Grahame selects the cryptic title, "The Magic Ring," which might mean many things. But he disregards all other magic rings for the sawdust ring, and his essay pictures with rare sympathy and understanding the heart of youth and its joy in the circus. So one must not expect to find a subject exhausted in the essay.

A fourth characteristic of the essay is its *distinctive style*. Ease and familiarity are its virtues. The essayist must at all times attend to his style. Finish and mastery, charm and naturalness mark this literary form. How a thing is said is equally important with what is said. In tone it may be serious, witty, rhetorical, satirical, light. Often the real charm of the essay lies in its dress. DeQuincey once wrote: "An essayist should make every sentence sparkle; he is never permitted to be a dull or slovenly workman. He should be always at his best; for the narrow limit within which the essayist works demands superior merit in the performance." The accomplished essayist has a unique style different from that of other writers and peculiar to his own personality. We read Lamb and Bacon and Hearn with pleasure, yet each charms us differently, for each has his distinctive fascination.

In this discussion of style, a caution should be voiced. Sincerity must never be sacrificed for style and polish. With some writers the desire to be too clever, too quaint, is strong, and some essayists yield to this tendency, but when the essay lacks sincerity and the tone of candor, its charm has fled. In frankness lies the fascination of the personal essay. Lamb was courageous and sincere; he never posed. A lesser spirit might have feared to write freely and frankly of his poverty and of his family, but because Lamb was in perfect sympathy with his reader and trusted him, he gave freely and sincerely intimate confidences to us. This candor has earned for him the highest rank in the familiar essay.

Generally, essays have a cultured, aristocratic flavor. They are addressed to cultivated, leisurely, and tranquil persons. The essayist is usually a man of scholarly tastes, mature in his wisdom, sound in his judgments. He is fond of literary allusion and illustration. "Literary echoing" is frequently found within the pages of an essay, and the miracle of reading many books when there is only one before the eyes takes place each day. The reader must understand and follow these references or else there is pleasure lost. When we read Stevenson's "An Apology for Idlers," we must know Falstaff, Colonel Newcomb, Pharaoh, Joan of Arc, Shakespeare, and Sir Thomas Lucy if we understand all that the author wished to communicate. When Stevenson, in the same essay, says, "Atlas was just a gentleman with a protracted nightmare," he recalls for us the whole biography of Atlas. When speaking of pleasures he says, "Like the quality of mercy they are not strained, and they are twice blest," he assumes that we know *The Merchant of Venice*.

Another characteristic of this literary form is its strong *personal* tone. Probably in this lies its greatest claim to distinction. Always is the essay a personal revelation of the author. We are given his whims, his hobbies, his opinions upon every possible kind of subject. His mood may be serious or trivial, grave or humorous, but we see the subject only as it is reflected through his eyes. The essayist is always personal, partly autobiographical. He sings of himself. The essay in prose corresponds to the lyric in poetry; it is an expression of subjective emotion. The writer says: "I think; I feel; I grieve; I joy; I scorn; I exult; I love." This personal, individual point of view is its distinguishing feature. It is a literary form devoted to self-revelation of the writer. "The perfection of the familiar essay is a conscious revelation of self done inadvertently." Montaigne, Bacon, Lamb, and Stevenson reveal interesting personalities turned on any number of subjects. And it is the man who arouses our interest finally, rather than the material he offers us. We know essayists as we become acquainted with no other writers.

It must be clearly recognized that the essayist shows perfect good taste when he writes thus freely of himself. In countless ways in our everyday conversation we speak of ourselves and of the things which interest us. If this is done with modesty and truthfulness, there is no offense. Stevenson tells us that more than half of all talkable subjects of conversation may be reduced to three: "That I am I; that you are you; and that there are other people dimly understood to be not quite the same as either." Again to quote Alexander Smith: "A modest, truthful man speaks better about himself than about anything else, and on that subject his speech is likely to be most profitable to his hearers. Certainly, there is no subject with which he is better acquainted, and on which he has a better title to be heard." And the charm of the essay lies in this pleasant egotism. We learn the whims, the foibles, and the prejudices of the writer. We enter into all of his moods. We become his intimate friend, for he shares with us the secrets of his mind and heart. Mr. William Allen White has unlocked his heart in the moving and tender revelation of grief expressed in "Mary White." Stevenson reveals his fine and buoyant attitude towards life and towards living in "Aes Triplex," and as we read this essay we know better this brave spirit who faced life and death courageously. In "Three Days to See" Helen Keller shows us her indomitable will to live richly despite her handicaps.

And finally, the essay must be a *literary whole*. It may be brief; it may not exhaust the subject, yet there must be a completeness in the author's treatment of his subject. The reader must feel the unity of its handling, and must recognize an underlying organization. It may be strictly planned, or it may digress and ramble, but it must be a literary whole.

THE ESSAY RESEMBLES CONVERSATION

The essay resembles good conversation. Good talk glances from one subject to another with no apparent method. Conversation may be entirely serious or wholly humorous, or it may be serious and humorous by turns. So it is with the essay. Some writers of this literary form are usually dignified and serious while others are humorous and light. And there are those who combine the two elements in delightful mixture. Bacon approached his subjects in serious mood, and he treated them with majestic dignity. It has been said that he seems to write with his ermine on. Mr. Stephen Leacock, even though he may have chosen some important idea, approaches it in a spirit of fun and satire. There is truth in his comparison of English and American universities in " Oxford as I See It," but he handles it humorously. Lamb was a master in the mingling of humor and pathos. A delightful example of this is found in " Old China," while " Dream Children" reveals Lamb's delicacy and pathos.

Montaigne recognized the kinship of the essay to good conversation. His comment is so sane and shrewd that it must be given in its entirety: " It is a natural, simple and unaffected speech that I love, so written as it is spoken, and such upon the paper as it is in the mouth, a pithy, sinewy, full, strong, compendious, and material speech, not so delicate and affected as vehement and piercing — rather difficult than tedious, void of affectation, free, loose, and bold, so that every member of it seems to make a body; not pedantical, nor friar-like, nor lawyer-like but rather downright soldier-like. I decided to walk with my pen as I go with my feet, and let my mind move with its own natural step, not the steps of the dancing school or as those who leap on horseback because they are not strong enough in their legs to march on foot. The titles of my chapters embrace not always the matter, they often but glance at it by some mark."

Like the conversationalist, the essayist too may select a subject and then spend most of his time in the discussion of apparently unrelated things. Bypaths are dear to both. The essay may be rambling, for the assigned title is not always important. Mr. Gilbert Chesterton's "On Running after One's Hat" is a charming example of this. He first touches upon floods in London and romantic views of inconveniences before he comes to his subject. After devoting two paragraphs to the sport of pursuing one's hat, he digresses, discussing the proper attitude towards some other minor frictions of life. Lamb begins "Old China" with a statement concerning his interest in old china, but he soon drifts into memories of his early days of poverty. He lives again those days of youth and happiness shared with his sister. The closing paragraphs echo once more old china, but there is a spirit and emotion in the essay which gives it unity of mood. The essayist may select any subject; cannibals, sundials, shower-baths, noses, gas lamps, solitude, or journeys may intrigue his interest for a time and his written observations on such varied themes become essays. From his announced subject he may wander far, but each writes of himself, and so, in spite of digressions, the essayist conforms to the laws of this type. He has no obligation to his subject once he has the inspiration from it.

The purpose of the essayist is varied. Like the talker, he may have a serious intent, or he may have no reason for writing other than the sheer love of self-expression. He may try to provoke thought in the reader; he may attempt to convince; he may write merely to please. The act of composition may have given him pleasure, and he is glad to share his enthusiasm with the reader. The tone may be light and trivial, for the essayist does not always aim to dispense knowledge, to inform, or to teach. His purpose is rather to delight his readers and to stimulate thought. Great truths may be presented in this attractive dress.

THE SUBJECT MATTER OF THE ESSAY

The essayist enjoys a freedom denied the dramatist, the novelist, or the writer of short stories. Subjects suitable to drama do not lend themselves to the restrictions of the novel and the short story. And all too frequently a great novel fails to conform to the laws of the drama. All of us have seen poor plays on the stage or screen made from successful novels. Dramatized novels and novelized dramas are frequently failures. The essayist, however, has no limitations in the selection of his subject matter. He is not cabined, cribbed, or confined in his choice of appropriate themes, for anything interesting or unusual which provokes his interest or curiosity is matter enough for his essay. "Anything is grist which comes to his mill." And no matter what his mood or his attitude towards his theme, he must jot down his ideas, and the world is richer by one essay. Scanning the table of contents of any collection of essays reveals the rich variety of subjects which may be treated. From the essays included in this book we find the serious treatment of great problems: "On War," "Independence," "Self-Reliance," "The New Freedom," "Aes Triplex," "The Strenuous Life." Reading, "the greatest of all indoor sports," is discussed in "My Silent Servants" and in "Translating Literature into Life." Our international relations are considered in "American and Briton," while a noteworthy experiment in living alone is recorded in "Where I Lived and What I Lived For." Our interest in composition, in expressing our thoughts in writing, is charmingly discussed in the essay, "To be Read Only by Serious Stupid Persons." "The Jungle Sluggard" presents scientific facts simply and with charm. The wide variety of material appealing to the essayist is revealed in this collection, for we find treatments of such subjects as roast pig, unanswering letters, kittens, canes, book agents, telephones, doors, baseball, and talk. The essayist is limited only by his interests, and they may compass all of life.

Most of our essayists today are interested in economical, social, and governmental problems, and magazines and books reflect this serious trend. You will undoubtedly find controversial essays outnumbering the informal familiar ones.

HISTORY OF THE ESSAY

Although its greatest growth and development has come since 1580, the essay is an ancient form of literature. Plato is sometimes called the first essayist. Cicero and Seneca used this form in Latin, and gave us treatments on life, patriotism, duty, death, friendship, old age, and immortality. Hebrew literature furnishes examples of this type. Ecclesiastes, Exodus, and Judges contain proverbs and clusters of proverbs which are nothing less than essays on subjects dealing with the problems of life — friendship, wisdom, pride, gossip, vengeance, and punishment. Moulton defines the Biblical essay as "a number of miscellaneous thoughts collected around a common theme." These early writings, however, were not given the name essay. "The word is late, though the thing is ancient."

In 1580 Montaigne published his first two volumes of *Essais*. In 1588 a third edition was issued. Montaigne was a Frenchman of rank and means. He had been influential in public affairs, but before he was forty, he retired from active life and spent his days in quiet contemplation and reading. The following quotations from his preface suggest that the reader must not expect important material. He says: "I have proposed unto myself no other than a familiar and a private end: I have no respect or consideration at all, either to thy service or to my glory." "Myself am the groundwork of my book. It is then no reason thou shouldst employ thy time about so frivolous and vain a subject." In this preface Montaigne has outlined the form and set the tone of the familiar and informal essay.

In Montaigne's book we find the open and friendly comment of a shrewd, kindly, and tolerant man on the experiences and happenings of life. There is no discoverable principle of arrangement, for his essays are just good talk on any matter which pleases him. Such subjects as idleness, envy, smells, hands, thumbs, fortune, cannibals, liars, names, and virtues have challenged his passing interest.

Thus early, Montaigne outlined the plan for this literary form; he gave it a name; he demonstrated its possibilities in his charming essays, and he is still regarded as its master, for essayists who followed him have acknowledged their debt. Bacon, Lamb, Hazlitt, and Stevenson pay glad homage to his genius.

When Montaigne's works were translated into English, their influence was immediate. The best translation is that of John Florio. Even before these French essays were published in the English language, Bacon used the word *essays* for the title of a book which contained brief prose statements of serious subjects. These essays were published in 1597. Later he issued other editions, and in 1625, *Essays, Counsels Civil and Moral* appeared. These were on general and serious subjects, such as studies, riches, love, truth. There were sixty of these brief treatments, ranging in length from two to ten pages. Bacon's essays are just as truly a reflection of his mind as are Montaigne's, for Bacon saw all things in a cold, dry, intellectual light. The affable and human quality of Montaigne is lacking. It is interesting to know that Bacon's monumental life work, scientific and philosophical treatises in fifteen large volumes, has been forgotten. His books lie dusty on the shelves. Only his essays are read today. His short, terse sayings, packed full of thought, are aphoristic and proverbial in style. The wise and prudent gentleman, who measured success in life by material prosperity, breathes in these pages, and his sound maxims have worldly wisdom as their keynote.

Although much of the subject matter of the seventeenth century is of the essay spirit and flavor, Montaigne and Bacon had little influence upon seventeenth-century writers. The form of the essay was not carefully developed. There is little in this period to interest the young reader. Mature students, who are interested in the development of the essay, are delighted to pore over the works of Thomas Fuller, Sir Thomas Browne, Izaak Walton, and Abraham Cowley. Of these men Cowley wrote with most distinction.

The development of the essay in the eighteenth century is

closely associated with the rise of periodical literature. How difficult for us to imagine living today without newspaper and magazine! Yet as late as 1688 in England there was neither magazine nor newspaper. The eighteenth century was a period of strenuous social activity. The tavern and the coffee house flourished. Englishmen were becoming interested in themselves, and they met in the coffee houses for conversation. This interesting talk was put on paper, little sheets were circulated, and Englishmen had a new interest, the current magazine. These sheets contained a review of the news, and a short story or editorial. In 1709, Richard Steele published the *Tatler,* a large sheet printed on both sides and issued once a week. Later, Joseph Addison helped his friend Steele, but after a time the *Tatler* was discontinued, and these two men established the *Spectator* in 1711. It was first issued three times a week, later as a daily. The paper did not treat politics seriously. An essay and some advertisements were included always. The editors discussed a wide range of topics; for example: slang, dueling, Italian opera, education, courtship, marriage, treatment of servants, style in women's dress. These essays brought to public attention some wrong or folly to be corrected. In purpose, they are similar to the editorial of today. Behavior and customs were criticized. Addison and Steele roamed about London, noting matters for comment. There were 555 numbers of this magazine published. These men have had many imitators.

Other men in this period aided in the development of this form. In 1704, Defoe, author of *Robinson Crusoe,* began a journal. In addition to news from Europe, he ran an essay or editorial. Dryden wrote prefaces to his dramatic and poetic works, in which he explained his literary principles and methods, thus establishing a form for the critical essay. Samuel Johnson, the famous lexicographer, wrote ponderous and lengthy essays on literary criticism, which are little read today, and his periodicals, the *Rambler* and the *Idler,* encouraged this literary form. Goldsmith, late in this period, wrote his charming "Citizen of the World" series. He used an old idea, but his own delightful personality so fills the pages that the essays are distinctive. He employed the device of having a Chinese gentleman who visits England write shrewd and pointed criticisms of the things he has observed. Goldsmith employed much narrative, as did Addison and Steele.

The nineteenth century contributed much to the advance of the essay. Newspapers and periodicals developed rapidly and furnished a reading public for rising young essayists. Contributors were paid liberally, for there was much rivalry between these publications. Personal essays, and those of critical and descriptive merit, were popular with the public. Lamb, DeQuincey, Macaulay, Hazlitt, and Hunt wrote for these journals. Such magazines as the *Edinburgh Review,* the *Quarterly Review, Blackwood's Magazine,* and the *London Magazine* encouraged the growth of this literary form. Stevenson's essays first appeared in the *Cornhill Magazine,* and later, *Scribner's* introduced them to American readers. Dr. Van Dyke's essays have appeared in the same publication. The *Atlantic* first introduced *The Autocrat of the Breakfast Table* to Holmes's admirers. The magazine of today caters to the spirit of the times. Much space is given to the discussion of governmental problems and to our world relationships.

Lamb is the chief master of the English familiar essay, for he is individual, personal, whimsical, and imaginative. He was a wide reader, and his mind retained out-of-the-way facts. He loved the past. Life and human beings interested him. But the most important of all the qualities which favored his success as an essayist are his sound judgment and essential wisdom. "The evidences of this wisdom are to be met with everywhere. It is the essence of Lamb's criticism. No one but a man endowed with the very genius of common sense could have been so uniformly right as he." Lamb's essays breathe a sound philosophy of life, and are filled with shrewd wisdom mixed with humor and wit. He is the best beloved of our essayists, the " more nearly unique." Canon Ainger says: " Thoroughly to enjoy Charles Lamb, one must come to entertain a feeling towards him almost like personal affection. . . .

It is necessary to come to the study of his writings in entire truthfulness, and having cast aside all prejudice." In all his "whim-whams," his quaint words and antique phrases, his charming comparisons, it is always Lamb, the man, we enjoy. His sympathy was universal.

As Lamb was distinguished for his sympathy, DeQuincey brought imagination to the essay, Carlyle, high moral purpose and seriousness, and Macaulay, a clear and forceful style. Macaulay developed the critical essay, or the book review. This consisted of a description of the book, followed by a discussion of the subject suggested by the book. Stevenson, a little later, viewed the essay as a recreation. He jotted down his worth-while interests and his observations on life.

In America the essay has developed parallel with the English essay. Irving's *Sketch Book* was modeled after Addison's *Spectator* papers and it was as popular in England as in America. Emerson, like Bacon, used the aphoristic form. He emphasized the sentence rather than the whole composition. His revelations of truth came to him one at a time, and thus the sentence was his unit of thought. Thoreau lived his unique life, solitary and original, and he wrote like no one else. He combined the serious and familiar in his essays. Because of the essential truth in his writings, Thoreau's influence is greater today than when he wrote. He saw clearly the effect of the machine age on our civilization even in his day. Holmes was a master in the free and intimate conversational essay. He wrote as he talked. All these men gave charming revelations of personality in their writings. Their characters were worth revealing, and they have loyal and devoted readers on both sides of the Atlantic. The writing of essays did not cease with the death of Emerson, Irving, and Thoreau. The selections in this book from living writers will testify that essays which have the power to stimulate, to soothe, or to delight are still being written.

RELATION OF THE ESSAY TO OTHER LITERARY TYPES

Because the essay has always evidenced a strong interest in character and personality, it has had influence upon literary forms in which character is an important element. The modern novel has been influenced by the essay. It is a fusion of essay and story. George Eliot combined the terse power of epigram with the creation of a story, and this union produced a novelist. She might easily have been an essayist. Agnes Repplier first wrote fiction, but was advised by a discerning publisher to try her hand at essays. The essay is like the familiar letter, it is the "direct exposure of the man behind the book." It is subjective, personal, full of gossip and of self-revelation. Dialogue and story are used in this literary form. The border line between the essay and the short story is sometimes slight, as in Mr. Heywood Broun's "The Fifty-First Dragon" or Simeon Strunsky's "Romance." Often the narrative essay has some serious purpose behind the story, as in Mr. Stephen Leacock's "Hoodoo McFiggin's Christmas." Mr. Christopher Morley says: "The essay is a mood rather than a form; the frontier between the essay and the short story is as imperceptible as is at present the once famous Mason and Dixon line. Indeed, in that pleasant lowland country between the two empires lie (to my way of thinking) some of the most fertile fields of prose — fiction that expresses feeling and character rather than action and plot; fiction beautifully ripened by the lingering mild sunshine of the essayist's mood." The essay is of the literature of personality; it resembles the lyric in its expression of personal emotion. The biography, the novel, and the short story all have some common ground with the essay.

TYPES OF ESSAYS

There will always be variety in the classification of essays into types. The complexity of subjects and the wide variety of their treatment give a scope to the essay which makes classification difficult. Following are some divisions which **may** prove helpful to the student:

1. Personal Essay. The personal or familiar essay aims primarily to entertain. It reveals the personality of the writer. Montaigne says: " It is myself I portray." Thackeray, Hazlitt, Lamb, and Stevenson are masters of this type.

2. Descriptive Essay. The descriptive essay may deal with a variety of subjects: nature, animals, things. In the exposition, however, one is always conscious of the author, of what he thinks and of what he interprets as well as of what he sees.

3. Character Sketch. This name defines itself. Here are we interested in man, not alone in his physical appearance, but in the spirit, the soul, the character, and the personality of the man. And the man may exist in actual life, or he may be a creature of the essayist's imagination.

4. Critical Essay. The critical essay has some work of art for its subject. Music, painting, or literature may engross the attention of the essayist. Young people are likely to be most familiar with literary criticism, or the book review. The writer may give unbiased and clear judgment upon the work in question. He may show the relation of the book to the subject in general. He may relate this book to the other works of the author. The reviewer should possess insight and sound critical judgment. The criticism may be written by an authority on the subject, who perchance knows more about the field than the author. We gain from the critical essay a knowledge about the work in question, and in addition, the praise or blame of the author.

5. Editorial Essay. These expository and editorial treatments present ideals. They may be written under strong feeling, with deep conviction. Their aim is to influence public opinion. The editorial writer [1] has something to say, and he knows how to say it. When the article aims solely to guide opinion, it is not an essay in the true sense.

6. Reflective Essay. The reflective essay is usually serious in tone. The essayist has thought deeply upon certain great

[1] Consult *Writing of Today,* Cunliffe & Lomer, The Century Company.

questions touching life, and he offers his convictions and philosophy to his readers. The subjects may be abstract, such as life, death, studies, character, self-reliance. Galsworthy considered seriously the relation of two kindred races in " American and Briton." Emerson pondered on one fundamental quality of character in " Self-Reliance."

More important than any classification of essays, is the time spent in extensive reading in this form. Young readers will find much of interest in the personal or familiar essay because of the variety of subjects treated. Wide reading should become a habit, and this book aims to encourage it.

ESSAYS OLD AND NEW

An essayist is not a mighty traveler. He does not run to grapple with a roaring lion. He desires neither typhoon nor tempest. He is content in his harbor to listen to the storm upon the rocks if now and then by lucky chance, he can shelter someone from the wreck. His hands are not red with revolt against the world. He has glanced upon the thoughts of many men; and as opposite philosophies point upon the truth, he is modest with his own and tolerant of the opinion of others. He looks at the stars and, knowing in what a dim immensity we travel, he writes of little things beyond dispute. There are enough to weep upon the shadows; he, like the dial, marks the light. The small clatter of the city beneath his window, the cry of peddlers, children chalking their games upon the pavement, laundry dancing on the roofs and smoke in the winter's wind — these are the things he weaves into the fabric of his thoughts. Or sheep upon the hillside — if his window is so lucky — or a sunny meadow, is a profitable speculation. An essay, therefore, cannot be writ hurriedly upon the knee.

CHARLES S. BROOKS, " Hints to Pilgrims "

ROBERT LOUIS STEVENSON

Fortunate the boy or girl who comes early upon the writings of Robert Louis Stevenson (1850–1894). For the young and really adventurous there waits the imperishable *Treasure Island,* with its sinister villain, Long John Silver, and that perfect sea-chanty, " Yo-ho, and a bottle of rum! " For the older and more sophisticated who no longer wish to run away to sea and meet the pirates on the Spanish main, but take their adventures soberly, on the Continent of Europe for example, there lie ready *Travels with a Donkey* and *An Inland Voyage.* And thereafter a whole series of narratives of travel in America, in the South Seas, and elsewhere. Further, when come the romantic and melancholy dreams of adolescence, these can be stimulated with *The New Arabian Nights* in company with Prince Florizel and the Suicide Club. And still the treasure-store of Stevenson's entertainment remains far from exhausted. Dr. Jekyll beckons for a cold and lonely night to thrill the reader with the creepy way in which he transforms himself into Mr. Hyde, but in this story the eerie must not be allowed to conceal the allegory. And beyond are still more stories and essays, all penned with the same frail charm.

For Stevenson was a frail and charming man who put his predominant characteristics into what he wrote. A delicate constitution was ill-treated by privation, and quickly disease leaped into the breach. Born and brought up in that most charming of gray old towns, Edinburgh, this charming and gay young man became a wanderer as soon as he could, and finally died an exile in Samoa of the South Seas, far, far away indeed from the old folks at home. He was only forty-four.

His father was well off, but Robert Louis wanted to support himself, and in his struggle to achieve such self-support he found the pen a stern taskmaster, particularly when he first stayed in the United States. But he certainly extracted from journeys and new scenery all the joy they had to give to him; he loved idling and moving from one place to another, not in conventional Pullmans or in monstrous st⌐amships, but gently on a donkey or in a canal barge. It was during his Inland Voyage (in the barge) that — he was twenty-eight then — he met the American woman ten years his senior who was to become his wife. There was a genuine Stevensonian touch about that meeting. Darkness had fallen ere he reached the house in the thick and mighty Forest of Fontaine-bleau, and as he marched into the patch of lamplight that came through the living-room window, he beheld her seated inside. Here was love at first sight.

But she was married, and they parted. Later he was in Scotland when he learned that she was ill, six thousand miles away in San Francisco, and forthwith he crossed the Atlantic to be at her side, going steerage because he could afford no better. Her husband died, and they were married. With her Stevenson lived for a time at Bournemouth, on the English South Coast, but that being yet too inclement for him, they eventually set out for Samoa, whence he was not to return. His remains lie buried at the summit of a knoll in that coral isle.

The two accompanying essays well express aspects of Stevenson's pensive philosophy.

AN APOLOGY FOR IDLERS[1]
(1877)

" BOSWELL: We grow weary when idle.

" JOHNSON: That is, Sir, because others being busy, we want company; but if we were idle, there would be no growing weary; we should all entertain one another."

JUST now, when every one is bound, under pain of a decree in absence convicting them of *lèse*-respectability, to enter on some lucrative profession, and labor therein with something not far short of enthusiasm, a cry from the opposite party who are content when they have enough, and like to look on and enjoy in the meanwhile, savors a little of bravado and gasconade. And yet this should not be. Idleness

[1] From *Virginibus Puerisque,* copyright by Charles Scribner's Sons.

so called, which does not consist in doing nothing, but in doing a great deal not recognized in the dogmatic formularies of the ruling class, has as good a right to state its position as industry itself. It is admitted that the presence of people who refuse to enter in the great handicap race for sixpenny pieces, is at once an insult and a disenchantment for those who do. A fine fellow (as we see so many) takes his determination, votes for the sixpences, and in the emphatic Americanism, " goes for " them. And while such a one is plowing distressfully up the road, it is not hard to understand his resentment, when he perceives cool persons in the meadows by the wayside, lying with a handkerchief over their ears and a glass at their elbow. Alexander is touched in a very delicate place by the disregard of Diogenes. Where was the glory of having taken Rome for these tumultuous barbarians, who poured into the Senate house, and found the Fathers sitting silent and unmoved by their success? It is a sore thing to have labored along and scaled the arduous hilltops, and when all is done, find humanity indifferent to your achievement. Hence physicists condemn the unphysical; financiers have only a superficial toleration for those who know little of stocks; literary persons despise the unlettered; and people of all pursuits combine to disparage those who have none.

But though this is one difficulty of the subject, it is not the greatest. You could not be put in prison for speaking against industry, but you can be sent to Coventry for speaking like a fool. The greatest difficulty with most subjects is to do them well; therefore, please to remember this is an apology. It is certain that much may be judiciously argued in favor of diligence; only there is something to be said against it, and that is what, on the present occasion, I have to say. To state one argument is not necessarily to be deaf to all others, and that a man has written a book of travels in Montenegro, is no reason why he should never have been to Richmond.

It is surely beyond a doubt that people should be a good deal idle in youth. For though here and there a Lord Macaulay may escape from school honors with all his wits about him, most boys pay so dear for their medals that they never afterward have a shot in their locker, and begin the world bankrupt. And the same holds true during all the time a lad is educating himself, or suffering others to educate him. It must have been a very foolish old gentleman who addressed Johnson at Oxford in these words: " Young man, ply your book diligently now, and acquire a stock of knowledge; for when years come upon you, you will find that poring upon books will be but an irksome task." The old gentleman seems to have been unaware that many other things besides reading grow irksome, and not a few become impossible, by the time a man has to use spectacles and cannot walk without a stick. Books are good enough in their own way, but they are a mighty bloodless substitute for life. It seems a pity to sit, like the Lady of Shalott, peering into a mirror, with your back turned on all the bustle and glamour of reality. And if a man reads very hard, as the old anecdote reminds us, he will have little time for thoughts.

If you look back on your own education, I am sure it will not be the full, vivid, instructive hours of truantry that you regret; you would rather cancel some lack-luster periods between sleep and waking in the class. For my own part, I have attended a good many lectures in my time. I still remember that the spinning of a top is a case of Kinetic Stability. I still remember that Emphyteusis is not a disease, nor Stillicide a crime. But though I would not willingly part with such scraps of science, I do not set the same store by them as by certain other odds and ends that I came by in the open street while I was playing truant. This is not the moment to dilate on that mighty place of education, which was the favorite school of Dickens and of Balzac, and turns out yearly many inglorious masters in the Science of the Aspects of Life. Suffice it to say this: if a lad does not learn in the streets, it is because he has no faculty of learning. Nor is the truant always in the streets, for if he prefers, he may go out by the gardened suburbs into the country. He may pitch on some tuft of lilacs over a burn, and smoke innumerable pipes to the tune of the water on the stones. A bird will sing in the thicket. And there he may fall into a vein of kindly thought, and see things in a new perspective. Why, if this be not education, what is? We may conceive Mr. Worldly Wiseman accosting such a one, and the conversation that should thereupon ensue:

" How, now, young fellow, what dost thou here? "

" Truly, sir, I take mine ease."

" Is this not the hour of the class? and should'st thou not be plying thy Book with diligence, to the end thou mayest obtain knowledge? "

" Nay, but thus also I follow after Learning, by your leave."

" Learning, quotha! After what fashion, I pray thee? Is it mathematics? "

" No, to be sure."

" Is it metaphysics? "

" Nor that."

" Is it some language? "

" Nay, it is no language."

" Is it a trade? "

" Nor a trade neither."

" Why, then, what is't? "

" Indeed, sir, as a time may soon come for me to go upon Pilgrimage, I am desirous to note what is commonly done by persons in my case, and where are the ugliest Sloughs and Thickets on the Road; as also, what manner of Staff is of the best service. Moreover, I lie here, by this water, to learn by root-of-heart a lesson which my master teaches me to call Peace, or Contentment."

Hereupon Mr. Worldly Wiseman was much commoved with passion, and shaking his cane with a very threatful countenance broke forth upon this wise: " Learning, quotha! " said he; " I would have all such rogues scourged by the Hangman! "

And so he would go his way, ruffling out his cravat with a crackle of starch, like a turkey when it spreads its feathers.

Now this, of Mr. Wiseman's, is the common opinion. A fact is not called a fact, but a piece of gossip, if it does not fall into one of your scholastic categories. An inquiry must be in some acknowledged direction, with a name to go by; or else you are not inquiring at all, only lounging; and the workhouse is too good for you. It is supposed that all knowledge is at the bottom of a well, or the far end of a telescope. Sainte-Beuve, as he grew older, came to regard all experience as a single great book, in which to study for a few years ere we go hence; and it seemed all one to him whether you should read in Chapter XX, which is the differential calculus, or in Chapter XXXIX, which is hearing the band play in the gardens. As a matter of fact, an intelligent person, looking out of his eyes and hearkening in his ears, with a smile on his face all the time, will get more true education than many another in a life of heroic vigils. There is certainly some chill and arid knowledge to be found upon the summits of formal and laborious science; but it is all round about you, and for the trouble of looking, that you will acquire the warm and palpitating facts of life. While others are filling their memory with a lumber of words, one-half of which they will forget before the week be out, your truant may learn some really useful art: to play the fiddle, to know a good cigar, or to speak with ease and opportunity to all varieties of men. Many who have "plied their book diligently," and know all about some one branch or another of accepted lore, come out of the study with an ancient and owl-like demeanor, and prove dry, stockish, and dyspeptic in all the better and brighter parts of life. Many make a large fortune, who remain underbred and pathetically stupid to the last. And meantime there goes the idler, who began life along with them — by your leave, a different picture. He has had time to take care of his health and his spirits; he has been a great deal in the open air, which is the most salutary of all things for both body and mind; and if he has never read the great Book in very recondite places, he has dipped into it and skimmed it over to excellent purpose. Might not the student afford some Hebrew roots, and the business man some of his half-crowns, for a share of the idler's knowledge of life at large, and Art of Living? Nay, and the idler has another and more important quality than these. I mean his wisdom. He who has much looked on at the childish satisfaction of other people in their hobbies, will regard his own with only a very ironical indulgence. He will not be heard among the dogmatists. He will have a great and cool allowance for all sorts of people and opinions. If he finds no out-of-the-way truths, he will identify himself with no very burning falsehood. His way takes him along a by-road, not much frequented, but very even and pleasant, which is called Commonplace Lane, and leads to the Belvedere of Commonsense. Thence he shall command an agreeable, if no very noble prospect; and while others behold the East and West, the Devil and the Sunrise, he will be contentedly aware of a sort of morning hour upon all sublunary things, with an army of shadows running speedily and in many different directions into the great daylight of Eternity. The shadows and the generations, the shrill doctors and the plangent wars, go by into ultimate silence and emptiness; but underneath all this, a man may see, out of the Belvedere windows, much green and peaceful landscape; many firelit parlors; good people laughing, drinking, and making love as they did before the Flood or the French Revolution; and the old shepherd telling his tale under the hawthorn.

Extreme *busyness,* whether at school or college, kirk or market, is a symptom of deficient vitality; and a faculty for idleness implies a catholic appetite and a strong sense of personal identity. There is a sort of dead-alive, hackneyed people about, who are scarcely conscious of living except in the exercise of some conventional occupation. Bring these fellows into the country, or set them aboard ship, and you will see how they pine for their desk or their study. They have no curiosity; they cannot give themselves over to random provocations; they do not take pleasure in the exercise of their faculties for its own sake; and unless Necessity lays about them with a stick, they will even stand still. It is no good speaking to such folk: they *cannot* be idle, their nature is not generous enough; and they pass those hours in a sort of coma, which are not dedicated to furious moiling in the gold-mill. When they do not require to go to the office, when they are not hungry and have no mind for drink, the whole breathing world is a blank to them. If they have to wait an hour or so for a train, they fall into a stupid trance with their eyes open. To see them, you would suppose there was nothing to look at and no one to speak with; you would imagine they were paralyzed or alienated; and yet very possibly they are hard workers in their own way, and have good eyesight for a flaw in a deed or a turn of the market. They have been to school and college, but all the time they had their eye on the medal; they have gone about in the world and mixed with clever people, but all the time they were thinking of their own affairs. As if a man's soul were not too small to begin with, they have dwarfed and narrowed theirs by a life of all work and no play; until here they are at forty, with a listless attention, a mind vacant of all material of amusement, and not one thought to rub against another, while they wait for the train. Before he was breeched, he might have clambered on the boxes; when he was twenty, he would have stared at the girls; but now the pipe is smoked out, the snuffbox empty, and my gentleman sits bolt upright upon a bench, with lamentable eyes. This does not appeal to me as being Success in Life.

But it is not only the person himself who suffers from his busy habits, but his wife and children, his friends and relations, and down to the very people he sits with in a railway carriage or an omnibus. Perpetual devotion to what a man calls his business, is only to be sustained by perpetual neglect of many other things. And it is not by any means certain that a man's business is the most important thing he has to do. To an impartial estimate it will seem clear that many of the wisest, most virtuous, and most beneficent parts that are to be played upon the Theater of Life are filled by gratuitous performers, and pass, among the world at large, as phases of idleness. For in that Theater, not only the walking gentleman, singing chambermaids, and diligent fiddlers in the orchestra, but those who look on and clap their hands from the benches, do really play a part and fulfill important offices toward the general result. You are no doubt very dependent on the care of your lawyer and stockbroker, of the guards and signalmen who convey you rapidly from place to place, and the policemen who walk the streets for your protection; but is there not a thought of gratitude in your heart for certain other benefactors who set you smiling when they fall in your way, or season your dinner with good company? Colonel Newcome helped to lose his friend's money; Fred Bayham had an ugly trick of borrowing shirts; and yet they were better people to fall among than Mr. Barnes. And though Falstaff was neither sober nor very honest, I think I could name one or two long-faced Barabbases whom the world could better have done without. Hazlitt mentions that he was more sensible of obligation to Northcote, who had never done him anything he could call a service, than to his whole circle of ostentatious friends; for he thought a good companion emphatically the greatest benefactor. I know there are people in the world who cannot feel grateful unless the favor has been done them at the cost of pain and difficulty. But this is a churlish disposition. A man may send you six sheets of letter-paper covered with the most entertaining gossip, or you may pass half an hour pleasantly, perhaps profitably, over an article of his; do you think the service would be greater, if he had made the manuscript in his heart's blood, like a compact with the devil? Do you really fancy you should be more beholden to your correspondent, if he had been damning you all the while for your importunity? Pleasures are more beneficial than duties because, like the quality of mercy, they are not strained, and they are twice blest. There must always be two to a kiss, and there may be a score in a jest; but wherever there is an element of sacrifice, the favor is conferred with pain, and, among generous people, received with confusion. There is no duty we so much underrate as the duty of being happy. By being happy, we sow anonymous benefits upon the world, which remain unknown even to ourselves, or when they are disclosed, surprise nobody so much as the benefactor. The other day, a ragged, barefoot boy ran down the street after a marble, with so jolly an air that he set every one he passed into a good humor; one of these persons, who had been delivered from more than usually black thoughts, stopped the little fellow and gave him some money with this remark: "You see what sometimes comes of looking pleased." If he had looked pleased before, he had now to look both pleased and mystified. For my part, I justify this encouragement of smiling rather than tearful children; I do not wish to pay for tears anywhere but upon the stage; but I am prepared to deal largely in the opposite commodity. A happy man or woman is a better thing to find than a five-pound note. He or she is a radiating focus of goodwill; and their entrance into a room is as though another candle had been lighted. We need not care whether they could prove the forty-seventh proposition; they do a better thing than that, they practically demonstrate the great Theorem of the Livableness of Life. Consequently, if a person cannot be happy without remaining idle, idle he should remain. It is a revolutionary precept; but thanks to hunger and the workhouse, one not easily to be abused; and within practical limits, it is one of the most incontestable truths in the whole Body of Morality. Look at one of your industrious fellows for a moment, I beseech you. He sows hurry and reaps indigestion; he puts a vast deal of activity out to interest, and receives a large measure of nervous derangement in return. Either he absents himself entirely from all fellowship, and lives a recluse in a garret, with carpet slippers and a leaden inkpot; or he comes among people swiftly and bitterly, in a contraction of his whole nervous system, to discharge some temper before he returns to work. I do not care how much or how well he works, this fellow is an evil feature in other people's lives. They would be happier if he were dead. They could easier do without his services in the Circumlocution Office, than they can tolerate his fractious spirits. He poisons life at the well-head. It is better to be beggared out of hand by a scapegrace nephew, than daily hag-ridden by a peevish uncle.

And what, in God's name, is all this pother about? For what cause do they embitter their own and other people's lives? That a man should publish three or thirty articles a year, that he should finish or not finish his great allegorical picture, are questions of little interest to the world. The ranks of life are full; and although a thousand fall, there are always some to go into the breach. When they told Joan of Arc she should be at home minding women's work, she answered there were plenty to spin and wash. And so, even with your own rare gifts! When nature is " so careless of the single life," why should we coddle ourselves into the fancy that our own is of exceptional importance? Suppose Shakespeare had been knocked on the head some dark night in Sir Thomas Lucy's preserves, the world would have wagged on better or worse, the pitcher gone to the well, the scythe to the corn, and the student to his book; and no one been any the wiser of the loss. There are not many works extant, if you look the alternative all over, which are worth the price of a pound of tobacco to a man of limited means. This is a sobering reflection for the proudest of our earthly vanities. Even a tobacconist may, upon consideration, find no great cause for personal vainglory in the phrase; for although tobacco is an admirable sedative, the qualities necessary for retailing it are neither rare nor precious in themselves. Alas and alas! you may take it how you will, but the services of no single individual are indispensable. Atlas was just a gentleman with a protracted nightmare! And yet you see merchants who go and labor themselves into a great fortune and thence into the bankruptcy court; scribblers who keep scribbling at little articles until their temper is a cross to all who come about them, as though Pharaoh should set the Israelites to make a pin instead of a pyramid; and fine young men who work themselves into a decline, and are driven off in a hearse with white plumes upon it. Would you not suppose these persons had been whispered, by the Master of the Ceremonies, the promise of some momentous destiny? and that this lukewarm bullet on which they play their farces was the bull's-eye and centerpoint of all the universe? And yet it is not so. The ends for which they give away their priceless youth, for all they know, may be chimerical or hurtful; the glory and riches they expect may never come, or may find them indifferent; and they and the world they inhabit are so inconsiderable that the mind freezes at the thought.

APPRECIATION HELPS

1. Discuss the effectiveness of the title. What do you know of Stevenson's habits of work? Did his life exemplify the idler? Why should this title attract him?
2. What definition does Stevenson give of idleness? Do you know very *busy* pupils, either in class or study hall, who might be included in this definition? Illustrate.
3. Why should people be a " good deal idle in youth "?
4. Discuss: " Books are good enough in their own way, but they are a mighty bloodless substitute for life."
5. In what sense is the street " that mighty place of education "?
6. What valuable information have you gathered away from school? Discuss the education which comes from experience.
7. Why does Stevenson place so high a value on curiosity? Lacking it, into what kind of persons do we develop? Illustrate.
8. In what sense may success in business narrow and cramp a man's development?
9. What is Stevenson's idea of the importance of any single person in the work of the world? Do you agree? Does this philosophy discourage individual effort? Why?
10. Read the last paragraph aloud many times. What makes it great literature?
11. What ideas of Stevenson are you going to keep as permanent possessions?

COMPOSITION HINTS

1. An Apology for Industry
2. " Instructive Hours of Truancy "
3. Odds and Ends Learned on the Streets
4. Dialogue between Idleness and Industry
5. Daydreaming: a Defense
6. The Pleasures of Loafing
7. Curiosity: an Asset

AES TRIPLEX[1]

by Robert Louis Stevenson

THE changes wrought by death are in themselves so sharp and final, and so terrible and melancholy in their consequences, that the thing stands alone in man's experience and has no parallel upon earth. It outdoes all other accidents because it is the last of them. Sometimes it leaps suddenly upon its victims, like a Thug; sometimes it lays a regular siege and creeps upon their citadel during a score of years. And when the business is done, there is sore havoc made in other people's lives, and a pin knocked out by which many subsidiary friendships hung together. There are empty chairs, solitary walks, and single beds at night. Again, in taking away our friends, death does not take them away utterly, but leaves behind a mocking, tragical, and soon intolerable residue, which must be hurriedly concealed. Hence a whole chapter of sights and customs striking to the mind, from the pyramids of Egypt to the gibbets and dule trees of medieval Europe. The poorest persons have a bit of pageant going towards the tomb; memorial stones are set up over the least memorable; and, in order to preserve some show of respect for what remains of our old loves and friendships, we must accompany it with much grimly ludicrous ceremonial, and the hired undertaker parades before the door. All this, and much more of the same sort, accompanied by the eloquence of poets, has gone a great way to put humanity in error; nay, in many philosophies the error has been embodied and laid down with every circumstance of logic; although in real life the bustle and swiftness, in leaving people little time to think, have not left them time enough to go dangerously wrong in practice.

As a matter of fact, although few things are spoken of with more fearful whisperings than this prospect of death, few have less influence on conduct under healthy circumstances. We

---

[1] From *Virginibus Puerisque*, copyright by Charles Scribner's Sons.

have all heard of cities of South America built upon the side
of fiery mountains, and how, even in this tremendous neighborhood, the inhabitants are not a jot more impressed by the
solemnity of mortal conditions than if they were delving gardens in the greenest corner of England. There are serenades
and suppers and much gallantry among the myrtles overhead;
and meanwhile the foundation shudders underfoot, the bowels
of the mountain growl, and at any moment living ruin may
leap sky-high into the moonlight, and tumble man and his
merry-making in the dust. In the eyes of very young people,
and very dull old ones, there is something indescribably reck-
less and desperate in such a picture. It seems not credible that
respectable married people, with umbrellas, should find appetite for a bit of supper within quite a long distance of a fiery
mountain; ordinary life begins to smell of high-handed debauch when it is carried on so close to a catastrophe; and even
cheese and salad, it seems, could hardly be relished in such
circumstances without something like a defiance of the Creator. It should be a place for nobody but hermits dwelling in
prayer and maceration, or mere born-devils drowning care in
a perpetual carouse.

And yet, when one comes to think upon it calmly, the situation of these South American citizens forms only a very pale
figure for the state of ordinary mankind. This world itself,
traveling blindly and swiftly in overcrowded space, among a
million other worlds traveling blindly and swiftly in contrary
directions, may very well come by a knock that would set it
into explosion like a penny squib. And what, pathologically
looked at, is the human body with all its organs, but a mere
bagful of petards? The least of these is as dangerous to the
whole economy as the ship's powder-magazine to the ship;
and with every breath we breathe, and every meal we eat, we
are putting one more of them in peril. If we clung as devotedly as some philosophers pretend we do to the abstract
idea of life, or were half as frightened as they make out we
are, for the subversive accident that ends it all, the trumpets
might sound by the hour and no one would follow them into

battle — the blue-peter might fly at the truck, but who would climb into a sea-going ship? Think (if these philosophers were right) with what a preparation of spirit we should affront the daily peril of the dinner-table: a deadlier spot than any battle-field in history, where the far greater proportion of our ancestors have miserably left their bones! What woman would ever be lured into marriage, so much more dangerous than the wildest sea? And what would it be to grow old? For, after a certain distance, every step we take in life we find the ice growing thinner below our feet, and all around us and behind us we see our contemporaries going through. By the time a man gets well into the seventies, his continued existence is a mere miracle; and when he lays his old bones in bed for the night, there is an overwhelming probability that he will never see the day. Do the old men mind it, as a matter of fact? Why, no. They were never merrier; they have their grog at night, and tell the raciest stories; they hear of the death of people about their own age, or even younger, not as if it was a grisly warning, but with a simple childlike pleasure at having outlived some one else; and when a draft might puff them out like a guttering candle, or a bit of a stumble shatter them like so much glass, their old hearts keep sound and unaffrighted, and they go on, bubbling with laughter, through years of man's age compared to which the valley at Balaklava was as safe and peaceful as a village cricket-green on Sunday. It may fairly be questioned (if we look at the peril only) whether it was a much more daring feat for Curtius to plunge into the gulf than for any old gentleman of ninety to doff his clothes and clamber into bed.

Indeed, it is a memorable subject for consideration, with what unconcern and gaiety mankind pricks on along the Valley of the Shadow of Death. The whole way is one wilderness of snares; and the end of it, for those who fear the last pinch, is irrevocable ruin. And yet we go spinning through it all, like a party for the Derby. Perhaps the reader remembers one of the humorous devices of the deified Caligula: how he encouraged a vast concourse of holiday-makers on to his bridge over

Baiae bay, and, when they were in the height of their enjoyment, turned loose the Pretorian guards among the company, and had them tossed into the sea. This is no bad miniature of the dealings of nature with the transitory race of man. Only, what a checkered picnic we have of it, even while it lasts! and into what great waters, not to be crossed by any swimmer, God's pale Pretorian throws us over in the end! .

We live the time that a match flickers; we pop the cork of a ginger-beer bottle, and the earthquake swallows us on the instant. Is it not odd, is it not incongruous, is it not in the highest sense of human speech, incredible, that we should think so highly of the ginger-beer and regard so little the devouring earthquake? The love of Life and the fear of Death are two famous phrases that grow harder to understand the more we think about them. It is a well-known fact that an immense proportion of boat accidents would never happen if people held the sheet in their hands instead of making it fast; and yet, unless it be some martinet of a professional mariner or some landsman with shattered nerves, every one of God's creatures makes it fast. A strange instance of man's unconcern and brazen boldness in the face of death!

We confound ourselves with metaphysical phrases, which we import into daily talk with noble inappropriateness. We have no idea of what death is, apart from its circumstances and some of its consequences to others; and although we have some experience of living, there is not a man on earth who has flown so high into abstraction as to have any practical guess at the meaning of the word *life*. All literature, from Job and Omar Khayam to Thomas Carlyle or Walt Whitman, is but an attempt to look upon the human state with such largeness of view as shall enable us to rise from the consideration of living to the Definition of Life. And our sages give us about the best satisfaction in their power when they say that it is a vapor, or a show, or made out of the same stuff with dreams. Philosophy, in its more rigid sense, has been at the same work for ages; and after a myriad bald heads have wagged over the problem, and piles of words have been heaped one upon another into dry and cloudy volumes without end, philosophy has the honor of laying before us, with modest pride, her contribution towards the subject: that life is a Permanent Possibility of Sensation. Truly a fine result! A man may very well love beef, or hunting, or a woman; but surely, surely, not a Permanent Possibility of Sensation! He may be afraid of a precipice, or a dentist, or a large enemy with a club, or even an undertaker's man; but not certainly of abstract death. We may trick with the word life in its dozen senses until we are weary of tricking; we may argue in terms of all the philosophies on earth; but one fact remains true throughout — that we do not love life, in the sense that we are greatly preoccupied about its conservation; that we do not, properly speaking, love life at all, but living. Into the views of the least careful there will enter some degree of providence; no man's eyes are fixed entirely on the passing hour; but although we have some anticipation of good health, good weather, wine, active employment, love, and self-approval, the sum of these anticipations does not amount to anything like a general view of life's possibilities and issues; nor are those who cherish them most vividly, at all the most scrupulous of their personal safety. To be deeply interested in the accidents of our existence, to enjoy keenly the mixed texture of human experience, rather leads a man to disregard precautions, and risk his neck against a straw. For surely the love of living is stronger in an Alpine climber roping over a peril, or a hunter riding merrily at a stiff fence, than in a creature who lives upon a diet and walks a measured distance in the interest of his constitution.

There is a great deal of very vile nonsense talked upon both sides of the matter; tearing divines reducing life to the dimensions of a mere funeral procession, so short as to be hardly decent; and melancholy unbelievers yearning for the tomb as if it were a world too far away. Both sides must feel a little ashamed of their performances now and again, when they draw in their chairs to dinner. Indeed, a good meal and a bottle of wine is an answer to most standard works upon the question. When a man's heart warms to his viands, he forgets a great deal of sophistry, and soars into a rosy zone of contemplation. Death may be knocking at the door, like the Commander's statue; we have something else in hand, thank God, and let him knock. Passing bells are ringing the world over. All the world over, and every hour, some one is parting company with all his aches and ecstasies. For us also the trap is laid. But we are so fond of life that we have no leisure to entertain the terror of death. It is a honeymoon with us all through, and none of the longest. Small blame to us if we give our whole hearts to this glowing bride of ours — to the appetites, to honor, to the hungry curiosity of the mind, to the pleasure of the eyes in nature, and the pride of our own nimble bodies.

We all of us appreciate the sensations; but as for caring about the Permanence of the Possibility, a man's head is generally very bald, and his senses very dull, before he comes to that. Whether we regard life as a lane leading to a dead wall — a mere bag's end, as the French say — or whether we think of it as a vestibule or gymnasium, where we wait our turn and prepare our faculties for some more noble destiny; whether we thunder in a pulpit, or pule in little atheistic poetry-books, about its vanity and brevity; whether we look justly for years of health and vigor, or are about to mount into a bath-chair, as a step towards the hearse; in each and all of these views and situations there is but one conclusion possible: that a man should stop his ears against paralyzing terror, and run the race that is set before him with a single mind. No one surely could have recoiled with more heartache and terror from the thought of death than our respected lexicographer; and yet we know how little it affected his conduct, how wisely and boldly he walked, and in what a fresh and lively vein he spoke of life. Already an old man, he ventured on his Highland tour; and his heart, bound with triple brass, did not recoil before twenty-seven individual cups of tea. As courage and intelligence are the two qualities best worth a good man's cultivation, so it is the first part of intelligence to recognize our precarious estate in life, and the first part of courage to be not at all abashed before the fact. A frank and somewhat headlong carriage, not looking too anxiously before, not dallying in maudlin regret over the past, stamps the man who is well armored for this world.

And not only well armored for himself, but a good friend and a good citizen to boot. We do not go to cowards for tender dealing; there is nothing so cruel as panic; the man who has least fear for his own carcase, has most time to consider others. That eminent chemist who took his walks abroad in tin shoes, and subsisted wholly upon tepid milk, had all his work cut out for him in considerate dealings with his own digestion. So soon as prudence has begun to grow up in the brain, like a dismal fungus, it finds its first expression in a paralysis of generous acts. The victim begins to shrink spiritually; he develops a fancy for parlors with a regulated temperature, and takes his morality on the principle of tin shoes and tepid milk. The care of one important body or soul becomes so engrossing that all the noises of the outer world begin to come thin and faint into the parlor with the regulated temperature; and the tin shoes go equably forward over blood and rain. To be otherwise is to ossify; and the scruple-monger ends by standing stock still. Now the man who has his heart on his sleeve, and a good whirling weathercock of a brain, who reckons his life as a thing to be dashingly used and cheerfully hazarded, makes a very different acquaintance of the world, keeps all his pulses going true and fast, and gathers impetus as he runs, until, if he be running towards anything better than wildfire, he may shoot up and become a constellation in the end. Lord look after his health, Lord have a care of his soul, says he; and he has at the key of the position, and swashes through incongruity and peril towards his aim. Death is on all sides of him with pointed batteries, as he is on all sides of all of us; unfortunate surprises gird him round; mim-mouthed friends and relations hold up their hands in quite a little elegiacal synod about his path: and what cares he for all this? Being a true lover of living, a fellow with something pushing and spontaneous in his inside, he must, like any other soldier, in any other stirring, deadly warfare, push on at his best pace until he touch the goal. " A peerage or Westminster Abbey! " cried Nelson in his bright, boyish, heroic manner. These are great incentives; not for any of these, but for the plain satisfaction of living, of being about their business in some sort or other, do the brave, serviceable men of every nation tread down the nettle danger, and pass flying over all the stumbling-blocks of prudence. Think of the heroism of Johnson, think of that superb indifference to mortal limitation that set him upon his dictionary, and carried him through triumphantly until the end! Who, if he were wisely considerate of things at large, would ever embark upon any work much more considerable than a halfpenny postcard? Who would project a serial novel, after Thackeray and Dickens had each fallen in mid-course? Who would find heart enough to begin to live, if he dallied with the consideration of death?

And, after all, what sorry and pitiful quibbling all this is! To forgo all the issues of living, in a parlor with a regulated temperature — as if that were not to die a hundred times over, and for ten years at a stretch! As if it were not to die in one's own lifetime, and without even the sad immunities of death! As if it were not to die, and yet to be the patient spectators of our own pitiable change! The Permanent Possibility is preserved, but the sensations carefully held at arm's length, as if one kept a photographic plate in a dark chamber. It is better to lose health like a spendthrift than to waste it like a miser. It is better to live and be done with it, than to die daily in the sick room. By all means begin your folio; even if the doctor does not give you a year, even if he hesitates about a month, make one brave push and see what can be accomplished in a week. It is not only in finished undertakings that we ought to honor useful labor. A spirit goes out of the man who means execution, which outlives the most untimely ending. All who have meant good work with their whole hearts, have done good work, although they may die before they have the time to sign it. Every heart that has beat strong and cheerfully has left a hopeful impulse behind it in the world, and bettered the tradition of mankind. And even if death catch people, like an open pitfall, and in mid-career, laying out vast projects, and planning monstrous foundations, flushed with hope, and their mouths full of boastful language, they should be at once tripped up and silenced: is there not something brave and spirited in such a termination? and does not life go down with a better grace, foaming in full body over a precipice, than miserably straggling to an end in sandy deltas? When the Greeks made their fine saying that those whom the gods love die young, I cannot help believing they had this sort of death also in their eye. For surely, at whatever age it overtake the man, this is to die young. Death has not been suffered to take so much as an illusion from his heart. In the hot-fit of life, a-tiptoe on the highest point of being, he passes at a bound on to the other side. The noise of the mallet and chisel is scarcely quenched, the trumpets are hardly done blowing, when, trailing with him clouds of glory, this happy-starred, full-blooded spirit shoots into the spiritual land.

APPRECIATION HELPS

1. What are the circumstances of Stevenson's life which make this essay on death significant?
2. How does the author show that we are little influenced by the fear of death? What things do people do today which reveal that they have no fear of death?
3. What is the attitude of old persons towards death?
4. List the historical and literary allusions found in the essay. Comment on their effectiveness. Do you enjoy the ones you understand? Does this suggest the pleasure which comes from a broad reading background? Watch for "literary echoing" in all your reading for the week.
5. Point out places in the essay which reveal the deeper qualities of Stevenson's nature. Essays are a revelation of personality. Have you discovered differences in the personality of the authors studied? Illustrate.
6. What distinction does Stevenson make between the "love of life" and the "love of living"?

7. List five essays you have enjoyed which furnish material for interesting discussion. List five which merely amuse. What is the value in reading " Aes Triplex "?
8. The last paragraph is one of the finest passages in all literature. Why? Comment on Stevenson's philosophy towards life and work.

COMPOSITION HINTS

1. The Daily Peril of the Dinner Table. (Write a humorous account of the dangers met at the table — mince pie, and so on.)
2. Courage and Intelligence, the Chief Assets in Life
3. Stumbling-blocks of prudence. (Show that too much caution hinders progress.)

THEODORE ROOSEVELT

If one is to be strong, healthy, and energetic, it would seem to be almost an advantage to start frail and puny, judging by the career of Theodore Roosevelt (1858–1919), twenty-sixth President of the United States. Provided, of course, one has the will to alter one's condition.

Roosevelt was born a weakling. He became asthmatic, had to remain in bed for weeks on end, proved too delicate to go to school and so had to get his schooling at home. His condition and his dependence disgusted him. He decided to vanquish them. Other men had triumphed over such handicaps, and he would too. By the time he was twenty-eight he had definitely succeeded.

This is how he did it. He began building up his physical strength as a boy by boxing daily. When he was of age, he found himself equal to going to Harvard, and there continued his efforts. He fenced and he played football. More, he did forcible unconventional things, such as wearing whiskers, because the ridicule which this entailed was good for his character. Then he went to Europe and at twenty-two climbed the Matterhorn, just after he had met two Englishmen who claimed that they had been the first people ever to do so. At twenty-six he turned cowpuncher and trick rider out on a ranch in North Dakota near the Missouri River, and for two years there he lived really hard. At the end of that period the weakling was no more; he had become a big-chested, iron-sinewed man of action, a fellow of vigor and stamina. Thereafter Roosevelt's life was one which only a man of extremely powerful physique could endure.

Born at Sagamore Hill, near Oyster Bay, Long Island, which remained his home all his life, he was essentially a New Yorker. Failing to be elected Mayor of New York, he became Police Commissioner and conducted what he called " a grimy struggle." In 1897 he was made Assistant Secretary of the Navy, but resigned in a year to form with Surgeon Leonard Wood the First U. S.

Cavalry, which was known as Roosevelt's Rough Riders. With this regiment he served in the Spanish-American War in Cuba and became its colonel. He captured San Juan Hill and when he returned to New York was welcomed as a hero and was elected Governor of New York State. In 1901 he became Vice President against his desires. That same year, on September 6, President McKinley was shot; he died eight days later, and Roosevelt automatically succeeded him, the youngest man to assume the office. He was elected to a second term and so occupied the White House until 1909, when, leisured quiet now being impossible for him, he plunged into Equatorial Africa on a big-game hunting expedition, supporting himself by writing. In 1912 he ran as third (Progressive) candidate for the presidency, with the result that Woodrow Wilson was elected. During the campaign at Milwaukee he was shot and wounded by a crank. Nobody would have suspected then that he had been born frail and puny. Though wounded, he delivered the speech he had prepared! Since he was not to have office again, he must have other adventure, and in 1913 he faced the privations of exploring South America, where he discovered a hitherto unknown river which the Brazilian Government named the Rio Roosevelt. Next came what we know now as the World War, and from its outset Roosevelt vigorously demanded American participation. He sought to raise troops as he had done before, but was not allowed to do so. All through the struggle he was as active as ever, on behalf of the Allied cause. Yet when his end came, this man of many battles died quietly in his sleep.

Roosevelt was also the author of some twenty volumes and twice he undertook journalism; he edited the *Outlook* from 1910 to 1912.

As President he settled several international problems, including the peace between the two belligerents in the Russo-Japanese War. For this he was awarded the Nobel Prize for Peace.

Having read so far, you will not be surprised to see the title of the following essay.

THE STRENUOUS LIFE [1]

Gentlemen: — In speaking to you, men of the greatest city of the West, men of the State which gave to the country Lincoln and Grant, men who preëminently and distinctly embody all that is most American in the American character, I wish to preach not the doctrine of ignoble ease but the doctrine of the strenuous life; the life of toil and effort; of labor and strife; to preach that highest form of success which comes not to the man who desires mere easy peace but to the man who does not shrink from danger, from hardship, or from bitter toil, and who out of these wins the splendid ultimate triumph.

A life of ignoble ease, a life of that peace which springs merely from lack either of desire or of power to strive after great things, is as little worthy of a nation as of an individual. I ask only that what every self-respecting American demands from himself, and from his sons, shall be demanded of the American nation as a whole. Who among you would teach your boys that ease, that peace is to be the first consideration in your eyes — to be the ultimate goal after which they strive? You men of Chicago have made this city great, you men of Illinois have done your share, and more than your share, in making America great, because you neither preach nor practice such a doctrine. You work yourselves, and you bring up your sons to work. If you are rich, and are worth your salt, you will teach your sons that though they may have leisure, it is not to be spent in idleness; for wisely used leisure merely means that those who possess it, being free from the necessity of working for their livelihood, are all the more bound to carry on some kind of non-remunerative work in science, in letters, in art, in exploration, in historical research — work of the type we most need in this country, the successful carrying out of which reflects most honor upon the nation.

We do not admire the man of timid peace. We admire the

[1] From *The Strenuous Life,* published by The Century Company, 1900.

man who embodies victorious effort; the man who never wrongs his neighbor; who is prompt to help a friend; but who has those virile qualities necessary to win in the stern strife of actual life. It is hard to fail; but it is worse never to have tried to succeed. In this life we get nothing save by effort. Freedom from effort in the present, merely means that there has been stored up effort in the past. A man can be freed from the necessity of work only by the fact that he or his fathers before him have worked to good purpose. If the freedom thus purchased is used aright, and the man still does actual work, though of a different kind, whether as a writer or a general, whether in the field of politics or in the field of exploration and adventure, he shows he deserves his good fortune. But if he treats this period of freedom from the need of actual labor as a period not of preparation but of mere enjoyment, he shows that he is simply a cumberer on the earth's surface; and he surely unfits himself to hold his own with his fellows if the need to do so should again arise. A mere life of ease is not in the end a satisfactory life, and above all it is a life which ultimately unfits those who follow it for serious work in the world.

As it is with the individual so it is with the nation. It is a base untruth to say that happy is the nation that has no history. Thrice happy is the nation that has a glorious history. Far better it is to dare mighty things, to win glorious triumphs, even though checkered by failure, than to take rank with those poor spirits who neither enjoy much nor suffer much because they live in the gray twilight that knows neither victory nor defeat. If in 1861 the men who loved the Union had believed that peace was the end of all things and war and strife the worst of all things, and had acted up to their belief, we would have saved hundreds of thousands of lives, we would have saved hundreds of millions of dollars. Moreover, besides saving all the blood and treasure we then lavished, we would have prevented the heartbreak of many women, the dissolution of many homes; and we would have spared the country those months of gloom and shame when it seemed as if our armies marched only to defeat. We could have avoided all this suffering simply by shrinking from strife. And if we had thus avoided it we would have shown that we were weaklings and that we were unfit to stand among the great nations of the earth. Thank God for the iron in the blood of our fathers, the men who upheld the wisdom of Lincoln and bore sword or rifle in the armies of Grant! Let us, the children of the men who proved themselves equal to the mighty days — let us, the children of the men who carried the great Civil War to a triumphant conclusion, praise the God of our fathers that the ignoble counsels of peace were rejected, that the suffering and loss, the blackness of sorrow and despair, were unflinchingly faced and the years of strife endured; for in the end the slave was freed, the Union restored, and the mighty American Republic placed once more as a helmeted queen among nations.

We of this generation do not have to face a task such as that our fathers faced, but we have our tasks, and woe to us if we fail to perform them! We cannot, if we would, play the part of China, and be content to rot by inches in ignoble ease within our borders, taking no interest in what goes on beyond them; sunk in a scrambling commercialism; heedless of the higher life, the life of aspiration, of toil and risk; busying ourselves only with the wants of our bodies for the day; until suddenly we should find, beyond a shadow of question, what China has already found, that in this world the nation that has trained itself to a career of unwarlike and isolated ease is bound in the end to go down before other nations which have not lost the manly and adventurous qualities. If we are to be a really great people, we must strive in good faith to play a great part in the world. We cannot avoid meeting great issues. All that we can determine for ourselves is whether we shall meet them well or ill. Last year we could not help being brought face to face with the problem of war with Spain. All we could decide was whether we should shrink like cowards from the contest or enter into it as beseemed a brave and high-spirited people; and, once in, whether failure or success should crown our banners. So it is now. We cannot avoid the responsibilities that confront us in Hawaii, Cuba, Porto Rico, and the Philippines.

All we can decide is whether we shall meet them in a way that will redound to the national credit, or whether we shall make of our dealings with these new problems a dark and shameful page in our history. To refuse to deal with them at all merely amounts to dealing with them badly. We have a given problem to solve. If we undertake the solution there is, of course, always danger that we may not solve it aright, but to refuse to undertake the solution simply renders it certain that we cannot possibly solve it aright.

The timid man, the lazy man, the man who distrusts his country, the overcivilized man, who has lost the great fighting, masterful virtues, the ignorant man and the man of dull mind, whose soul is incapable of feeling the mighty lift that thrills " stern men with empires in their brains " — all these, of course, shrink from seeing the nation undertake its new duties; shrink from seeing us build a navy and army adequate to our needs; shrink from seeing us do our share of the world's work by bringing order out of chaos in the great, fair tropic islands from which the valor of our soldiers and sailors has driven the Spanish flag. These are the men who fear the strenuous life, who fear the only national life which is really worth leading. They believe in that cloistered life which saps the hardy virtues in a nation, as it saps them in the individual; or else they are wedded to that base spirit of gain and greed which recognizes in commercialism the be-all and end-all of national life, instead of realizing that, though an indispensable element, it is after all but one of the many elements that go to make up true national greatness. No country can long endure if its foundations are not laid deep in the material prosperity which comes from thrift, from business energy and enterprise, from hard unsparing effort in the fields of industrial activity; but neither was any nation ever yet truly great if it relied upon material prosperity alone. All honor must be paid to the architects of our material prosperity; to the great captains of industry who have built our factories and our railroads; to the strong men who toil for wealth with brain or hand; for great is the debt of the nation to these and their kind. But our debt is yet greater to the men whose highest type is to be found in a statesman like Lincoln, a soldier like Grant. They showed by their lives that they recognized the law of work, the law of strife; they toiled to win a competence for themselves and those dependent upon them; but they recognized that there were yet other and even loftier duties — duties to the nation and duties to the race.

We cannot sit huddled within our own borders and avow ourselves merely an assemblage of well-to-do hucksters who care nothing for what happens beyond. Such a policy would defeat even its own end; for as the nations grow to have ever wider and wider interests and are brought into closer and closer contact, if we are to hold our own in the struggle for naval and commercial supremacy, we must build up our power without our own borders. We must build the Isthmian canal, and we must grasp the points of vantage which will enable us to have our say in deciding the destiny of the oceans of the East and the West. . . .

I preach to you, then, my countrymen, that our country calls not for the life of ease, but for the life of strenuous endeavor. The Twentieth Century looms before us big with the fate of many nations. If we stand idly by, if we seek merely swollen, slothful ease, and ignoble peace, if we shrink from the hard contests where men must win at hazard of their lives and at the risk of all they hold dear, then the bolder and stronger peoples will pass us by and will win for themselves the domination of the world. Let us therefore boldly face the life of strife, resolute to do our duty well and manfully; resolute to uphold righteousness by deed and by word; resolute to be both honest and brave, to serve high ideals, yet to use practical methods. Above all, let us shrink from no strife, moral or physical, within or without the nation, provided we are certain that the strife is justified; for it is only through strife, through hard and dangerous endeavor, that we shall ultimately win the goal of true national greatness.

APPRECIATION HELPS

1. Give facts concerning Roosevelt's life which gave him the right to speak on the " strenuous life."
2. Discuss the statement that rich men are under obligation to carry on " some kind of non-remunerative work in science, in letters, in art, in exploration, in historical research."
3. Has there been any change in attitude towards the " human parasite " in your time?
4. What in the essay shows that Roosevelt was interested in the problems of his day? If he were living now, what things would he be defending or opposing?
5. What is Roosevelt's conception of the responsibility of the United States?
6. Explain: " the overcivilized man "; " the man of timid peace "; " architects of material prosperity."
7. Has the essay made you better acquainted with the man Roosevelt?

COMPOSITION HINTS

1. " Thrice Happy Is the Nation that Has a Glorious History "
2. " Iron in the Blood." (Write a character sketch of a courageous person.)
3. Our Debt to Lincoln
4. Success Comes through Labor and Strife

WASHINGTON IRVING

When in 1832 Washington Irving (1783–1859) returned to America from Europe, where he had been living since 1815, he was welcomed home as a national hero. And indeed that is what he was. He had not led troops to victory nor routed an enemy's navy, but he had achieved something very similar. One of the effects of a successful battle is to raise a nation's prestige, and raising America's prestige is what Irving had done. America then was still a young country — a mere fifty-six years old. She was naturally eager to gain the respect and admiration of the older European nations, just as a new boy at school wants the other fellows to think well of him. That Europeans should agree that Americans were first-class pioneers and could fight Indians, and if necessary Britons, was not enough. America wanted Europe to reckon with her in the arts. And hitherto that was what Europe had failed to do; it seemed to people in Europe that America was only a nation of roughnecks, of men too busy struggling with nature to be artists. But Irving made them change their minds. He was the first American to whom Europe did homage as a man of letters. He was compared with the great English essayist, Joseph Addison, whom he took as his model. Well did he deserve the triumphant homecoming, just as much as if he had been a great statesman or a great soldier! And America will always remember his name for that noble service.

At sixteen he had been set to study law, but his health did not allow him to become a lawyer, and meanwhile writing had already proved more attractive. He began as a humorist. While still a lad, he had some amusing letters printed in the New York *Morning Chronicle*. They were signed Jonathan Oldstyle. The name alone makes one smile. In 1809 appeared a burlesque of a pompous and pedantic guidebook. Irving called it *The History of New York*, by Diedrich Knickerbocker (another pen name).

It was business that called Irving to Liverpool in 1815. He remained in England for some years and during that time aroused the admiration of English literary circles with *The Sketchbook*, by Geoffrey Crayon, from which the following essay is taken. From England he went to Spain, where he was America's ambassador, and was inspired there to write a *Life of Christopher Columbus*. Thereafter he devoted himself chiefly to biography, producing histories of Oliver Goldsmith (the author of *The Vicar of Wakefield*), Mahomet and his successors (the great Arab preachers), and George Washington. His writing is droll rather than broadly funny, refined rather than vigorous, but it is always simple and direct.

TRAITS OF INDIAN CHARACTER

I appeal to any white man, if ever he enter Logan's cabin hungry, and he gave him not to eat — if ever he came cold and naked, and he clothed him not.
— Speech of Indian Chief.

THERE is something in the character and habits of the North American savage, taken in connection with the scenery over which he is accustomed to range, its vast lakes, boundless forests, majestic rivers, and trackless plains, that is to my mind wonderfully striking and sublime. He is formed for the wilderness, as the Arab is for the desert. His nature is stern, simple, and enduring; fitted to grapple with difficulties, and to support privations. There seems but little soil in his heart for the support of the kindly virtues; and yet, if we would but take the trouble to penetrate through that proud stoicism and habitual taciturnity, which lock up his character from casual observation, we should find him linked to his fellowman of civilized life by more of those sympathies and affections than are usually ascribed to him.

It has been the lot of the unfortunate aborigines of America, in the early periods of colonization, to be doubly wronged by the white men. They have been dispossessed of their hereditary possessions by mercenary and frequently wanton warfare;

and their characters have been traduced by bigoted and interested writers. The colonist often treated them like beasts of the forest; and the author has endeavored to justify him in his outrages. The former found it easier to exterminate than to civilize; the latter to vilify than to discriminate. The appellations of savage and pagan were deemed sufficient to sanction the hostilities of both; and thus the poor wanderers of the forest were persecuted and defamed, not because they were guilty, but because they were ignorant.

The rights of the savage have seldom been properly appreciated or respected by the white man. In peace he has often been the dupe of artful traffic; in war he has been regarded as a ferocious animal, whose life or death was a question of mere precaution and convenience. Man is cruelly wasteful of life when his own safety is endangered, and he is sheltered by impunity; and little mercy is to be expected from him, when he feels the sting of the reptile and is conscious of the power to destroy.

The same prejudices, which were indulged thus early, exist in common circulation at the present day. Certain learned societies have, it is true, with laudable diligence, endeavored to investigate and record the real characters and manners of the Indian tribes; the American government, too, has wisely and humanely exerted itself to inculcate a friendly and forbearing spirit towards them, and to protect them from fraud and injustice.[1] The current opinion of the Indian character, however, is too apt to be formed from the miserable hordes which infest the frontiers, and hang on the skirts of the settlements. These are too commonly composed of degenerate beings, corrupted and enfeebled by the vices of society, without being benefited by its civilization. That proud independence, which formed the main pillar of savage virtue, has been

[1] The American government has been indefatigable in its exertions to ameliorate the situation of the Indians, and to introduce among them the arts of civilization, and civil and religious knowledge. To protect them from the frauds of the white traders, no purchase of land from them by individuals is permitted; nor is any person allowed to receive lands from them as a present, without the express sanction of government. These precautions are strictly enforced.

shaken down, and the whole moral fabric lies in ruins. Their spirits are humiliated and debased by a sense of inferiority, and their native courage cowed and daunted by the superior knowledge and power of their enlightened neighbors. Society has advanced upon them like one of those withering airs, that will sometimes breed desolation over a whole region of fertility. It has enervated their strength, multiplied their diseases, and superinduced upon their original barbarity the low vices of artificial life. It has given them a thousand superfluous wants, whilst it has diminished their means of mere existence. It has driven before it the animals of the chase, who fly from the sound of the axe and the smoke of the settlement, and seek refuge in the depths of the remotest forests and yet untrodden wilds. Thus do we too often find the Indians on our frontiers to be the mere wrecks and remnants of once powerful tribes, who have lingered in the vicinity of the settlements, and sunk into precarious and vagabond existence. Poverty, repining and hopeless poverty, a canker of the mind unknown in savage life, corrodes their spirits and blights every free and noble quality of their natures. They become drunken, indolent, feeble, thievish, and pusillanimous. They loiter like vagrants about the settlements, among spacious dwellings replete with elaborate comforts, which only render them sensible of the comparative wretchedness of their own condition. Luxury spreads its ample board before their eyes; but they are excluded from the banquet. Plenty revels over the fields; but they are starving in the midst of its abundance; the whole wilderness has blossomed into a garden; but they feed as reptiles that infest it.

How different was their state while yet the undisputed lords of the soil! Their wants were few, and the means of gratification within their reach. They saw every one around them sharing the same lot, enduring the same hardships, feeding on the same aliments, arrayed in the same rude garments. No roof then rose, but was open to the homeless stranger; no smoke curled among the trees, but he was welcome to sit down by its fire and join the hunter in his repast. "For," says an old historian of New England, "their life is so void of care, and they are so loving also that they make use of those things they enjoy as common goods, and are therein so compassionate that rather than one should starve through want they would starve all; thus they pass their time merrily, not regarding our pomp, but are better content with their own, which some men esteem so meanly of." Such were the Indians whilst in the pride and energy of their primitive natures; they resembled those wild plants which thrive best in the shades of the forest, but shrink from the hand of cultivation, and perish beneath the influence of the sun.

In discussing the savage character, writers have been too prone to indulge in vulgar prejudice and passionate exaggeration, instead of the candid temper of true philosophy. They have not sufficiently considered the peculiar circumstances in which the Indians have been placed, and the peculiar principles under which they have been educated. No being acts more rigidly from rule than the Indian. His whole conduct is regulated according to some general maxims early implanted in his mind. The moral laws that govern him are, to be sure, but few; but then he conforms to them all; — the white man abounds in laws of religion, morals, and manners, but how many does he violate!

A frequent ground of accusation against the Indians is their disregard of treaties, and the treachery and wantonness with which, in time of apparent peace, they will suddenly fly to hostilities. The intercourse of the white men with the Indians, however, is too apt to be cold, distrustful, oppressive, and insulting. They seldom treat them with that confidence and frankness which are indispensable to real friendship; nor is sufficient caution observed not to offend against those feelings of pride or superstition, which often prompt the Indian to hostility quicker than mere considerations of interest. The solitary savage feels silently, but acutely. His sensibilities are not diffused over so wide a surface as those of the white man; but they run in steadier and deeper channels. His pride, his affections, his superstitions are all directed towards fewer objects; but the wounds inflicted on them are proportionably severe, and furnish motives of hostility which we cannot sufficiently appreciate.   Where a community is also limited in number, and forms one great patriarchal family, as in an Indian tribe, the injury of an individual is the injury of the whole; and the sentiment of vengeance is almost instantaneously diffused.   One council-fire is sufficient for the discussion and arrangement of a plan of hostilities.   Here all the fighting men and sages assemble.   Eloquence and superstition combine to inflame the minds of the warriors.   The orator awakens their martial ardor, and they are wrought up to a kind of religious desperation, by the visions of the prophet and the dreamer.

An instance of one of those sudden exasperations, arising from a motive peculiar to the Indian character, is extant in an old record of the early settlement of Massachusetts.   The planters of Plymouth had defaced the monuments of the dead at Passonagessit, and had plundered the grave of the Sachem's mother of some skins with which it had been decorated.   The Indians are remarkable for the reverence which they entertain for the sepulchres of their kindred.   Tribes that have passed generations exiled from the abodes of their ancestors, when by chance they have been traveling in the vicinity, have been known to turn aside from the highway, and, guided by wonderfully accurate tradition, have crossed the country for miles, to some tumulus, buried perhaps in woods, where the bones of their tribe were anciently deposited; and there have passed hours in silent meditation.   Influenced by this sublime and holy feeling, the Sachem whose mother's tomb had been violated, gathered his men together, and addressed them in the following beautifully simple and pathetic harangue; a curious specimen of Indian eloquence, and an affecting instance of filial piety in a savage: —

"When last the glorious light of all the sky was underneath this globe, and birds grew silent, I began to settle, as my custom is, to take repose.   Before mine eyes were fast closed, methought I saw a vision, at which my spirit was much troubled; and trembling at that doleful sight, a spirit cried aloud, ' Behold, my son, whom I have cherished, see the breasts that gave thee suck, the hands that lapped thee warm, and fed thee oft. Canst thou forget to take revenge of those wild people who have defaced my monument in a despiteful manner, disdaining our antiquities and honorable customs? See, now, the Sachem's grave lies like the common people, defaced by an ignoble race. Thy mother doth complain, and implores thy aid against this thievish people, who have newly intruded on our land. If this be suffered, I shall not rest quiet in my everlasting habitation.' This said, the spirit vanished, and I, all in a sweat, not able scarce to speak, began to get some strength, and recollect my spirits that were fled, and determined to demand your counsel and assistance."

I have adduced this anecdote at some length, as it tends to show how these sudden acts of hostility, which have been attributed to caprice and perfidy, may often arise from deep and generous motives, which our inattention to Indian character and customs prevents our properly appreciating.

Another ground of violent outcry against the Indians is their barbarity to the vanquished. This had its origin partly in policy and partly in superstition. The tribes, though sometimes called nations, were never so formidable in their numbers, but that the loss of several warriors was sensibly felt; this was particularly the case when they had been frequently engaged in warfare; and many an instance occurs in Indian history, where a tribe, that had long been formidable to its neighbors, has been broken up and driven away, by the capture and massacre of its principal fighting men. There was a strong temptation, therefore, to the victor to be merciless; not so much to gratify any cruel revenge, as to provide for future security. The Indians had also the superstitious belief, frequent among barbarous nations, and prevalent also among the ancients, that the manes of their friends who had fallen in battle were soothed by the blood of the captives. The prisoners, however, who are not thus sacrificed, are adopted into their families in the place of the slain, and are treated with the confidence and affection of relatives and friends; nay, so hospitable and tender is their entertainment, that when the alternative is offered them, they will often prefer to remain with their adopted brethren, rather than return to the home and the friends of their youth.

The cruelty of the Indians towards their prisoners has been heightened since the colonization of the whites. What was formerly a compliance with policy and superstition, has been exasperated into a gratification of vengeance. They cannot but be sensible that the white men are the usurpers of their ancient dominion, the cause of their degradation, and the gradual destroyers of their race. They go forth to battle, smarting with injuries and indignities which they have individually suffered, and they are driven to madness and despair by the wide-spreading desolation, and the overwhelming ruin of European warfare. The whites have too frequently set them an example of violence, by burning their villages, and laying waste their slender means of subsistence; and yet they wonder that savages do not show moderation and magnanimity towards those who have left them nothing but mere existence and wretchedness.

We stigmatize the Indians, also, as cowardly, and treacherous, because they use stratagem in warfare, in preference to open force; but in this they are fully justified by their rude code of honor. They are early taught that stratagem is praiseworthy; the bravest warrior thinks it no disgrace to lurk in silence, and take every advantage of his foe; he triumphs in the superior craft and sagacity by which he has been enabled to surprise and destroy an enemy. Indeed, man is naturally more prone to subtlety than open valor, owing to his physical weakness in comparison with other animals. They are endowed with natural weapons of defense; with horns, with tusks, with hoofs, and talons; but man has to depend on his superior sagacity. In all his encounters with these, his proper enemies, he resorts to stratagem; and when he perversely turns his hostility against his fellow-man, he at first continues the same subtle mode of warfare.

The natural principle of war is to do the most harm to our enemy with the least harm to ourselves; and this of course is to be effected by stratagem. That chivalrous courage which induces us to despise the suggestions of prudence, and to rush in the face of certain danger, is the offspring of society, and produced by education. It is honorable, because it is, in fact, the triumph of lofty sentiment over an instinctive repugnance to pain and over those yearnings after personal ease and security, which society has condemned as ignoble. It is kept alive by pride and the fear of shame; and thus the dread of real evil is overcome by the superior dread of an evil which exists but in the imagination. It has been cherished and stimulated also by various means. It has been the theme of spirit-stirring song and chivalrous story. The poet and minstrel have delighted to shed round it the splendors of fiction; and even the historian has forgotten the sober gravity of narration, and broken forth into enthusiasm and rhapsody in its praise. Triumphs and gorgeous pageants have been its reward: monuments, on which art has exhausted its skill, and opulence its treasures, have been erected to perpetuate a nation's gratitude and admiration. Thus artificially excited, courage has risen to an extraordinary and factitious degree of heroism, and, arrayed in all the glorious " pomp and circumstance of war," this turbulent quality has even been able to eclipse many of those quiet, but invaluable virtues, which silently ennoble the human character, and swell the tide of human happiness.

But if courage intrinsically consists in the defiance of danger and pain, the life of the Indian is a continual exhibition of it. He lives in a state of perpetual hostility and risk. Peril and adventure are congenial to his nature; or rather seem necessary to arouse his faculties and to give an interest to his existence. Surrounded by hostile tribes, whose mode of warfare is by ambush and surprisal, he is always prepared for fight, and lives with his weapons in his hands. As the ship careers in fearful singleness through the solitudes of ocean; as the bird mingles among clouds and storms, and wings its way, a mere speck, across the pathless fields of air; — so the Indian holds his course, silent, solitary, but undaunted, through the boundless bosom of the wilderness. His expeditions may vie in distance and danger with the pilgrimage of the devotee, or the crusade of the knight-errant. He traverses vast forests, exposed to the hazards of lonely sickness, of lurking enemies, and pining famine. Stormy lakes — those great inland seas — are no obstacles to his wanderings; in his light canoe of bark he sports, like a feather, on their waves; and darts, with the swiftness of an arrow, down the roaring rapids of the rivers. His very subsistence is snatched from the midst of toil and peril. He gains his food by the hardships and dangers of the chase; he wraps himself in the spoils of the bear, the panther, and the buffalo, and sleeps among the thunders of the cataract.

No hero of ancient or modern days can surpass the Indian in his lofty contempt of death, and the fortitude with which he sustains its cruelest affliction. Indeed, we here behold him rising superior to the white man, in consequence of his peculiar education. The latter rushes to glorious death at the cannon's mouth; the former calmly contemplates its approach, and triumphantly endures it, amidst the varied torments of surrounding foes and the protracted agonies of fire. He even takes a pride in taunting his persecutors, and provoking their ingenuity of torture; and as the devouring flames prey on his very vitals, and the flesh shrinks from the sinews, he raises his last song of triumph, breathing the defiance of an unconquered heart, and invoking the spirits of his fathers to witness that he dies without a groan.

Notwithstanding the obloquy with which the early historians have overshadowed the characters of the unfortunate natives, some bright gleams occasionally break through, which throw a degree of melancholy luster on their memories. Facts are occasionally to be met with in the rude annals of the eastern provinces, which, though recorded with the coloring of prejudice and bigotry, yet speak for themselves, and will be dwelt on with applause and sympathy, when prejudice shall have passed away.

In one of the homely narratives of the Indian wars in New

England, there is a touching account of the desolation carried into the tribe of the Pequod Indians. Humanity shrinks from the cold-blooded detail of indiscriminate butchery. In one place we read of the surprisal of an Indian fort in the night, when the wigwams were wrapt in flames, and the miserable inhabitants shot down and slain in attempting to escape, " all being despatched and ended in the course of an hour." After a series of similar transactions, " our soldiers," as the historian piously observes, " being resolved by God's assistance to make a final destruction of them," the unhappy savages being hunted from their homes and fortresses, and pursued with fire and sword, a scanty, but gallant band, the sad remnant of the Pequod warriors, with their wives and children, took refuge in a swamp.

Burning with indignation, and rendered sullen by despair; with hearts bursting with grief at the destruction of their tribe, and spirits galled and sore at the fancied ignominy of their defeat, they refused to ask their lives at the hands of an insulting foe and preferred death to submission.

As the night drew on they were surrounded in their dismal retreat, so as to render escape impracticable. Thus situated, their enemy " plied them with shot all the time, by which means many were killed and buried in the mire." In the darkness and fog that preceded the dawn of day, some few broke through the besiegers and escaped into the woods; " the rest were left to the conquerors, of which many were killed in the swamp, like sullen dogs who would rather, in their self-willedness and madness, sit still and be shot through, or cut to pieces," than implore for mercy. When the day broke upon this handful of forlorn but dauntless spirits, the soldiers, we are told, entering the swamp, " saw several heaps of them sitting close together upon whom they discharged their pieces laden with ten or twelve pistol bullets at a time, putting the muzzles of the pieces under the boughs, within a few yards of them; so as, besides those that were found dead, many more were killed and sunk into the mire, and never were minded more by friend or foe."

Can any one read this plain unvarnished tale without admiring the stern resolution, the unbending pride, the loftiness of spirit, that seemed to nerve the hearts of these self-taught heroes, and to raise them above the instinctive feelings of human nature? When the Gauls laid waste the city of Rome, they found the senators clothed in their robes, and seated with stern tranquillity in their curule chairs; in this manner they suffered death without resistance or even supplication. Such conduct was, in them, applauded as noble and magnanimous; in the hapless Indian it was reviled as obstinate and sullen. How truly are we the dupes of show and circumstance! How different is virtue, clothed in purple and enthroned in state, from virtue, naked and destitute, and perishing obscurely in a wilderness!

But I forbear to dwell on these gloomy pictures. The eastern tribes have long since disappeared; the forests that sheltered them have been laid low; and scarce any traces remain of them in the thickly-settled states of New England, excepting here and there the Indian name of a village or a stream. And such must, sooner or later, be the fate of those other tribes which skirt the frontiers, and have occasionally been inveigled from their forests to mingle in the wars of white men. In a little while, and they will go the way that their brethren have gone before. The few hordes which still linger about the shores of Huron and Superior, and the tributary streams of the Mississippi, will share the fate of those tribes that once spread over Massachusetts and Connecticut, and lorded it along the proud banks of the Hudson; of that gigantic race said to have existed on the borders of the Susquehanna; and of those various nations that flourished about the Potomac and the Rappahannock, and that peopled the forests of the vast valley of Shenandoah. They will vanish like a vapor from the face of the earth; their very history will be lost in forgetfulness; and " the places that now know them will know them no more forever." Or, if, perchance, some dubious memorial of them should survive, it may be in the romantic dreams of the poet, to people in imagination his glades and groves like the fauns and satyrs and sylvan deities of antiquity. But should he venture upon the dark story of their wrongs and wretchedness; should he tell how they were invaded, corrupted, despoiled, driven from their native abodes and the sepulchres of their fathers, hunted like wild beasts about the earth, and sent down with violence and butchery to the grave, posterity will either turn with horror and incredulity from the tale, or blush with indignation at the inhumanity of their forefathers, — "We are driven back," said an old warrior, "until we can retreat no farther — our hatchets are broken, our bows are snapped, our fires are nearly extinguished — a little longer and the white man will cease to persecute us — for we shall cease to exist."

APPRECIATION HELPS

1. What qualities make the Indian at home in the wilderness?
2. What prejudices have the white men always held against the Indian?
3. Discuss the attitude of the United States Government towards the Indian, both in Irving's time and at present.
4. Has the Indian been truthfully pictured in literature? With what pictures of Indian life are you familiar?
5. Discuss Irving's statements concerning treaties between the Indians and the white men.
6. Were the author's statements regarding the barbarity of the Indian to the vanquished convincing to you?
7. What admirable traits of character are found in the Indian?
8. Do you feel that this is a truthful or a biased review of Indian character?

COMPOSITION HINTS

1. Indians I Have Known
2. Grandfather's Experience with Indians
3. The Indian in Literature
4. The Indian of Today
5. Indian Beliefs and Superstitions
6. Indian Character
7. Relations Between the Indians and the White Man
8. The Influence of the Indian upon Our Geographical Names

CHARLES LAMB

If you had been riding in a certain London omnibus one cold winter's night at the beginning of the nineteenth century you would have decided that the little man seated in the corner next the entrance was a humorist. He remained quiet and inconspicuous enough until, at the first stop, a stranger poked his head in from the step, and inquired, "Full up inside?" At once the little man came to life. His eye lit, his chin lifted from his heavy muffler, he glanced round the two rows of tightly wedged travelers, and he stammered: "I — I — d-d-don't know ab-ab-about these others, b-b-but that last p-p-piece of p-p-pie quite fin-f-finished m-m-me!" And if, thereupon, you had learned that the little man was no other than the famous Mr. Charles Lamb (1775–1834), the author of the delightful *Essays of Elia* then appearing in the *London Magazine,* you would have said to yourself: That is just what I expected him to be in private life, a blithe, frolicsome fellow, evidently (though he stutters) without a care in the world.

But you would have been wrong. At least, while certainly he was invariably bright and whimsical amid the conviviality of parties or under the inspiration of pen and paper, deep down in his heart he was sad, with a sadness beyond remedy. It was the old story of the clown, so merry in the ring, so melancholy at the fireside. But in Lamb's case there was good reason for his sadness, and, further, he allied to it a rare nobility of spirit, so that one may well rate him as one of those few fine men whose existence redeems the petty meannesses and cowardices of a million human beings.

Three occupations filled his life. First, of course, he was an author, but his talent developed and blossomed slowly, and never would he have been able to make a living from it. Moreover, he was a poor man's son, and while he became a poet young — at twenty-one — the necessity of earning his keep sent him out into the world younger still. It took him from the London Charity

School and perched him as a mere child of fourteen upon a junior clerk's high stool in a gloomy lair such as merchants of the city of London in those days called their offices. Three years after that, on April 5, 1792, he entered another office, the accountant's office of the renowned East India House, and there he was destined to remain, arriving punctually each morning for thirty-three years and producing, as he used to say, the one hundred official folios of his " true works." He retired in 1825 with a pension. So much for occupation number two. The first was a hobby, the second a means of livelihood. And now for the third. That was entirely a labor of love, bringing him neither fame nor cash, yet to it he really dedicated his life. This third occupation was guarding the freedom of his sister.

On September 22, 1796, when Charles was twenty-one, this sister, Mary, suddenly stabbed their mother dead. She had gone mad. Charles moved heaven and earth to obtain her release from the lunatic asylum, and at last succeeded on one condition — that he himself would always look after her. Gladly, without hesitation, he agreed. Possibly at the time he did not realize the extent of the sacrifice he was making, but never once afterwards did he flinch from it. Her loving and attentive custodian he remained until a skin disease ended his life. Think what it meant for her: instead of the desolation of an asylum cell, the sinister companionship of other lunatics, the rough treatment of callous keepers, she had the comforts of a home, the solace of a brother's constant care, and that most precious of all human possessions, liberty. Think what it meant for him: instead of marrying and watching his children grow up, of devoting all his leisure to sharpening his pen, he consecrated himself to his vigil, being always on the alert for a fresh outbreak of insanity; virtually he became the prisoner that Mary might be free.

It is true that most of the time she was to all intents perfectly sane and was able to collaborate with him upon that charming book for the young, *Tales from Shakespeare,* which was published in 1807. But the threat was always there. When at last marriage did seem possible to Charles, and, with Mary's consent, he aspired to the hand of an actress, Fanny Kelly, it was too late: the clerk of forty-four found his suit rejected. So to the end he bore his burden.

Here is the most popular of those *Essays of Elia* upon which Lamb's reputation so firmly rests.

A DISSERTATION UPON ROAST PIG

Mankind, says a Chinese manuscript, which my friend M. was obliging enough to read and explain to me, for the first seventy thousand ages ate their meat raw, clawing or biting it from the living animal, just as they do in Abyssinia to this day. This period is not obscurely hinted at by their great Confucius in the second chapter of his Mundane Mutations, where he designates a kind of golden age by the term Cho-fang, literally the Cook's holiday. The manuscript goes on to say that the art of roasting, or rather broiling (which I take to be the elder brother), was accidentally discovered in the manner following. The swineherd, Ho-ti, having gone out into the woods one morning, as his manner was, to collect mast for his hogs, left his cottage in the care of his eldest son, Bo-bo, a great lubberly boy, who being fond of playing with fire, as younkers of his age commonly are, let some sparks escape into a bundle of straw, which kindling quickly, spread the conflagration over every part of their poor mansion, till it was reduced to ashes. Together with the cottage (a sorry antediluvian makeshift of a building, you may think it), what was of much more importance a fine litter of new-farrowed pigs, no less than nine in number, perished. China pigs have been esteemed a luxury all over the East from the remotest periods that we read of. Bo-bo was in utmost consternation, as you may think, not so much for the sake of the tenement, which his father and he could easily build up again with a few dry branches, and the labor of an hour or two, at any time, as for the loss of the pigs. While he was thinking what he should say to his father, and wringing his hands over the smoking remnants of one of those untimely sufferers, an odor assailed his nostrils, unlike any scent which he had before experienced. What could it proceed from? — not from the burnt cottage — he had smelt that smell before — indeed this was by no means the first accident of the kind which had occurred through the negligence of this unlucky young firebrand. Much less did it

resemble that of any known herb, weed, or flower. A premoni-
tory moistening at the same time overflowed his nether lip.
He knew not what to think. He next stooped down to feel the
pig, if there were any signs of life in it. He burnt his fingers,
and to cool them he applied them in his booby fashion to his
mouth. Some of the crumbs of the scorched skin had come
away with his fingers, and for the first time in his life (in the
world's life indeed, for before him no man had known it) he
tasted — *crackling!* Again he felt and fumbled at the pig. It
did not burn him so much now, still he licked his fingers from
a sort of habit. The truth at length broke into his slow understanding, that it was the pig that smelt so, and the pig that
tasted so delicious; and, surrendering himself up to the new-
born pleasure, he fell to tearing up whole handfuls of the
scorched skin with the flesh next it, and was cramming it down
his throat in his beastly fashion, when his sire entered amid
the smoking rafters, armed with retributory cudgel, and finding how affairs stood, began to rain blows upon the young
rogue's shoulders, as thick as hailstones, which Bo-bo heeded
not any more than if they had been flies. The tickling pleasure, which he experienced in his lower regions, had rendered
him quite callous to any inconveniences he might feel in those
remote quarters. His father might lay on, but he could not
beat him from his pig, till he had fairly made an end of it,
when, becoming a little more sensible of his situation, something like the following dialogue ensued.

"You graceless whelp, what have you got there devouring?
Is it not enough that you have burnt me down three houses
with your dog's tricks, and be hanged to you, but you must be
eating fire, and I know not what — what have you got there,
I say?"

"O, father, the pig, the pig, do come and taste how nice the
burnt pig eats."

The ears of Ho-ti tingled with horror. He cursed his son,
and he cursed himself that ever he should beget a son that
should eat burnt pig.

Bo-bo, whose scent was wonderfully sharpened since morning, soon raked out another pig, and fairly rending it asunder, thrust the lesser half by main force into the fists of Ho-ti, still shouting out, " Eat, eat, eat the burnt pig, father, only taste — O Lord," — with such-like barbarous ejaculations, cramming all the while as if he would choke.

Ho-ti trembled in every joint while he grasped the abominable thing, wavering whether he should not put his son to death for an unnatural young monster, when the crackling scorching his fingers, as it had done his son's, and applying the same remedy to them, he in his turn tasted some of its flavor, which, make what sour mouths he would for a pretense, proved not altogether displeasing to him. In conclusion (for the manuscript here is a little tedious) both father and son fairly sat down to the mess, and never left till they had despatched all that remained of the litter.

Bo-bo was strictly enjoined not to let the secret escape, for the neighbors would certainly have stoned them for a couple of abominable wretches, who could think of improving upon the good meat which God had sent them. Nevertheless strange stories got about. It was observed that Ho-ti's cottage was burnt down now more frequently than ever. Nothing but fires from this time forward. Some would break out in broad day, others in the nighttime. As often as the sow farrowed, so sure was the house of Ho-ti to be in a blaze; and Ho-ti himself, which was the more remarkable, instead of chastising his son, seemed to grow more indulgent to him than ever. At length they were watched, the terrible mystery discovered, and father and son summoned to take their trial at Pekin, then an inconsiderable assize town. Evidence was given, the obnoxious food itself produced in court, and verdict about to be pronounced, when the foreman of the jury begged that some of the burnt pig, of which the culprits stood accused, might be handed into the box. He handled it, and they all handled it, and burning their fingers, as Bo-bo and his father had done before them, and Nature prompting to each of them the same remedy, against the face of all the facts, and the clearest charge which judge had ever given, — to the surprise of the whole court.

townsfolk, strangers, reporters, and all present — without leaving the box, or any manner of consultation whatever, they brought in a simultaneous verdict of Not Guilty.

The judge, who was a shrewd fellow, winked at the manifest iniquity of the decision; and, when the court was dismissed, went privily, and bought up all the pigs that could be had for love or money. In a few days his Lordship's town house was observed to be on fire. The thing took wing, and now there was nothing to be seen but fires in every direction. Fuel and pigs grew enormously dear all over the district. The insurance offices one and all shut up shop. People built slighter and slighter every day, until it was feared that the very science of architecture would in no long time be lost to the world. Thus this custom of firing houses continued, till in process of time, says my manuscript, a sage arose, like our Locke, who made a discovery, that the flesh of swine, or indeed of any other animal, might be cooked (*burnt,* as they called it) without the necessity of consuming a whole house to dress it. Then first began the rude form of a gridiron. Roasting by the string, or spit, came in a century or two later, I forget in whose dynasty. By such slow degrees, concludes the manuscript, do the most useful, and seemingly the most obvious arts, make their way among mankind. —

Without placing too implicit faith in the account above given, it must be agreed that if a worthy pretext for so dangerous an experiment as setting houses on fire (especially in these days) could be assigned in favor of any culinary object, that pretext and excuse might be found in ROAST PIG.

Of all the delicacies in the whole *mundus edibilis,* I will maintain it to be the most delicate — *princeps obsoniorum.*

I speak not of your grown porkers — things between pig and pork — those hobbydehoys — but a young and tender suckling — under a moon old — guiltless as yet of the sty — with no original speck of the *amor immunditiæ,* the hereditary failing of the first parent, yet manifest — his voice as yet not broken, but something between a childish treble, and a grumble — the mild forerunner or *præludium,* of a grunt.

He must be roasted. I am not ignorant that our ancestors ate them seethed, or boiled — but what a sacrifice of the exterior tegument!

There is no flavor comparable, I will contend, to that of the crisp, tawny, well-watched, not over-roasted, *crackling,* as it is well called — the very teeth are invited to their share of the pleasure at this banquet in overcoming the coy, brittle resistance — with the adhesive oleaginous — O call it not fat — but an indefinable sweetness growing up to it — the tender blossoming of fat — fat cropped in the bud — taken in the shoot — in the first innocence — the cream and quintessence of the child-pig's yet pure food —— the lean, no lean, but a kind of animal manna — or, rather, fat and lean (if it must be so), so blended and running into each other, that both together make but one ambrosian result, or common substance.

Behold him, while he is doing — it seemed rather a refreshing warmth, than a scorching heat, that he is so passive to. How equably he twirleth round the string! — Now he is just done. To see the extreme sensibility of that tender age, he hath wept out his pretty eyes — radiant jellies — shooting stars —

See him in the dish, his second cradle, how meek he lieth! — wouldst thou have had this innocent grow up to the grossness and indocility which too often accompany maturer swinehood? Ten to one he would have proved a glutton, a sloven, an obstinate, disagreeable animal — wallowing in all manner of filthy conversation — from these sins he is happily snatched away —

> Ere sin could blight, or sorrow fade,
> Death came with timely care —

his memory is odoriferous — no clown curseth, while his stomach half rejecteth, the rank bacon — no coal-heaver bolteth him in reeking sausages — he hath a fair sepulchre in the grateful stomach of the judicious epicure — and for such a tomb might be content to die.

He is the best of Sapors. Pineapple is great. She is indeed

almost too transcendent — a delight, if not sinful, yet so like to sinning, that really a tender-conscienced person would do well to pause — too ravishing for mortal taste, she woundeth and excoriateth the lips that approach her — like lovers' kisses, she biteth — she is a pleasure bordering on pain from the fierceness and insanity of her relish — but she stoppeth at the palate — she meddleth not with the appetite — and the coarsest hunger might barter her consistently for a mutton chop.

Pig — let me speak his praise — is no less provocative of the appetite, than he is satisfactory to the criticalness of the censorious palate. The strong man may batten on him, and weakling refuseth not his mild juices.

Unlike to mankind's mixed characters, a bundle of virtues and vices, inexplicably intertwisted, and not to be unraveled without hazard, he is — good throughout. No part of him is better or worse than another. He helpeth, as far as his little means extend, all around. He is the least envious of banquets. He is all neighbors' fare.

I am one of those who freely and ungrudgingly impart a share of the good things of this life which fall to their lot (few as mine are in this kind) to a friend. I protest I take as great an interest in my friend's pleasures, his relishes, and proper satisfactions, as in mine own. "Presents," I often say, "endear Absents." Hares, pheasants, partridges, snipes, barndoor chickens (those "tame vilatic fowl"), capons, plovers, brawn, barrels of oysters, I dispense as freely as I receive them. I love to taste them, as it were, upon the tongue of my friend. But a stop must be put somewhere. One would not, like Lear, "give everything." I make stand upon pig. Methinks it is an ingratitude to the Giver of all good flavors, to extra-domiciliate, or send out of the house, slightly (under pretext of friendship, of I know not what), a blessing so particularly adapted, predestined, I may say, to my individual palate — it argues an insensibility.

I remember a touch of conscience in this kind at school. My good old aunt, who never parted from me at the end of a holiday without stuffing a sweetmeat, or some nice thing, into my pocket, had dismissed me one evening with a smoking plum-cake, fresh from the oven. In my way to school (it was over London Bridge) a gray-headed old beggar saluted me (I have no doubt at this time of day that he was a counterfeit). I had no pence to console him with, and in the vanity of self-denial, and the very coxcombry of charity, schoolboy like, I made him a present of — the whole cake. I walked on a little, buoyed up, as one is on such occasions, with a sweet soothing of self-satisfaction; but before I had got to the end of the bridge, my better feelings returned, and I burst into tears, thinking how ungrateful I had been to my good aunt, to go and give her good gift away to a stranger, that I had never seen before, and who might be a bad man for aught I knew; and then I thought of the pleasure my aunt would be taking in thinking that I — I myself, and not another — would eat her nice cake — and what should I say to her the next time I saw her — how naughty I was to part with her pretty present — and the odor of that spicy cake came back upon my recollection, and the pleasure and the curiosity I had taken in seeing her make it, and her joy when she sent it to the oven, and how disappointed she would feel that I had never had a bit of it in my mouth at last — and I blamed my impertinent spirit of alms-giving, and out-of-place hypocrisy of goodness, and above all I wished never to see the face again of that insidious, good-for-nothing, old gray impostor.

Our ancestors were nice in their method of sacrificing these tender victims. We read of pigs whipped to death with something of a shock, as we hear of any other obsolete custom. The age of discipline is gone by, or it would be curious to inquire (in a philosophical light merely) what effect this process might have towards intenerating and dulcifying a substance, naturally so mild and dulcet as the flesh of young pigs. It looks like refining a violet. Yet we should be cautious, while we condemn the inhumanity, how we censure the wisdom of the practice. It might impart a gusto —

I remember an hypothesis, argued upon by the young students, when I was at St. Omer's, and maintained with much learning and pleasantry on both sides, "Whether, supposing that the flavor of a pig who obtained his death by whipping (*per flagellationem extremam*) superadded a pleasure upon the palate of a man more intense than any possible suffering we can conceive in the animal, is man justified in using that method of putting the animal to death?" I forget the decision.

His sauce should be considered. Decidedly, a few bread crumbs, done up with his liver and brains, and a dash of mild sage. But banish, dear Mrs. Cook, I beseech you, the whole onion tribe. Barbecue your whole hogs to your palate, steep them in shalots, stuff them out with plantations of the rank and guilty garlic; you cannot poison them, or make them stronger than they are — but consider, he is a weakling — a flower.

APPRECIATION HELPS

1. Can you explain why this essay of Lamb's is included in almost every collection of essays for schools?
2. Select any other custom or institution which has become commonplace and make up an explanation of its social origin.
3. How is Lamb's personality revealed in this essay?
4. Find passages which show keenness, precision, humor, reverence for the past.
5. Find quaint turns of speech, good phrasing.
6. Does the narrative element help the essay?
7. In what mood does Lamb leave you? What is your personal feeling toward him?

COMPOSITION HINTS

1. A Dissertation on ——. (Give the origin of any other common thing or custom, as Lamb explains roast pig.)
2. The Pleasures of Eating
3. The Humor of Charles Lamb
4. Proper Topics of Conversation at the Dinner Table
5. The Importance of Food in Books I Have Read. (For example the Cratchets' Christmas dinner in Dickens's "Christmas Carol.")

MARK TWAIN

It is a significant thing that the three really great books written by Mark Twain — *The Adventures of Tom Sawyer, Huckleberry Finn, The Tragedy of Pudd'nhead Wilson* — are books that can be enjoyed alike by growing boy and experienced man. Their keynote is simplicity, and yet with humor and pathos they preserve vividly for all time the memory of a vanished civilization, that of the Mississippi Valley in the days before the Civil War. All great work is simple.

The Mississippi Valley is where the author of those three books was born and reared and where he passed the happiest days of his manhood. Mark Twain was the penname of Samuel Langhorne Clemens (1835–1910), who was born at Florida, Missouri, and grew up at Hannibal, another Missouri town on the banks of the Mississippi. His father, a country merchant hailing from Tennessee, died when Sam was twelve, and the boy went out early into the world to earn money. He wandered widely as a journeyman printer.

Then at seventeen he became the pilot of a Mississippi River boat. Those were happy days, as he has recalled in his *Life on the Mississippi,* which was published in 1883. They lasted for an all too brief nine years, and then the outbreak of the Civil War in 1861 put an end to the occupation of pilot.

Sam went to the Nevada gold mines, found no gold, and sought money instead by writing contributions to the newspapers. The contributions that were funny got accepted, and Clemens found himself becoming a humorist. For a time he worked on a newspaper in San Francisco, then in 1867 he joined a party bound on a holiday jaunt to the Mediterranean. The result of that tour was his first book, *Innocents Abroad.* It attained a great popularity. He next edited a paper in Buffalo, where he met Olivia Langdon, the girl whom he married. They went to live in Hartford, Connecticut. (Later he lived at Redding Ridge in the same state.)

He lost a great deal of money in the collapse of a publishing house of which he was a member, but soon recouped himself with his earnings as a writer and paid the debts of the firm in full, although under no legal obligation to do so.

He acquired wide fame, not only in the United States, but all over the world, and when he visited Europe he was received with great pomp. While he lived he was known chiefly as a comic writer, but it is in the books mentioned above that he did his best work. On their account is he to be set beside Cervantes, the greatest of Spanish authors, and Molière, the greatest of French writers of comedy.

The following is an essay from Mark Twain's *In Defense of Harriet Shelley and Other Essays,* in which, albeit with a light touch, he treats the savior of France in the fifteenth century with the greatest respect.

SAINT JOAN OF ARC[1]

THE evidence furnished at the Trials and Rehabilitation sets forth Joan of Arc's strange and beautiful history in clear and minute detail. Among all the multitude of biographies that freight the shelves of the world's libraries, *this is the only one whose validity is confirmed to us by oath.* It gives us a vivid picture of a career and a personality of so extraordinary a character that we are helped to accept them as actualities by the very fact that both are beyond the inventive reach of fiction. The public part of the career occupied only a mere breath of time — it covered but two years; but what a career it was! The personality which made it possible is one to be reverently studied, loved, and marveled at, but not to be wholly understood and accounted for by even the most searching analysis.[2]

[1] From *In Defense of Harriet Shelley and Other Essays,* published by Harper and Brothers, 1918.

[2] The Official Record of the Trials and Rehabilitation of Joan of Arc is the most remarkable history that exists in any language; yet there are few people in the world who can say they have read it: in England and America it has hardly been heard of.

Three hundred years ago Shakespeare did not know the true story of

In Joan of Arc at the age of sixteen there was no promise of a romance. She lived in a dull little village on the frontiers of civilization; she had been nowhere and had seen nothing; she knew none but simple shepherd folk; she had never seen a person of note; she hardly knew what a soldier looked like; she had never ridden a horse, nor had a warlike weapon in her hand; she could neither read nor write: she could spin and sew; she knew her catechism and her prayers and the fabulous histories of the saints, and this was all her learning. That was Joan of sixteen. What did she know of law? of evidence? of courts? of the attorney's trade? of legal procedure? Nothing. Less than nothing. Thus exhaustively equipped with ignorance, she went before the court at Toul to contest a false charge of breach of promise of marriage; she conducted her cause herself, without any one's help or advice or any one's friendly sympathy, and won it. She called no witnesses of her own, but vanquished the prosecution by using with deadly effectiveness its own testimony. The astonished judge threw the case out of court, and spoke of her as "this marvelous child."

She went to the veteran Commandant of Vaucouleurs and demanded an escort of soldiers, saying she must march to the help of the King of France, since she was commissioned of God to win back his lost kingdom for him and set the crown upon his head. The Commandant said, "What, you? You are only a child." And he advised that she be taken back to her village and have her ears boxed. But she said she must obey God, and would come again, and again, and yet again, and finally she would get the soldiers. She said truly. In time he yielded, after months of delay and refusal, and gave her the soldiers; and took off his sword and gave her that, and said,

Joan of Arc; in his day it was unknown even in France. For four hundred years it existed rather as a vaguely defined romance than as definite and authentic history. The true story remained buried in the official archives of France from the Rehabilitation of 1456 until Quicherat dug it out and gave it to the world two generations ago, in lucid and understandable modern French. It is a deeply fascinating story. But only in the Official Trials and Rehabilitation can it be found in its entirety. — M. T.

"Go—and let come what may." She made her long and perilous journey through the enemy's country, and spoke with the King, and convinced him. Then she was summoned before the University of Poitiers to prove that she *was* commissioned of God and not of Satan, and daily during three weeks she sat before that learned congress unafraid, and capably answered their deep questions out of her ignorant but able head and her simple and honest heart; and again she won her case, and with it the wondering admiration of all that august company.

And now, aged seventeen, she was made Commander-in-Chief, with a prince of the royal house and the veteran generals of France for subordinates; and at the head of the first army she had ever seen, she marched to Orleans, carried the commanding fortresses of the enemy by storm in three desperate assaults, and in ten days raised a siege which had defied the might of France for seven months.

After a tedious and insane delay caused by the King's instability of character and the treacherous counsels of his ministers, she got permission to take the field again. She took Jargeau by storm; then Meung; she forced Beaugency to surrender; then—in the open field—she won the memorable victory of Patay against Talbot, "the English lion," and broke the back of the Hundred Years' War. It was a campaign which cost but seven weeks of time; yet the political results would have been cheap if the time expended had been fifty years. Patay, that unsung and now long-forgotten battle, was the Moscow of the English power in France; from the blow struck that day it was destined never to recover. It was the beginning of the end of an alien dominion which had ridden France intermittently for three hundred years.

Then followed the great campaign of the Loire, the capture of Troyes by assault, and the triumphal march past surrendering towns and fortresses to Rheims, where Joan put the crown upon her King's head in the Cathedral, amid wild public rejoicings, and with her old peasant father there to see these things and believe his eyes if he could. She had restored the crown and the lost sovereignty; the King was grateful for once in his shabby poor life, and asked her to name her reward and have it. She asked for nothing for herself, but begged that the taxes of her native village might be remitted forever. The prayer was granted, and the promise kept for three hundred and sixty years. Then it was broken, and remains broken today. France was very poor then, she is very rich now; but she has been collecting those taxes for more than a hundred years.

Joan asked one other favor: that now that her mission was fulfilled she might be allowed to go back to her village and take up her humble life again with her mother and the friends of her childhood; for she had no pleasure in the cruelties of war, and the sight of blood and suffering wrung her heart. Sometimes in battle she did not draw her sword, lest in the splendid madness of the onset she might forget herself and take an enemy's life with it. In the Rouen Trials, one of her quaintest speeches — coming from the gentle and girlish source it did — was her naïve remark that she had "never killed any one." Her prayer for leave to go back to the rest and peace of her village home was not granted.

Then she wanted to march at once upon Paris, take it, and drive the English out of France. She was hampered in all the ways that treachery and the King's vacillation could devise, but she forced her way to Paris at last, and fell badly wounded in a successful assault upon one of the gates. Of course her men lost heart at once — she was the only heart they had. They fell back. She begged to be allowed to remain at the front, saying victory was sure. "I will take Paris now or die!" she said. But she was removed from the field by force; the King ordered a retreat, and actually disbanded his army. In accordance with a beautiful old military custom Joan devoted her silver armor and hung it up in the Cathedral of St. Denis. Its great days were over.

Then, by command, she followed the King and his frivolous court and endured a gilded captivity for a time, as well as her free spirit could; and whenever inaction became unbearable she gathered some men together and rode away and assaulted a stronghold and captured it.

At last in a sortie against the enemy, from Compiègne, on the 24th of May (when she was turned eighteen), she was herself captured, after a gallant fight. It was her last battle. She was to follow the drums no more.

Thus ended the briefest epoch-making military career known to history. It lasted only a year and a month, but it found France an English province, and furnishes the reason that France is France today and not an English province still. Thirteen months! It was, indeed, a short career; but in the centuries that have since elapsed five hundred millions of Frenchmen have lived and died blest by the benefactions it conferred; and so long as France shall endure, the mighty debt must grow. And France is grateful; we often hear her say it. Also thrifty: she collects the Domremy taxes.

TWENTY-FIVE years afterward the Process of Rehabilitation was instituted, there being a growing doubt as to the validity of a sovereignty that had been rescued and set upon its feet by a person who had been proven by the Church to be a witch and a familiar of evil spirits. Joan's old generals, her secretary, several aged relations and other villagers of Domremy, surviving judges and secretaries of the Rouen and Poitiers Processes — a cloud of witnesses, some of whom had been her enemies and persecutors — came and made oath and testified; and what they said was written down. In that sworn testimony the moving and beautiful history of Joan of Arc is laid bare, from her childhood to her martyrdom. From the verdict she rises stainlessly pure, in mind and heart, in speech and deed and spirit, and will so endure to the end of time.

She is the Wonder of the Ages. And when we consider her origin, her early circumstances, her sex, and that she did all the things upon which her renown rests while she was still a young girl, we recognize that while our race continues she will be also the *Riddle* of the Ages. When we set about accounting for a Napoleon or a Shakespeare or a Raphael or a Wagner or an Edison or other extraordinary person, we understand that the measure of his talent will not explain the whole result, nor even the largest part of it; no, it is the atmosphere in which the talent was cradled that explains; it is the training which it received while it grew, the nurture it got from reading, study, example, the encouragement it gathered from self-recognition and recognition from the outside at each stage of its development: when we know all these details, then we know why the man was ready when his opportunity came. We should expect Edison's surroundings and atmosphere to have the largest share in discovering him to himself and to the world; and we should expect him to live and die undiscovered in a land where an inventor could find no comradeship, no sympathy, no ambition-rousing atmosphere of recognition and applause — Dahomey, for instance. Dahomey could not find an Edison out; in Dahomey an Edison could not find himself out. Broadly speaking, genius is not born with sight, but blind; and it is not itself that opens its eyes, but the subtle influences of a myriad of stimulating exterior circumstances.

We all know this to be not a guess, but a mere commonplace fact, a truism. Lorraine was Joan of Arc's Dahomey. And there the Riddle confronts us. We can understand how she could be born with military genius, with leonine courage, with incomparable fortitude, with a mind which was in several particulars a prodigy — a mind which included among its specialties the lawyer's gift of detecting traps laid by the adversary in cunning and treacherous arrangements of seemingly innocent words, the orator's gift of eloquence, the advocate's gift of presenting a case in clear and compact form, the judge's gift of sorting and weighing evidence, and finally, something recognizable as more than a mere trace of the statesman's gift of understanding a political situation and how to make profitable use of such opportunities as it offers; we can comprehend how she could be born with these great qualities, but we cannot comprehend how they became immediately usable and effective without the developing forces of a sympathetic atmosphere and the training which comes of teaching, study, practice — years of practice — and the crowning and perfecting help of a thousand mistakes. We can understand how the possibilities of the future perfect peach are all lying hid in the humble bitter-almond, but we cannot conceive of the peach springing directly from the almond without the intervening long seasons of patient cultivation and development. Out of a cattle-pasturing peasant village lost in the remotenesses of an unvisited wilderness and atrophied with ages of stupefaction and ignorance we cannot see a Joan of Arc issue equipped to the last detail for her amazing career and hope to be able to explain the riddle of it, labor at it as we may.

It is beyond us. All the rules fail in this girl's case. In the world's history she stands alone — quite alone. Others have been great in their first public exhibitions of generalship, valor, legal talent, diplomacy, fortitude; but always their previous years and associations had been in a larger or smaller degree a preparation for these things. There have been no exceptions to the rule. But Joan was competent in a law case at sixteen without ever having seen a law book or a courthouse before; she had no training in soldiership and no associations with it, yet she was a competent general in her first campaign; she was brave in her first battle, yet her courage had had no education — not even the education which a boy's courage gets from never-ceasing reminders that it is not permissible in a boy to be a coward, but only in a girl; friendless, alone, ignorant, in the blossom of her youth, she sat week after week, a prisoner in chains, before her assemblage of judges, enemies hunting her to her death, the ablest minds in France, and answered them out of an untaught wisdom which overmatched their learning, baffled their tricks and treacheries with a native sagacity which compelled their wonder, and scored every day a victory against these incredible odds and camped unchallenged on the field. In the history of the human intellect, untrained, inexperienced, and using only its birthright equipment of untried capacities, there is nothing which approaches this. Joan of Arc stands alone, and must continue to stand alone, by reason of the unfellowed fact that in the things wherein she was great she was so without shade or suggestion of help from preparatory teaching, practice, environment, or experience. There is no one to compare her with, none to measure her by; for all others among the illustrious *grew* toward their high place in an atmosphere and surroundings which discovered their gift to them and nourished it and promoted it, intentionally or unconsciously. There have been other young generals, but they were not girls; young generals, but they had been soldiers before they were generals: she *began* as a general; she commanded the first army she ever saw; she led it from victory to victory, and never lost a battle with it; there have been young commanders-in-chief, but none so young as she: she is the only soldier in history who has held the supreme command of a nation's armies at the age of seventeen.

Her history has still another feature which sets her apart and leaves her without fellow or competitor: there have been many uninspired prophets, but she was the only one who ever ventured the daring detail of naming, along with a foretold event, the event's precise nature, the special time-limit within which it would occur, and the place — *and scored fulfillment.* At Vaucouleurs she said she must go to the King and be made his general, and break the English power, and crown her sovereign — " at Rheims." It all happened. It was all to happen " next year " — and it did. She foretold her first wound and its character and date a month in advance, and the prophecy was recorded in a public record-book three weeks in advance. She repeated it the morning of the date named, and it was fulfilled before night. At Tours she foretold the limit of her military career — saying it would end in one year from the time of its utterance — and she was right. She foretold her martyrdom — using *that word,* and naming a time three months away — and again she was right. At a time when France seemed hopelessly and permanently in the hands of the English she twice asserted in her prison before her judges that within seven years the English would meet with a mightier disaster than had been the fall of Orleans: it happened within five — the fall of Paris. Other prophecies of hers came true, both as to the event named and the time-limit prescribed.

She was deeply religious, and believed that she had daily speech with angels; that she saw them face to face, and that they counseled her, comforted and heartened her, and brought commands to her direct from God. She had a childlike faith in the heavenly origin of her apparitions and her Voices, and not any threat of any form of death was able to frighten it out of her loyal heart. She was a beautiful and simple and lovable character. In the records of the Trials this comes out in clear and shining detail. She was gentle and winning and affectionate; she loved her home and friends and her village life; she was miserable in the presence of pain and suffering; she was full of compassion: on the field of her most splendid victory she forgot her triumphs to hold in her lap the head of a dying enemy and comfort his passing spirit with pitying words; in an age when it was common to slaughter prisoners she stood dauntless between hers and harm, and saved them alive; she was forgiving, generous, unselfish, magnanimous; she was pure from all spot or stain of baseness. And always she was a *girl;* and dear and worshipful, as is meet for that estate: when she fell wounded, the first time, she was frightened, and cried when she saw her blood gushing from her breast; but she was Joan of Arc! and when presently she found that her generals were sounding the retreat, she staggered to her feet and led the assault again and took that place by storm.

There is no blemish in that rounded and beautiful character.

How strange it is! — that almost invariably the artist remembers only one detail — one minor and meaningless detail of the personality of Joan of Arc: to wit, that she was a peasant girl — and forgets all the rest; and so he paints her as a strapping middle-aged fishwoman, with costume to match, and in her face the spirituality of a ham. He is slave to his one idea, and forgets to observe that the supremely great souls are never lodged in gross bodies. No brawn, no muscle, could endure the work that their bodies must do; they do their miracles by the spirit, which has fifty times the strength and staying-power of brawn and muscle. The Napoleons are little, not big; and they work twenty hours in the twenty-four, and come up fresh, while the big soldiers with the little hearts faint around them with fatigue. We know what Joan of Arc was like, without asking — merely by what she did. The artist should paint her *spirit* — then he could not fail to paint her body aright. She would rise before us, then, a vision to win us, not repel: a lithe young slender figure, instinct with " the unbought grace of youth," dear and bonny and lovable, the face beautiful, and transfigured with the light of that lustrous intellect and the fires of that unquenchable spirit.

Taking into account, as I have suggested before, all the circumstances — her origin, youth, sex, illiteracy, early environment, and the obstructing conditions under which she exploited her high gifts and made her conquests in the field and before the courts that tried her for her life — she is easily and by far the most extraordinary person the human race has ever produced.

APPRECIATION HELPS

1. In what ways does Mark Twain make you feel a sympathy for Joan? How does he reveal his own attitude towards his subject?
2. In what way is Joan's biography unique among biographies of the world? Why is this distinction so important to Mark Twain?
3. What were the facts of her early life which seemed to give no hint of any future greatness?
4. Point out the obstacles that continually made her work difficult.
5. In what sense is Joan " the Wonder and the Riddle of the ages "?
6. Discuss Mark Twain's treatment of her supernatural powers.
7. What does the author think of the portraits artists have given us of Joan? How should she look?
8. Do the illustrators of books usually please you with their conceptions of your favorite characters? Why?

9. What kind of writing do you associate with the author? Did this serious essay interest and please you? Why?
10. List five books of Mark Twain which high-school students would enjoy reading.

COMPOSITION HINTS

1. A Pen Picture of Joan of Arc
2. The Child Joan
3. Joan of Arc in Pictures
4. Dialogue between Two Soldiers after Joan's Victory
5. Joan of Arc, the Dreamer

CHRISTOPHER MORLEY

Mr. Christopher Morley (b. 1890) is of English parentage. His father, Mr. Frank Morley, who has been professor of mathematics in Johns Hopkins University since 1900, was born at Woodbridge. Suffolk, and his mother comes from Sussex. Also, after he had wrested an A.B. from Haverford College, Pennsylvania, he himself, as a Rhodes scholar, resided from 1910 to 1913 at New College, Oxford. From these sources, no doubt, did he acquire his love of those favorite old English institutions, shandygaff, mince pie, plum pudding, and pipefuls, a love so real that he has given their names to four of his many volumes of charming essays. Among those loves perhaps the greatest is Mr. Morley's love of pipefuls; in the subway or in his sleep are the only times, so his intimates declare, when he is not puffing at a formidable contrivance with wide, curved stem and deep-bellied bowl. That certainly is a true English habit, and English too are his taste for George Santayana's writings and his gift for light fantastic prose or verse of his own. The quality of this prose is well shown in *Where the Blue Begins,* that tale of the dog who left home, as a boy might do, in search of adventure.

Essays, verse, fantasies, and short stories — the number of books to Mr. Morley's name would do credit to any man of his age. The amazing thing is that almost all have been written while he performed the daily duties of a job. From the time he came back from Oxford until 1917 he was with Doubleday, Page and Company; he left that firm for the *Ladies' Home Journal,* which in turn he abandoned a year later for the Philadelphia *Evening Public Ledger.* Then in 1920 he joined the New York *Evening Post* as its columnist, conducting therein " The Bowling Green " for the delectation of all who shared his catholic tastes for books, tobacco, and such seafaring men as Captain David W. Bone, the author of *The Lookout Man,* and William McFee, the novelist, not to mention the great Joseph Conrad. Even the three years in

Philadelphia yielded its harvest in the volume *Travels in Philadelphia*. But the prophets might have predicted early that Mr. Morley would have no difficulty in writing books while getting to an office each morning and spending most of the day there. For during his arduous career as an Oxford undergraduate he found opportunity for his very first excursion between covers, *The Eighth Sin,* which was published when he was twenty-two. Five years then elapsed before the next book, *Parnassus on Wheels*.

In 1924 he left the *Evening Post* and settled to his most ambitious feat so far, the writing of a novel, *Thunder on the Left*. It came out late in 1925 and proved a huge success, 60,000 copies being sold in the first six weeks of its existence. Since then he has published several other books, and more will surely follow.

ON UNANSWERING LETTERS[1]

THERE are a great many people who really believe in answering letters the day they are received, just as there are people who go to the movies at nine o'clock in the morning; but these people are stunted and queer.

It is a great mistake. Such crass and breathless promptness takes away a great deal of the pleasure of correspondence.

The psychological didoes involved in receiving letters and making up one's mind to answer them are very complex. If the tangled process could be clearly analyzed and its component involutions isolated for inspection we might reach a clearer comprehension of that curious bag of tricks, the efficient Masculine Mind.

Take Bill F., for instance, a man so delightful that even to contemplate his existence puts us in good humor and makes us think well of a world that can exhibit an individual equally comely in mind, body and estate. Every now and then we get a letter from Bill, and immediately we pass into a kind of trance, in which our mind rapidly enunciates the ideas, thoughts, surmises and contradictions that we would like to

[1] From *Mince Pie*, copyright, 1919, by the George H. Doran Company.

write to him in reply. We think what fun it would be to sit right down and churn the inkwell, spreading speculation and cynicism over a number of sheets of foolscap to be wafted Billward.

Sternly we repress the impulse for we know that the shock to Bill of getting so immediate a retort would surely unhinge the well-fitted panels of his intellect.

We add his letter to the large delta of unanswered mail on our desk, taking occasion to turn the mass over once or twice and run through it in a brisk, smiling mood, thinking of all the jolly letters we shall write some day.

After Bill's letter has lain on the pile for a fortnight or so it has been gently silted over by about twenty other pleasantly postponed manuscripts. Coming upon it by chance, we reflect that any specific problems raised by Bill in that manifesto will by this time have settled themselves. And his random speculations upon household management and human destiny will probably have taken a new slant by now, so that to answer his letter in its own tune will not be congruent with his present fevers. We had better bide a wee until we really have something of circumstance to impart.

We wait a week.

By this time a certain sense of shame has begun to invade the privacy of our brain. We feel that to answer that letter now would be an indelicacy. Better to pretend that we never got it. By and by Bill will write again and then we will answer promptly. We put the letter back in the middle of the heap and think what a fine chap Bill is. But he knows we love him, so it doesn't really matter whether we write or not.

Another week passes by, and no further communication from Bill. We wonder whether he does love us as much as we thought. Still — we are too proud to write and ask.

A few days later a new thought strikes us. Perhaps Bill thinks we have died and he is annoyed because he wasn't invited to the funeral. Ought we to wire him? No, because after all we are not dead, and even if he thinks we are, his subsequent relief at hearing the good news of our survival will outweigh his bitterness during the interval. One of these days we will write him a letter that will really express our heart, filled with all the grindings and gear-work of our mind, rich in affection and fallacy. But we had better let it ripen and mellow for a while. Letters, like wines, accumulate bright fumes and bubblings if kept under cork.

Presently we turn over that pile of letters again. We find in the lees of the heap two or three that have gone for six months and can safely be destroyed. Bill is still on our mind, but in a pleasant, dreamy kind of way. He does not ache or twinge us as he did a month ago. It is fine to have old friends like that and keep in touch with them. We wonder how he is and whether he has two children or three. Splendid old Bill!

By this time we have written Bill several letters in imagination and enjoyed doing so, but the matter of sending him an actual letter has begun to pall. The thought no longer has the savor and vivid sparkle it had once. When one feels like that it is unwise to write. Letters should be spontaneous outpourings: they should never be undertaken merely from a sense of duty. We know that Bill wouldn't want to get a letter that was dictated by a feeling of obligation.

Another fortnight or so elapsing, it occurs to us that we have entirely forgotten what Bill said to us in that letter. We take it out and con it over. Delightful fellow! It is full of his own felicitous kinks of whim, though some of it sounds a little old-fashioned by now. It seems a bit stale, has lost some of its freshness and surprise. Better not answer it just yet, for Christmas will soon be here and we shall have to write then anyway. We wonder, can Bill hold out until Christmas without a letter?

We have been rereading some of those imaginary letters to Bill that have been dancing in our head. They are full of all sorts of fine stuff. If Bill ever gets them he will know how we love him. To use O. Henry's immortal joke, we have days of Damon and Knights of Pythias writing those uninked letters to Bill. A curious thought has come to us. Perhaps it would be better if we never saw Bill again. It is very difficult to talk to a man when you like him so much. It is much easier to write in the sweet fantastic strain. We are so inarticulate when face to face. If Bill comes to town we will leave word that we have gone away. Good old Bill! He will always be a precious memory.

A few days later a sudden frenzy sweeps over us, and though we have many pressing matters on hand, we mobilize pen and paper and literary shock troops and prepare to hurl several battalions at Bill. But, strangely enough, our utterance seems stilted and stiff. We have nothing to say. *My dear Bill,* we begin, *it seems a long time since we heard from you. Why don't you write? We still love you, in spite of all your shortcomings.*

That doesn't seem very cordial. We muse over the pen and nothing comes. Bursting with affection, we are unable to say a word.

Just then the phone rings. " Hello? " we say.

It is Bill, come to town unexpectedly.

" Good old fish! " we cry, ecstatic. " Meet you at the corner of Tenth and Chestnut in five minutes."

We tear up the unfinished letter. Bill will never know how much we love him. Perhaps it is just as well. It is very embarrassing to have your friends know how you feel about them. When we meet him we will be a little bit on our guard. It would not be well to be betrayed into any extravagance of cordiality.

And perhaps a not altogether false little story could be written about a man who never visited those most dear to him, because it panged him so to say good-by when he had to leave.

APPRECIATION HELPS

1. Just where has the author described your own emotions in " unanswering letters "? If you are prompt in answering letters, what are the pleasurable emotions resulting from promptness?
2. Describe your own emotional stages in " unanswering " a letter.

3. Describe your feeling in rereading old letters, those you have written as well as those you have received.
4. List several titles for essays which the reading of this stimulated.
5. Would you enjoy knowing Christopher Morley? Why?
6. What are the qualities of a good letter?
7. Write a letter which embodies these attractive qualities.

COMPOSITION HINTS

1. On " Unpreparing " Lessons
2. On Postponing a Dreaded Interview
3. My Favorite Correspondent
4. Uninked Letters
5. The Jolly Letters I Am Going to Write Some Day
6. Christmas Card Correspondents
7. If My Desk Could Speak

WHAT MEN LIVE BY[1]

by Christopher Morley

WHAT a delicate and rare and gracious art is the art of conversation! With what a dexterity and skill the bubble of speech must be maneuvered if mind is to meet and mingle with mind.

There is no sadder disappointment than to realize that a conversation has been a complete failure. By which we mean that it has failed in blending or isolating for contrast the ideas, opinions, and surmises of two eager minds. So often a conversation is shipwrecked by the very eagerness of one member to contribute. There must be give and take, parry and thrust, patience to hear and judgment to utter. How uneasy is the qualm as one looks back on an hour's talk and sees that the opportunity was wasted; the precious instant of intercourse gone forever: the secrets of the heart still incommunicate! Perhaps we were too anxious to hurry the moment, to enforce

[1] From *Mince Pie*, copyright, 1919, by the George H. Doran Company.

our own theory, to adduce instance from our own experience. Perhaps we were not patient enough to wait until our friend could express himself with ease and happiness. Perhaps we squandered the dialogue in tangent topics, in a multitude of irrelevances.

How few, how few are those gifted for real talk! There are fine merry fellows, full of mirth and shrewdly minted observation, who will not abide by one topic, who must always be lashing out upon some new byroad, snatching at every bush they pass. They are too excitable, too ungoverned for the joys of patient intercourse. Talk is so solemn a rite it should be approached with prayer and must be conducted with nicety and forbearance. What steadiness and sympathy are needed if the thread of thought is to be unwound without tangles or snapping! What forbearance, while each of the pair, after tentative gropings here and yonder, feels his way toward truth as he sees it. So often two in talk are like men standing back to back, each trying to describe to the other what he sees and disputing because their visions do not tally. It takes a little time for minds to turn face to face.

Very often conversations are better among three than between two, for the reason that then one of the trio is always, unconsciously, acting as umpire, interposing fair play, recalling wandering wits to the nub of the argument, seeing that the aggressiveness of one does no foul to the reticence of another. Talk in twos may, alas! fall into speaker and listener: talk in threes rarely does so.

It is little realized how slowly, how painfully, we approach the expression of truth. We are so variable, so anxious to be polite, and alternately swayed by caution or anger. Our mind oscillates like a pendulum: it takes some time for it to come to rest. And then, the proper allowance and correction has to be made for our individual vibrations that prevent accuracy. Even the compass needle doesn't point the true north, but only the magnetic north. Similarly our minds at best can but indicate magnetic truth, and are distorted by many things that act as iron filings do on the compass. The necessity of holding one's job: what an iron filing that is on the compass card of a man's brain!

We are all afraid of truth: we keep a battalion of our pet prejudices and precautions ready to throw into the argument as shock troops, rather than let our fortress of Truth be stormed. We have smoke bombs and decoy ships and all manner of cunning colorizations by which we conceal our innards from our friends, and even from ourselves. How we fume and fidget, how we bustle and dodge rather than commit ourselves.

In days of hurry and complication, in the incessant pressure of human problems that thrust our days behind us, does one never dream of a way of life in which talk would be honored and exalted to its proper place in the sun? What a zest there is in that intimate unreserved exchange of thought, in the pursuit of the magical bluebird of joy and human satisfaction that may be seen flitting distantly through the branches of life. It was a sad thing for the world when it grew so busy that men had no time to talk. There are such treasures of knowledge and compassion in the minds of our friends, could we only have time to talk them out of their shy quarries. If we had our way, we would set aside one day a week for talking. In fact, we would reorganize the week altogether. We would have one day for Worship (let each man devote it to worship of whatever he holds dearest); one day for Work; one day for Play (probably fishing); one day for Talking; one day for Reading, and one day for Smoking and Thinking. That would leave one day for Resting, and (incidentally) interviewing employers.

The best week of our life was one in which we did nothing but talk. We spent it with a delightful gentleman who has a little bungalow on the shore of a lake in Pike County. He had a great many books and cigars, both of which are conversational stimulants. We used to lie out on the edge of the lake, in our oldest trousers, and talk. We discussed ever so many subjects; in all of them he knew immensely more than we did. We built up a complete philosophy of indolence and good will, according to Food and Sleep and Swimming their proper share of homage. We rose at ten in the morning and began talking;

we talked all day and until three o'clock at night. Then we went to bed and regained strength and combativeness for the coming day. Never was a week better spent. We committed no crimes, planned no secret treaties, devised no annexations or indemnities. We envied no one. We examined the entire world and found it worth while. Meanwhile our wives, who were watching (perhaps with a little quiet indignation) from the veranda, kept on asking us, "What on earth do you talk about?"

Bless their hearts, men don't have to have anything to talk *about*. They just talk.

And there is only one rule for being a good talker: learn how to listen.

APPRECIATION HELPS

1. What are the conditions of good talk? What things hinder good talk? Have you discovered some not mentioned by the author?
2. Do you agree with the author when he says that few persons are gifted for real talk? Explain.
3. Does your experience lead you to agree that conversations are better among three than between two persons? Why?
4. Read Stevenson's "Talks and Talkers," in *Memories and Portraits*. Compare it with this essay.
5. Why is it hard to express truth in conversation? Is this merely an adult view? Where have you found it difficult to be truthful in conversation?
6. What are the values of good talk?
7. Discuss: "And there is only one rule for being a good talker: learn how to listen."

COMPOSITION HINTS

1. On the Gentle Art of Conversation
2. Shipwrecked Conversations I Have Had
3. When Conversations Develop into Monologues
4. When Three Was a Crowd
5. The Best Week of My Life
6. On the Conversation of Children
7. Pet Prejudices

8. Silent Talkers
9. Etiquette for Talkers
10. Bypaths in Conversation
11. Conversational Stimulants
12. Bores

ON DOORS[1]

by Christopher Morley

THE opening and closing of doors are the most significant actions of man's life. What a mystery lies in doors! No man knows what awaits him when he opens a door. Even the most familiar room, where the clock ticks and the hearth grows red at dusk, may harbor surprises. The plumber may actually have called (while you were out) and fixed that leaking faucet. The cook may have had a fit of the vapors and demanded her passports. The wise man opens his front door with humility and a spirit of acceptance.

Which one of us has not sat in some anteroom and watched the inscrutable panels of a door that was full of meaning? Perhaps you were waiting to apply for a job; perhaps you had some " deal " you were ambitious to put over. You watched the confidential stenographer flit in and out, carelessly turning that mystic portal which, to you, revolved on hinges of fate. And then the young woman said, " Mr. Cranberry will see you now." As you grasped the knob the thought flashed, " When I open this door again, what will have happened? "

There are many kinds of doors. Revolving doors for hotels, shops, and public buildings. These are typical of the brisk, bustling ways of modern life. Can you imagine John Milton or William Penn skipping through a revolving door? Then there are the curious little slatted doors that still swing outside denatured barrooms, and extend only from shoulder to knee. There are trapdoors, sliding doors, double doors, stage doors, prison doors, glass doors. But the symbol and mystery of a

[1] From *Mince Pie*, copyright, 1919, by the George H. Doran Company.

door resides in its quality of concealment. A glass door is not a door at all, but a window. The meaning of a door is to hide what lies inside; to keep the heart in suspense.

Also, there are many ways of opening doors. There is the cheery push of elbow with which the waiter shoves open the kitchen door when he bears in your tray of supper. There is the suspicious and tentative withdrawal of a door before the unhappy book agent or peddler. There is the genteel and carefully modulated recession with which footmen swing wide the oaken barriers of the great. There is the sympathetic and awful silence of the dentist's maid who opens the door into the operating room and, without speaking, implies that the doctor is ready for you. There is the brisk cataclysmic opening of a door when the nurse comes in, very early in the morning — "It's a boy!"

Doors are the symbol of privacy, of retreat, of the mind's escape into blissful quietude or sad secret struggle. A room without doors is not a room, but a hallway. No matter where he is, a man can make himself at home behind a closed door. The mind works best behind closed doors. Men are not horses to be herded together. Dogs know the meaning and anguish of doors. Have you ever noticed a puppy yearning at a shut portal? It is a symbol of human life.

The opening of doors is a mystic act: it has in it some flavor of the unknown, some sense of moving into a new moment, a new pattern of the human rigmarole. It includes the highest glimpses of mortal gladness: reunions, reconciliations, the bliss of lovers long parted. Even in sadness, the opening of a door may bring relief: it changes and redistributes human forces. But the closing of doors is far more terrible. It is a confession of finality. Every door closed brings something to an end. And there are degrees of sadness in the closing of doors. A door slammed is a confession of weakness. A door gently shut is often the most tragic gesture in life. Every one knows the seizure of anguish that comes just after the closing of a door, when the loved one is still near, within sound of voice, and yet already far away.

The opening and closing of doors is a part of the stern fluency of life. Life will not stay still and let us alone. We are continually opening doors with hope, closing them with despair. Life lasts not much longer than a pipe of tobacco, and destiny knocks us out like the ashes.

The closing of a door is irrevocable. It snaps the packthread of the heart. It is no avail to reopen, to go back. Pinero spoke nonsense when he made Paula Tanqueray say, " The future is only the past entered through another gate." Alas, there is no other gate. When the door is shut, it is shut forever. There is no other entrance to that vanished pulse of time. " The moving finger writes, and having writ — "

There is a certain kind of door-shutting that will come to us all. The kind of door-shutting that is done very quietly, with the sharp click of the latch to break the stillness. They will think then, one hopes, of our unfulfilled decencies rather than of our pluperfected misdemeanors. Then they will go out and close the door.

APPRECIATION HELPS

1. Why are the opening and the closing of doors significant in man's life? They symbolize what to the author?
2. When, in your own experience, have doors been " momentous "? Describe a visit to the office of the principal.
3. Discuss the revelation of individuality as shown by the manner of opening and closing doors.
4. Read Emily Dickinson's poem " Suspense."
5. How is the genial, kindly spirit of Morley reflected in this essay?
6. With what essays of Morley are you familiar? List five that your classmates would enjoy.

COMPOSITION HINTS

1. On Windows
2. On Revolving Doors
3. Open Doors of Youth
4. Two-Headed Janus, God of Doors
5. Closed Doors

AGNES REPPLIER

To a recent request for biographical confidences Miss Agnes Repplier (b. 1858) replied:

" Biographical material there is none. My life affords no salient feature for narration. I have been badly injured by an accident, but half the world is injured by accidents. I have been robbed by burglars; but all Philadelphians are robbed sooner or later by burglars. I am going to Europe in the spring, but who isn't going to Europe in the spring? In these incidents there is no shadow of distinction."

But during her uneventful life Miss Repplier has written four teen volumes of essays, two biographical sketches, and four miscellaneous volumes, so that today she ranks as a foremost American woman author. Her latest volume is *To Think of Tea!* (1932) (Houghton Mifflin Company).

She was brought up in a convent in Pennsylvania, a strict place where *Chambers' Miscellany,* she asserts, was her only means of approach to the intellectual. And not only was her brain allowed to develop untended, her nerves were put to severe tests. For instance, by a triumph of monastic discipline she was always placed next to a girl to whom she could find nothing to say, a good girl with medals hanging around her neck. Her first book, a compilation still much used, appeared in 1892, *A Book of Famous Verse.*

Miss Repplier is devoted to cats, and has written a whole book about them, *The Fireside Sphinx* (1902).

A KITTEN[1]

If

The child is father of the man,

why is not the kitten father of the cat? If in the little boy there lurks the infant likeness of all that manhood will complete, why does not the kitten betray some of the attributes common to the adult puss? A puppy is but a dog, plus high spirits, and minus common sense. We never hear our friends say they love puppies, but cannot bear dogs. A kitten is a thing apart; and many people who lack the discriminating enthusiasm for cats, who regard these beautiful beasts with aversion and mistrust, are won over easily, and cajoled out of their prejudices by the deceitful wiles of kittenhood.

The little actor cons another part,

and is the most irresistible comedian in the world. Its wide-open eyes gleam with wonder and mirth. It darts madly at nothing at all, and then, as though suddenly checked in the pursuit, prances sideways on its hind legs with ridiculous agility and zeal. It makes a vast pretense of climbing the rounds of a chair, and swings by the curtain like an acrobat. It scrambles up a table leg, and is seized with comic horror at finding itself full two feet from the floor. If you hasten to its rescue, it clutches you nervously, its little heart thumping against its furry sides, while its soft paws expand and contract with agitation and relief;

And all their harmless claws disclose,
Like prickles of an early rose.

Yet the instant it is back on the carpet it feigns to be suspicious of your interference, peers at you out of " the tail o' its ee," and scampers for protection under the sofa, from which

[1] From *In the Dozy Hours*, published by the Houghton Mifflin Company, 1894.

asylum it presently emerges with cautious trailing steps, as though encompassed by fearful dangers and alarms. Its baby innocence is yet unseared. The evil knowledge of uncanny things which is the dark inheritance of cathood has not yet shadowed its round infant eyes. Where did witches find the mysterious beasts that sat motionless by their fires, and watched unblinkingly the waxen manikins dwindling in the flame? They never reared these companions of their solitude, for no witch could have endured to see a kitten gamboling on her hearthstone. A witch's kitten! That one preposterous thought proves how wide, how unfathomed, is the gap between feline infancy and age.

So it happens that the kitten is loved and cherished and caressed as long as it preserves the beguiling mirthfulness of youth. Richelieu, we know, was wont to keep a family of kittens in his cabinet, that their grace and gayety might divert him from the cares of state, and from black moods of melancholy. Yet, with short-sighted selfishness, he banished these little friends when but a few months old, and gave their places to younger pets. The first faint dawn of reason, the first indication of soberness and worldly wisdom, the first charming and coquettish pretenses to maturity, were followed by immediate dismissal. Richelieu desired to be amused. He had no conception of the finer joy which springs from mutual companionship and esteem. Even humbler and more sincere admirers, like Joanna Baillie, in whom we wish to believe Puss found a friend and champion, appear to take it for granted that the kitten should be the spoiled darling of the household, and the cat a social outcast, degraded into usefulness, and expected to work for her living. What else can be understood from such lines as these?

> Ah! many a lightly sportive child,
> Who hath, like thee, our wits beguiled,
> To dull and sober manhood grown,
> With strange recoil our hearts disown.
> Even so, poor Kit! must thou endure,
> When thou becomest a cat demure,

Full many a cuff and angry word,
Chid roughly from the tempting board.
And yet, for that thou hast, I ween,
So oft our favored playmate been,
Soft be the change which thou shalt prove,
When time hath spoiled thee of our love;
Still be thou deemed, by housewife fat,
A comely, careful, mousing cat,
Whose dish is, for the public good,
Replenished oft with savory food.

Here is a plain exposition of the utilitarian theory which Shakespeare is supposed to have countenanced because Shylock speaks of the " harmless, necessary cat." Shylock, forsooth! As if he, of all men in Christendom or Jewry, knew anything about cats! Small wonder that he was outwitted by Portia and Jessica, when an adroit little animal could so easily beguile him. But Joanna Baillie should never have been guilty of those snug commonplaces concerning the

comely, careful, mousing cat,

remembering her own valiant Tabby who won Scott's respectful admiration by worrying and killing a dog. It ill became the possessor of an Amazonian cat, distinguished by Sir Walter's regard, to speak with such patronizing kindness of the race.

We can make no more stupid blunder than to look upon our pets from the standpoint of utility. Puss, as a rule, is another Nimrod, eager for the chase, and unwearyingly patient in pursuit of her prey. But she hunts for her own pleasure, not for our convenience; and when a life of luxury has relaxed her zeal, she often declines to hunt at all. I knew intimately two Maryland cats, well born and of great personal attractions. The sleek, black Tom was named Onyx, and his snow-white companion Lilian. Both were idle, urbane, fastidious, and self-indulgent as Lucullus. Now, into the house honored, but not served, by these charming creatures came a rat, which secured permanent lodgings in the kitchen, and speedily evicted the maid servants. A reign of terror followed, and after a few days of hopeless anarchy it occurred to the cook that the cats might be brought from their comfortable cushions upstairs and shut in at night with their hereditary foe. This was done, and the next morning, on opening the kitchen door, a tableau rivaling the peaceful scenes of Eden was presented to the view. On one side of the hearth lay Onyx, on the other, Lilian; and ten feet away, upright upon the kitchen table, sat the rat, contemplating them both with tranquil humor and content. It was apparent to him, as well as to the rest of the household, that he was an object of absolute, contemptuous indifference to those two lordly cats.

There is none of this superb unconcern in the joyous eagerness of infancy. A kitten will dart in pursuit of everything that is small enough to be chased with safety. Not a fly on the window-pane, not a moth in the air, not a tiny crawling insect on the carpet, escapes its unwelcome attentions. It begins to "take notice" as soon as its eyes are open, and its vivacity, outstripping its dawning intelligence, leads it into infantile perils and wrong doing. I own that when Agrippina brought her first-born son — aged two days — and established him in my bedroom closet, the plan struck me at the start as inconvenient. I had prepared another nursery for the little Claudius Nero, and I endeavored for a while to convince his mother that my arrangements were best. But Agrippina was inflexible. The closet suited her in every respect; and, with charming and irresistible flattery, she gave me to understand, in the mute language I knew so well, that she wished her baby boy to be under my immediate protection. "I bring him to you because I trust you," she said as plainly as looks can speak. "Downstairs they handle him all the time, and it is not good for kittens to be handled. Here he is safe from harm, and here he shall remain." After a few weak remonstrances, the futility of which I too clearly understood, her persistence carried the day. I removed my clothing from the closet, spread a shawl upon the floor, had the door taken from its hinges, and resigned myself, for the first time in my life, to the daily and hourly companionship of an infant.

I was amply rewarded. People who require the household cat to rear her offspring in some remote attic, or dark corner of the cellar, have no idea of all the diversion and pleasure that they lose. It is delightful to watch the little blind, sprawling, feeble, helpless things develop swiftly into the grace and agility of kittenhood. It is delightful to see the mingled pride and anxiety of the mother, whose parental love increases with every hour of care, and who exhibits her young family as if they were infant Gracchi, the hope of all their race. During Nero's extreme youth, there were times, I admit, when Agrippina wearied both of his companionship and of her own maternal duties. Once or twice she abandoned him at night for the greater luxury of my bed, where she slept tranquilly by my side, unmindful of the little wailing cries with which Nero lamented her desertion. Once or twice the heat of early summer tempted her to spend the evening on the porch roof which lay beneath my windows, and I have passed some anxious hours awaiting her return, and wondering what would happen if she never came back, and I were left to bring up the baby by hand.

But as the days sped on, and Nero grew rapidly in beauty and intelligence, Agrippina's affection for him knew no bounds. She could hardly bear to leave him even for a little while, and always came hurrying back to him with a loud frightened mew, as if fearing he might have been stolen in her absence. At night she purred over him for hours, or made little gurgling noises expressive of ineffable content. She resented the careless curiosity of strangers, and was a trifle supercilious when the cook stole softly in to give vent to her fervent admiration. But from first to last she shared with me her pride and pleasure; and the joy in her beautiful eyes, as she raised them to mine, was frankly confiding and sympathetic. When the infant Claudius rolled for the first time over the ledge of the closet, and lay sprawling on the bedroom floor, it would have been hard to say which of us was the more elated at his prowess. A narrow pink ribbon of honor was at once tied around the small adventurer's neck, and he was pronounced the most daring and agile of kittens. From that day his brief career was a series of brilliant triumphs. He was a kitten of parts. Like one of Miss Austen's heroes, he had air and countenance. Less beautiful than his mother, whom he closely resembled, he easily eclipsed her in vivacity and the specious arts of fascination. Never were mother and son more unlike in character and disposition, and the inevitable contrast between kittenhood and cathood was enhanced in this case by a strong natural dissimilarity which no length of years could have utterly effaced.

Agrippina had always been a cat of manifest reserves. She was only six weeks old when she came to me, and had already acquired that gravity of demeanor, that air of gentle disdain, that dignified and somewhat supercilious composure, which won the respectful admiration of those whom she permitted to enjoy her acquaintance. Even in moments of self-forgetfulness and mirth her recreations resembled those of the little Spanish Infanta, who, not being permitted to play with her inferiors, and having no equals, diverted herself as best she could with sedate and solitary sport. Always chary of her favors, Agrippina cared little for the admiration of her chosen circle; and, with a single exception, she made no friends beyond it.

Claudius Nero, on the contrary, thirsted for applause. Affable, debonair, and democratic to the core, the caresses and commendations of a chance visitor or of a housemaid were as valuable to him as were my own. I never looked at him " showing off," as children say, — jumping from chair to chair, balancing himself on the bedpost, or scrambling rapturously up the forbidden curtains, — without thinking of the young Emperor who contended in the amphitheater for the worthless plaudits of the crowd. He was impulsive and affectionate, — so, I believe was the Emperor for a time, — and as masterful as if born to the purple. His mother struggled hard to maintain her rightful authority, but it was in vain. He woke her from her sweetest naps; he darted at her tail, and leaped down on her from sofas and tables with the grace of a diminutive

panther. Every time she attempted to punish him for these
misdemeanors he cried piteously for help, and was promptly
and unwisely rescued by some kind-hearted member of the
family. After a while Agrippina took to sitting on her tail,
in order to keep it out of his reach, and I have seen her many
times carefully tucking it out of sight. She had never been
a cat of active habits or of showy accomplishments, and the
daring agility of the little Nero amazed and bewildered her.
"A Spaniard," observes that pleasant gossip, James Howell,
"walks as if he marched, and seldom looks upon the ground,
as if he contemned it. I was told of a Spaniard who, having
got a fall by a stumble, and broke his nose, rose up, and in a
disdainful manner said, 'This comes of walking on the earth.'"
    Now Nero seldom walked on the earth. At least, he never,
if he could help it, walked on the floor; but traversed a room
in a series of flying leaps from chair to table, from table to
lounge, from lounge to desk, with an occasional dash at the
mantelpiece, just to show what he could do. It was curious to
watch Agrippina during the performance of these acrobatic
feats. Pride, pleasure, the anxiety of a mother, and the faint
resentment of conscious inferiority struggled for mastership in
her little breast. Sometimes, when Nero's radiant self-satisfaction grew almost insufferable, I have seen her eyelids narrow
sullenly, and have wondered whether the Roman Empress
ever looked in that way at her brilliant and beautiful son, when
maternal love was withering slowly under the shadow of coming evil. Sometimes, when Nero had been prancing and pad-
dling about with absurd and irresistible glee, attracting and
compelling the attention of everybody in the room, Agrippina
would jump up on my lap, and look in my face with an expression I thought I understood. She had never before valued
my affection in all her little petted, pampered life. She had
been sufficient for herself, and had merely tolerated me as a
devoted and useful companion. But now that another had
usurped so many of her privileges, I fancied there were moments when it pleased her to know that one subject, at least,
was not to be beguiled from allegiance; that to one friend, at

least, she always was and always would be the dearest cat in
the world.

I am glad to remember that love triumphed over jealousy,
and that Agrippina's devotion to Nero increased with every
day of his short life. The altruism of a cat seldom reaches
beyond her kittens; but she is capable of heroic unselfishness
where they are concerned. I knew of a London beast, a homeless, forlorn vagrant, who constituted herself an out-door pen-
sioner at the house of a friendly man of letters. This cat had
a kitten, whose youthful vivacity won the hearts of a neigh-
boring family. They adopted it willingly, but refused to harbor the mother, who still came for her daily dole to her only
benefactor. Whenever a bit of fish or some other especial
dainty was given her, this poor mendicant scaled the wall, and
watched her chance to share it with her kitten, her little
wealthy, greedy son, who gobbled it up as remorselessly as if
he were not living on the fat of the land.

Agrippina would have been swift to follow such an example
of devotion. At dinner time she always yielded the precedence
to Nero, and it became one of our daily tasks to compel the
little lad to respect his mother's privileges. He scorned his
saucer of milk, and from tenderest infancy aspired to adult
food, making predatory incursions upon Agrippina's plate, and
obliging us finally to feed them in separate apartments. I
have seen him, when a very young kitten, rear himself upon
his baby legs, and with his soft and wicked little paw strike
his mother in the face until she dropped the piece of meat she
had been eating, when he tranquilly devoured it. It was to
prevent the recurrence of such scandalous scenes that two din-
ing-rooms became a necessity in the family. Yet he was so
loving and so lovable, poor little Claudius Nero! Why do I
dwell on his faults, remembering, as I do, his winning sweetness and affability? Day after day, in the narrow city garden,
the two cats played together, happy in each other's society, and
never a yard apart. Night after night they retired at the same
time, and slept upon the same cushion, curled up inextricably
into one soft, furry ball. Many times I have knelt by their

chair to bid them both good-night; and always, when I did so, Agrippina would lift her charming head, purr drowsily for a few seconds, and then nestle closer still to her first-born, with sighs of supreme satisfaction. The zenith of her life had been reached. Her cup of contentment was full.

It is a rude world, even for little cats, and evil chances lie in wait for the petted creatures we strive to shield from harm. Remembering the pangs of separation, the possibilities of unkindness or neglect, the troubles that hide in ambush on every unturned page, I am sometimes glad that the same cruel and selfish blow struck both mother and son, and that they lie together, safe from hurt or hazard, sleeping tranquilly and always, under the shadow of the friendly pines.

APPRECIATION HELPS

1. Point out descriptive passages which make you know that Miss Repplier loved cats and kittens.
2. Comment upon the distinction drawn between the kitten and the cat. Does your observation agree with that of the author?
3. Why is it a " stupid blunder to look upon pets from the standpoint of utility "?
4. Do you like the names bestowed upon the pets? What is the most attractive name you know for a cat? For a dog?
5. How was the author " amply rewarded " for giving up her closet to her pets?
6. Point out passages where the essay has gained by the use of literary and historical allusions.
7. What human qualities are given to these pets?
8. Name some interesting books which depict the life or habits of animals.
9. List subjects for essays which characterize some pets you have enjoyed.
10. Read Stevenson's " The Character of Dogs," in *Memories and Portraits*.
11. Read Kipling's " The Cat That Walked by Himself," in *Just-So Stories*.

COMPOSITION HINTS

1. The Harmless, Necessary Cat
2. How to Name a Family Pet
3. The Playfulness of My Favorite Kitten
4. Pets I Have Wished to Own
5. The Character of Dogs
6. Why Every Boy Should Own a Dog
7. When I Was the Chief Mourner
8. Childhood Pets

STEPHEN LEACOCK

The tragedy of so many people is that they laugh at the wrong time. As a result, when they should be serious they are ludicrous, and when they should be amusing they are dull. This is a mournful mistake of which Professor Stephen Leacock has never been guilty. When he wrote *Elements of Political Science* (1906), *Essays and Literary Studies* (1916), or *The Unsolved Riddle of Social Justice* (1920), he easily invested his subject with the dignity it deserved. In this domain assuredly he has been taken seriously, since for years he has been head of the department of political economy in McGill University at Montreal. Yet, at the same time, he has contrived to become a most popular humorous writer. In 1910 Mr. John Lane, the London publisher, got hold of a volume entitled *Literary Lapses,* published in Canada and written by a Stephen Leacock very different from the brilliant professor. No doubt it had been thrown off as a holiday joke. Mr. Lane promptly reissued it, and at once the whole English-speaking world was set aroar. The success was so great that Mr. Leacock had to go on writing funny books, and he did so with such side-splitting skill that nobody would believe that this laughter-raising fellow and the learned man at McGill were the same person. He had succeeded in restricting his solemnity and his jocularity to their respective fields.

Nevertheless, in such an amusing book as *My Discovery of England,* there are some evident and important points, as you may be left to discover. Humor need not obliterate purpose even though there are purposes for which it is unsuited.

Mr. Leacock was born at Swanmoor in Hampshire, England, in 1869 and educated at the Upper Canada College, the staff of which he joined in 1891. In 1899 he went to the Graduate School of the University of Chicago, and since 1903 he has been at McGill. In 1907 and 1908 he toured the British Empire, lecturing on imperial organization under the auspices of the Cecil Rhodes Trust.

OXFORD AS I SEE IT [1]

Y private profession being that of a university professor, I was naturally deeply interested in the system of education in England. I was therefore led to make a special visit to Oxford and to submit the place to a searching scrutiny. Arriving one afternoon at four o'clock, I stayed at the Mitre Hotel and did not leave until eleven o'clock next morning. The whole of this time, except for one hour spent in addressing the undergraduates, was devoted to a close and eager study of the great university. When I add to this that I had already visited Oxford in 1907 and spent a Sunday at All Souls with Colonel L. S. Amery, it will be seen at once that my views on Oxford are based upon observations extending over fourteen years.

At any rate, I can at least claim that my acquaintance with the British university is just as good a basis for reflection and judgment as that of the numerous English critics who come to our side of the water. I have known a famous English author arrive at Harvard University in the morning, have lunch with President Lowell, and then write a whole chapter on the Excellence of Higher Education in America. I have known another one to come to Harvard, have lunch with President Lowell, and do an entire book on the Decline of Serious Study in America. Or take the case of my own university. I remember Mr. Rudyard Kipling coming to McGill and saying in his address to the undergraduates at 2:30 P.M., "You have here a great institution." But how could he have gathered this information? So far as I knew, he spent the entire morning with Sir Andrew Macphail in his house beside the campus, smoking cigarettes. When I add that he distinctly refused to visit the Palaeontologic Museum, that he saw nothing of our new hydraulic apparatus or of our classes in domestic science, his judgment that we had here a great institution seems a

[1] From *My Discovery of England,* copyright by Dodd, Mead & Company, Inc., 1922.

little bit superficial. I can only put beside it, to redeem it in some measure, the hasty and ill-formed judgment expressed by Lord Milner, "McGill is a noble university," and the rash and indiscreet expression of the Prince of Wales, when we gave him an LL.D. degree, "McGill has a glorious future."

To my mind these unthinking judgments about our great college do harm, and I determined, therefore, that anything that I said about Oxford should be the actual observation and real study based upon a bona fide residence in the Mitre Hotel.

On the strength of this basis of experience I am prepared to make the following positive and emphatic statements.

Oxford is a noble university. It has a great past. It is at present the greatest university in the world; and it is quite possible that it has a great future. Oxford trains scholars of the real type better than any other place in the world. Its methods are antiquated. It despises science. It has professors who never teach and students who never learn. It has no order, no arrangement, no system. Its curriculum is unintelligible. It has no present. It has no state legislature to tell it how to teach, and yet — it gets there. Whether we like it or not, Oxford gives something to its students, a life and a mode of thought, which in America as yet we can emulate, but not equal.

If anybody doubts this let him go and take a room at the Mitre Hotel (ten and six for a wainscoted bedroom, period of Charles I) and study the place for himself.

These singular results achieved at Oxford are all the more surprising when one considers the distressing conditions under which the students work. The lack of an adequate building fund compels them to go on working in the same old buildings which they have had for centuries. The buildings at Wadham College have not been renewed since the year 1605. In Merton and Magdalen the students are still housed in the old buildings erected in the fourteenth century. At Christ Church College I was shown a kitchen which had been built at the expense of Cardinal Wolsey in 1525. Incredible though it may seem, they have no other place to cook in than this, and are compelled to use it today. On the day when I saw this kitchen, four cooks were busy roasting an ox whole for the students' lunch — this, at least, is what I presumed they were doing, from the size of the fireplace used; but it may not have been an ox; perhaps it was a cow. On a huge table, twelve feet by six and made of slabs of wood five inches thick, two other cooks were rolling out a game pie. I estimated it as measuring three feet across. In this rude way, unchanged since the time of Henry VIII, the unhappy Oxford students are fed. I could not help contrasting it with the cozy little boarding houses on Cottage Grove Avenue where I used to eat when I was a student at Chicago, or the charming little basement dining rooms of the students' boarding houses in Toronto. But then, of course, Henry VIII never lived in Toronto.

The same lack of a building fund necessitates the Oxford students' living in the identical old boarding houses they had in the sixteenth and seventeenth centuries. Technically they are called quadrangles, closes, and "rooms," but I am so broken in to the usage of my student days that I can't help calling them boarding houses. In many of these the old stairway has been worn down by the feet of ten generations of students; the windows have little latticed panes; there are old names carved here and there upon the stone, and a thick growth of ivy covers the walls. The boarding house at St. John's College dates from 1555; the one at Brasenose, from 1509. A few hundred thousand pounds would suffice to replace these old buildings with neat steel-and-brick structures like the normal school at Schenectady, New York, or the Peel Street High School at Montreal. But nothing is done. A movement was, indeed, attempted last autumn toward removing the ivy from the walls, but the result was unsatisfactory and they are putting it back. Any one could have told them beforehand that the mere removal of the ivy would not brighten Oxford up, unless at the same time one cleared the stones of the old inscriptions, put in steel fire escapes, and, in fact, brought the boarding houses up to date.

But Henry VIII being dead, nothing was done. Yet, in spite

of its dilapidated buildings and its lack of fire escapes, ventilation, sanitation, and up-to-date kitchen facilities, I persist in my assertion that I believe that Oxford, in its way, is the greatest university in the world. I am aware that this is an extreme statement and needs explanation. Oxford is much smaller in numbers, for example, than the State University of Minnesota, and is much poorer. It has, or had till yesterday, fewer students than the University of Toronto. To mention Oxford beside the 26,000 students of Columbia University sounds ridiculous. In point of money, the $30,000,000 endowment of the University of Chicago, and the $35,000,000 one of Columbia, and the $43,000,000 one of Harvard seem to leave Oxford nowhere. Yet the peculiar thing is that it is not nowhere. By some queer process of its own it seems to get there every time. It was, therefore, of the very greatest interest to me, as a profound scholar, to try to investigate just how this peculiar excellence of Oxford arises.

It has hardly been due to anything in the curriculum or program of studies. Indeed, to any one accustomed to the best models of a university curriculum as it flourishes in the United States and Canada, the program of studies is frankly quite laughable. There is less applied science in the place than would be found with us in a theological college. Hardly a single professor at Oxford would recognize a dynamo if he met it in broad daylight. The Oxford student learns nothing of chemistry, physics, heat, plumbing, electric wiring, gas fitting, or the use of a blow torch. Any American college student can run a motor car, take a gasoline engine to pieces, fix a washer on a kitchen tap, mend a broken electric bell, and give an expert opinion on what has gone wrong with the furnace. It is these things, indeed, which stamp him as a college man and occasion a very pardonable pride in the minds of his parents. But in all these things the Oxford student is the merest amateur.

This is bad enough. But, after all, one might say this is only the mechanical side of education. True; but one searches in vain in the Oxford curriculum for any adequate recognition of the higher and more cultured studies. Strange though it seems to us on this side of the Atlantic, there are no courses at Oxford in Housekeeping, or in Salesmanship, or in Advertising, or on Comparative Religion, or on the Influence of the Press. There are no lectures whatever on Human Behavior, on Altruism, or Egotism, or on the Play of Wild Animals. Apparently, the Oxford student does not learn these things. This cuts him off from a great deal of the larger culture of our side of the Atlantic. "What are you studying this year?" I once asked a fourth-year student at one of our great colleges. "I am electing Salesmanship and Religion," he answered. Here was a young man whose training was destined inevitably to turn him into a moral business man; either that or nothing. At Oxford salesmanship is not taught and religion takes the feeble form of the New Testament. The more one looks at these things the more amazing it becomes that Oxford can produce any results at all.

The effect of the comparison is heightened by the peculiar position occupied at Oxford by the professor's lectures. In the colleges of Canada and the United States the lectures are supposed to be a really necessary and useful part of the student's training. Again and again I have heard the graduates of my own college assert that they had got as much, or nearly as much, out of the lectures at college as out of athletics or the Greek-letter society or the Banjo and Mandolin Club. In short, with us the lectures form a real part of the college life. At Oxford it is not so. The lectures, I understand, are given and may even be taken. But they are quite worthless and are not supposed to have anything much to do with the development of the student's mind. "The lectures here," said a Canadian student to me, "are punk." I appealed to another student to know if this was so. "I don't know whether I'd call them exactly punk," he answered, "but they're certainly rotten." Other judgments were that the lectures were of no importance; that nobody took them; that they don't matter; that you can take them if you like; that they do you no harm.

It appears further that the professors themselves are not keen on their lectures. If the lectures are called for they give them; if not, the professor's feelings are not hurt. He merely waits and rests his brain until in some later year the students call for his lectures. There are men at Oxford who have rested their brains this way for over thirty years; the accumulated brain power thus dammed up is said to be colossal.

I understand that the key to this mystery is found in the operations of the person called the tutor. It is from him, or rather with him, that the students learn all that they know; one and all are agreed on that. Yet it is a little odd to know just how he does it. "We go over to his rooms," said one student, "and he just lights a pipe and talks to us." "We sit round with him," said another, "and he simply smokes and goes over our exercises with us." From this and other evidence I gather that what an Oxford tutor does is to get a little group of students together and smoke at them. Men who have been systematically smoked at for four years turn into ripe scholars. If anybody doubts this, let him go to Oxford and he can see the thing actually in operation. A well-smoked man speaks and writes English with a grace that can be acquired in no other way.

In what was said above I seem to have been directing criticism against the Oxford professors as such; but I have no intention of doing so. For the Oxford professor and his whole manner of being I have nothing but a profound respect. Here is indeed the greatest difference between the modern up-to-date American idea of a professor and the English type. Even with us in older days, in the bygone time when such people as Henry Wadsworth Longfellow and William Cullen Bryant were professors, we had the English idea: a professor was supposed to be a venerable kind of person, with snow-white whiskers reaching to his stomach. He was expected to moon around the campus, oblivious of the world around him. If you nodded to him he failed to see you. Of money he knew nothing; of business, far less. He was, as his trustees were proud to say of him, "a child."

On the other hand, he contained within him a reservoir of learning of such depth as to be practically bottomless. None of this learning was supposed to be of any material or commercial benefit to anybody. Its use was in saving the soul and enlarging the mind.

At the head of such a group of professors was one whose beard was even whiter and longer, whose absence of mind was even still greater, and whose knowledge of money, business, and practical affairs was below zero. Him they made the president.

All this is changed in America. A university professor is now a busy, hustling person, approximating as closely to a business man as he can manage to do. It is on the business man that he models himself. He has a little place that he calls his "office," with a typewriter machine and stenographer. Here he sits and dictates letters, beginning after the best business models, "In re yours of the eighth ult., would say, etc., etc." He writes there letters to students, to his fellow professors, to the president, indeed to any people who will let him write to them. The number of letters that he writes each month is duly counted and set to his credit. If he writes enough he will get a reputation as an "executive" and big things may happen to him. He may even be asked to step out of the college and take a post as an "executive" in a soap company or an advertising firm. The man, in short, is a "hustler," an "advertiser" whose highest aim is to be a "live wire." If he is not he will presently be dismissed, or, to use the business term, be "let go," by a board of trustees who are themselves hustlers and live wires. As to the professor's soul, he no longer needs to think of it, as it has been handed over, along with all the others, to a board of censors.

The American professor deals with his students according to his lights. It is his business to chase them along over a prescribed ground at a prescribed pace, like a flock of sheep. They all go humping together over the hurdles, with the professor chasing them with a set of "tests" and "recitations," "marks" and "attendances," the whole apparatus obviously

copied from the time clock of the business man's factory. This
process is what is called "showing results." The pace set is
necessarily that of the slowest, and this results in what I have
heard Mr. Edward Beatty describe as the "convoy system of
education."

In my own opinion, reached after fifty-two years of profound
reflection, this system contains in itself the seeds of destruction.
It puts a premium on dullness and a penalty on genius. It
circumscribes that attitude of mind which is the real spirit of
learning. If we persist in it we shall presently find that true
learning will fly away from our universities and will take rest
wherever some individual and inquiring mind can mark out
its path for itself.

Now the principal reason why I am led to admire Oxford
is that the place is little touched as yet by the measuring of
"results," and this passion for visible and provable "efficiency." The whole system at Oxford is such as to put a
premium on genius and to let mediocrity and dullness go their
way. On the dull student Oxford, after a proper lapse of time,
confers a degree which means nothing more than that he lived
and breathed at Oxford and kept out of jail. This for many
students is as much as society can expect. But for the gifted
student Oxford offers great opportunities. There is no question of his hanging back till the last sheep has jumped over
the fence. He need wait for no one. He may move forward
as fast as he likes, following the bent of his genius. If he has
in him any ability beyond that of the common herd, his tutor,
interested in his studies, will smoke at him until he kindles him
into a flame. For the tutor's soul is not harassed by herding
dull students, with dismissal hanging by a thread over his head
in the classroom. The American professor has no time to be
interested in a clever student. He has time to be interested in
his "department," his letter writing, his executive work, and
his organizing ability and his hope of promotion to a soap
factory. But with that his mind is exhausted. The student of
genius merely means to him a student who gives no trouble,
who passes all his "tests" and is present at all his "recitations";

such a student also, if he can be trained to be a hustler and an advertiser, will undoubtedly " make good." But beyond that the professor does not think of him. The everlasting principle of equality has inserted itself in a place where it has no right to be and where irregularity is the breath of life.

American or Canadian college trustees would be horrified at the notion of professors who apparently do no work, give few or no lectures, and draw their pay merely for existing. Yet these are really the only kind of professors worth having; I mean men who can be trusted with a vague general mission in life, with a salary guaranteed at least till their death, and a sphere of duties intrusted solely to their own conscience and the promptings of their own desires. Such men are rare, but a single one of them when found is worth ten " executives " and a dozen " organizers."

The excellence of Oxford, then, as I see it, lies in the peculiar vagueness of the organization of its work. It starts from the assumption that the professor is a really learned man whose sole interest lies in his own sphere; and that a student, or at least the only student with whom the university cares to reckon seriously, is a young man who desires to know. This is an ancient medieval attitude long since buried in more up-to-date places under successive strata of compulsory education, state teaching, the democratization of knowledge, and the substitution of the shadow for the substance, and the casket for the gem. No doubt, in newer places the thing has got to be so. Higher education in America flourishes chiefly as a qualification for entrance into a money-making profession, and not as a thing in itself. But in Oxford one can still see the surviving outline of a nobler type and structure and a higher inspiration.

The real thing for the student is the life and environment that surround him. All that he really learns he learns, in a sense, by the active operation of his own intellect and not as the passive recipient of lectures. And for this active operation what he really needs most is the continued and intimate contact with his fellows. Students must live together and eat together, talk and smoke together. Experience shows that that is how their minds really grow. And they must live together in a rational and comfortable way. They must eat in a big dining room or hall, with oak beams across the ceiling, and stained glass in the windows, and with a shield or tablet here or there upon the wall to remind them between times of the men who went before them and left a name worthy of the memory of the college. If a student is to get from his college what it ought to give him, a college dormitory with the life in common that it brings is his absolute right. A university that fails to give it to him is cheating him.

If I were founding a university — and I say it with all the seriousness of which I am capable — I would found first a smoking room; then when I had a little more money in hand I would found a dormitory; then after that, or more probably with it, a decent reading room and a library. After that, if I still had more money that I couldn't use, I would hire a professor and get some textbooks.

This article has sounded for the most part like a continuous eulogy of Oxford, with but little in favor of our American colleges. I turn, therefore, with pleasure to the more congenial task of showing what is wrong with Oxford and with the English university system generally, and the aspect in which our American universities far excel the British.

The point is that Henry VIII is dead. The English are so proud of what Henry VIII and the benefactors of earlier centuries did for the universities that they forget the present. There is little or nothing in the English to compare with the magnificent generosity of individuals, provinces, and states which is building up the colleges of the United States and Canada. There used to be. But by some strange confusion of thought, the English people admire the noble gifts of Cardinal Wolsey and Henry VIII and Queen Margaret, and do not realize that the Carnegies and Rockefellers and the William Macdonalds are the Cardinal Wolseys of today. The University of Chicago was founded upon oil. McGill University rests largely on a basis of tobacco. In America the world of commerce and business levies on itself a noble tribute in favor of the higher learning. In England, with a few conspicuous exceptions, such as that at Bristol, there is little of the sort. The feudal families are content with what their remote ancestors have done; they do not try to emulate it in any great degree.

In the long run this must count. Of all the various reforms that are talked of at Oxford, and of all the imitations of American methods that are suggested, the only one worth while, to my thinking, is to capture a few millionaires, give them honorary degrees at a million pounds sterling apiece, and tell them to imagine that they are Henry VIII. I give Oxford warning that if this is not done the place will not last another two centuries.

APPRECIATION HELPS

1. Under all the humor of the essay, what truth is Leacock trying to drive home?
2. Discuss Leacock's criticism of English visitors who pronounce judgment on American institutions with only scant acquaintance with them.
3. What criticisms of America by visiting Englishmen have you read?
4. Read Bennett's *Your United States* and Kipling's *American Notes*.
5. Read Price Collier's *England and the English from an American Point of View*.
6. Analyze the author's criticism of Oxford. What makes Oxford a great university?
7. What does the Oxford tutor accomplish in the three years " he smokes at the student "?
8. What does Leacock see in the American college president to criticize?
9. What disadvantages may there be to the student in a system where " results are measured "?
10. What advantages does Oxford offer its gifted students?
11. Do the high schools of today offer opportunities to gifted students?

COMPOSITION HINTS

1. My School as I See It
2. " You Have Here a Great Institution "
3. " —— Has a Glorious Future "
4. My Ideal University
5. " Hustlers and Advertisers " I Have Known in School
6. Write a satire on the duties of some school or class officer, in imitation of Leacock's satire on the duties of college presidents.

A, B, AND C—THE HUMAN ELEMENT IN MATHEMATICS[1]

by Stephen Leacock

THE student of arithmetic who has mastered the first four rules of his art and successfully striven with money sums and fractions finds himself confronted by an unbroken expanse of questions known as problems. These are short stories of adventure and industry with the end omitted, and though betraying a strong family resemblance, are not without a certain element òf romance.

The characters in the plot of a problem are three people called A, B, and C, the form of the question is generally of this sort:

" A, B, and C do a certain piece of work. A can do as much work in one hour as B in two, or C in four. Find how long they work at it."

Or thus: " A, B, and C are employed to dig a ditch. A can dig as much in one hour as B can dig in two, and B can dig twice as fast as C. Find how long, etc., etc."

Or after this wise: " A lays a wager that he can walk faster than B or C. A can walk half as fast again as B, and C is only an indifferent walker. Find how far, and so forth."

The occupations of A, B, and C are many and varied. In

[1] From *Literary Lapses,* published by Dodd, Mead & Company, Inc., 1910.

the older arithmetics they contented themselves with doing a "certain piece of work." This statement of the case, however, was found too sly and mysterious, or possibly lacking in romantic charm. It became the fashion to define the job more clearly and to set them at walking matches, ditch-digging, regattas, and piling cordwood. At times, they became commercial and entered into partnership, having, with their old mystery, a "certain" capital. Above all they revel in motion. When they tire of walking matches, A rides on horseback, or borrows a bicycle and competes with his weaker-minded associates on foot. Now they race on locomotives; now they row; or again they become historical and engage stagecoaches; or at times they are aquatic and swim. If their occupation is actual work, they prefer to pump water into cisterns, two of which leak through holes in the bottom and one of which is water-tight. A, of course, has the good one; he also takes the bicycle, and the best locomotive, and the right of swimming with the current. Whatever they do they put money on it, being all three sports. A always wins.

In the early chapters of the arithmetic, their identity is concealed under the names of John, William, and Henry, and they wrangle over the division of marbles. In algebra they are often called X, Y, Z. But these are only their Christian names, and they are really the same people.

Now to one who has followed the history of these men through countless pages of problems, watched them in their leisure hours dallying with cordwood, and seen their panting sides heave in the full frenzy of filling a cistern with a leak in it, they become something more than mere symbols. They appear as creatures of flesh and blood, living men with their own passions, ambitions, and aspirations like the rest of us.

A is full-blooded, hot-headed and strong-willed. It is he who proposes everything, challenges B to work, makes the bets, and bends the others to his will. He is a man of great physical strength and phenomenal endurance. He has been known to walk forty-eight hours at a stretch, and to pump ninety-six. His life is arduous and full of peril. A mistake in the working of a sum may keep him digging a fortnight without sleep. A repeating decimal in the answer might kill him.

B is a quiet, easy-going fellow, afraid of A and bullied by him, but very gentle and brotherly to little C, the weakling. He is quite in A's power, having lost all his money in bets.

Poor C is an undersized, frail man, with a plaintive face. Constant walking, digging, and pumping has broken his health and ruined his nervous system. His joyless life has driven him to drink and smoke more than is good for him, and his hand often shakes as he digs ditches. He has not the strength to work as the others do, in fact, as Hamlin Smith has said, " A can do more work in one hour than C in four."

The first time that ever I saw these men was one evening after a regatta. They had all been rowing in it, and it had transpired that A could row as much in one hour as B in two, or C in four. B and C had come in dead fagged and C was coughing badly. " Never mind, old fellow," I heard B say, " I'll fix you up on the sofa and get you some hot tea." Just then A came blustering in and shouted, " I say, you fellows, Hamlin Smith has shown me three cisterns in his garden and he says we can pump them until tomorrow night. I bet I can beat you both. Come on. You can pump in your rowing things, you know. Your cistern leaks a little, I think, C." I heard B growl that it was a dirty shame and that C was used up now, but they went and presently I could tell from the sound of the water that A was pumping four times as fast as C.

For years after that I used to see them constantly about the town and always busy. I never heard of any of them eating or sleeping. After that, owing to a long absence from home, I lost sight of them. On my return I was surprised to find A, B, and C no longer at their old tasks; on inquiry I heard that work in this line was now done by N, M, and O, and that some people were employing for algebraical jobs four for-eigners called Alpha, Beta, Gamma, and Delta.

Now it chanced one day that I stumbled upon old D, in the

little garden in front of his cottage, hoeing in the sun. D is an aged laboring man who used occasionally to be called in to help A, B, and C. " Did I know 'em, sir? " he answered. " Why I knowed 'em ever since they was little fellows in brackets. Master A, he were a fine-hearted lad, sir, though I always said, give me Master B for kind-heartedness-like. Many's the job as we've been on together, sir, though I never did no racing nor aught of that, but just the plain labor, as you might say. I'm getting a bit too old and stiff for it nowadays, sir, — just scratch about in the garden here and grow a bit of a logarithm, or raise a common denominator or two. But Mr. Euclid he uses me still for propositions, he do."

From the garrulous old man I learned the melancholy end of my former acquaintances. Soon after I left town, he told me, C had been ill. It seems that A and B had been rowing on the river for a wager, and C had been running on the bank and then sat in a draught. Of course the bank had refused the draught and C was taken ill. A and B came home and found C lying helpless in bed. A shook him roughly and said, " Get up, C, we're going to pile wood." C looked so worn and pitiful that B said, " Look here, A, I won't stand this, he isn't fit to pile wood tonight." C smiled feebly and said, " Perhaps I might pile a little if I sat up in bed." Then B, thoroughly alarmed, said, " See here, A, I'm going to fetch a doctor; he's dying." A flared up and answered, " You've got no money to fetch a doctor." " I'll reduce him to his lowest terms," B said firmly, " that'll fetch him." C's life might even then have been saved but they made a mistake about the medicine. It stood at the head of the bed on a bracket, and the nurse accidentally removed it from the bracket without changing the sign. After the fatal blunder C seems to have sunk rapidly. On the evening of the next day, it was clear, as the shadows deepened, that the end was near. I think that even A was affected at the last as he stood with bowed head, aimlessly offering to bet with the doctor on C's labored breathing. " A," whispered C, " I think I'm going fast." " How fast do you think you'll go, old man? " murmured A. " I don't know," said C, "but I'm going at any rate." The end came soon after that. C rallied for a moment and asked for a certain piece of work that he had left downstairs. A put it in his arms and he expired. As his soul sped heavenward, A watched its flight with melancholy admiration. B burst into a passionate flood of tears and sobbed, "Put away his little cistern and the rowing clothes he used to wear, I feel as if I could hardly ever dig again." — The funeral was plain and unostentatious. It differed in nothing from the ordinary, except that out of deference to sporting men, and mathematicians, A engaged two hearses. Both vehicles started at the same time, B driving the one which bore the sable parallelopiped containing the last remains of his ill-fated friend. A on the box of the empty hearse generously consented to a handicap of a hundred years, but arrived first at the cemetery by driving four times as fast as B. (Find the distance to the cemetery.) As the sarcophagus was lowered, the grave was surrounded by the broken figures of the first book of Euclid.

It was noticed that after the death of C, A became a changed man. He lost interest in racing with B, and dug but languidly. He finally gave up his work and settled down to live on the interest of his bets. — B never recovered from the shock of C's death; his grief preyed upon his intellect and it became deranged. He grew moody and spoke only in monosyllables. His disease became rapidly aggravated, and he presently spoke in words whose spelling was regular and which presented no difficulty to the beginner. Realizing his precarious condition he voluntarily submitted to be incarcerated in an asylum, where he abjured mathematics and devoted himself to writing the History of the Swiss Family Robinson in words of one syllable.

APPRECIATION HELPS

1. What pleases you in this admirable satire on mathematics?
2. Find in your algebra text some "short stories of adventure and industry with the end omitted."
3. Do A, B, and C still engage in the same sports and occupations

Leacock found them doing, or have your texts become thoroughly modern?

4. In your town or school library find some old texts in mathematics, and read them to discover the variety of activities indulged in by A, B, and C.

5. How are character and individuality given to these abstractions?

6. Ask several of the oldest persons you know who Hamlin Smith is.

7. Note the interesting use of words and expressions from mathematics.

COMPOSITION HINTS

1. " A Can Do More Work in One Hour than C in Four "

2. Study the notes and questions in any text, this one if you choose, and write a satire on the foolish things you find. Sometimes the notes take more space than the original matter.

3. Why not satirize some other school subject, such as Latin, history, chemistry, physics?

4. Criticize the vocabulary of any one of your texts, then rewrite one paragraph in words of one syllable.

5. Discover, from the attic or storeroom, some texts used by your father and mother. Study all the marginal notes, and then write a sketch of father and mother when they were young, Were they frivolous?

WOODROW WILSON

It would be presumptuous to attempt to tell intelligent American schoolboys or schoolgirls much about Woodrow Wilson (1856–1924), twenty-eighth President of the United States. For Wilson was in office at the White House during the most exciting period through which so far they have lived, the time when America was sharing so tremendously in the winning of the World War, and they are not likely to forget those days or the portrait of the tall, pale, white-haired, thin-lipped, and spectacled man who decided upon the country's entry into the struggle. He served two terms as President, you remember, and thus was the country's chief executive for eight years, from 1913 to 1921.

But Wilson has other claims to remembrance besides the supreme one of having declared war on Germany in 1917. Other Presidents have had wide knowledge of men and affairs; he, perhaps, was the greatest scholar of all. Had he not gone to the White House he would in any case have won for himself a place in history as a man of profound learning and of high academic distinction. It is as a scholar that he appears before you now. "The New Freedom," herewith, is a speech, a discussion, to use his own description, "in the free form of extemporaneously spoken words," a scholarly way of saying that the speech was made up as it was spoken, and not written in advance and learned by heart, or read from a manuscript. Yet see how deep is the learning it displays, how grammatically correct and pleasantly rhythmical its sentences.

Strange to relate, Mr. Wilson himself esteemed "The New Freedom" ill-suited for inclusion in a collection of school essays, as some correspondence with him in 1924 shortly before his death revealed. But it continues to be extremely popular in the school world.

The salient features of Wilson's life may just be recalled briefly. He was born in Virginia, and after graduating at Princeton studied law at the University of Virginia. But he preferred the academic life, and went to Princeton as professor of jurisprudence and political economy, and in 1902 was made president of the university. In 1911 he became Governor of New Jersey. At Paris during the Peace Conference of 1919 he insisted that the Covenant of the League of Nations should be made an integral part of the Peace Treaty concluded between the Allies and Germany, and won his point. In the same year the Nobel Prize for Peace was awarded to him. Campaigning in the West in 1920 to arouse public sentiment in favor of his Covenant and the Peace Treaty — favor he failed to win — he was stricken and partly paralyzed. Thereafter he was an invalid, and he succumbed to heart disease just over three years later. Throughout his life his Scotch Presbyterian ancestry showed its influence.

THE NEW FREEDOM[1]

No matter how often we think of it, the discovery of America must each time make a fresh appeal to our imaginations. For centuries, indeed from the beginning, the face of Europe had been turned toward the east. All the routes of trade, every impulse and energy, ran from west to east. The Atlantic lay at the world's back door. Then, suddenly, the conquest of Constantinople by the Turk closed the route to the Orient. Europe had either to face about or lack any outlet for her energies; the unknown sea at the west at last was ventured upon, and the earth learned that it was twice as big as it had thought. Columbus did not find, as he had expected, the civilization of Cathay; he found an empty continent. In that part of the world, upon that new-found half of the globe, mankind, late in its history, was thus afforded an opportunity to set up a new civilization; here it was strangely privileged to make a new human experiment.

Never can that moment of unique opportunity fail to excite the emotion of all who consider its strangeness and richness; a

[1] From *The New Freedom,* published by Harper and Brothers.

thousand fanciful histories of the earth might be contrived without the imagination daring to conceive such a romance as the hiding away of half the globe until the fullness of time had come for a new start in civilization. A mere sea captain's ambition to trace a new trade route gave way to a moral adventure for humanity. The race was to found a new order here on this delectable land, which no man approached without receiving, as the old voyagers relate, you remember, sweet airs out of woods aflame with flowers and murmurous with the sounds of pellucid waters. The hemisphere lay waiting to be touched with life, — life from the old centers of living, surely, but cleansed of defilement, and cured of weariness, so as to be fit for the virgin purity of a new bride. The whole thing springs into the imagination like a wonderful vision, an exquisite marvel which once only in all history could be vouchsafed.

One other thing only compares with it; only one other thing touches the springs of emotion as does the picture of the ships of Columbus drawing near the bright shores, — and that is the thought of the choke in the throat of the immigrant of today as he gazes from the steerage deck at the land where he has been taught to believe he in his turn shall find an earthly paradise, where, a free man, he shall forget the heartaches of the old life, and enter into the fulfillment of the hope of the world. For has not every ship that has pointed her prow westward borne hither the hopes of generation after generation of the oppressed of other lands? How always have men's hearts beat as they saw the coast of America rise to their view! How it has always seemed to them that the dweller there would at last be rid of kings, of privileged classes, and of all those bonds which had kept men depressed and helpless, and would there realize the full fruition of his sense of honest manhood, would there be one of a great body of brothers, not seeking to defraud and deceive one another, but seeking to accomplish the general good!

What was in the writings of the men who founded America, — to serve the selfish interests of America? Do you find that in their writings? No; to serve the cause of humanity, to bring liberty to mankind. They set up their standards here in America in the tenet of hope, as a beacon of encouragement to all the nations of the world; and men came thronging to these shores with an expectancy that never existed before, with a confidence they never dared feel before, and found here for generations together a haven of peace, of opportunity, of equality.

God send that in the complicated state of modern affairs we may recover the standards and repeat the achievements of that heroic age!

For life is no longer the comparatively simple thing it was. Our relations one with another have been profoundly modified by the new agencies of rapid communication and transportation, tending swiftly to concentrate life, widen communities, fuse interests, and complicate all the processes of living. The individual is dizzily swept about in a thousand new whirlpools of activities. Tyranny has become more subtle, and has learned to wear the guise of mere industry, and even of benevolence. Freedom has become a somewhat different matter. It cannot, — eternal principle that it is, — it cannot have altered, yet it shows itself in new aspects. Perhaps it is only revealing its deeper meaning.

What is liberty?

I have long had an image in my mind of what constitutes liberty. Suppose that I were building a great piece of powerful machinery, and suppose that I should so awkwardly and unskillfully assemble the parts of it that every time one part tried to move it would be interfered with by the others, and the whole thing would buckle up and be checked. Liberty for the several parts would consist in the best possible assembling and adjustment of them all, would it not? If you want the great piston of the engine to run with absolute freedom, give it absolutely perfect alignment and adjustment with the other parts of the machine, so that it is free, not because it is let alone or isolated, but because it has been associated most skillfully and carefully with the other parts of the great structure.

What is liberty? You say of the locomotive that it runs free. What do you mean? You mean that its parts are so assembled and adjusted that friction is reduced to a minimum, and that it has perfect adjustment. We say of a boat skimming the water with light foot, "How free she runs," when we mean, how perfectly she is adjusted to the force of the wind, how perfectly she obeys the great breath out of the heavens that fills her sails. Throw her head up into the wind and see how she will halt and stagger, how every sheet will shiver and her whole frame be shaken, how instantly she is "in irons," in the expressive phrase of the sea. She is free only when you have let her fall off again and have recovered once more her nice adjustment to the forces she must obey and cannot defy.

Human freedom consists in perfect adjustments of human interests and human activities and human energies.

Now, the adjustments necessary between individuals, between individuals and the complex institutions amidst which they live, and between those institutions and the government, are infinitely more intricate today than ever before. No doubt this is a tiresome and roundabout way of saying the thing, yet perhaps it is worth while to get somewhat clearly in our mind what makes all the trouble today. Life has become complex; there are many more elements, more parts, to it than ever before. And, therefore, it is harder to find out where the trouble lies when the machine gets out of order.

You know that one of the interesting things that Mr. Jefferson said in those early days of simplicity which marked the beginnings of our government was that the best government consisted in as little governing as possible. And there is still a sense in which that is true. It is still intolerable for a government to interfere with our individual activities except where it is necessary to interfere with them in order to free them. But I feel confident that if Jefferson were living in our day he would see what we see; that the individual is caught in a great confused nexus of all sorts of complicated circumstances, and that to let him alone is to leave him helpless as against the obstacles with which he has to contend; and that, therefore, law in our day must come to the assistance of the individual. It must come to his assistance to see that he gets fair play; that is all, but that is much. Without the watchful interference, the resolute interference, of the government, there can be no fair play between individuals and such powerful institutions as the trusts. Freedom today is something more than being let alone. The program of a government of freedom must in these days be positive, not negative merely.

Well, then, in this new sense and meaning of it, are we preserving freedom in this land of ours, the hope of all the earth?

Have we, inheritors of this continent and of the ideals to which the fathers consecrated it,—have we maintained them, realizing them, as each generation must, anew? Are we, in the consciousness that the life of man is pledged to higher levels here than elsewhere, striving still to bear aloft the standards of liberty and hope, or, disillusioned and defeated, are we feeling the disgrace of having had a free field in which to do new things and of not having done them?

The answer must be, I am sure, that we have been in a fair way of failure,—tragic failure. And we stand in danger of utter failure yet except we fulfil speedily the determination we have reached, to deal with the new and subtle tyrannies according to their deserts. Don't deceive yourselves for a moment as to the power of the great interests which now dominate our development. They are so great that it is almost an open question whether the government of the United States can dominate them or no. Go one step further, make their organized power permanent, and it may be too late to turn back. The roads diverge at the point where we stand. They stretch their vistas out to regions where they are very far separated from one another; at the end is the old tiresome scene of government tied up with special interests; and at the other shines the liberating light of individual initiative, of individual liberty, of individual freedom, the light of untrammeled enterprise. I believe that that light shines out of the heavens itself that God has created. I believe in human liberty as I believe in the wine of life. There is no salvation for men in the pitiful condescensions of industrial masters. Guardians have no place in a land of freemen. Prosperity guaranteed by trustees has no prospect of endurance. If monopoly persists, monopoly will always sit at the helm of the government. I do not expect to see monopoly restrain itself. If there are men in this country big enough to own the government of the United States, they are going to own it; what we have to determine now is whether we are big enough, whether we are men enough, whether we are free enough, to take possession again of the government which is our own. We haven't had free access to it, our minds have not touched it by way of guidance, in half a generation, and now we are engaged in nothing less than the recovery of what was made with our own hands, and acts only by our delegated authority.

I tell you, when you discuss the question of the tariffs and of the trusts, you are discussing the very lives of yourselves and your children. I believe that I am preaching the very cause of some of the gentlemen whom I am opposing when I preach the cause of free industry in the United States, for I think they are slowly girding the tree that bears the inestimable fruits of our life, and that if they are permitted to gird it entirely nature will take her revenge and the tree will die.

I do not believe that America is securely great because she has great men in her now. America is great in proportion as she can make sure of having great men in the next generation. She is rich in her unborn children; rich, that is to say, if those unborn children see the sun in a day of opportunity, see the sun when they are free to exercise their energies as they will. If they open their eyes in a land where there is no special privilege, then we shall come into a new era of American greatness and American liberty; but if they open their eyes in a country where they must be employees or nothing, if they open their eyes in a land of merely regulated monopoly, where all the conditions of industry are determined by small groups of men, then they will see an America such as the founders of this Republic would have wept to think of. The only hope is in the release of the forces which philanthropic trust presidents want to monopolize. Only the emancipation, the freeing and heartening of the vital energies of all the people will redeem us. In all that I may have to do in public affairs in the United States I am going to think of towns such as I have seen in Indiana, towns of the old American pattern, that own and operate their own industries, hopefully and happily. My thought is going to be bent upon the multiplication of towns of that kind and the prevention of the concentration of industry in this country in such a fashion and upon such a scale that towns that own themselves will be impossible. You know what the vitality of America consists of. Its vitality does not lie in New York, nor in Chicago; it will not be sapped by anything that happens in St. Louis. The vitality of America lies in the brains, the energies, the enterprise of the people throughout the land; in the efficiency of their factories and in the richness of the fields that stretch beyond the borders of the town; in the wealth which they extract from nature and originate for themselves through the inventive genius characteristic of all free American communities.

That is the wealth of America, and if America discourages the locality, the community, the self-contained town, she will kill the nation. A nation is as rich as her free communities; she is not as rich as her capital city or her metropolis. The amount of money in Wall Street is no indication of the wealth of the American people. That indication can be found only in the fertility of the American mind and the productivity of American industry everywhere throughout the United States. If America were not rich and fertile, there would be no money in Wall Street. If Americans were not vital and able to take care of themselves, the great money exchanges would break down. The welfare, the very existence of the nation, rests at last upon the great mass of the people; its prosperity depends at last upon the spirit in which they go about their work in their several communities throughout the broad land. In proportion as her towns and her countrysides are happy and hopeful will America realize the high ambitions which have marked her in the eyes of all the world.

The welfare, the happiness, the energy and spirit of the men and women who do the daily work in our mines and factories, on our railroads, in our offices and ports of trade, on our farms and on the sea, is the underlying necessity of all prosperity. There can be nothing wholesome unless their life is wholesome; there can be no contentment unless they are contented. Their physical welfare affects the soundness of the whole nation. How would it suit the prosperity of the United States, how would it suit business, to have a people that went every day sadly or sullenly to their work? How would the future look to you if you felt that the aspiration had gone out of most men, the confidence of success, the hope that they might improve their condition? Do you not see that just as soon as the old self-confidence of America, just so soon as her old boasted advantage of individual liberty and opportunity, is taken away, all the energy of her people begins to subside, to slacken, to grow loose and pulpy, without fiber, and men simply cast about to see that the day does not end disastrously with them?

So we must put heart into the people by taking the heartlessness out of politics, business, and industry. We have got to make politics a thing in which an honest man can take his part with satisfaction because he knows that his opinion will count as much as the next man's, and that the boss and the interests have been dethroned. Business we have got to untrammel, abolishing tariff favors, and railroad discrimination, and credit denials, and all forms of unjust handicaps against the little man. Industry we have got to humanize,— not through the trusts,— but through the direct action of law guaranteeing protection against dangers and compensation for injuries, guaranteeing sanitary conditions, proper hours, the right to organize, and all the other things which the conscience of the country demands as the workingman's right. We have got to cheer and inspirit our people with the sure prospects of social justice and due reward, with the vision of the open gates of opportunity for all. We have got to set the energy and the initiative of this great people absolutely free, so that the future of America will be greater than the past, so that the pride of America will grow with achievement, so that America will know as she advances from generation to generation that each brood of her sons is greater and more enlightened than that which preceded it, know that she is fulfilling the promise that she has made to mankind.

Such is the vision of some of us who now come to assist in its realization. For we Democrats would not have endured this long burden of exile if we had not seen a vision. We could have traded; we could have got into the game; we could have surrendered and made terms; we could have played the rôle of patrons to the men who wanted to dominate the interests of the country, — and here and there gentlemen who pretended to be of us did make those arrangements. They couldn't stand privation. You never can stand it unless you have within you some imperishable food upon which to sustain life and courage, the food of those visions of the spirit where a table is set before us laden with palatable fruits, the fruits of hope, the fruits of imagination, those invisible things of the spirit which are the only things upon which we can sustain ourselves through this weary world without fainting. We have carried in our minds, after you had thought you had obscured and blurred them, the ideals of those men who first set their foot upon America, those little bands who came to make a foothold in the wilderness, because the great teeming nations that they had left behind them had forgotten what human liberty was, liberty of thought, liberty of residence, liberty of action.

Since their day the meaning of liberty has deepened. But it has not ceased to be a fundamental demand of the human spirit, a fundamental necessity for the life of the soul. And the day is at hand when it shall be realized on this consecrated soil, — a New Freedom, — a Liberty widened and deepened to match the broadened life of man in modern America, restoring to him in very truth the control of his government, throwing wide all gates of lawful enterprise, unfettering his energies, and warming the generous impulses of his heart,— a process of release, emancipation, and inspiration, full of a breath of life as sweet and wholesome as the airs that filled the sails of the caravels of Columbus, and gave the promise and boast of magnificent Opportunity in which America *dare not fail.*

APPRECIATION HELPS

1. "Where the President excels," says Colonel House, "is in his union of the capabilities of the dreamer, the seer, and the man of action." Where does this essay give evidence of these three abilities?

2. Explain: "A mere sea captain's ambition to trace a new trade route gave way to a moral adventure for humanity."

3. What is the attitude of the immigrant as he looks upon America for the first time?

4. What is liberty? Comment on the nice distinctions made by the author in his examples of the locomotive and of the boat.

5. In what does the real vitality of America consist?

6. What is the new spirit of politics as embodied in this essay?

7. Discuss: "America is great in proportion as she can make sure of having great men in the next generation." "A nation is as rich as her free communities." "The program of a government of freedom must in these days be positive, not negative merely."

COMPOSITION HINTS

1. Complicating the Problem of Living
2. A Modern Utopia
3. Dominating Forces in American Life
4. Old American Towns
5. The Cornerstones of American Life
6. Visions of the Spirit
7. Achievements of the Next Generation
8. "You Are the Hope of the World"

SAMUEL McCHORD CROTHERS

Dr. Samuel McChord Crothers (1857–1927) was aged eleven when first he saw his own words in print in the local newspaper of Springfield, Illinois. Taking the *Biglow Papers* of James Russell Lowell as his model, he had written a series of short essays and sent them to the newspaper anonymously. The secret of authorship leaked out and Springfield was delighted with its boy prodigy. After such a success, he simply had to become a professional author.

But in his blood was a more insistent call. For generations his forbears had been clergymen. His father had died when the son was in infancy, and his mother left him free to shape his career himself. Thus it was without outside influence that he elected to study for the church. As was to be expected of such a precocious author, he was a most promising scholar. At twelve he was ready to attend classes at Wittenburg University, and thence he went to Princeton, the Union Theological Seminary, and the Harvard Divinity School.

Once he was a minister, he felt that he should carry the preaching of the Gospel into unsheltered places, and he went out as pastor to a succession of churches in the Kansas prairies and the silver camps of Nevada. In 1891, however, he returned East, accepting a call to the First Unitarian Church of Cambridge, Massachusetts. There he remained until his death. In the Cambridge literary atmosphere his early desires to write reasserted themselves, and he found that with the years his pen had lost none of its cunning. He sent in an essay to a magazine. It was printed. After that he was a frequent contributor to similar periodicals. This essay is one of his most characteristic.

EVERY MAN'S NATURAL DESIRE TO
BE SOMEBODY ELSE[1]

SEVERAL years ago a young man came to my study with a manuscript which he wished me to criticize.

"It is only a little bit of my work," he said modestly, "and it will not take you long to look it over. In fact it is only the first chapter, in which I explain the Universe."

I suppose that we have all had moments of sudden illumination when it occurred to us that we had explained the Universe, and it was so easy for us that we wondered why we had not done it before. Some thought drifted into our mind and filled us with vague forebodings of omniscience. It was not an ordinary thought, that explained only a fragment of existence. It explained everything. It proved one thing and it proved the opposite just as well. It explained why things are as they are, and if it should turn out that they are not that way at all, it would prove that fact also. In the light of our great thought chaos seemed rational.

Such thoughts usually occur about four o'clock in the morning. Having explained the Universe, we relapse into satisfied slumber. When, a few hours later, we rise, we wonder what the explanation was.

Now and then, however, one of these highly explanatory ideas remains to comfort us in our waking hours. Such a thought is that which I here throw out, and which has doubtless at some early hour occurred to most of my readers. It is that every man has a natural desire to be somebody else.

This does not explain the universe, but it explains that perplexing part of it which we call Human Nature. It explains why so many intelligent people, who deal skillfully with matters of fact, make such a mess of it when they deal with their fellow creatures. It explains why we get on as well as we do with strangers, and why we do not get on better with our

---

[1] From *The Dame School of Experience,* published by the Houghton Mifflin Company, 1920.

friends. It explains why people are so often offended when we say nice things about them, and why it is that, when we say harsh things about them, they take it as a compliment. It explains why people marry their opposites and why they live happily ever afterwards. It also explains why some people don't. It explains the meaning of tact and its opposite.

The tactless person treats a person according to a scientific method as if he were a thing. Now, in dealing with a thing, you must first find out what it is, and then act accordingly. But with a person, you must find out what he is and then carefully conceal from him the fact that you have made the discovery.

The tactless person can never be made to understand this. He prides himself on taking people as they are without being aware that that is not the way they want to be taken.

He has a keen eye for the obvious, and calls attention to it. Age, sex, color, nationality, previous condition of servitude, and all the facts that are interesting to the census-taker are apparent to him and are made the basis of his conversation. When he meets one who is older than he, he is conscious of the fact, and emphasizes by every polite attention the disparity in years. He has an idea that at a certain period in life the highest tribute of respect is to be urged to rise out of one chair and take another that is presumably more comfortable. It does not occur to him that there may remain any tastes that are not sedentary. On the other hand, he sees a callow youth and addresses himself to the obvious callowness, and thereby, makes himself thoroughly disliked. For, strange to say, the youth prefers to be addressed as a person of precocious maturity.

The literalist, observing that most people talk shop, takes it for granted that they like to talk shop. This is a mistake. They do it because it is the easiest thing to do, but they resent having attention called to their limitations. A man's profession does not necessarily coincide with his natural aptitude or with his predominant desire. When you meet a member of the Supreme Court you may assume that he is gifted with a judicial mind. But it does not follow that that is the only quality of mind he has; nor that when, out of court, he gives you a piece of his mind, it will be a piece of his judicial mind that he gives.

My acquaintance with royalty is limited to photographs of royal groups, which exhibit a high degree of domesticity. It would seem that the business of royalty when pursued as a steady job becomes tiresome, and that when they have their pictures taken they endeavor to look as much like ordinary folks as possible — and they usually succeed.

The member of one profession is always flattered by being taken for a skilled practitioner of another. Try it on your minister. Instead of saying, "That was an excellent sermon of yours this morning," say, "As I listened to your cogent argument, I thought what a successful lawyer you would have made." Then he will say, "I did think of taking to the law."

If you had belonged to the court of Frederick the Great, you would have proved a poor courtier indeed if you had praised His Majesty's campaigns. Frederick knew that he was a Prussian general, but he wanted to be a French literary man. If you wished to gain his favor, you should have told him that in your opinion he excelled Voltaire.

We do not like to have too much attention drawn to our present circumstances. They may be well enough in their way, but we can think of something which would be more fitting for us. We have either seen better days or we expect them.

Suppose you had visited Napoleon in Elba and had sought to ingratiate yourself with him.

"Sire," you would have said, "this is a beautiful little empire of yours, so snug and cozy and quiet. It is just such a domain as is suited to a man in your condition. The climate is excellent. Everything is peaceful. It must be delightful to rule where everything is arranged for you and the details are taken care of by others. As I came to your dominion I saw a line of British frigates guarding your shores. The evidences of such thoughtfulness are everywhere.

Your praise of his present condition would not have endeared you to Napoleon. You were addressing him as the

Emperor of Elba. In his own eyes he was Emperor, though in Elba.

It is such a misapprehension which irritates any mature human being when his environment is taken as the measure of his personality.

The man with a literal mind moves in a perpetual comedy of errors. It is not a question of two Dromios. There are half a dozen Dromios under one hat.

How casually introductions are made, as if it were the easiest thing in the world to make two human beings acquainted: Your friend says, "I want you to know Mr. Stifflekin," and you say that you are happy to know him. But does either of you know the enigma that goes under the name of Stifflekin? You may know what he looks like and where he resides and what he does for a living. But that is all in the present tense. To really know him you must not only know what he is but what he used to be; what he used to think he was; what he used to think he ought to be and might be if he worked hard enough. You must know what he might have been if certain things had happened otherwise, and you must know what might have happened otherwise if he had been otherwise. All these complexities are a part of his own dim apprehension of himself. They are what make him so much more interesting to himself than he is to anyone else.

It is this consciousness of the inadequacy of our knowledge which makes us so embarrassed when we offer any service to another. Will he take it in the spirit in which it is given?

That was an awkward moment when Stanley, after all his hardships in his search for Dr. Livingstone, at last found the Doctor by a lake in Central Africa. Stanley held out his hand and said stiffly, "Dr. Livingstone, I presume?" Stanley had heroically plunged through the equatorial forests to find Livingstone and to bring him back to civilization. But Livingstone was not particularly anxious to be found, and had a decided objection to being brought back to civilization. What he wanted was a new adventure. Stanley did not find the real Livingstone till he discovered that the old man was as young at heart as himself. The two men became acquainted only when they began to plan a new expedition to find the source of the Nile.

II

The natural desire of every man to be somebody else explains many of the minor irritations of life. It prevents that perfect organization of society in which everyone should know his place and keep it. The desire to be somebody else leads us to practice on work that does not strictly belong to us. We all have aptitudes and talents that overflow the narrow bounds of our trade or profession. Every man feels that he is bigger than his job, and he is all the time doing what theologians call " works of supererogation."

The serious-minded housemaid is not content to do what she is told to do. She has an unexpended balance of energy. She wants to be a general household reformer. So she goes to the desk of the titular master of the house and gives it a thorough reformation. She arranges the papers according to her idea of neatness. When the poor gentleman returns and finds his familiar chaos transformed into a hateful order, he becomes a reactionary.

The serious manager of a street railway company is not content with the simple duty of transporting passengers cheaply and comfortably. He wants to exercise the functions of a lecturer in an ethical culture society. While the transported victim is swaying precariously from the end of a strap he reads a notice urging him to practice Christian courtesy and not to push. While the poor wretch pores over his counsel of perfection, he feels like answering as did Junius to the Duke of Grafton, " My Lord, injuries may be atoned for and forgiven, but insults admit of no compensation."

A man enters a barber's shop with the simple desire of being shaved. But he meets with the more ambitious desires of the barber. The serious barber is not content with any slight contribution to human welfare. He insists that his client shall be shampooed, manicured, massaged, steamed beneath boiling towels, cooled off by electric fans, and, while all this is going on, that he shall have his boots blacked.

Have you ever marveled at the patience of people in having so many things done to them that they don't want, just to avoid hurting the feelings of professional people who want to do more than is expected of them? You watch the stoical countenance of the passenger in a Pullman car as he stands up to be brushed. The chances are that he doesn't want to be brushed. He would prefer to leave the dust on his coat rather than to be compelled to swallow it. But he knows what is expected of him. It is a part of the solemn ritual of traveling. It precedes the offering.

The fact that every man desires to be somebody else explains many of the aberrations of artists and literary men. The painters, dramatists, musicians, poets, and novelists are just as human as housemaids and railway managers and porters. They want to do " all the good they can to all the people they can in all the ways they can." They get tired of the ways they are used to and like to try new combinations. So they are continually mixing things. The practitioner of one art tries to produce effects that are proper to another art.

A musician wants to be a painter and use his violin as if it were a brush. He would have us see the sunset glories that he is painting for us. A painter wants to be a musician and paint symphonies, and he is grieved because the uninstructed cannot hear his pictures, although the colors do swear at each other. Another painter wants to be an architect and build up his picture as if it were made of cubes of brick. It looks like brick-work, but to the natural eye it doesn't look like a picture. A prose-writer gets tired of writing prose, and wants to be a poet. So he begins every line with a capital letter, and keeps on writing prose.

You go to the theater with the simple-minded Shakespearean idea that the play's the thing. But the playwright wants to be a pathologist. So you discover that you have dropped into a gruesome clinic. You sought innocent relaxation, but you are one of the non-elect and have gone to the place prepared for you. You must see the thing through. The fact that you

have troubles of your own is not a sufficient claim for exemp‐
tion.

Or you take up a novel expecting it to be a work of fiction.
But the novelist has other views. He wants to be your spirit‐
ual adviser. He must do something to your mind, he must
rearrange your fundamental ideas, he must massage your soul,
and generally brush you off. All this in spite of the fact that
you don't want to be brushed off and set to rights. You don't
want him to do anything to your mind. It's the only mind
you have and you need it in your own business.

III

But if the desire of every man to be somebody else accounts
for the many whimsicalities of human conduct and for many
aberrations in the arts, it cannot be lightly dismissed as be‐
longing only to the realm of comedy. It has its origin in the
nature of things. The reason why every man wants to be
somebody else is that he can remember the time when he was
somebody else. What we call personal identity is a very
changeable thing, as all of us realize when we look over old
photographs and read old letters.

The oldest man now living is but a few years removed from
the undifferentiated germ-plasm, which might have developed
into almost anything. In the beginning he was a bundle of
possibilities. Every actuality that is developed means a de‐
crease in the rich variety of possibilities. In becoming one
thing it becomes impossible to be something else.

The delight in being a boy lies in the fact that the possi‐
bilities are still manifold. The boy feels that he can be any‐
thing that he desires. He is conscious that he has capacities
that would make him a successful banker. On the other hand,
there are attractions in a life of adventure in the South Seas.
It would be pleasant to lie under a breadfruit tree and let the
fruit drop into his mouth, to the admiration of the gentle
savages who would gather about him. Or he might be a saint
— not a commonplace modern saint who does chores and

attends tiresome committee meetings, but a saint such as one reads about, who gives away his rich robes and his purse of gold to the first beggar he meets, and then goes on his carefree way through the forest to convert interesting robbers. He feels that he might practice that kind of unscientific charity, if his father would furnish him with the money to give away.

But by and by he learns that making a success in the banking business is not consistent with excursions to the South Seas or with the more picturesque and unusual forms of saintliness. If he is to be in a bank he must do as the bankers do.

Parents and teachers conspire together to make a man of him, which means making a particular kind of man of him. All mental processes which are not useful must be suppressed. The sum of their admonitions is that he must pay attention. That is precisely what he is doing. He is paying attention to a variety of things that escape the adult mind. As he wriggles on the bench in the schoolroom, he pays attention to all that is going on. He attends to what is going on out-of-doors; he sees the weak points of his fellow pupils, against whom he is planning punitive expeditions; and he is delightfully conscious of the idiosyncrasies of the teacher. Moreover, he is a youthful artist and his sketches from life give acute joy to his contemporaries when they are furtively passed around.

But the schoolmaster says sternly, " My boy, you must learn to pay attention; that is to say, you must not pay attention to so many things, but you must pay attention to one thing, namely, the second declension."

Now, the second declension is the least interesting thing in the room, but unless he confines his attention to it he will never learn it. Education demands narrowing of attention in the interest of efficiency.

A man may, by dint of application to a particular subject, become a successful merchant or real-estate man or chemist or overseer of the poor. But he cannot be all of these things at the same time. He must make his choice. Having in the presence of witnesses taken himself for better or worse, he must, forsaking all others, cleave to that alone. The consequence is that, by the time he is forty, he has become one kind of man, and is able to do one kind of work. He has acquired a stock of ideas true enough for his purposes, but not so transcendently true as to interfere with his business. His neighbors know where to find him, and they do not need to take a spiritual elevator. He does business on the ground floor. He has gained in practicality, but has lost in the quality of interestingness.

The old prophet declared that the young men dream dreams and the old men see visions, but he did not say anything about the middle-aged men. *They* have to look after the business end.

But has the man whose working hours are so full of responsibilities changed so much as he seems to have done? When he is talking shop is he " all there " ? I think not. There are elusive personalities that are in hiding. As the rambling mansions of the old Catholic families had secret panels opening into the " priest's hole," to which the family resorted for spiritual comfort, so in the mind of the most successful man there are secret chambers where are hidden his unsuccessful ventures, his romantic ambitions, his unfulfilled promises. All that he dreamed of as possible is somewhere concealed in the man's heart. He would not for the world have the public know how much he cares for the selves that have not had a fair chance to come into the light of day. You do not know a man until you know his lost Atlantis, and his Utopia for which he still hopes to set sail.

When Dogberry asserted that he was " as pretty a piece of flesh as any is in Messina," and " one that hath two gowns and everything handsome about him," he was pointing out what he deemed to be quite obvious. It was in a more intimate tone that he boasted, " and a fellow that hath had losses."

When Julius Caesar rode through the streets of Rome in his chariot, his laurel crown seemed to the populace a symbol of his present greatness. But gossip has it that Caesar at that time desired to be younger than he was, and that before appearing in public he carefully arranged his laurel wreath so as to conceal the fact that he had had losses.

Much that passes for pride in the behavior of the great

comes from the fear of the betrayal of emotions that belong to a simpler manner of life. When the sons of Jacob saw the great Egyptian officer to whom they appealed turn away from them, they little knew what was going on. "And Joseph made haste, for his bowels did yearn upon his brother: and he sought where to weep, and he entered into his chamber, and wept there. And he washed his face, and went out, and refrained himself." Joseph didn't want to be a great man. He wanted to be human. It was hard to refrain himself.

What of the lost arts of childhood, the lost audacities and ambitions and romantic admirations of adolescence? What becomes of the sympathies which make us feel our kinship to all sorts of people? What becomes of the early curiosity in regard to things which were none of our business? We ask as Saint Paul asked of the Galatians, "Ye began well; who did hinder you?"

The answer is not wholly to our discredit. We do not develop all parts of our nature because we are not allowed to do so. Walt Whitman might exult over the Spontaneous Me. But nobody is paid for being spontaneous. A spontaneous switchman on the railway would be a menace to the traveling public. We prefer someone less temperamental.

As civilization advances and work becomes more specialized, it becomes impossible for anyone to find free and full development for all his natural powers in any recognized occupation. What then becomes of the other selves? The answer must be that playgrounds must be provided for them outside the confines of daily business. As work becomes more engrossing and narrowing, the need is more urgent for recognized and carefully guarded periods of leisure.

The old Hebrew sage declared, "Wisdom cometh from the opportunity of leisure." It does not mean that a wise man must belong to what we call the leisure classes. It means, that, if one has only a little free time at his disposal, he must use that time for the refreshment of his hidden selves. If he cannot have a sabbath rest of twenty-four hours, he must learn to sanctify little sabbaths, it may be of ten minutes' length.

In them he shall do no manner of work. It is not enough that the self that works and receives wages shall be recognized and protected; the world must be made safe for our other selves. Does not the Declaration of Independence say that every man has an inalienable right to the pursuit of happiness?

The old-time minister, after he had exhorted the believers at considerable length, used to turn to a personage who for homiletical purposes was known as the Objector. To him, he addressed his most labored arguments. At this point I am conscious of the presence of the Objector.

"All you say," he remarks, "in praise of your favorite platitude is true to a fault. But what has all this to do with the War? There is only one thing in these days worth thinking about — at least, it is the only thing we *can* think about."

"I agree with you, courteous Objector. No matter where we start, we all come back to this point: Who was to blame for the War, and how is it coming out? Our explanatory idea has a direct bearing on the question before us. The Prussian militarists had a painstaking knowledge of facts, but they had a contempt for human nature. Their tactlessness was almost beyond belief. They treated persons as if they were things. They treated facts with deadly seriousness, but had no regard for feelings. They had spies all over the world to report all that could be seen, but they took no account of what could not be seen. So, while they were dealing scientifically with the obvious facts and forces, all the hidden powers of the human soul were being turned against them. Prussianism insists on highly specialized men who have no sympathies to interfere with their efficiency. Having adopted a standard, all variation must be suppressed. It is against this effort to suppress the human variations that we are fighting. We don't want all men to be reduced to one pattern."

"But what about the Kaiser? Does your formula explain him? Does he want to be somebody else?"

"I confess, dear Objector, that it is probably a new idea to him; but he may come to it."

APPRECIATION HELPS

1. Discuss the profound truth underlying the title.
2. What does the author accomplish in the first two paragraphs?
3. When do your most illuminating thoughts occur?
4. Recall the various times when you desired to be somebody else.
5. Why does the tactless person have difficulty in human relationships? What are his difficulties in meeting those older or younger than he?
6. Discuss the prevalence of " shop talk."
7. What suggestions have you gained from the essay on proper topics of conversation?
8. What is implied in really knowing a man?
9. Point out humorous passages. Which are due to the thought? which to the phrasing?
10. Where is the author good-naturedly criticizing the follies and fads of the age?
11. Does the essayist show an understanding of youth in his third section? Compare this part with Kipling's " Independence " (p. 135).
12. Discuss the narrowing effect education has upon a man.
13. What " elusive personalities " have you found hiding in your friends and in yourself?
14. Discuss: " Nobody is paid for being spontaneous."

COMPOSITION HINTS

1. A Moment of Sudden Illumination
2. My Selves
3. My Life History as Revealed by Photographs
4. Elusive Personalities in My Secret Chamber
5. When " Spontaneous Me " Caused Trouble
6. My Literal-Minded Friend
7. Persons I Have Wished to Be
8. The Boy I Should Have Been
9. The Familiar Chaos of My Desk

RUDYARD KIPLING

Two important things should be borne in mind concerning Mr. Rudyard Kipling. First, he is one of the most famous prose writers and poets alive; second, he is the author of that rarity, a school story that lives, the tale of his own boyhood at the United Services College on the rocky coast of North Devon.

Let the story be taken first. It is entitled *Stalky and Co.* The heroes are Three Musketeers of school life assisted by their friend Beetle, the short-sighted wearer of gig-lamps who is no other than Kipling himself. Stalky today is a famous British general named Dunsterville and the other two Musketeers have also distinguished themselves as soldiers. Buy, beg, borrow, or steal *Stalky and Co.* and get to know a delightful quartet from real life, indulging in rollicking adventures and evading with uncanny dexterity the restraints of authority. Learn from it, too, how Beetle as a lad always was stringing words together and how his great delight was in messing about a printing office, setting type, pulling proofs, and correcting galleys.

That brings one to his subsequent fame as a writer. He went to the United Services College because that is where boys go to prepare to enter the British Army or Navy. But Kipling's eyesight was not good enough for soldiering, so at sixteen he returned to India (he was born in Bombay in 1865) and took a job within smell of the printer's ink so dear to him. He became a copy-reader on the *Civil and Military Gazette.* The glamour of the vast Indian Empire and the miraculous manner in which a mere handful of Englishmen there dominated, either as civilians or soldiers, millions of dusky natives, captivated his imagination and worked upon it until, when he was twenty-one, he burst forth in a new kind of verse with the lilt of bugles and the beat of drums in it. *Departmental Ditties* was the title of the volume. The next year followed *Plain Tales from the Hills,* supremely clever short stories of Anglo-Indian life. At an age when many are just leaving college Kipling found that his name was made. Thereafter he was able to travel, wandering throughout the East, and later to go home to live at Brighton in England.

It was in the heyday of the good reign of Queen Victoria when to English people the British Empire, that Empire " upon which the sun never sets," seemed the most wonderful creation of all time. Kipling became the poet of Empire, and the singer of its glories in prose as well. He was peculiarly well fitted for such duties. He is a little man with shaggy eyebrows and shaggy mustache, and somehow his own frailty makes him admire doughty deeds in distant lands, the fixed determination of gritted teeth, the nobility of silent heroism. Further, he is the apostle of efficiency, and it seemed to him in those days that the chief characteristics of the British empire-builder were the neatness and thoroughness with which he did his job. So it was that Kipling turned up, the right man for the right moment, and his popularity seemed to know no bounds.

But the real secret of his success lay in his own amazing talent. He was first and foremost a workman, in his own striking word; over everything he set his hand to, ballad, solemn poem, short story, novel, or fantasy for children, craftsmanship, supreme and admirable, invariably presided. He was also as versatile as he was efficient, producing novels such as *Kim,* animal stories like *The Jungle Book,* fairy tales such as *Puck of Pook's Hill,* short tales like " The Night Mail," and, during the Boer War, patriotic verse, grave as " Recessional " or lightly tragic as " The Absent-Minded Beggar."

In later years, however, with the decline of English excitement in Empire, his own powers seemed somewhat to dwindle too. His only son was killed in the World War, and he himself recently was gravely ill. He has written less and less. But his gospel remains unaltered. It is expressed vigorously in the rectorial address he delivered at the Scottish University of St. Andrews on October 10, 1923, part of which is given here.

INDEPENDENCE[1]

THE amount of Truth open to Mankind has always been limited. Substantially, it comes to no more than the axiom quoted by the Fool in *Twelfth Night,* on the authority of the witty Hermit of Prague, " That that is, is." Conversely, " That that is not, isn't." But it is just this Truth which Man most bitterly resents being brought to his notice. He will do, suffer, and permit anything rather than acknowledge it. He desires that the waters which he has digged and canalized should run uphill by themselves when it suits him. He desires that the numerals which he has himself counted on his fingers and christened " two and two " should make three and five according to his varying needs or moods. Why does he want this? Because, subconsciously, he still scales himself against his age-old companions, the beasts, who can only act lies. Man knows that, at any moment, he can tell a lie which, for a while, will delay or divert the workings of cause and effect. Being an animal who is still learning to reason, he does not yet understand why with a little more, or a little louder, lying he should not be able permanently to break the chain of that law of cause and effect — the Justice without the Mercy — which he hates, and to have everything both ways in every relation of his life.

In other words, we want to be independent of facts, and the younger we are, the more intolerant are we of those who tell us that this is impossible. When I wished to claim my independence and to express myself according to the latest lights of my age (for there were lights even then), it was disheartening to be told that I could not expect to be clothed, fed, taught, amused, and comforted — not to say preached at — by others, and at the same time to practice towards them a savage and thorny independence.

I imagine that you, perhaps, may have assisted at domestic

[1] From the book of this name, copyright by Doubleday, Page and Company, 1923; published in England by A. P. Watt & Son.

conferences on these lines; but I maintain that we are not the unthinking asses that our elders called us. Our self-expression may have been a trifle crude, but the instinct that prompted it was that primal instinct of independence which antedates the social one, and makes the young at times a little difficult. It comes down from the dumb and dreadful epoch when all that Man knew was that he was himself, and not another, and therefore the loneliest of created beings; and *you* know that there is no loneliness to equal the loneliness of youth at war with its surroundings in a world that does not care.

I can give you no great comfort in your war, but, if you will allow me, I will give you a scientific parallel that may bear on the situation.

Not once upon a time, but at many different times in different places and ages, it came over some one Primitive Man that he desired, above everything, to escape for a while from the sight and sound and the smell of his Tribe. It may have been an excellent Tribe, or it may have been an abominable one, but whichever it was he had had enough of it for a time. Knowing no more than the psychology of his age (whereas we, of course, know the psychology of all the ages), he referred his impulse to the direct orders, guidance, or leading of his Totem, his Guardian Spirit, his Disembodied Ancestor, or other Private God, who had appeared to him in a dream and inspired his action.

Herein our ancestor was as logical as a man taking his Degree on the eve of a professional career — not to say as practical as a Scot. He accepted Spirits and Manifestations of all kinds as part of his highly organized life, which had its roots in the immemorial past; but, outside that, the amount of truth open to him was limited. He only knew that if he did not provide himself with rations in advance, for his proposed excursion away from the Tribe, he would surely starve.

Consequently, he took some pains and practiced a certain amount of self-denial to get and prepare these rations. He may have wished to go forth on some utterly useless diversion, such as hacking down a tree or piling up stones, but whatever his object was, he intended to undertake it without the advice, interference, or even the privity of his Tribe. He might appreciate the dear creatures much better on his return; he might hatch out wonderful schemes for their advantage during his absence. But that would be a side-issue. The power that possessed him was the desire to own himself for a while, even as his ancestors, whose spirits had, he believed, laid this upon him, had owned themselves, before the Tribal idea had been evolved.

Morally his action was unassailable; his personal God had dictated it. Materially, his justification for his departure from the normal was the greasy, inconspicuous packet of iron rations on his shoulder, the trouble he had taken to get them, and the extent to which he was prepared not to break into them except as a last resort. For, without that material, backed by those purposes, his visions of his Totem, Spirit, or God would have melted back into the ruck of unstable, unfulfilled dreams; and his own weariness of his Tribe would have returned upon himself in barrenness of mind and bitterness of soul.

Because if a man has *not* his rations in advance, for any excursion of any kind that he proposes to himself, he must stay with his Tribe. He may swear at it aloud or under his breath. He may tell himself and his friends what splendid things he would do were he his own master, but as his Tribe goes so must he go — for his belly's sake. When and as it lies, so must he lie. Its people must be his people, and its God must be his God. Some men may accept this dispensation; some may question it. It is to the latter that I would speak.

Remember always that, except for the appliances we make, the rates at which we move ourselves and our possessions through space, and the words which we use, nothing in life changes. The utmost any generation can do is to rebaptize each spiritual or emotional rebirth in its own tongue. Then it goes to its grave hot and bothered, because no new birth has been vouchsafed for its salvation, or even its relief.

And your generation succeeds to an unpromising and disheveled heritage. In addition to your own sins, which will be numerous but quite normal, you have to carry the extra handicap of the sins of your fathers. This, it is possible that many of you have already made clear to your immediate circle. But the point you probably omitted (as our generation did, when we used to deliver *our* magnificent, unpublished orations De Juventute) is that no shortcomings on the part of others can save us from the consequences of our own shortcomings.

It is also true that you were brought into this world without being consulted. But even this disability, from which, by the way, Adam suffered, though it may justify our adopting a critical attitude towards First Causes, will not in the long run nourish our physical or mental needs. There seems, moreover, to be an unscientific objection on the part of First Causes against being inquired of.

Even so, there is no need for the individual who intends to own himself to be too pessimistic. Let us, as our forefathers used, count our blessings.

You, my constituents, enjoy three special ones. First, thanks to the continuity of self-denial on the part of your own forbears, the bulk of you will enter professions and callings in which you will be free men — free to be paid what your work is worth in the open market, irrespective of your alleged merits or your needs. Free, moreover, to work without physical molestation of yourself or your family as long and as closely as you please — free to exploit your own powers and your own health to the uttermost for your own ends.

Your second blessing is that you carry in your land's history and in your hearts the strongest instinct of inherited continuity, which expresses itself in your passionate interest in your own folk, your own race and all its values. History shows that, from remote ages, the Scots would descend from their heather and associate together on the flat for predatory purposes; these now take the form of raiding the world in all departments of life — and governments. But at intervals your race, more than others, feels the necessity for owning itself. Therefore it returns, in groups, to its heather, where, under camouflage of

" games " and " gatherings," it fortifies itself with the rites, incantations, pass-words, raiment, dances, food and drink of its ancestors, and re-initiates itself into its primal individualism. These ceremonies, as the Southern races know to their cost, give its members fresh strength for renewed forays.

And that same strength is your third and chief blessing. I have already touched on the privilege of being broken by birth, custom, precept, and example to doing without things. This is where the sons of the small houses who have borne the yoke in their youth hold a cumulative advantage over those who have been accustomed to life with broad margins. Such men can and do accommodate themselves to straitened circumstances at a pinch, and for an object; but they are as aware of their efforts afterwards as an untrained man is aware of his muscles on the second morning of a walking tour; and when they have won through what they consider hardship they are apt to waste good time and place by subconsciously approving, or even remembering, their own efforts. On the other hand, the man who has been used to shaving, let us say, in cold water at seven o'clock the year round, takes what one may call the minor damnabilities of life in his stride, without either making a song about them or writing home about them. And that is the chief reason why the untrained man always has to pay more for the privilege of owning himself than the man trained to the little things. It is the little things, in microbes or morale, that make us, as it is the little things that break us.

Also, men in any walk of life who have been taught not to waste or muddle material under their hand are less given to muddle or mishandle moral, intellectual, and emotional issues than men whose wastage has never been checked, or who look to have their wastage made good by others. The proof is plain.

Among the generations that have preceded you at this University were men of your own blood — many and many — who did their work on the traditional sack of peasemeal or oatmeal behind the door — weighed out and measured with their own hands against the cravings of their natural appetites.

These were men who intended to own themselves, in obedience to some dream, leading, or word which had come to them. They knew that it would be a hard and long task, so they set about it with their own iron rations on their own backs, and they walked along the sands here to pick up driftwood to keep the fire going in their lodgings.

Now, what in this World, or the next, can the World, or any Tribe in it, do with or to people of this temper? Bribe them by good dinners to take larger views of life? They would probably see their hosts under the table first and argue their heads off afterwards. Offer 'em money to shed a conviction or two? A man doesn't lightly sell what he has paid for with his hide. Stampede them, or coax them, or threaten them into countenancing the issue of false weights and measures? It is a little hard to liberalize persons who have done their own weighing and measuring with broken teacups by the light of tallow candles. No! Those thrifty souls must have been a narrow and an anfractuous breed to handle; but, by their God, in whose Word they walked, they owned themselves! And their ownership was based upon the truth that if you have not your own rations you must feed out of your Tribe's hands — with all that that implies.

Should any of you care to own yourselves on these lines, your insurances ought to be effected in those first ten years of a young man's life when he is neither seen nor heard. This is the period — one mostly spends it in lodgings, alone — that corresponds to the time when Man in the making began to realize that he was himself and not another.

The initial payments on the policy of one's independence, then, must be financed, by no means for publication, but as a guarantee of good faith towards oneself, primarily out of the drinks that one does not too continuously take; the maidens in whom one does not too extravagantly rejoice; the entertainments that one does not too systematically attend or conduct; the transportation one does not too magnificently employ; the bets one does not too generally place, and the objects of beauty and desire that one does not too generously buy. Secondarily, those revenues can be added to by extra work undertaken at hours before or after one's regular work, when one would infinitely rather rest or play. That involves the question of how far you can drive yourself without breaking down, and if you do break down, how soon you can recover and carry on again. This is for you to judge, and to act accordingly.

No one regrets — no one has regretted — more than I that these should be the terms of the policy. It would better suit the spirit of the age if personal independence could be guaranteed for all by some form of coördinated action combined with public assistance and so forth. Unfortunately there are still a few things in this world that a man must manage for himself: his own independence is one of them; and the obscure, repeated shifts and contrivances and abstentions necessary to the manufacture of it are too personal and intimate to expose to the inspection of any Department, however sympathetic.

If you have a temperament that can accommodate itself to cramping your style while you are thus saving, you are lucky. But, anyway, you will be more or less uncomfortable until it presently dawns on you that you have put enough by to give you food and housing for, say, one week ahead. It is both sedative and anti-spasmodic — it makes for calm in the individual and forbearance towards the Tribe — to know that you hold even seven days' potential independence in reserve — and owed to no man. One is led on to stretch that painfully extorted time to one month if possible; and as one sees that this is possible, the possibilities grow. Bit by bit, one builds up and digs oneself into a base whence one can move in any direction, and fall back upon in any need. The need may be merely to sit still and consider, as did our first ancestors, what manner of animal we are; or it may be to cut loose at a minute's notice from a situation which has become intolerable or unworthy; but, whatever it may be, it is one's own need, and the opportunity of meeting it has been made by one's own self.

After all, yourself is the only person you can by no possibility get away from in this life, and, may be, in another. It is worth a little pains and money to do good to him. For it is he, and not our derivatively educated minds or our induced emotions, who preserves in us the undefeated senior instinct of independence. You can test this by promising yourself *not* to do a thing, and noticing the scandalous amount of special pleading that you have to go through with yourself if you break your promise. A man does not always remember, or follow up, the great things which he has promised himself or his friends to do; but he rarely forgets or forgives when he has promised himself *not* to do even a little thing. This is because Man has lived with himself as an individual, vastly longer than he has lived with himself under tribal conditions. Consequently, facts about his noble solitary self and his earliest achievements had time to get well fixed in his memory. He knew he was not altogether one with the beasts. His amazing experiences with his first lie had shown him that he was something of a magician, if not a miracle-worker; and his first impulse towards self-denial, for ends not immediately in sight, must have been a revelation of himself to himself as stupendous as a belief in a future life, which it was possibly intended to herald. It is only natural, then, that individuals who first practiced this apparently insane and purposeless exercise came later to bulk in the legends of their Tribe as demigods, who went forth and bearded the gods themselves for gifts — for fire, wisdom, or knowledge of the arts.

But one thing that stands outside exaggeration or belittlement — through all changes in shapes of things and the sounds of words — is the bidding, the guidance, that drives a man to own himself and upholds him through his steps on that road. That bidding comes, direct as a beam of light, from that Past when man had grown into his present shape, which Past, could we question it, would probably refer us to a Past immeasurably remoter still, whose Creature, not yet Man, felt within him that it was not well for him to jackal round another brute's kill, even if he went hungry for a while.

It is not such a far cry from that Creature, howling over his empty stomach in the dark, to the Heir of all the Ages counting over his coppers in front of a cookshop, to see if they will run to a full meal — as some few here have had to do; and the principle is the same: "At any price that I can pay, let me own myself."

And the price *is* worth paying if you keep what you have bought. For the eternal question still is whether the profit of any concession that a man makes to his Tribe, against the Light that is in him, outweighs or justifies his disregard of that Light. A man may apply his independence to what is called worldly advantage, and discover too late that he laboriously has made himself dependent on a mass of external conditions, for the maintenance of which he has sacrificed himself. So he may be festooned with the whole haberdashery of success, and go to his grave a castaway.

Some men hold that this risk is worth taking. Others do not. It is to these that I have spoken.

" Let the council of thy own heart stand, for there is no man more faithful unto thee than it. For a man's mind is sometime wont to show him more than seven watchmen who sit above in a high tower."

APPRECIATION HELPS

1. Has Kipling successfully come within the experience of his audience? Point out places which make you feel that he understands young people.
2. If you are interested in this abridgment, read the speech entire.
3. Explain the first sentence.
4. Why is it impossible to be " independent of facts "?
5. Explain: " There is no loneliness to equal the loneliness of youth at war with its surroundings in a world that does not care."
6. What books have you read which take the above quotation for a theme?
7. Discuss: " As his Tribe goes so must he go — for his belly's sake."
8. What are the " three special blessings " enjoyed by the young people of today?
9. How are the " initial payments on the policy of one's independence " financed?

10. Why does Kipling set so high a value on being able to do without things?
11. Select five quotations that embody the finest thoughts of the essay.

COMPOSITION HINTS

1. Youth at War with Its Surroundings
2. The Hardness of a World That Does not Care
3. The Pleasures of Escape
4. Departures and Arrivals
5. Independence as I Understand It
6. On Being Misunderstood by My Family
7. The Intolerance of Age towards Youth
8. Without Interference from the Family
9. " Count Your Blessings "
10. " There is Nothing New under the Sun "
11. Handicaps Which Help

KENNETH GRAHAME

For fifteen years Mr. Kenneth Grahame (1859–1932) was an important bank official. After being educated at Oxford, he became a servant of the Old Lady of Threadneedle Street. (That is the affectionate name by which from time immemorial the merchants and business men of the City of London have known the Bank of England, greatest of all banks in the world after the Federal Reserve Bank of America.) He became the acting secretary and later the secretary. Then in 1908 — at the age of forty-nine — he retired. He gave up living in London and went to live in the country to write. After that until his death in 1932 he dwelt mostly in Berkshire, a county of lovely woodlands within easy reach of London.

Mr. Grahame, as his name indicates, was a Scot. He was also a born essayist, with a deep and engaging insight into the joyful anticipations and poignant disappointments of the young, as you may verify for yourself now. Two delightful books of his about children for grown-ups are *Dream Days* (1898) and *The Golden Age* (1899).

THE MAGIC RING[1]

GROWN-UP people really ought to be more careful. Among themselves it may seem but a small thing to give their word and take back their word. For them there are so many compensations. Life lies at their feet, a party-colored india-rubber ball; they may kick it this way or kick it that, it turns up blue, yellow, or green, but always colored and glistening. Thus one sees it happen almost every day, and, with a jest and a laugh, the thing is over, and the disappointed

[1] From *Dream Days,* copyright by Dodd, Mead & Company, Inc., 1898.

one turns to fresh pleasure, lying ready to his hand. But with those who are below them, whose little globe is swayed by them, who rush to build star-pointing alhambras on their most casual word, they really ought to be more careful.

In this case of the circus, for instance, it was not as if we had led up to the subject. It was they who began it entirely — prompted thereto by the local newspaper. "What, a circus!" said they, in their irritating, casual way: "that would be nice to take the children to. Wednesday would be a good day. Suppose we go on Wednesday. Oh, and pleats are being worn again, with rows of deep braid," etc.

What the others thought I know not; what they said, if they said anything, I did not comprehend. For me the house was bursting, walls seemed to cramp and to stifle, the roof was jumping and lifting. Escape was the imperative thing — to escape into the open air, to shake off bricks and mortar, and to wander in the unfrequented places of the earth, the more properly to take in the passion and the promise of the giddy situation.

Nature seemed prim and staid that day, and the globe gave no hint that it was flying round in a circus ring of its own. Could they really be true, I wondered, all those bewildering things I had heard tell of circuses? Did long-tailed ponies really walk on their hind-legs and fire off pistols? Was it humanly possible for clowns to perform one-half of the bewitching drolleries recorded in history? And how, oh, how dare I venture to believe that, from off the backs of creamy Arab steeds, ladies of more than earthly beauty discharged themselves through paper hoops? No, it was not altogether possible, there must have been some exaggeration. Still, I would be content with very little, I would take a low percentage — a very small proportion of the circus myth would more than satisfy me. But again, even supposing that history were, once in a way, no liar, could it be that I myself was really fated to look upon this thing in the flesh and to live through it, to survive the rapture? No, it was altogether too much. Something was bound to happen, one of us would develop measles, the world would blow up with a loud explosion. I must not dare, I must not presume, to entertain the smallest hope. I must endeavor sternly to think of something else.

Needless to say, I thought, I dreamed of nothing else, day or night. Waking, I walked arm-in-arm with a clown, and cracked a portentous whip to the brave music of a band. Sleeping, I pursued — perched astride of a coal-black horse — a princess all gauze and spangles, who always managed to keep just one unattainable length ahead. In the early morning Harold and I, once fully awake, cross-examined each other as to the possibilities of this or that circus tradition, and exhausted the lore long ere the first housemaid was stirring. In this state of exaltation we slipped onward to what promised to be a day of all white days — which brings me right back to my text, that grown-up people really ought to be more careful.

I had known it could never really be; I had said so to myself a dozen times. The vision was too sweetly ethereal for embodiment. Yet the pang of the disillusionment was none the less keen and sickening, and the pain was as that of a corporeal wound. It seemed strange and foreboding, when we entered the breakfast-room, not to find everybody cracking whips, jumping over chairs, and whooping in ecstatic rehearsal of the wild reality to come. The situation became grim and pallid indeed, when I caught the expressions " garden-party " and " my mauve tulle," and realized that they both referred to that very afternoon. And every minute, as I sat silent and listened, my heart sank lower and lower, descending relentlessly like a clock-weight into my boot soles.

Throughout my agony I never dreamed of resorting to a direct question, much less a reproach. Even during the period of joyful anticipation some fear of breaking the spell had kept me from any bald circus talk in the presence of them. But Harold, who was built in quite another way, so soon as he discerned the drift of their conversation and heard the knell of all his hopes, filled the room with wail and clamor of bereavement. The grinning welkin rang with " Circus! " " Circus! " shook the window-panes; the mocking walls reëchoed

"Circus!" Circus he would have, and the whole circus, and nothing but the circus. No compromise for him, no evasions, no fallacious, unsecured promises to pay. He had drawn his check on the Bank of Expectation, and it had got to be cashed then and there; else he would yell, and yell himself into a fit, and come out of it and yell again. Yelling should be his profession, his art, his mission, his career. He was qualified, he was resolute, and he was in no hurry to retire from the business.

The noisy ones of the world, if they do not always shout themselves into the imperial purple, are sure at least of receiving attention. If they cannot sell everything at their own price, one thing — silence — must, at any cost, be purchased of them. Harold accordingly had to be consoled by the employment of every specious fallacy and base-born trick known to those whose doom it is to handle children. For me their hollow cajolery had no interest, I could pluck no consolation out of their bankrupt though prodigal pledges. I only waited till that hateful, well-known "Some other time, dear!" told me that hope was finally dead. Then I left the room without any remark. It made it worse — if anything could — to hear that stale, worn-out old phrase, still supposed by those dullards to have some efficacy.

To nature, as usual, I drifted by instinct, and there, out of the track of humanity, under a friendly hedgerow had my black hour unseen. The world was a globe no longer, space was no more filled with whirling circuses of spheres. That day the old beliefs rose up and asserted themselves, and the earth was flat again — ditch-riddled, stagnant, and deadly flat. The undeviating roads crawled straight and white, elms dressed themselves stiffly along inflexible hedges, all nature, centrifugal no longer, sprawled flatly in lines out to its farthest edge, and I felt just like walking out to that terminus, and dropping quietly off. Then, as I sat there, morosely chewing bits of stick, the recollection came back to me of certain fascinating advertisements I had spelled out in the papers — advertisements of great and happy men, owning big ships of tonnage running into four figures, who yet craved, to the extent of public supplication, for the sympathetic coöperation of youths as apprentices. I did not rightly know what apprentices might be, nor whether I was yet big enough to be styled a youth, but one thing seemed clear, that, by some such means as this, whatever the intervening hardships, I could eventually visit all the circuses of the world — the circuses of merry France and gaudy Spain, of Holland and Bohemia, of China and Peru. Here was a plan worth thinking out in all its bearings; for something had presently to be done to end this intolerable state of things.

Mid-day, and even feeding-time, passed by gloomily enough, till a small disturbance occurred which had the effect of releasing some of the electricity with which the air was charged. Harold, it should be explained, was of a very different mental mold, and never brooded, moped, nor ate his heart out over any disappointment. One wild outburst — one dissolution of a minute into his original elements of air and water, of tears and outcry — so much insulted nature claimed. Then he would pull himself together, iron out his countenance with a smile, and adjust himself to the new condition of things.

If the gods are ever grateful to man for anything, it is when he is so good as to display a short memory. The Olympians were never slow to recognize this quality of Harold's, in which, indeed, their salvation lay, and on this occasion their gratitude had taken the practical form of a fine fat orange, tough-rinded as oranges of those days were wont to be. This he had eviscerated in the good old-fashioned manner, by biting out a hole in the shoulder, inserting a lump of sugar therein, and then working it cannily till the whole soul and body of the orange passed glorified through the sugar into his being. Thereupon, filled full of orange-juice and iniquity, he conceived a deadly snare. Having deftly patted and squeezed the orange-skin till it resumed its original shape, he filled it up with water, inserted a fresh lump of sugar in the orifice, and, issuing forth, blandly proffered it to me as I sat moodily in the doorway dreaming of strange wild circuses under tropic skies.

Such a stale old dodge as this would hardly have taken me in at ordinary moments. But Harold had reckoned rightly upon the disturbing effect of ill-humor, and had guessed, perhaps, that I thirsted for comfort and consolation, and would not criticize too closely the source from which they came. Unthinkingly I grasped the golden fraud, which collapsed at my touch, and squirted its contents into my eyes and over my collar, till the nethermost parts of me were damp with the water that had run down my neck. In an instant I had Harold down, and, with all the energy of which I was capable, devoted myself to grinding his head into the gravel; while he, realizing that the closure was applied, and that the time for discussion or argument was past, sternly concentrated his powers on kicking me in the stomach.

Some people can never allow events to work themselves out quietly. At this juncture one of Them swooped down on the scene, pouring shrill, misplaced abuse on both of us: on me for ill-treating my younger brother, whereas it was distinctly I who was the injured and the deceived; on him for the high offense of assault and battery on a clean collar — a collar which I had myself deflowered and defaced, shortly before, in sheer desperate ill-temper. Disgusted and defiant we fled in different directions, rejoining each other later in the kitchen-garden; and as we strolled along together, our short feud forgotten, Harold observed, gloomily: "I should like to be a caveman, like Uncle George was tellin' us about: with a flint hatchet and no clothes, and live in a cave and not know anybody!"

"And if anyone came to see us we didn't like," I joined in, catching on to the points of the idea, "we'd hit him on the head with the hatchet till he dropped down dead."

"And then," said Harold, warming up, "we'd drag him into the cave and *skin him!*"

For a space we gloated silently over the fair scene our imaginations had conjured up. It was *blood* we felt the need of just then. We wanted no luxuries, nothing dear-bought nor far-fetched. Just plain blood, and nothing else, and plenty of it.

Blood, however, was not to be had. The time was out of

joint, and we had been born too late. So we went off to the greenhouse, crawled into the heating arrangement underneath, and played at the dark and dirty and unrestricted life of cavemen till we were heartily sick of it. Then we emerged once more into historic times, and went off to the road to look for something living and sentient to throw stones at.

Nature, so often a cheerful ally, sometimes sulks and refuses to play. When in this mood she passes the word to her underlings, and all the little people of fur and feather take the hint and slip home quietly by back streets. In vain we scouted, lurked, crept, and ambuscaded. Everything that usually scurried, hopped, or fluttered — the small society of the undergrowth — seemed to have engagements elsewhere. The horrid thought that perhaps they had all gone off to the circus occurred to us simultaneously, and we humped ourselves up on the fence and felt bad. Even the sound of approaching wheels failed to stir any interest in us. When you are bent on throwing stones at something, humanity seems obtrusive and better away. Then suddenly we both jumped off the fence together, our faces clearing. For our educated ear had told us that the approaching rattle could only proceed from a dogcart, and we felt sure it must be the funny man.

We called him the funny man because he was sad and serious, and said little, but gazed right into our souls, and made us tell him just what was on our minds at the time, and then came out with some magnificently luminous suggestion that cleared every cloud away. What was more, he would then go off with us at once and play the thing right out to its finish, earnestly and devotedly, putting all other things aside. So we called him the funny man, meaning only that he was different from those others who thought it incumbent on them to play the painful mummer. The ideal as opposed to the real man was what we meant, only we were not acquainted with the phrase. Those others, with their labored jests and clumsy contortions, doubtless flattered themselves that *they* were funny men; we, who had to sit through and applaud the painful performance, knew better.

He pulled up to a walk as soon as he caught sight of us, and

the dogcart crawled slowly along till it stopped just opposite.
Then he leant his chin on his hand and regarded us long and
soulfully, yet said he never a word; while we jigged up and
down in the dust, grinning bashfully but with expectation.
For you never knew exactly what this man might say or do.

"You look bored," he remarked presently; "thoroughly
bored. Or else — let me see; you're not married, are you?"

He asked this in such sad earnestness that we hastened to
assure him we were not married, though we felt he ought to
have known that much; we had been intimate for some time.

"Then it's only boredom," he said. "Just satiety and world-
weariness. Well, if you assure me you aren't married you can
climb into this cart and I'll take you for a drive. I'm bored, too.
I want to do something dark and dreadful and exciting."

We clambered in, of course, yapping with delight and tread-
ing all over his toes; and as we set off, Harold demanded of
him imperiously whither he was going.

"My wife," he replied, "has ordered me to go and look up
the curate and bring him home to tea. Does that sound sufficiently exciting for you?"

Our faces fell. The curate of the hour was not a success,
from our point of view. He was not a funny man, in any sense
of the word.

"— But I'm not going to," he added, cheerfully. "Then
I was to stop at some cottage and ask — what was it? There
was *nettle-rash* mixed up in it, I'm sure. But never mind, I've
forgotten, and it doesn't matter. Look here, we're three desperate young fellows who stick at nothing. Suppose we go off
to the circus?"

Of certain supreme moments it is not easy to write. The
varying shades and currents of emotion may indeed be put into
words by those specially skilled that way; they often are, at
considerable length. But the sheer, crude article itself — the
strong, live thing that leaps up inside you and swells and
strangles you, the dizziness of revulsion that takes the breath
like cold water — who shall depict this and live? All I knew
was that I would have died then and there, cheerfully, for the

funny man; that I longed for red Indians to spring out from the hedge on the dogcart, just to show what I would do; and that, with all this, I could not find the least little word to say to him.

Harold was less taciturn. With shrill voice, uplifted in solemn chant, he sang the great spheral circus-song, and the undying glory of the Ring. Of its timeless beginning he sang, of its fashioning by cosmic forces, and of its harmony with the stellar plan. Of horses he sang, of their strength, their swiftness, and their docility as to tricks. Of clowns again, of the glory of knavery, and of the eternal type that shall endure. Lastly he sang of Her — the Woman of the Ring — flawless, complete, untrammeled in each subtly curving limb; earth's highest output, time's noblest expression. At least, he doubtless sang all these things and more — he certainly seemed to; though all that was distinguishable was, " We're-goin'-to-the-circus! " and then, once more, " We're-goin'-to-the-circus " — the sweet rhythmic phrase repeated again and again. But indeed I cannot be quite sure, for I heard confusedly, as in a dream. Wings of fire sprang from the old mare's shoulders. We whirled on our way through purple clouds, and earth and the rattle of wheels were far away below.

The dream and the dizziness were still in my head when I found myself, scarce conscious of intermediate steps, seated actually in the circus at last, and took in the first sniff of that intoxicating circus smell that will stay by me while this clay endures. The place was beset by a hum and a glitter and a mist; suspense brooded large o'er the blank, mysterious arena. Strung up to the highest pitch of expectation, we knew not from what quarter, in what divine shape, the first surprise would come.

A thud of unseen hoofs first set us a-quiver; then a crash of cymbals, a jangle of bells, a hoarse applauding roar, and Cora-lie was in the midst of us, whirling past 'twixt earth and sky, now erect, flushed, radiant, now crouched to the flowing mane; swung and tossed and molded by the maddening dance-music of the band. The mighty whip of the count in the frock-coat

marked time with pistol-shots; her war-cry, whooping clear
above the music, fired the blood with a passion for splendid
deeds, as Coralie, laughing, exultant, crashed through the paper
hoops. We gripped the red cloth in front of us, and our souls
sped round and round with Coralie, leaping with her, prone
with her, swung by mane or tail with her. It was not only the
ravishment of her delirious feats, nor her cream-colored horse
of fairy breed, long-tailed, roe-footed, an enchanted prince
surely, if ever there was one! It was her more than mortal
beauty — displayed, too, under conditions never vouchsafed to
us before — that held us spellbound. What princess had arms
so dazzlingly white, or went delicately clothed in such pink and
spangles? Hitherto we had known the outward woman as but
a drab thing, hour-glass shaped, nearly legless, bunched here,
constricted there; slow of movement, and given to deprecating
lusty action of limb. Here was a revelation! From henceforth our imaginations would have to be revised and corrected
up to date. In one of those swift rushes the mind makes in
high-strung moments, I saw myself and Coralie, close enfolded,
pacing the world together, o'er hill and plain, through storied
cities, past rows of applauding relations, — I in my Sunday
knickerbockers, she in her pink and spangles.

Summers sicken, flowers fail and die, all beauty but rides
round the ring and out at the portal; even so Coralie passed
in her turn, poised sideways, panting, on her steed; lightly
swayed as a tulip-bloom, bowing on this side and on that
as she disappeared; and with her went my heart and my soul,
and all the light and the glory and the entrancement of the
scene.

Harold woke up with a gasp. "Wasn't she beautiful?" he
said, in quite a subdued way for him. I felt a momentary
pang. We had been friendly rivals before, in many an exploit;
but here was altogether a more serious affair. Was this, then,
to be the beginning of strife and coldness, of civil war on the
hearthstone and the sundering of old ties? Then I recollected
the true position of things, and felt very sorry for Harold; for
it was inexorably written that he would have to give way to

me, since I was the elder. Rules were not made for nothing, in a sensibly constructed universe.

There was little more to wait for, now Coralie had gone; yet I lingered still, on the chance of her appearing again. Next moment the clown tripped up and fell flat, with magnificent artifice, and at once fresh emotions began to stir. Love had endured its little hour, and stern ambition now asserted itself. Oh, to be a splendid fellow like this, self-contained, ready of speech, agile beyond conception, braving the forces of society, his hand against everyone, yet always getting the best of it! What freshness of humor, what courtesy to dames, what triumphant ability to discomfit rivals, frock-coated and mustached though they might be! And what a grand, self-confident straddle of the legs! Who could desire a finer career than to go through life thus gorgeously equipped! Success was his keynote, adroitness his panoply, and the mellow music of laughter his instant reward. Even Coralie's image wavered and receded. I would come back to her in the evening, of course; but I would be a clown all the working hours of the day.

The short interval was ended: the band, with long-drawn chords, sounded a prelude touched with significance; and the program, in letters overtopping their fellows, proclaimed Zephyrine, the Bride of the Desert, in her unequaled bareback equestrian interlude. So sated was I already with beauty and wit, that I hardly dared hope for a fresh emotion. Yet her title was tinged with romance, and Coralie's display had aroused in me an interest in her sex which even herself had failed to satisfy entirely.

Brayed in by trumpets, Zephyrine swung passionately into the arena. With a bound she stood erect, one foot upon each of her supple, plunging Arabs; and at once I knew that my fate was sealed, my chapter closed, and the Bride of the Desert was the one bride for me. Black was her raiment, great silver stars shone through it, caught in the dusky twilight of her gauze; black as her own hair were the two mighty steeds she bestrode. In a tempest they thundered by, in a whirlwind, a *scirocco* of tan; her cheeks bore the kiss of an Eastern sun, and the sand-storms of her native desert were her satellites. What was Coralie, with her pink silk, her golden hair and slender limbs, beside this magnificent, full-figured Cleopatra? In a twinkling we were scouring the desert — she and I and two coal-black horses. Side by side, keeping pace in our swinging gallop, we distanced the ostrich, we outstrode the zebra; and, as we went, it seemed the wilderness blossomed like the rose.

I know not rightly how we got home that evening. On the road there were everywhere strange presences, and the thud of phantom hoofs encircled us. In my nose was the pungent circus-smell; the crack of the whip and the frank laugh of the clown were in my ears. The funny man thoughtfully abstained from conversation, and left our illusion quite alone, sparing us all jarring criticism and analysis; and he gave me no chance, when he deposited us at our gate, to get rid of the clumsy expressions of gratitude I had been laboriously framing. For the rest of the evening, distraught and silent, I only heard the march-music of the band, playing on in some corner of my brain. When at last my head touched the pillow, in a trice I was with Zephyrine, riding the boundless Sahara, cheek to cheek, the world well lost; while at times, through the sand-clouds that encircled us, glimmered the eyes of Coralie, touched, one fancied, with something of a tender reproach.

APPRECIATION HELPS

1. In what does the charm of this essay consist? Discuss the author's sympathy with the point of view of children.
2. Why ought " grown-up people to be more careful in promising things to children "? What early disappointments do you recall that were the result of broken promises?
3. Describe from your early experience the days of anticipation preceding any important event.
4. Do the members of your own family differ as much in temper and temperament as the two boys described in this essay? Illustrate.

5. Did you ever plan to run away from home after an indignity suffered at the hands of an unsympathetic adult? When?
6. What qualities of the " funny man " endeared him to children?
7. Discuss the changing ambitions which swayed the boy at the circus. Is the picture overdrawn? Illustrate from your own experience.
8. Point out passages of charm, of humor, and of pathos.

COMPOSITION HINTS

1. Childhood Anticipations
2. Childhood Disappointments
3. An Unpaid Check on the Bank of Expectation
4. " Some Other Time, Dear! "
5. Why I Planned to Run Away from Home
6. People Who Make-Believe
7. Childish Misconceptions
8. Sights and Sounds and Smells of the Circus
9. The Pleasures of Escape
10. Crabbed Age and Youth
11. The Tendency to Exaggerate Misfortune

OLIVER WENDELL HOLMES

One often hears people reproached for talking too much. This is because they have nothing real to say, no bright ways of expression, and are content with retailing idle gossip or reporting trivial happenings. In short, because they are bores. Let a man have something interesting to impart, and wit and humor in his speech, and nobody will ever complain that he talks too much. On the contrary, everybody will want to hear more from him. Such a man was Oliver Wendell Holmes (1809–1894). He was professor of anatomy at Harvard, and so fresh, lively, and witty were his lectures that the students were sent to him at the end of the day when they were fagged, for he alone at that hour could make them alert and attentive again. At dinner parties he was always in demand, not only for speeches, but also for the sparkling give-and-take, the sallies and repartees of conversation.

He soon showed too that he could do more than talk well; he could write as if he were talking. That is a wonderful gift. Publishers of books and editors of magazines and papers are always wishing and praying for an author who will write in that way. But it is indeed rarely that they find one. When they do, the authors are at once on what is known as Easy Street. In 1856, the Boston publishers, Phillips, Sampson, and Co., asked James Russell Lowell to edit a new magazine named *The Atlantic Monthly*. You will still see it on the news stands. He consented, provided that Holmes should be a regular contributor. Holmes agreed and supplied the first of those famous papers collected under the title of *The Autocrat of the Breakfast Table*. At once they made a success of the magazine.

The following essay is one of them. When you are reading it, picture to yourself the author sitting at his dining-room table and chatting away to his friends in the delightful fashion he has written down. And whenever you see or hear the name, Oliver Wendell Holmes, think at once of the man who could write as he talked. It is true that Holmes, in *The Autocrat,* is not actually quite so good as he was when he was speaking. The warmth of good fellowship, the presence of listeners, their apt suggestions and responses, all stimulated him in conversation. But nevertheless with his pen he is very good indeed. *The Autocrat* came out in book form in 1857. Two years later Holmes put another boarder in the Autocrat's chair and produced a book entitled *The Professor at the Breakfast Table.* Finally in 1872 came a third of the series, *The Poet at the Breakfast Table.* Holmes himself was a poet, and he also wrote a novel, *Elsie Venner.*

Altogether he was one of those immortals of whom America may justly be proud.

BOATING

A YOUNG friend has lately written an admirable article in one of the journals, entitled, "Saints and Their Bodies." Approving of his general doctrines, and grateful for his records of personal experience, I cannot refuse to add my own experimental confirmation of his eulogy of one particular form of active exercise and amusement, namely, boating. For the past nine years I have rowed about, during a good part of the summer, on fresh or salt water. My present fleet on the River Charles consists of three row-boats. 1. A small flat-bottomed skiff in the shape of a flat-iron, kept mainly to lend to boys. 2. A fancy "dory" for two pairs of sculls, in which I sometimes go out with my young folks. 3. My own particular water-sulky, a "skeleton" or "shell" race-boat, twenty-two feet long, with huge outriggers, which boat I pull with ten-foot sculls, — alone, of course, as it holds but one, and tips him out if he doesn't mind what he is about. In this I glide around the Back Bay, down the stream, up the Charles to Cambridge and Watertown, up the Mystic, round the wharves, in the wake of steamboats, which leave a swell after them delightful to rock upon; I linger under the bridges, — those "caterpillar bridges," as my brother professor so happily called them; rub against the black sides of old wood-schooners; cool down under the overhanging stern of some tall Indiaman; stretch across to the Navy Yard, where the sentinel warns me off from the *Ohio,*—just as if I should hurt her by lying in her shadow; then strike out into the harbor, where the water gets clear and the air smells of the ocean,—till all at once I remember that, if a west wind blows up of a sudden, I shall drift along past the islands, out of sight of the dear old State-house,—plate, tumbler, knife and fork all waiting at home, but no chair drawn up at the table,—all the dear people waiting, waiting, waiting, while the boat is sliding, sliding, sliding into the great desert, where there is no tree and no fountain. As I don't want my wreck to be washed up on one of the beaches in company with devil's-aprons, bladder-weeds, dead horse-shoes, and bleached crab-shells, I turn about and flap my long, narrow wings for home. When the tide is running out swiftly, I have a splendid fight to get through the bridges, but always make it a rule to beat,—though I have been jammed up into pretty tight places at times, and was caught once between a vessel swinging round and the pier, until our bones (the boat's, that is) cracked as if we had been in the jaws of Behemoth. Then back to my moorings at the foot of the Common, off with the rowing-dress, dash under the green translucent wave, return to the garb of civilization, walk through my Garden, take a look at my elms on the Common, and, reaching my habitat, in consideration of my advanced period of life, indulge in the Elysian abandonment of a huge recumbent chair.

When I have established a pair of well-pronounced feathering-calluses on my thumbs, when I am in training so that I can do my fifteen miles at a stretch without coming to grief in any way, when I can perform my mile in eight minutes or a little more, then I feel as if I had old Time's head in chancery, and could give it to him at my leisure.

I do not deny the attraction of walking. I have bored this ancient city through and through in my travels, until I know it as an old inhabitant of a Cheshire knows his cheese. Why, it was I who, in the course of these rambles, discovered that remarkable avenue called Myrtle Street, stretching in one long

line from east of the Reservoir to a precipitous and rudely
paved cliff which looks down on the grim abode of Science, and
beyond it to the far hills; a promenade so delicious in its repose, so cheerfully varied with glimpses down the northern
slope into busy Cambridge Street with its iron river of the
horse-railroad, and wheeled barges gliding back and forward
over it, — so delightfully closing at its western extremity in
sunny courts and passages where I know peace, and beauty,
and virtue, and serene old age must be perpetual tenants, —
so alluring to all who desire to take their daily stroll, in the
words of Dr. Watts,

> Alike unknowing and unknown, —

that nothing but a sense of duty would have prompted me to
reveal the secret of its existence. I concede, therefore, that
walking is an immeasurably fine invention, of which old
age ought constantly to avail itself.

Saddle-leather is in some respects even preferable to sole-
leather. The principal objection to it is of a financial character. But you may be sure that Bacon and Sydenham did not
recommend it for nothing. One's *hepar,* or, in vulgar language, liver, — a ponderous organ, weighing some three or four
pounds, — goes up and down like the dasher of a churn in the
midst of the other vital arrangements, at every step of a
trotting horse. The brains are also shaken up like coppers in
a money-box. Riding is good, for those that are born with a
silver-mounted bridle in their hand, and can ride as much and
as often as they like, without thinking all the time they hear
that steady grinding sound as the horse's jaws triturate with
calm lateral movement the bank-bills and promises to pay upon
which it is notorious that the profligate animal in question
feeds day and night.

Instead, however, of considering these kinds of exercise in
this empirical way, I will devote a brief space to an examination
of them in a more scientific form.

The pleasure of exercise is due first to a purely physical
impression, and secondly to a sense of power in action. The

first source of pleasure varies of course with our condition and the state of the surrounding circumstances; the second with the amount of kind of power, and the extent and kind of action. In all forms of active exercise there are three powers simultaneously in action, — the will, the muscles, and the intellect. Each of these predominates in different kinds of exercise. In walking, the will and muscles are so accustomed to work together, and perform their task with so little expenditure of force, that the intellect is left comparatively free. The mental pleasure in walking, as such, is in the sense of power over all our moving machinery. But in riding, I have the additional pleasure of governing another will, and my muscles extend to the tips of the animal's ears and to his four hoofs, instead of stopping at my hands and feet. Now in this extension of my volition and my physical frame into another animal, my tyrannical instincts and my desire for heroic strength are at once gratified. When the horse ceases to have a will of his own and his muscles require no special attention on your part, then you may live on horseback as Wesley did, and write sermons or take naps, as you like. But you will observe that in riding on horseback you always have a feeling that, after all, it is not you that do the work, but the animal, and this prevents the satisfaction from being complete.

Now let us look at the conditions of rowing. I won't suppose you to be disgracing yourself in one of those miserable tubs, tugging in which is to rowing the true boat what riding a cow is to bestriding an Arab. You know the Esquimau *kayak* (if that is the name of it), don't you? Look at that model of one over my door. Sharp, rather? — On the contrary it is a lubber to the one you and I must have; a Dutch fishwife to Psyche, contrasted with what I will tell you about. Our boat, then, is something of the shape of a pickerel, as you look down upon his back, he lying in the sunshine just where the sharp edge of the water cuts in among the lily-pads. It is a kind of giant pod, as one may say, — tight everywhere, except in a little place in the middle, where you sit. Its length is from seven to ten yards, and as it is only from sixteen to thirty inches wide in its widest part, you understand why you want those "outriggers," or projecting iron frames with the rowlocks in which the oars play. My rowlocks are five feet apart; double or more than double the greatest width of the boat.

Here you are, then, afloat with a body a rod and a half long, with arms, or wings, as you may choose to call them, stretching more than twenty feet from tip to tip; every volition of yours extending as perfectly into them as if your spinal cord ran down the center strip of your boat, and the nerves of your arms tingled as far as the broad blades of your oars, — oars of spruce, balanced, leathered, and ringed under your own special direction. This, in sober earnest, is the nearest approach to flying that man has ever made or perhaps ever will make. As the hawk sails without flapping his pinions, so you drift with the tide when you will, in the most luxurious form of locomotion indulged to an embodied spirit. But if your blood wants rousing, turn around that stake in the river, which you see a mile from here; and when you come in in sixteen minutes (if you do, for we are old boys, and not champion scullers, you remember), then say if you begin to feel a little warmed up or not. You can row easily and gently all day, and you can row yourself blind and black in the face in ten minutes, just as you like. It has been long agreed that there is no such way in which a man can accomplish so much labor with his muscles as in rowing. It is in the boat, then, that man finds the largest extension of his volitional and muscular existence; and yet he may tax both of them so slightly, in that most delicious of exercises, that he shall mentally write his sermon, or his poem, or recall the remarks he has made in company and put them in form for the public, as well as in his easy-chair.

I dare not publicly name the rare joys, the infinite delights, that intoxicate me on some sweet June morning when the river and bay are smooth as a sheet of beryl-green silk, and I run along ripping it up with my knife-edged shell of a boat, the rent closing after me like those wounds of angels which Milton tells of, but the seam still shining for many a long rood behind me. To lie still over the Flats, where the waters are shallow, and see the crabs crawling and the sculpins gliding busily and silently beneath the boat, — to rustle in through the long harsh grass that leads up some tranquil creek, — to take shelter from the sunbeams under one of the thousand-footed bridges, and look down its interminable colonnades, crusted with green and oozy growths, studded with minute barnacles, and belted with rings of dark mussels, while overhead streams and thunders that other river whose every wave is a human soul flowing to eternity as the river below flows to the ocean, — lying there moored unseen, in loneliness so profound that the columns of Tadmor in the Desert could not seem more remote from life — the cool breeze on one's forehead, the stream whispering against the half-sunken pillars, — why should I tell of these things, that I should live to see my beloved haunts invaded, and the waves blackened with boats as with a swarm of water-beetles? What a city of idiots we must be not to have covered this glorious bay with gondolas and wherries, as we have just learned to cover the ice in winter with skaters!

APPRECIATION HELPS

1. How important a factor is *locality* in contributing to the charm of this essay?
2. Why are you glad that he owned three boats? What does it reveal of the man?
3. About what age was Holmes when he wrote the essay? Quote passages to support your claim.
4. Discuss his estimate on walking; on riding.
5. What cities have you " bored through and through "?
6. Where are your favorite haunts in *your* locality?
7. Point out passages which tell you that the essay was not written in the nineteen-hundreds.
8. Were Holmes writing today, what additional forms of exercise might he include? List the ones you would include in such an essay.
9. Discuss his contention that rowing is the superlative exercise.
10. In what passages describing rowing does he " put you there "?

COMPOSITION HINTS

1. What I Have Discovered in My Rambles
2. Saddle-Leather versus Sole-Leather
3. My Favorite Exercise
4. Among the Lily-Pads
5. Drifting
6. Things Seen from My Boat
7. Favorite Haunts in My Neighborhood

JOHN GALSWORTHY

In England the practice of the law is sharply divided. On the one hand are the pleaders in the courts, who are called barristers or counsel. To become a pleader a man, before he can sit for the examinations, must join one of the old Inns of Court in London, and, after the examinations, he must eat a prescribed number of dinners in the Hall of the Inn. Then he is *called* to the Bar. On the other hand are the lawyers who instruct counsel, who look after wills and conduct all legal business outside the courts. These are called solicitors. To become a solicitor a young man usually is articled to some well-established solicitor, and, after passing his examinations, he is *admitted* to the roll of solicitors. In Scotland solicitors are known as writers to the Signet. Mr. John Galsworthy (1867–1933) one of three leading English novelists of his generation — the others being Mr. H. G. Wells and Mr. Arnold Bennett — came of a line of family solicitors and he himself was brought up to succeed his father. His youth was dominated by a consciousness of the legal affairs of wealthy merchant families in England. He grew up not in contact with the spectacular side of the law, the notorious suits, the noisy divorces, the criminal prosecutions, but in the quiet, secret atmosphere of deeds, conveyances, mortgages, wills, family histories, and family skeletons. All this seemed to him so interesting, so filled with a kind of repressed drama, that instead of becoming a solicitor himself, he decided to write about it. The very titles of some of his novels, *The Man of Property* (1906), *In Chancery* (1920), *To Let* (1921), have a legal sound about them.

He was born in 1867 and was sent to Harrow School. This school and Eton College are the two most exclusive in England. To have been at either is a guarantee of one's family's social position. They are two of the public schools to which Mr. Galsworthy refers in his essay. These are not public schools in the American sense; they correspond to private American academies, and their fees usually are large. They are called public schools because the oldest were founded to be open to all, because they are not managed by one individual, but superintended by a board of governors, and generally are regulated by laws known as the Public Schools Acts. Many famous statesmen, lawyers, and authors have attended Harrow, which is situated in what now is a London suburb, but until recently was a picturesque village. It stands on a hill crowned by trees, and these trees and the church steeple are a landmark for miles. From Harrow young Galsworthy went to Oxford University, and afterwards continued to read for the law. It was at this time that he decided to become a writer. But first he went off to see the world, traveling for two years in Russia, the Orient, the Fiji Islands, Australia, Canada, and South America. His first book was published in 1898.

He came to America several times and had a great admiration for both the country and its people. He was a quiet, unassuming, slight man, with a pale face and not much hair. If he were in the same room, you might easily not notice that he was there. Yet he excelled as a novelist, essayist, short-story writer, and lecturer, and all these things add to his reputation as a writer of prose. His most famous work is the series of novels collected under one title as *The Forsyte Saga*.

AMERICAN AND BRITON[1]

ON the mutual understanding of each other by Britons and Americans the future happiness of nations depends more than on any other world cause.

I have never held a whole-hearted brief for the British character. There is a lot of good in it, but much which is repellent. It has a kind of deliberate unattractiveness, setting out on its journey with the words: " Take me or leave me." One may respect a person of this sort, but it is difficult either to know or to like him. I am told that an American officer said recently to a British staff officer in a friendly voice: " So we're going to clean up Brother Boche together! " and the

[1] From *Addresses in America,* copyright by Charles Scribner's Sons, 1919.

British staff officer replied " Really! " No wonder Americans sometimes say: " I've got no use for those fellows."

The world is consecrate to strangeness and discovery, and the attitude of mind concreted in that " Really! " seems unforgivable, till one remembers that it is manner rather than matter which divides the hearts of American and Briton.

In a huge, still half-developed country, where every kind of national type and habit comes to run a new thread into the rich tapestry of American life and thought, people must find it almost impossible to conceive the life of a little old island where traditions persist generation after generation without anything to break them up; where blood remains undoctored by new strains; demeanor becomes crystallized for lack of contrasts and manner gets set like a plaster mask. The English manner of today, of what are called the classes, is the growth of only a century or so. There was probably nothing at all like it in the days of Elizabeth or even of Charles II. The English manner was still racy when the inhabitants of Virginia, as we are told, sent over to ask that there might be despatched to them some hierarchical assistance for the good of their souls, and were answered: " D——n your souls, grow tobacco! " The English manner of today could not even have come into its own when that epitaph of a lady, quoted somewhere by Gilbert Murray, was written: " Bland, passionate, and deeply religious, she was second cousin to the Earl of Leitrim; of such are the Kingdom of Heaven." About that gravestone motto was a certain lack of the self-consciousness which is now the foremost characteristic of the English manner.

But this British self-consciousness is no mere fluffy *gaucherie,* it is our special form of what Germans would call " Kultur." Behind every manifestation of thought or emotion the Briton retains control of self, and is thinking: " That's all I'll let them see "; even " That's all I'll let myself feel." This stoicism is good in its refusal to be foundered; bad in that it fosters a narrow outlook; starves emotion, spontaneity, and frank sympathy; destroys grace and what one may describe roughly as the lovable side of personality. The English hardly ever say

just what comes into their heads. What we call " good form,"
the unwritten law which governs certain classes of the Briton,
savors of the dull and glacial; but there lurks within it a core
of virtue. It has grown up like callous shell round two fine
ideals — suppression of the ego lest it trample on the corns of
other people, and exaltation of the maxim: " Deeds before
words." Good form, like any other religion, starts well with
some ethical truth, but soon gets commonized and petrified till
we can hardly trace its origin, and watch with surprise its
denial and contradiction of the root idea.

Without doubt good form had become a kind of disease in
England. A French friend told me how he witnessed in a
Swiss hotel the meeting between an Englishwoman and her
son, whom she had not seen for two years; she was greatly
affected — by the fact that he had not brought a dinner jacket.
The best manners are no " manners," or at all events no
mannerisms; but many Britons who have even attained to this
perfect purity are yet not free from the paralytic effects of
" good form " ; are still self-conscious in the depths of their
souls, and never do or say a thing without trying not to show
what they are feeling. All this guarantees a certain decency
in life; but in intimate intercourse with people of other nations
who have not this particular cult of suppression, we English
disappoint, and jar, and often irritate. Nations have their
differing forms of snobbery. At one time the English all
wanted to be second cousins to the Earl of Leitrim, like that
lady bland and passionate. Nowadays it is not so simple.
The Earl of Leitrim has become etherealized. We no longer
care how a fellow is born so long as he behaves as the Earl of
Leitrim would have, never makes himself conspicuous or ridiculous, never shows too much what he's really feeling, never
talks of what he's going to do, and always " plays the game."
The cult is centered in our public schools and universities.

At a very typical and honored old public school the writer of
this essay passed on the whole a happy time; but what a curious
life, educationally speaking! We lived rather like young
Spartans; and were not encouraged to think, imagine, or see

anything that we learned in relation to life at large. It's very difficult to teach boys, because their chief object in life is not to be taught anything, but I should say we were crammed, not taught at all. Living as we did the herd-life of boys with little or no intrusion from our elders, and they men who had been brought up in the same way as ourselves, we were debarred from any real interest in philosophy, history, art, literature and music, or any advancing notions in social life or politics. I speak of the generality, not of the few black swans among us. We were reactionaries almost to a boy. I remember one summer term Gladstone came down to speak to us, and we repaired to the Speech Room with white collars and dark hearts, muttering what we would do to that Grand Old Man if we could have our way. But he contrived to charm us, after all, till we cheered him vociferously. In that queer life we had all sorts of unwritten rules of suppression. You must turn up your trousers; must not go out with your umbrella rolled. Your hat must be worn tilted forward; you must not walk more than two abreast till you reached a certain form, nor be enthusiastic about anything, except such a supreme matter as a drive over the pavilion at cricket, or a run the whole length of the ground at football. You must not talk about yourself or your home people, and for any punishment you must assume complete indifference.

I dwell on these trivialities because every year thousands of British boys enter these mills which grind exceeding small, and because these boys constitute in after life the great majority of the official, military, academic, professional, and a considerable proportion of the business classes of Great Britain. They become the Englishmen who say: " Really! " and they are for the most part the Englishmen who travel and reach America. The great defense I have always heard put up for our public schools is that they form character. As oatmeal is supposed to form bone in the bodies of Scotsmen, so our public schools are supposed to form good, sound moral fiber in British boys. And there is much in this plea. The life does make boys enduring, self-reliant, good-tempered and honorable, but it most carefully endeavors to destroy all original sin of individuality, spontaneity, and engaging freakishness. It implants, moreover, in the great majority of those who have lived it the mental attitude of that swell, who when asked where he went for his hats, replied: "Blank's, of course. Is there another fellow's?"

To know all is to excuse all — to know all about the bringing up of English public school boys makes one excuse much. The atmosphere and tradition of those places is extraordinarily strong, and persists through all modern changes. Thirty-seven years have gone since I was a new boy, but cross-examining a young nephew who left not long ago, I found almost precisely the same features and conditions. The war, which has changed so much of our social life, will have some, but no very great, effect on this particular institution. The boys still go there from the same kind of homes and preparatory schools and come under the same kind of masters. And the traditional unemotionalism, the cult of a dry and narrow stoicism, is rather fortified than diminished by the times we live in. . . .

We are, deep down, under all our lazy mentality, the most combative and competitive race in the world, with the exception, perhaps, of the American. This is at once a spiritual link with America, and yet one of the great barriers to friendship between the two peoples. We are not sure whether we are better men than Americans. Whether we are really better than French, Germans, Russians, Italians, Chinese, or any other race is, of course, more than a question; but those peoples are all so different from us that we are bound, I suppose, secretly to consider ourselves superior. But between Americans and ourselves, under all differences, there is some mysterious deep kinship which causes us to doubt and makes us irritable, as if we were continually being tickled by that question: Now am I really a better man than he? Exactly what proportion of American blood at this time of day is British, I know not; but enough to make us definitely cousins — always an awkward relationship. We see in Americans a sort of image of ourselves; feel near enough, yet far enough, to criticise and carp

at the points of difference. It is as though a man went out
and encountered, in the street, what he thought for the moment
was himself, and, wounded in his *amour propre,* instantly began to disparage the appearance of that fellow. Probably community of language rather than of blood accounts for our sense
of kinship, for a common means of expresssion cannot but
mold thought and feeling into some kind of unity. One can
hardly overrate the intimacy which a common literature brings.
The lives of great Americans, Washington and Franklin, Lincoln and Lee and Grant, are unsealed for us, just as to Americans are the lives of Marlborough and Nelson, Pitt and Gladstone and Gordon. Longfellow and Whittier and Whitman
can be read by the British child as simply as Burns and Shelley
and Keats. Emerson and William James are no more difficult
to us than Darwin and Spencer to Americans. Without an
effort we rejoice in Hawthorne and Mark Twain, Henry James
and Howells, as Americans can in Dickens and Thackeray,
Meredith and Thomas Hardy. And, more than all, Americans
own with ourselves all literature in the English tongue before
the Mayflower sailed; Chaucer and Spenser and Shakespeare,
Raleigh, Ben Jonson, and the authors of the English Bible
Version are their spiritual ancestors as much as ever they are
ours. The tie of language is all-powerful — for language is
the food formative of minds. A volume could be written on
the formation of character by literary humor alone. The
American and Briton, especially the British townsman, have a
kind of bone-deep defiance of Fate, a readiness for anything
which may turn up, a dry, wry smile under the blackest sky,
and an individual way of looking at things which nothing can
shake. Americans and Britons both, we must and will think
for ourselves, and know why we do a thing before we do it.
We have that ingrained respect for the individual conscience
which is at the bottom of all free institutions. Some years
before the war an intelligent and cultivated Austrian, who had
lived long in England, was asked for his opinion of the British.
" In many ways," he said, " I think you are inferior to us; but
one great thing I have noticed about you which we have not.

You think and act and speak for yourselves." If he had passed those years in America instead of in England he must needs have pronounced the same judgment of Americans. Free speech, of course, like every form of freedom, goes in danger of its life in war-time. The other day, in Russia, an Englishman came on a street meeting shortly after the first revolution had begun. An extremist was addressing the gathering and telling them that they were fools to go on fighting, that they ought to refuse and go home, and so forth. The crowd grew angry, and some soldiers were for making a rush at him; but the chairman, a big burly peasant, stopped them with these words: " Brothers, you know that our country is now a country of free speech. We must listen to this man, we must let him say anything he will. But, brothers, when he's finished, we'll bash his head in! "

I cannot assert that either Britons or Americans are incapable in times like these of a similar interpretation of " free speech." Things have been done in our country, and will be done in America, which should make us blush. But so strong is the free instinct in both countries that some vestiges of it will survive even this war, for democracy is a sham unless it means the preservation and development of this instinct of thinking for oneself throughout a people. " Government of the people, by the people, for the people " means nothing unless individuals keep their consciences unfettered and think freely. Accustom people to be nose-led and spoon-fed, and democracy is a mere pretense. The measure of democracy is the measure of the freedom and sense of individual responsibility in its humblest citizens. And democracy — I say it with solemnity — has yet to prove itself. . . .

Ever since the substantial introduction of democracy nearly a century and a half ago with the American War of Independence, Western civilization has been living on two planes or levels — the autocratic plane, with which is bound up the idea of nationalism, and the democratic, to which has become conjoined the idea of internationalism. Not only little wars, but great wars such as this, come because of inequality in growth.

dissimilarity of political institutions between states; because this state or that is basing its life on different principles from its neighbors. The decentralization, delays, critical temper, and the importance of home affairs prevalent in democratic countries make them at once slower, weaker, less apt to strike, and less prepared to strike than countries where bureaucratic brains subject to no real popular check devise world policies which can be thrust, prepared to the last button, on the world at a moment's notice. The free and critical spirit in America, France, and Britain has kept our democracies comparatively unprepared for anything save their own affairs.

We fall into glib usage of words like democracy and make fetiches of them without due understanding. Democracy is inferior to autocracy from the aggressively national point of view; it is not necessarily superior to autocracy as a guarantee of general well-being; it may even turn out to be inferior unless we can improve it. But democracy is the rising tide; it may be dammed or delayed, but cannot be stopped. It seems to be a law in human nature that where, in any corporate society, the idea of self-government sets foot it refuses to take that foot up again. State after state, copying the American example, has adopted the democratic principle; the world's face is that way set. And civilization is now so of a pattern that the Western world may be looked on as one state and the process of change therein from autocracy to democracy regarded as though it were taking place in a single old-time country such as Greece or Rome. If throughout Western civilization we can secure the single democratic principle of government, its single level of state morality in thought and action, we shall be well on our way to unanimity throughout the world; for even in China and Japan the democratic virus is at work. It is my belief that only in a world thus uniform, and freed from the danger of pounce by autocracies, have states any chance to develop the individual conscience to a point which shall make democracy proof against anarchy and themselves proof against dissolution; and only in such a world can a League of Nations to enforce peace succeed.

But even if we do secure a single plane for Western civilization and ultimately for the world, there will be but slow and difficult progress in the lot of mankind. And unless we secure it, there will be only a march backward.

For this advance to a uniform civilization the solidarity of the English-speaking races is vital. Without that there will be no bottom on which to build.

The ancestors of the American people sought a new country because they had in them a reverence for the individual conscience; they came from Britain, the first large state in the Christian era to build up the idea of political freedom. The instincts and ideals of our two races have ever been the same. That great and lovable people, the French, with their clear thought and expression, and their quick blood, have expressed those ideals more vividly than either of us. But the phlegmatic and the dry tenacity of our English and American temperaments has ever made our countries the most settled and safe homes of the individual conscience, and of its children — Democracy, Freedom, and Internationalism. Whatever their faults — and their offenses cry aloud to such poor heaven as remains of chivalry and mercy — the Germans are in many ways a great race, but they possess two qualities dangerous to the individual conscience — unquestioning obedience and exaltation. When they embrace the democratic idea they may surpass us all in its logical development, but the individual conscience will still not be at ease with them. We must look to our two countries to guarantee its strength and activity, and if we English-speaking races quarrel and become disunited, civilization will split up again and go its way to ruin. We are the ballast of the new order.

I do not believe in formal alliances or in grouping nations to exclude and keep down other nations. Friendships between countries should have the only true reality of common sentiment, *and be animated by desire for the general welfare of mankind.* We need no formal bonds, but we have a sacred charge in common, to let no petty matters, differences of manner, or divergences of material interest, destroy our spiritual agreement. Our pasts, our geographical positions, our temperaments make us, beyond all other races, the hope and trustees of mankind's advance along the only lines now open — democratic internationalism. It is childish to claim for Americans or Britons virtues beyond those of other nations, or to believe in the superiority of one national culture to another; they are different, that is all. It is by accident that we find ourselves in this position of guardianship to the main line of human development; no need to pat ourselves on the back about it. But we are at a great and critical moment in the world's history — how critical none of us alive will ever realize. The civilization slowly built since the fall of Rome has either to break up and dissolve into jagged and isolated fragments through a century of war; or, unified and reanimated by a single idea, to move forward on one plane and attain greater height and breadth.

Under the pressure of this war there is, beneath the lip-service we pay to democracy, a disposition to lose faith in it because of its undoubted weakness and inconvenience in a struggle with states autocratically governed; there is even a sort of secret reaction to autocracy. On those lines there is no way out of a future of bitter rivalries, chicanery and wars, and the probable total failure of our civilization. The only cure which I can see lies in democratizing the whole world and removing the present weaknesses and shams of democracy by education of the individual conscience in every country. Good-by to that chance if Americans and Britons fall foul of each other, refuse to pool their thoughts and hopes, and to keep the general welfare of mankind in view. They have got to stand together, not in aggressive and jealous policies, but in defense and championship of the self-helpful, self-governing, " live and let live " philosophy of life.

The house of the future is always dark. There are few cornerstones to be discerned in the temple of our fate. But of these few one is the brotherhood and bond of the English-speaking races, not for narrow purposes, but that mankind may yet see faith and good-will enshrined, yet breathe a sweeter air, and know a life where Beauty passes, with the sun on her wings.

We want in the lives of men a " Song of Honor," as in Ralph Hodgson's poem:

> The song of men all sorts and kinds,
> As many tempers, moods and minds
>   As leaves are on a tree,
> As many faiths and castes and creeds,
> As many human bloods and breeds,
>   As in the world may be.

In the making of that song the English-speaking races will assuredly unite. What made this world we know not; the principle of life is inscrutable and will forever be; but we know that Earth is yet on the up-grade of existence, the mountain top of man's life not reached, that many centuries of growth are yet in front of us before Nature begins to chill this planet till it swims, at last, another moon, in space. In the climb to that mountain top of a happy life for mankind our two great nations are as guides who go before, roped together in perilous ascent. On their nerve, loyalty, and wisdom the adventure now hangs. What American or British knife will sever the rope?

He who ever gives a thought to the life of man at large, to his miseries and disappointments, to the waste and cruelty of existence, will remember that if American or Briton fail himself, or fail the other, there can but be for us both, and for all other peoples, a hideous slip, a swift and fearful fall into an abyss, whence all shall be to begin over again.

We shall not fail — neither ourselves, nor each other. Our comradeship will endure.

APPRECIATION HELPS

1. What was Galsworthy's purpose in writing the essay?
2. Do you agree with the thought in the first sentence? Why?
3. Does the author write as an Englishman who understands America? Does he seem prejudiced?

4. Discuss the part the English schools play in developing the character of the Briton; the influence of the American schools in molding the national character.
5. Where could the American high school do more in training its pupils for citizenship?
6. What are the bonds of kinship between American and Briton? Why should they be protected?

COMPOSITION HINTS

1. The Unwritten Rules of My Social Group
2. My Friendship with a Foreigner
3. When My Originality Led Me Astray
4. When My Self-Love Was Wounded
5. My Spiritual Ancestors
6. Free Speech in America
7. Forms of Snobbery
8. My Curious Life, Educationally Speaking
9. Advantages and Disadvantages of Concealing One's Feelings
10. England's Combative and Competitive Spirit

JOHN KENDRICK BANGS

" My Silent Servants," as you will find, is a serious and sensible disquisition, but it was written by a man who became popular as a humorous writer and lecturer. John Kendrick Bangs (1862–1922) produced in his lifetime nearly fifty volumes of amusing verse or prose and was in turn editor of *Life* and editor of " The Editor's Drawer " in *Harper's Magazine*. As a political, humorous, and wartime lecturer he addressed more than a thousand audiences. His book on his experiences on tour, *From Pillar to Post,* is entertaining reading.

Serious Bangs could be when he wished, and he held serious jobs, editor of *Harper's Weekly* and editor of the *Metropolitan Magazine*. But when he tried politics he failed. He once ran for mayor in Yonkers, New York, his native town, " and was returned by a comfortable majority to the bosom of my family, unwept, unhonored, and unsung."

MY SILENT SERVANTS[1]

I AM sorry for many kinds of folk. I am sorry for the distressed, the depressed, and the oppressed, whosoever they may be, or wheresoever found. I am sorry for the man of high aspiration thwarted at every point by the insurmountable steeps in the path of achievement. But when I find a man who has the means to build up a library in his own home, yet into whose home come only the most inconsequential of books, I don't know whether I am sorry for him or not. If he be one of those self-made persons whose supreme satisfaction with results is their most salient characteristic, who sneer at the real

[1] Published in *The Bookman*.

booklover and refer even to the reader of a Sunday comic supplement as a bookworm, and who hold themselves superior to books and their makers, I do not pity him at all. He has earned his wage of ignorance, and is entitled to its increment of dross. But if on the other hand he is one of those upon whose mental horizon the Sun of Letters and the Stars of Song have not yet shone, and who grope in darkness not by preference but merely because they do not know that the light is there, then I am sorry for him. I would do all that lies in my power to lead him to the light, for what light there is, indeed, in a well-selected library! What joy of song is there! What glowing comradeships with the noblest minds of all time lie within the silent covers of our books!

I think I have today a keener realization of the complete satisfaction of a library than ever before, for for three years I have been an exile from mine, and after much wandering have only just now returned to it. Coming back to my books was like returning to a home filled with old and devoted friends. It is true that when I first entered into their presence they all had their backs turned to me, but their welcome was none the less warm for that. And when I realized that on their backs they bore their title to my regard, it seemed to me that their seemingly ungracious posture was merely their tactful method of " presenting their cards " lest, perchance, in the presence of other matters I had forgotten their names. I wish all men would be as considerate. But there they stood, faithfully keeping watch, ready as ever to serve the need of each and every mood, giving me so warm a welcome, in truth, that with Shakespeare I was almost inclined to cry:

> My library was dukedom large enough!

I

And who would wish a greater? Is not the kingdom of mind fairer than all the principalities of earth? I would not deny the value of acres. I am not at all sure that if I could be the Duke of Devonshire and myself at the same time I should decline the honor, but for the riches of the spirit I would seek rather the pages of Emerson than the greening reaches of Chatsworth, Eaton, or Blenheim. Warwickshire is beautiful, but lovely as are its meadows, its gardens, trees, and leafy lanes, it is lovelier still for the romance of Kenilworth and the poetry of the Avon. It is indeed through the inspiration of Shakespeare and of Scott that pilgrims are inducted into a greater appreciation of the delights thereof, just as the song of Wordsworth is the primary lure that summons us to the sunny charms of Windermere and Rydal Mount.

Bovée tells us — and, by the way, I wish somebody would tell me who Bovée was, and what he did besides writing sayings for books of quotations, for I find no reference to him in the cyclopedias or other works of the cyclopedic, and I doubt not that to greater ignoramuses than I he is as well known as Captain John Smith or Daisy Ashford — Bovée tells us that

> Books are embalméd minds,

which is why I wish to know who he is or was, and where he may be addressed. I should like to drop him a postal and after paying my respects to his genius, tell him that *real books* are nothing of the sort. On the contrary, they are the vehicles by which the still living minds of dead men are carried on through the immortal years. They may be enshrined minds, or minds perpetuated, but their suggestion is not of death, but of life itself. Bulwer-Lytton has phrased it more happily and more truly in his lines:

> The Wise
> (Minstrel or Sage) out of their books are clay,
> But in their books, as from their graves they rise,
> Angels — that side by side upon our way
> Walk with, and warn us.

He might have added a tribute to the unwavering quality of their devotion to our interests, for our books, unlike some of our less constant friends, do not despair of our reformation if, perchance, heedless of their warnings, we sin and fall. **They** stand by faithfully, and though we fall seventy times **seventy** times, with persistent patience they again repeat their warnings, as if they knew that hopeless as we seem to be, there **is** yet hope for us.

> Silent companions of the lonely hour

Mrs. Norton calls them, and in their companionship they enable us to forget our trials, and sometimes in our perplexity they do our thinking, and point to right conclusions, for us.

> I love to lose myself in other men's minds.
> When I am not walking I am reading;
> I cannot sit and think. Books think for me,

says Lamb, who in his own sufferings found in books forgetfulness of pain, and who in his own books has brought forgetfulness of pain to others.

II

If I were a doctor I should make books a part of the *materia medica,* and prescribe them for my patients, according to their need. Over the door of the library at Thebes were inscribed the words "Medicine for the Soul," and Diodorus described books as "the medicine of the mind," wherefore I do not claim to have originated the idea, unless perchance in some earlier incarnation it was my privilege to be either Diodorus, or the sagacious trustee of the Theban library who suggested the inscription. I do not know if this were so or not. If it were, I can only say that it made no impression upon me. But I can personally testify out of a rich experience to the medical value of books. Many a time have I wakened in the deadly darkness of the night, gasping for breath, with an acute indigestion, and, feeling myself on the verge of dissolution, lit my lamp. And in the breathlessness of some great book, such for instance as Victor Hugo's indictment of "Napoleon the Little," I have as by some homeopathic magic found almost immediate cure of my own. A course of Mark Twain and Bernard Shaw is good for any man's liver; and I cannot even estimate the number of occasions when, afflicted by insomnia, I have wrested sleep from the pages of books which I shall not name, all freighted with the anodyne of slumber. Literature contains the herbage of thought that cures. Whether used as anesthetic to soothe a distraught nerve, or as tonic to stir to action a sluggish circulation, books serve the purpose, and justify the assertion of the already quoted Bovée that "the worth of a book is a matter of expressed juices."

III

But best of all the uses of a library are the contacts with great souls that having books always at hand makes possible. It has been said that man is judged by the company he keeps, and in nothing is this more clearly demonstrated than in the bookish companions one chooses for his constant friends. The right kind of man loves good company, and the nobler his choice the closer to nobility of soul does he himself come; and a well-selected library places all these great spirits within easy reach. Fielding has said that "we are as liable to be corrupted by books as by companions," and that is true, but it is no more true than the more genial view that we are as likely to be elevated by books as by inspiring associations. I know of no surer index to a man's character than the things that he laughs at, or the things that he reads. If I find a man whose shelves groan under the weight of books which he has to keep under lock and key for fear of their contaminating influence upon his children, I have a fairly clear line as to his type, and the quality of his soul. If on the other hand I find him enriching his mind with constant drafts upon the treasures of song, or feeding his soul upon the spiritual meat of the great masters of letters, or delving deep into the veins of the mines of philosophy, he seems to me to have become a promising initiate into the goodly company of the immortals. At any rate, association with the immortals is good, and it is through the open doorways of our libraries that they either come to us, or give us access to themselves.

At any time of the day or night I can follow the fortunes of Ulysses with no less a person than Homer himself for my guide. I can touch hands with all the gods of high Olympus on the cachet of his guidance, and all the splendors of the court of Zeus I am privileged to look upon, not through my purely mortal eyes alone, but with the vision of one who is himself immortal. If I desire to consort with men of power and purpose in ancient times, I have only to walk a foot or two from my desk to find in Plutarch a guide, who will introduce me to as many of the Caesars as I care to know, will present me at the court of Pericles, where I may have revealed to me the glory that was Greece; who will gossip to me engagingly of Solon and Themistocles, take me to dine with Lucullus, and give me the pleasing sense of having visited the Forum, and listened at the Agora. Time and space set no limit upon my associations, and though I dwell in a hemisphere they never knew, and in an age to theirs remote, Plato and Socrates through my books speak to me and pour their wisdom into my ears, while cynical old Diogenes with surprising agility leaps over seas and centuries to make me laugh. If I have need for song, Horace responds to my call, day or night. Omar Khayyam leaves his vine, drops his jug, and deserts his " thou " for a moment to charm me with verses, while if I be depressed in spirit a mere tap at the door of their books will bring Epictetus, or the Emperor Marcus himself to minister to my need of cheer.

If I be ill in bed, unable to stir abroad, books will take me to all the countries of earth, and in whatsoever company I may choose to go. I can visit the realms of the Grand Khan with Marco Polo, or week-end in Peru with Pizarro while that gallant bandit loots the treasury of the Incas. With Froude I can visit the West Indies without even lifting my head from my pillow or putting on my slippers. With Caesar I can travel from Rome to Britain, and find my way enlivened with many a stirring little scrap, and cross the Rubicon in the most invincible of company. With D'Artagnan, Porthos, Aramis, and the noble Athos, to whom my sleepless friend Dumas has introduced me, I can feed and sleep in fascinating roadside inns in France whenever the spirit moves. There is not a stone worth looking at in all of Venice that Ruskin will not pack into a small compass and for my delectation bring to my bedside, if I but open the cover of a book and let him out. Johnson and Boswell and I can go stamping through the Hebrides together if I am minded to summon them to that end. With Byron I can go singing along the Mediterranean and swim the Hellespont with none of the inconveniences of travel or dangers of the adventure, if so I choose to accept his lordship's standing invitation to participate at will in the enterprises he offers. Stevenson takes me with him on a joyous adventure with a donkey, or if I prefer conducts me through a Child's Garden of Verses, to the everlasting rejuvenation of my own aging spirit.

If I would sit upon the side lines of history, watching great events, observing epoch-making men at work at the very zenith of their fame, I can do it in a rocking-chair or swinging in a hammock, if I have books. I can participate in the fiercest battles of all time, from the fall of Jericho to the surgings to and from Ypres or Verdun, and not a hair of my head be imperiled. With Victor Hugo I can stand with the Old Guard at Waterloo. With Tennyson I can shamble through the hell and welter of Balaklava, charging with the Light Brigade. Shakespeare will lead me to the walls of Agincourt, where I may listen to the clarion tones of Harry of England summoning his men to the breach. A mere scrap of printed paper will carry me through shot and shell over the Bridge of Lodi with Napoleon, and with Gibbon as my guide Rome itself will rise and fall for me — and if in a whimsy mood I choose to read the opening chapters last, and the closing chapters first, the fall will precede the rise as if history were complacently willing to reverse herself to suit my pleasure.

Nor can any company exclude me if I have books. I can sit in with Ben Jonson at the Mermaid Tavern, and delight my soul with his witty discourse, and if he becomes discursive and bores me, it is my privilege to shut him off at will by the mere closing of a pasteboard cover. I may consume endless quantities of chops and brew of pleasing sort at the Cheshire Cheese with the author of *Rasselas,* or in the more modest company of Oliver Goldsmith. I can go with Monte Cristo to his cavern of riches, or with Aladdin summon the genii to do my bidding. I can sit alongside of Priscilla while John Alden makes love to her on behalf of his friend, without any uneasy sense of intrusion. I can introduce myself to Stanley as, in the heart of Africa, he utters his famous, "Dr. Livingstone, I believe?" and run no risk of rebuff. Sir Walter Scott will read his own journals to me if I ask him, and on top of his pillar I can stand with Simeon Stylites without danger of falling off, and privileged to come down whenever I choose. If my manners show signs of deterioration, having books, I can sit under Chesterfield while he delivers his fatherly injunctions as to the principles of deportment, or better still rub elbows with Colonel Newcome, who at my call never fails to answer, "Adsum!"

Who would not give a decade of his life to have known Lincoln? Well—Lincoln is not dead. It is only his habitation, the frame of which he was the immortal content, that has passed away. The man himself still lives, and stands over there upon my shelf—as he will stand upon yours if you choose to have him there—in all the splendor of his human sympathy and kingly character, his friend John Hay posted at the door ready to usher me into his presence. So, too, Emerson stands there, calling me constantly to a searching of the souls of the two of us, his and mine, I to find more of that which lies in mine by that which he reveals in his own as he talks to me of character and manners and the Oversoul, and of love and friendship. The gentle Elia walks with me, and talks to me. Thackeray and Dickens awaken me. Dante, Herrick, Shakespeare, Rossetti, and Wordsworth sing to me. Cervantes and Swift and Addison and Steele and Montaigne are never too busy to pause awhile to chat with me, and to ease the asperities of life with their gentle flashes of goodly humor. And why?

Merely to repay me for the paltry gift of hospitality. Merely because in the four square walls of a little room I have given them lodgment. I can in very truth sing with Proctor:

> All round my room my silent servants wait,
> My friends in every season, bright and dim.
>   Angels and Seraphim
> Come down and murmur to me, sweet and low,
> And spirits of the skies all come and go
>   Early and late.

It is a rich reward for so slight a service!

APPRECIATION HELPS

1. Do you like the title? Why?
2. Name some books you would classify as " inconsequential."
3. Make a list of twenty-five books you would place in a " well-selected library."
4. Prescribe some books for friends of yours who are ill either in body or mind.
5. What places would you like to visit because you have become acquainted with them through books?
6. Take the subject " If I Had a Wishing Carpet " and go to one of these places.
7. " I know of no surer index to a man's character than the things that he laughs at or the things that he reads." Is this true? Give examples from your own observation.
8. List the books and authors mentioned by Bangs familiar to you; those unfamiliar to you.
9. How many books do you own? Name five you value most highly. " Sell " one to the class.
10. Which quotation on books pleases you most?
11. Consult Dickinson's *One Thousand Best Books,* Doubleday & Page, 1924, to see if the five are included.
12. Consult these books on reading and contribute something to the class from what you gather:
    Companionable Books by Henry Van Dyke, Scribner's.
    A Reader's Guide Book by May L. Becker, Holt.

What Books Can Do for You by Jesse Lee Bennett, Doran.
How to Read by J. B. Kerfoot, Houghton.
What Can Literature Do for Me? by C. A. Smith, Doubleday.

COMPOSITION HINTS

1. Inconsequential Books
2. My Literary Debauches
3. Bedside Books
4. My Adventures in Bookland
5. " Magic Casements "
6. Illicit Delights. (Write an account of the reading you did which was not sanctioned by your parents.)
7. My Literary Successes
8. Old Favorites
9. Best-Sellers
10. The Joys of a Collector

HENRY DAVID THOREAU

" Where I Lived, and What I Lived For," the following paper, is from *Walden; or, Life in the Woods* (1854), the book upon which rests the fame of Henry David Thoreau (1817–1862), the American recluse. It is the account of how for two years he lived alone in a hut built with his own hands on a pine slope on the shores of Walden Pond, a short distance outside of Concord, and of how he supported himself during that time with a little surveying (he was a surveyor by profession) and the produce of his own vegetable garden. He went into this voluntary retirement ostensibly in fulfillment of a philosophy of life which he had evolved himself, a philosophy that has much to recommend it to a normal healthy schoolboy or schoolgirl. He held that there is too much work done in the world, and that the less each man labored the better it would be for mankind in general. He wanted to reverse the week as it was divided by Moses (Exodus 23:12) and have instead a week of six days' rest and one day's labor. To that extent he will carry the whole class with him. But to justify his contention, he went on to argue that an individual really needed very little of the fruits of the earth or of the luxuries of civilization and could easily minister unto himself. This does not sound so attractive. And Thoreau himself, when he set out to live up to this philosophy, at once broke the rules. For example, into his solitude he carried a vast number of books, the very luxuries which it was most obvious a man in a state of nature could not have. The fact is that he was just pretending. He liked to be alone. As a boy he had driven the cows to pasture, and alone in the fields acquired a taste for the delights of solitude. That is why he went away into his hut. Nevertheless, during those two years he had many interesting experiences, and hence the book he wrote about them is still read. He came to know the birds, beasts, and fishes better even than that other great lover of animals, St. Francis of Assisi, had done, and they came to know and love him.

But his writing is not stimulating. Thoreau gave off no sparks; he absorbed intensely, but when called upon to illuminate in turn, was found wanting.

He was of Jersey descent, Jersey, one of the little islands off the coast of Brittany, belonging to Britain, where English is the official language, but the peasants all speak the Breton dialect. He was a great friend of Emerson. He died at the early age of forty-five.

WHERE I LIVED, AND WHAT I LIVED FOR

A T a certain season of our life we are accustomed to consider every spot as the possible site of a house. I have thus surveyed the country on every side within a dozen miles of where I live. In imagination I have bought all the farms in succession, for all were to be bought, and I knew their price. I walked over each farmer's premises, tasted his wild apples, discoursed on husbandry with him, took his farm at his price, at any price, mortgaging it to him in my mind — even put a higher price on it; took everything but a deed of it; took his word for his deed, for I dearly love to talk; cultivated it, and him too to some extent, I trust, and withdrew when I had enjoyed it long enough, leaving him to carry it on. This experience entitled me to be regarded as a sort of realestate broker by my friends. Wherever I sat, there I might live, and the landscape radiated from me accordingly. What is a house but a *sedes*, a seat? — better if a country seat. I discovered many a site for a house not likely to be soon improved, which some might have thought too far from the village, but to my eyes the village was too far from it. Well, there I might live, I said; and there I did live, for an hour, a summer and a winter life; saw how I could let the years run off, buffet the winter through, and see the spring come in. The future inhabitants of this region, wherever they may place their houses, may be sure that they have been anticipated. An afternoon sufficed to lay out the land into orchard, woodlot, and pasture, and to decide what fine oaks or pines should be left to stand before the door, and whence each blasted tree could be seen to the best advantage; and then I let it lie, fallow perchance, for a man is rich in proportion to the number of things which he can afford to let alone.

My imagination carried me so far that I even had the refusal of several farms — the refusal was all I wanted — but I never got my fingers burned by actual possession. The nearest that I came to actual possession was when I bought the Hollowell place, and had begun to sort my seeds, and collected materials with which to make a wheelbarrow to carry it on or off with; but before the owner gave me a deed of it, his wife — every man has such a wife — changed her mind and wished to keep it, and he offered me ten dollars to release him. Now, to speak the truth, I had but ten cents in the world, and it surpassed my arithmetic to tell, if I was that man who had ten cents, or who had a farm, or ten dollars, or all together. However, I let him keep the ten dollars and the farm too, for I had carried it far enough; or rather, to be generous, I sold him the farm for just what I gave for it, and, as he was not a rich man, made him a present of ten dollars, and still had my ten cents, and seeds, and materials for a wheelbarrow left. I found thus that I had been a rich man without any damage to my poverty. But I retained the landscape, and I have since annually carried off what it yielded without a wheelbarrow. With respect to landscapes,

> I am monarch of all I *survey,*
> My right there is none to dispute.

I have frequently seen a poet withdraw, having enjoyed the most valuable part of a farm, while the crusty farmer supposed that he had got a few wild apples only. Why, the owner does not know it for many years when a poet has put his farm in rhyme, the most admirable kind of invisible fence, has fairly impounded it, milked it, skimmed it, and got all the cream, and left the farmer only the skimmed milk.

The real attractions of the Hollowell farm, to me, were: its complete retirement, being about two miles from the village, half a mile from the nearest neighbor, and separated from the highway by a broad field; its bounding on the river, which the owner said protected it by its fogs and frosts in the spring, though that was nothing to me; the gray color and ruinous state of the house and barn, and the dilapidated fences, which put such an interval between me and the last occupant; the hollow and lichen-covered apple trees, gnawed by rabbits, showing what kind of neighbors I should have; but above all, the recollection I had of it from my earliest voyages up the river, when the house was concealed behind a dense grove of red maples, through which I heard the house-dog bark. I was in haste to buy it, before the proprietor finished getting out some rocks, cutting down the hollow apple trees, and grubbing up some young birches which had sprung up in the pasture, or, in short, had made any more of his improvements. To enjoy these advantages I was ready to carry it on, like Atlas, to take the world on my shoulders — I never heard what compensation he received for that — and do all those things which had no other motive or excuse but that I might pay for it and be unmolested in my possession of it; for I knew all the while that it would yield the most abundant crop of the kind I wanted if I could only afford to let it alone. But it turned out as I have said.

All that I could say, then, with respect to farming on a large scale (I have always cultivated a garden) was that I had had my seeds ready. Many think that seeds improve with age. I have no doubt that time discriminates between the good and the bad; and when at last I shall plant, I shall be less likely to be disappointed. But I would say to my fellows, once for all: as long as possible live free and uncommitted. It makes but little difference whether you are committed to a farm or the county jail.

Old Cato, whose "De Re Rustica" is my "Cultivator," says, and the only translation I have seen makes sheer nonsense of the passage, "When you think of getting a farm, turn it thus in your mind, not to buy greedily; nor spare your pains to look at it, and do not think it enough to go around it once. The oftener you go there the more it will please you, if it is good." I think I shall not buy greedily, but go round and round it as long as I live, and be buried in it first, that it may please me the more at last.

The present was my next experiment of this kind, which I purpose to describe more at length, for convenience putting the experience of two years into one. As I have said, I do not propose to write an ode to dejection, but to brag as lustily as chanticleer in the morning standing on his roost, if only to wake my neighbors up.

When first I took up my abode in the woods, that is, began to spend my nights as well as days there, which, by accident, was on Independence day, or the fourth of July, 1845, my house was not finished for winter, but was merely a defense against the rain, without plastering or chimney, the walls being of rough weather-stained boards, with wide chinks, which made it cool at night. The upright white hewn studs and freshly planed door and window casings gave it a clean and airy look, especially in the morning, when its timbers were saturated with dew, so that I fancied that by noon some sweet gum would exude from them. To my imagination it retained throughout the day more or less of this auroral character, reminding me of a certain house on a mountain which I had visited the year before. This was an airy and unplastered cabin, fit to entertain a traveling god, and where a goddess might trail her garments. The winds which passed over my dwelling were such as sweep over the ridges of mountains, bearing the broken strains, or celestial parts only, of terrestrial music. The morning wind forever blows, the poem of creation is uninterrupted; but few are the ears that hear it. Olympus is but the outside of the earth everywhere.

The only house I had been the owner of before, if I except a boat, was a tent, which I used occasionally when making excursions in the summer, and this is still rolled up in my garret; but the boat, after passing from hand to hand, has gone down the stream of time. With this more substantial shelter about me, I had made some progress toward settling in the world. This frame, so slightly clad, was a sort of crystallization around me, and reacted on the builder. It was suggested somewhat as a picture in outlines. I did not need to go outdoors to take the air, for the atmosphere within had lost none of its freshness. It was not so much within doors as behind a door where I sat, even in the rainiest weather. The Harivansa says, "An abode without birds is like a meat without seasoning." Such was not my abode, for I found myself suddenly neighbor to the birds, not by having imprisoned one, but having caged myself near them. I was not only nearer to some of those which commonly frequent the garden and the orchard, but to those wilder and more thrilling songsters of the forest which never, or rarely, serenade a villager: the woodthrush, the veery, the scarlet tanager, the field-sparrow, the whippoorwill, and many others.

I was seated by the shore of a small pond, about a mile and a half south of the village of Concord and somewhat higher than it, in the midst of an extensive wood between that town and Lincoln, and about two miles south of that our only field known to fame, Concord Battle Ground; but I was so low in the woods that the opposite shore, half a mile off, like the rest, covered with wood, was my most distant horizon. For the first week, whenever I looked out on the pond, it impressed me like a tarn high up on the side of a mountain, its bottom far above the surface of other lakes, and as the sun arose, I saw it throwing off its nightly clothing of mist, and here and there, by degrees, its soft ripples or its smooth reflecting surface was revealed, while the mists, like ghosts, were stealthily withdrawing in every direction into the woods, as at the breaking up of some nocturnal conventicle. The very dew seemed to hang upon the trees later into the day than usual, as on the sides of mountains.

This small lake was of most value as a neighbor in the intervals of a gentle rain storm in August, when, both air and water being perfectly still, but the sky overcast, mid-afternoon had all the serenity of evening, and the wood-thrush sang around, and was heard from shore to shore. A lake like this is never smoother than at such a time; and, the clear portion of the air above it being shallow and darkened by clouds, the water, full of light and reflections, becomes a lower heaven itself so much the more important. From a hilltop near by, where the wood had been recently cut off, there was a pleasing vista southward across the pond, through a wide indentation in the hills which form the shore there, where their opposite sides sloping toward each other suggested a stream flowing out in that direction through a wooded valley, but stream there was none. That way I looked between and over the near green hills to some distant and higher ones in the horizon, tinged with blue. Indeed, by standing on tiptoe I could catch a glimpse of some of the peaks of the still bluer and more distant mountain ranges in the northwest, those true-blue coins from heaven's own mint, and also of some portion of the village. But in other directions, even from this point, I could not see over or beyond the woods which surrounded me. It is well to have some water in your neighborhood to give buoyancy to and float the earth. One value even of the smallest well is that when you look into it you see that earth is not continent but insular. This is as important as that it keeps butter cool. When I looked across the pond from this peak toward the Sudbury meadows, which in time of flood I distinguished elevated perhaps by a mirage in their seething valley, like a coin in a basin, all the earth beyond the pond appeared like a thin crust insulated and floated even by this small sheet of intervening water, and I was reminded that this on which I dwelt was but dry land.

Though the view from my door was still more contracted, I did not feel crowded or confined in the least. There was pasture enough for my imagination. The low shrub-oak plateau to which the opposite shore arose stretched away toward the prairies of the West and the steppes of Tartary, affording ample room for all the roving families of men. "There are none happy in the world but beings who enjoy freely a vast horizon," said Damodara, when his herds required new and larger pastures.

Both place and time were changed, and I dwelt nearer to those parts of the universe and to those eras in history which had most attracted me. Where I lived was as far off as many a region viewed nightly by astronomers. We are wont to imagine rare and delectable places in some remote and more celestial corner of the system, behind the constellation of Cassiopeia's Chair, far from noise and disturbance. I discovered that my house actually had its site in such a withdrawn, but forever new and unprofaned, part of the universe. If it were worth the while to settle in those parts near to the Pleiades or the Hyades, to Aldebaran or Altair, then I was really there, or at an equal remoteness from the life which I had left behind, dwindled and twinkling with as fine a ray to my nearest neighbor, and to be seen only in moonless nights by him. Such was that part of creation where I had squatted:

> There was a shepherd that did live,
> And held his thoughts as high
> As were the mounts whereon his flocks
> Did hourly feed him by.

What should we think of the shepherd's life if his flocks always wandered to higher pastures than his thoughts?

Every morning was a cheerful invitation to make my life of equal simplicity, and I may say innocence, with Nature herself. I have been as sincere a worshiper of Aurora as the Greeks. I got up early and bathed in the pond; that was a religious exercise, and one of the best things which I did. They say that characters were engraven on the bathing tub of King Tching-thang to this effect: "Renew thyself completely each day; do it again and again, and forever again." I can understand that. Morning brings back the heroic ages. I was as much affected by the faint hum of a mosquito making its invisible and unimaginable tour through my apartments at earliest dawn, when I was sitting with door and windows open, as I could be by any trumpet that ever sang of fame. It was Homer's requiem;

itself an Iliad and Odyssey in the air, singing its own wrath and wanderings. There was something cosmical about it, a standing advertisement, till forbidden, of the everlasting vigor and fertility of the world. The morning, which is the most memorable season of the day, is the awakening hour. Then there is least somnolence in us; and for an hour, at least, some part of us awakes which slumbers all the rest of the day and night. Little is to be expected of that day, if it can be called a day, to which we are not awakened by our Genius, but by the mechanical nudgings of some servitor, are not awakened by our own newly acquired force and aspirations from within, accompanied by the undulations of celestial music, instead of factory bells, and a fragrance filling the air — to a higher life than we fell asleep from; and thus the darkness bears its fruit, and proves itself to be good, no less than the light. That man who does not believe that each day contains an earlier, more sacred, and auroral hour than he has yet profaned has despaired of life, and is pursuing a descending and darkening way. After a partial cessation of his sensuous life, the soul of man, or its organs rather, are reinvigorated each day, and his Genius tries again what noble life it can make. All memorable events, I should say, transpire in morning time and in a morning atmosphere. The Vedas say, " All intelligences awake with the morning." Poetry and art and the fairest and most memorable of the actions of men date from such an hour. All poets and heroes, like Memnon, are the children of Aurora and emit their music at sunrise. To him whose elastic and vigorous thought keeps pace with the sun the day is a perpetual morning. It matters not what the clocks say or the attitudes and labors of men. Morning is when I am awake and there is a dawn in me. Moral reform is the effort to throw off sleep. Why is it that men give so poor an account of their day if they have not been slumbering? They are not such poor calculators. If they had not been overcome with drowsiness they would have performed something. The millions are awake enough for physical labor; but only one in a million is awake enough for effective intellectual exertion, only one in a hundred millions to a poetic or divine life. To be awake is to be alive. I have never yet met a man who was quite awake. How could I have looked him in the face?

We must learn to reawaken and keep ourselves awake, not by mechanical aids, but by an infinite expectation of the dawn, which does not forsake us in our soundest sleep. I know of no more encouraging fact than the unquestionable ability of man to elevate his life by a conscious endeavor. It is something to be able to paint a particular picture, or to carve a statue, and so to make a few objects beautiful; but it is far more glorious to carve and paint the very atmosphere and medium through which we look, which morally we can do. To affect the quality of the day, that is the highest of arts. Every man is tasked to make his life, even in its details, worthy of the contemplation of his most elevated and critical hour. If we refused, or rather used up, such paltry information as we get, the oracles would distinctly inform us how this might be done.

I went to the woods because I wished to live deliberately, to front only the essential facts of life, and see if I could not learn what it had to teach, and not, when I came to die, discover that I had not lived. I did not wish to live what was not life, living is so dear; nor did I wish to practice resignation, unless it was quite necessary. I wanted to live deep and suck out all the marrow of life, to live so sturdily and Spartan-like as to put to rout all that was not life, to cut a broad swath and shave close, to drive life into a corner, and reduce it to its lowest terms, and, if it proved to be mean, why then to get the whole and genuine meanness of it, and publish its meanness to the world; or if it were sublime, to know it by experience, and be able to give a true account of it in my next excursion. For most men, it appears to me, are in a strange uncertainty about it, whether it is of the devil or of God, and have somewhat hastily concluded that it is the chief end of man here to " glorify God and enjoy him forever."

Still we live meanly, like ants, though the fable tells us that we were long ago changed into men; like pygmies we fight with cranes; it is error upon error, and clout upon clout, and our best virtue has for its occasion a superfluous and evitable wretchedness. Our life is frittered away by detail. An honest man has hardly need to count more than his ten fingers, or in extreme cases he may add his ten toes, and lump the rest. Simplicity, simplicity, simplicity! I say, let your affairs be as two or three, and not a hundred or a thousand; instead of a million count half a dozen, and keep your accounts on your thumb nail. In the midst of this chopping sea of civilized life, such are the clouds and storms and quicksands and thousand-and-one items to be allowed for, that a man has to live, if he would not founder and go to the bottom and not make his port at all, by dead reckoning, and he must be a great calculator indeed who succeeds. Simplify, simplify. Instead of three meals a day, if it be necessary eat but one; instead of a hundred dishes, five; and reduce other things in proportion. Our life is like a German Confederacy, made up of petty states, with its boundary forever fluctuating so that even a German cannot tell you how it is bounded at any moment. The nation itself, with all its so-called internal improvements, which, by the way, are all external and superficial, is just such an unwieldy and overgrown establishment, cluttered with furniture and tripped up by its own traps, ruined by luxury and heedless expense, by want of calculation and a worthy aim, as the million households in the land; and the only cure for it, as for them, is in a rigid economy, a stern and more than Spartan simplicity of life and elevation of purpose. It lives too fast. Men think that it is essential that the nation have commerce, and export ice, and talk through a telegraph, and ride thirty miles an hour, without a doubt, whether they do or not; but whether we should live like baboons or like men is a little uncertain. If we do not get out sleepers, and forge rails, and devote days and nights to the work, but go to tinkering upon our lives to improve them, who will build railroads? And if railroads are not built, how shall we get to heaven in season? But if we stay at home and mind our business, who will want railroads? We do not ride on the railroad; it rides upon us. Did you ever think what those sleepers are that underlie the railroad? Each one is a man, an Irishman, or a Yankee man. The rails are laid on them, and they are covered with sand, and the cars run smoothly over them. They are sound sleepers, I assure you. And every few years a new lot is laid down and run over; so that, if some have the pleasure of riding on a rail, others have the misfortune to be ridden upon. And when they run over a man that is walking in his sleep, a supernumerary sleeper in the wrong position, and wake him up, they suddenly stop the cars and make a hue and cry about it, as if this were an exception. I am glad to know that it takes a gang of men for every five miles to keep the sleepers down and level in their beds as it is, for this is a sign that they may sometime get up again.

Why should we live with such hurry and waste of life? We are determined to be starved before we are hungry. Men say that a stitch in times saves nine, and so they take a thousand stitches today to save nine tomorrow. As for work, we haven't any of any consequence. We have the Saint Vitus's dance, and cannot possibly keep our heads still. If I should only give a few pulls at the parish bell-rope, as for a fire, that is, without setting the bell, there is hardly a man on his farm in the out-skirts of Concord, notwithstanding that press of engagements which was his excuse so many times this morning, nor a boy, nor a woman, I might almost say, but would forsake all and follow that sound, not mainly to save property from the flames, but, if we will confess the truth, much more to see it burn, since burn it must, and we, be it known, did not set it on fire —or to see it put out, and have a hand in it, if that is done as handsomely; yes, even if it were the parish church itself. Hardly a man takes a half hour's nap after dinner but when he wakes he holds up his head and asks, "What's the news?" as if the rest of mankind had stood his sentinels. Some give directions to be waked every half hour, doubtless for no other purpose; and then, to pay for it, they tell what they have dreamed. After a night's sleep the news is as indispensable as the breakfast. "Pray tell me anything new that has happened to a man anywhere on this globe," and he reads it over his coffee and rolls that a man has had his eyes gouged out this morning on the Wachito River, never dreaming the while that he lives in the dark unfathomed mammoth cave of this world and has but the rudiment of an eye himself.

For my part, I could easily do without the post office. I think that there are very few important communications made through it. To speak critically, I never received more than one or two letters in my life — I wrote this some years ago — that were worth the postage. The pennypost is, commonly, an institution through which you seriously offer a man that penny for his thoughts which is too often safely offered in jest. And I am sure that I never read any memorable news in a newspaper. If we read of one man robbed, or murdered, or killed by accident, or one house burned, or one vessel wrecked, or one steamboat blown up, or one cow run over on the Western Railroad, or one mad dog killed, or one lot of grasshoppers in the winter, we never need read of another. One is enough. If you are acquainted with the principle, what do you care for a myriad instances and applications? To a philosopher all *news,* as it is called, is gossip, and they who edit and read it are old women over their tea. Yet not a few are greedy after this gossip. There was such a rush, as I hear, the other day at one of the offices to learn the foreign news by the last arrival that several large squares of plate glass belonging to the establishment were broken by the pressure, news which I seriously think a ready wit might write a twelvemonth, or twelve years, beforehand with sufficient accuracy. As for Spain, for instance, if you know how to throw in Don Carlos and the Infanta, and Don Pedro and Seville and Granada, from time to time in the right proportions — they may have changed the names a little since I saw the papers — and serve up a bull-fight when other entertainments fail, it will be true to the letter, and give us as good an idea of the exact state or ruin of things in Spain as the most succinct and lucid reports under this head in the newspapers; and as for England, almost the last significant scrap of news from that quarter was the revolution of 1649; and if you have learned the history of her crops for an average year, you never need attend to that thing again, unless your speculations are of a merely pecuniary character. If one may judge who rarely looks into the newspapers, nothing new does ever happen in foreign parts, a French revolution not excepted.

What news! how much more important to know what that is which was never old! " Kieou-he-yu (great dignitary of the state of Wei) sent a man to Khoung-tseu to know his news. Khoung-tseu caused the messenger to be seated near him, and questioned him in these terms: What is your master doing? The messenger answered with respect: My master desires to diminish the number of his faults, but he cannot come to the end of them. The messenger being gone, the philosopher re-marked: What a worthy messenger! What a worthy mes-senger! " The preacher, instead of vexing the ears of drowsy farmers on their day of rest at the end of the week -- for Sunday is the fit conclusion of an ill-spent week, and not the fresh and brave beginning of a new one — with this one other draggletail of a sermon, should shout with thundering voice, " Pause! Avast! Why so seeming fast, but deadly slow? "

Shams and delusions are esteemed for soundest truths, while reality is fabulous. If men would steadily observe realities only and not allow themselves to be deluded, life, to compare it with such things as we know, would be like a fairy tale and the Arabian Nights' Entertainments. If we respected only what is inevitable and has a right to be, music and poetry would resound along the streets. When we are unhurried and wise, we perceive that only great and worthy things have any permanent and absolute existence, that petty fears and petty pleasures are but the shadow of the reality. This is always exhilarating and sublime. By closing the eyes and slumbering, and consenting to be deceived by shows, men establish and confirm their daily life of routine and habit everywhere, which still is built on purely illusory foundations. Children, who play life, discern its true law and relations more clearly than men, who fail to live it worthily, but who think that they are wiser by experience, that is, by failure. I have read in a Hindoo book, that " there was a king's son, who, being expelled in infancy from his native city, was brought up by a forester, and, growing up to maturity in that state, imagined himself to belong to the barbarous race with which he lived. One of his father's ministers, having discovered him, revealed to him what he was, and the misconception of his character was removed, and he knew himself to be a prince." " So the soul," continues the Hindoo philosopher, " from the circumstances in which it is placed, mistakes its own character, until the truth is revealed to it by some holy teacher, and then it knows itself to be *Brahm.*" I perceive that we inhabitants of New England live this mean life that we do because our vision does not penetrate the surface of things. (We think that that *is* which *appears* to be.) If a man should walk through this town and see only the reality, where, think you, would the " Mill-dam " go to? If he should give us an account of the realities he beheld there, we should not recognize the place in his description. Look at a meeting-house, or a court-house, or a jail, or a shop, or a dwelling-house, and say what that thing really is before a true gaze, and they would all go to pieces in your account of them. Men esteem truth remote, in the outskirts of the system, behind the farthest star, before Adam and after the last man. In eternity there is indeed something true and sublime. But all these times and places and occasions are now and here. God himself culminates in the present moment, and will never be more divine in the lapse of all the ages. And we are enabled to apprehend at all what is sublime and noble only by the perpetual instilling and drenching of the reality that surrounds us. The universe constantly and obediently answers to our conceptions; whether we travel fast or slow, the track is laid for us. Let us spend our lives in conceiving them. The poet or the artist never yet had so fair and noble a design but some of his posterity at least could accomplish it.

Let us spend one day as deliberately as Nature, and not be thrown off the track by every nutshell and mosquito's wing that falls on the rails. Let us rise early and fast, or breakfast gently and without perturbation; let company come and let company go, let the bells ring and the children cry — determined to make a day of it. Why should we knock under and go with the stream? Let us not be upset and overwhelmed in that terrible rapid and whirlpool called a dinner, situated in the meridian shallows. Weather this danger and you are safe, for the rest of the way is down hill. With unrelaxed nerves, with morning vigor, sail by it, looking another way, tied to the mast like Ulysses. If the engine whistles, let it whistle till it is hoarse for its pains. If the bell rings, why should we run? We will consider what kind of music they are like. Let us settle ourselves and work and wedge our feet downward through the mud and slush of opinion, and prejudice, and tradition, and delusion, and appearances, that allusion which covers the globe, through Paris and London, through New York and Boston and Concord, through church and state, through poetry and philosophy and religion, till we come to a hard bottom and rocks in place, which we can call reality, and say, This is, and no mistake; and then begin, having a *point d'appui,* below freshet and frost and fire, a place where you might found a wall or a state, or set a lamp-post safely, or perhaps a gauge, not a nilometer, but a "realometer," that future ages might know how deep a freshet of shams and appearances had gathered from time to time. If you stand right fronting and face to face to a fact, you will see the sun glimmer on both its surfaces, as if it were a cimeter, and feel its sweet edge dividing you through the heart and marrow, and so you will happily conclude your mortal career. Be it life or death, we crave only reality. If we are really dying, let us hear the rattle in our throats and feel cold in the extremities; if we are alive, let us go about our business.

Time is but the stream I go a-fishing in. I drink at it; but while I drink I see the sandy bottom and detect how shallow it is. Its thin current slides away, but eternity remains. I would drink deeper; fish in the sky, whose bottom is pebbly with stars. I cannot count one. I know not the first letter of the alphabet. I have always been regretting that I was not as wise as the day I was born. The intellect is a cleaver; it discerns and rifts its way into the secret of things. I do not wish to be any more busy with my hands than is necessary. My head is hands and feet. I feel all my best faculties concentrated in it. My instinct tells me that my head is an organ for burrowing, as some creatures use their snout and fore-paws, and with it I would mine and burrow my way through these hills. I think that the richest vein is somewhat hereabouts; so by the divining rod and thin rising vapors I judge; and here I will begin to mine.

APPRECIATION HELPS

1. Why did Thoreau go to the woods?
2. What, according to him, are the inconveniences of property? Does his attitude appeal to you as reasonable?
3. Do you discover places where the author is inconsistent?
4. What did he learn from his experience?
5. Discuss his estimate of the post office.
6. Discuss: " A man is rich in proportion to the number of things which he can afford to let alone."
7. Explain: " I retained the landscape and I have since annually carried off what it yielded without a wheelbarrow."
8. Explain: " We do not ride on the railroad; it rides upon us."
9. Do you agree that our " life is frittered away by detail "?
10. Has there been any value to others in this experiment of Thoreau's? Give reasons for your answer.
11. Explain: " My head is hands and feet."

COMPOSITION HINTS

1. Things I Could Do Without
2. Hunting with a Camera
3. Harvesting the Landscape
4. My Summer in the Woods
5. Shams and Delusions
6. The Streams I Go A-Fishing In
7. The Pleasures of Early Rising

BENJAMIN FRANKLIN

Of the great men who created the United States of America, Benjamin Franklin (1706–1790) is probably the one whose life most closely resembles the ideal fruitful career which, it is laid down, the Republic holds open to even the least of its citizens. Those other founders all started as somebodies. Franklin was the son of a small Boston tallow chandler and soapboiler, he went out into the world to work for his living at the age of thirteen, and yet, notwithstanding those humble beginnings, he became a hero of the War of Independence, the greatest of American diplomatists, and the only American scientist of his day.

His elder brother James was a printer and it was to him that little Ben was apprenticed. He developed rapidly into the splendid type of craftsman printer now all too rare in these days of linotypes. He not only took a craftsman's delight in the type which he set; he was also interested in the words into which that type grew. Thus, after trying out his pen in anonymous articles contributed to his brother's newspaper, the *New England Courant,* he actually wrote a pamphlet to refute a book which he had been setting. In the year 1934, when each compositor has to set so fast and gets only fragmentary takes, such a feat would be impossible, but two hundred years ago, in spite of the time which the hand setter perforce spent on his copy, and the custom of letting one man set a whole book, for a printer to turn in such a way on the hand that fed him, as it were, was very remarkable, and the author of this pamphlet attracted more attention than did the contents of his book.

Franklin found printing a very useful trade. For example, when he paid his first visit to London in 1724, he had been promised a letter of credit, but the bank knew nothing of it. So, instead of starving or seeking charity, he at once took a job as printer in the city.

He set up in business for himself in 1728 in Philadelphia and made a name with *Poor Richard's Almanac.* In 1736 he became clerk of the General Assembly of Pennsylvania and in 1751 an Assemblyman. From 1753 to 1774 he did pioneer work in building up a post office in the Keystone State. As a diplomatist, he visited London on two missions, the first in 1757 being successful, but the second, in 1774, leading to his loss of the post office. When he went to France in June, 1776, he found himself the most talked-of man in the world at Paris, and brought off his most notable diplomatic achievement, the conclusion of the treaty of alliance with France. As a scientist he devised the lightning-rod and bifocal glasses for the eyes. He was an early advocate of the abolition of slavery.

But his life was so filled with interesting events that the only thing for any boy or girl to do is to get hold of his *Autobiography* and read about them in his own words.

THE ART OF PROCURING PLEASANT DREAMS

As a great part of our life is spent in sleep during which we have sometimes pleasant and sometimes painful dreams, it becomes of some consequence to obtain the one kind and avoid the other; for whether real or imaginary, pain is pain and pleasure is pleasure. If we can sleep without dreaming, it is well that painful dreams are avoided. If while we sleep we can have any pleasing dream, it is, as the French say, *autant de gagné,* so much added to the pleasure of life.

To this end it is, in the first place, necessary to be careful in preserving health, by due exercise and great temperance; for, in sickness, the imagination is disturbed, and disagreeable, sometimes terrible, ideas are apt to present themselves. Exercise should precede meals, not immediately follow them; the first promotes, the latter, unless moderate, obstructs digestion. If, after exercise, we feed sparingly, the digestion will be easy and good, the body lightsome, the temper cheerful, and all the animal functions performed agreeably. Sleep, when it follows, will be natural and undisturbed; while indolence, with full feeding, occasions nightmares and horrors inexpressible; we fall from precipices, are assaulted by wild beasts, murderers, and demons, and experience every variety of distress. Observe, however, that the quantities of food and exercise are relative things; those who move much may, and indeed ought to eat more; those who use little exercise should eat little. In general, mankind, since the improvement of cookery, eat about twice as much as nature requires. Suppers are not bad, if we have not dined; but restless nights naturally follow hearty suppers after full dinners. Indeed, as there is a difference in constitutions, some rest well after these meals; it costs them only a frightful dream and an apoplexy, after which they sleep till doomsday. Nothing is more common in the newspapers, than instances of people who, after eating a hearty supper, are found dead abed in the morning.

Another means of preserving health, to be attended to, is the having a constant supply of fresh air in your bedchamber. It has been a great mistake, the sleeping in rooms exactly closed, and in beds surrounded by curtains. No outward air that may come in to you is so unwholesome as the unchanged air, often breathed, of a close chamber. As boiling water does not grow hotter by longer boiling, if the particles that receive greater heat can escape; so living bodies do not putrefy, if the particles, so fast as they become putrid, can be thrown off. Nature expels them by the pores of the skin and the lungs, and in a free, open air they are carried off; but in a close room we receive them again and again, though they become more and more corrupt. A number of persons crowded into a small room thus spoil the air in a few minutes, and even render it mortal, as in the Black Hole at Calcutta. A single person is said to spoil only a gallon of air per minute, and therefore requires a longer time to spoil a chamber-full; but it is done, however, in proportion, and many putrid disorders hence have their origin. It is recorded of Methusalem, who, being the longest liver, may be supposed to have best preserved his health, that he slept always in the open air; for, when he had lived five hundred years, an angel said to him: " Arise, Methusalem, and build thee an house, for thou shalt live yet five hundred years longer." But Methusalem answered, and said, "If I am to live but five hundred years longer, it is not worth while to build me an house; I will sleep in the air, as I have been used to do." Physicians, after having for ages contended that the sick should not be indulged with fresh air, have at length discovered that it may do them good. It is therefore to be hoped, that they may in time discover likewise, that it is not hurtful to those who are in health, and that we may be then cured of the *aërophobia,* that at present distresses weak minds, and makes them choose to be stifled and poisoned, rather than leave open the window of a bedchamber, or put down the glass of a coach.

Confined air, when saturated with perspirable matter, will not receive more; and that matter must remain in our bodies, and occasion diseases; but it gives some previous notice of its being about to be hurtful, by producing certain uneasiness, slight indeed at first, which as with regard to the lungs is a trifling sensation, and to the pores of the skin a kind of restlessness, which is difficult to describe, and few that feel it know the cause of it. But we may recollect, that sometimes on waking in the night, we have, if warmly covered, found it difficult to get asleep again. We turn often without finding repose in any position. This fidgettiness (to use a vulgar expression for want of a better) is occasioned wholly by an uneasiness in the skin, owing to the retention of the perspirable matter — the bedclothes having received their quantity, and, being saturated, refusing to take any more. To become sensible of this by an experiment, let a person keep his position in the bed, but throw off the bedclothes, and suffer fresh air to approach the part uncovered of his body; he will then feel that part suddenly refreshed; for the air will immediately relieve the skin, by receiving, licking up, and carrying off, the load of perspirable matter that incommoded it. For every portion of cool air that approaches the warm skin, in receiving its part of that vapor, receives therewith a degree of heat that rarefies and renders it lighter, when it will be pushed away with its burthen, by cooler and therefore heavier fresh air, which for a moment supplies its place, and then, being likewise changed and warmed, gives way to a succeeding quantity. This is the order of nature, to prevent animals being infected by their own perspiration. He will now be sensible of the difference between the part exposed to the air and that which, remaining sunk in the bed, denies the air access; for this part now manifests its uneasiness more distinctly by the comparison, and the seat of the uneasiness is more plainly perceived than when the whole surface of the body was affected by it.

Here, then, is one great and general cause of unpleasing dreams. For when the body is uneasy, the mind will be disturbed by it, and disagreeable ideas of various kinds will in sleep be the natural consequences. The remedies, preventive and curative, follow:

1. By eating moderately (as before advised for health's sake) less perspirable matter is produced in a given time; hence the bedclothes receive it longer before they are saturated, and we may therefore sleep longer before we are made uneasy by their refusing to receive any more.

2. By using thinner and more porous bedclothes, which will suffer the perspirable matter more easily to pass through them, we are less incommoded, such being longer tolerable.

3. When you are awakened by this uneasiness, and find you cannot easily sleep again, get out of bed, beat up and turn your pillow, shake the bedclothes well, with at least twenty shakes, then throw the bed open and leave it to cool; in the meanwhile, continuing undrest, walk about your chamber till your skin has had time to discharge its load, which it will do sooner as the air may be dried and colder. When you begin to feel the cold air unpleasant, then return to your bed, and you will soon fall asleep, and your sleep will be sweet and pleasant. All the scenes presented to your fancy will be too of the pleasing kind. I am often as agreeably entertained with them, as by the scenery of an opera. If you happen to be too indolent to get

out of bed, you may, instead of it, lift up your bedclothes with one arm and leg, so as to draw in a good deal of fresh air, and by letting them fall force it out again. This, repeated twenty times, will so clear them of the perspirable matter they have imbibed, as to permit your sleeping well for sometime afterwards. But this latter method is not equal to the former.

Those who do not love trouble, and can afford to have two beds, will find great luxury in rising, when they wake in a hot bed, and going into the cool one. Such shifting of beds would also be of great service to persons ill of a fever, as it refreshes and frequently procures sleep. A very large bed, that will admit a removal so distant from the first situation as to be cool and sweet, may in a degree answer the same end.

One or two observations more will conclude this little piece. Care must be taken, when you lie down, to dispose your pillow so as to suit your manner of placing your head, and to be perfectly easy; then place your limbs so as not to bear inconveniently hard upon one another, as, for instance, the joints of your ankles; for, though a bad position may at first give but little pain and be hardly noticed, yet a continuance will render it less tolerable, and the uneasiness may come on while you are asleep, and disturb your imagination. These are the rules of the art. But, though they will generally prove effectual in producing the end intended, there is a case in which the most punctual observance of them will be totally fruitless. I need not mention the case to you, my dear friend, but my account of the art would be imperfect without it. The case is, when the person who desires to have pleasant dreams has not taken care to preserve, what is necessary above all things,

A GOOD CONSCIENCE.

APPRECIATION HELPS

1. What entertained you in this good-natured discussion of pleasant dreams?
2. Point out details which show Franklin as a practical man.
3. Do his opinions on sleep check with your own experience?

4. Do you find any health hints here that do not agree with modern science?
5. Illustrate from experience and observation: " the quantities of food and exercise are relative things."
6. Discuss the very revolutionary ideas on fresh air offered by Franklin.
7. Discuss our changing beliefs on bathing, cold baths, exercise, heavy clothing.

COMPOSITION HINTS

1. Good and Bad Dreams
2. The Art of Procuring Lively Conversation
3. The Art of Procuring Permission from Parents
4. Five Hundred Years of Living — A Blessing or a Curse
5. Plain Living — High Thinking — Happy Dreaming
6. Bedside Books
7. A Dialogue with My Conscience
8. When I Took a Bad Conscience to Bed

WILLIAM ALLEN WHITE

The following father's tribute to his dead daughter, written on the day she was buried, is a piece of work best left to itself. But something must be said about its remarkable author. It was written for the Emporia *Gazette,* of which Mr. William Allen White (b. 1868) has been owner and editor since 1895. Emporia is a town in Kansas with a population of about 10,000, and the *Gazette* is the newspaper of that small community. Yet this newspaper and its editor are known and admired throughout the United States. Such exceptional renown results from the " canny, straightforward, humane, and humorous simplicity " with which Mr. White's pen deals with local, national, or international affairs, politics, literature, or morals. Simplicity it is, of course, that keeps Mr. White in Emporia, when with his talents Kansas City, Chicago, or New York, would be only too glad to have him, although one suspects that there must be something very attractive about Emporia to retain such a clever man there. But this simplicity is of a kind that is equal to the most complex matters, and one may gauge the value placed upon Mr. White's advice in the counsels of the nation from the fact that he was to have been a representative of the United States at the abortive conference with the Bolsheviks in the island of Prinkipo in 1919. He is also a distinguished novelist, *The Court of Boyville* (1899) containing illuminating episodes of small town life and *A Certain Rich Man* (1909) being deemed one of the best American novels. He is a national figure of independence, courage, and talent. He was educated at the University of Kansas.

MARY WHITE[1]

THE Associated Press reports carrying the news of Mary White's death declared that it came as the result of a fall from a horse. How she would have hooted at that! She never fell from a horse in her life. Horses have fallen on her and with her — " I'm always trying to hold 'em in my lap," she used to say. But she was proud of few things, and one was that she could ride anything that had four legs and hair. Her death resulted not from a fall, but from a blow on the head which fractured her skull, and the blow came from the limb of an overhanging tree on the parking.

The last hour of her life was typical of its happiness. She came home from a day's work at school, topped off by a hard grind with the copy on the High School Annual, and felt that a ride would refresh her. She climbed into her khakis, chattering to her mother about the work she was doing, and hurried to get her horse and be out on the dirt roads for the country air and the radiant green fields of the spring. As she rode through the town on an easy gallop she kept waving at passers-by. She knew every one in town. For a decade the little figure with the long pigtail and the red hair ribbon has been familiar on the streets of Emporia, and she got in the way of speaking to those who nodded at her. She passed the Kerrs, walking the horse, in front of the Normal Library, and waved at them; passed another friend a few hundred feet farther on, and waved at her. The horse was walking and as she turned into North Merchant Street she took off her cowboy hat, and the horse swung into a lope. She passed the Tripletts and waved her cowboy hat at them, still moving gaily north on Merchant Street. A *Gazette* carrier passed — a high-school boy friend — and she waved at him, but with her bridle hand; the horse veered quickly, plunged into the parking where the low-hanging limb faced her, and, while she still looked back waving, the blow came. But she did not fall from the horse; she

[1] From the Emporia *Gazette*, by permission of the author.

slipped off, dazed a bit, staggered, and fell in a faint. She never quite recovered consciousness.

But she did not fall from the horse, neither was she riding fast. A year or so ago she used to go like the wind. But that habit was broken, and she used the horse to get into the open to get fresh, hard exercise, and to work off a certain surplus energy that welled up in her and needed a physical outlet. That need has been in her heart for years. It was back of the impulse that kept the dauntless, little brown-clad figure on the streets and country roads of this community and built into a strong, muscular body what had been a frail and sickly frame during the first years of her life. But the riding gave her more than a body. It released a gay and hardy soul. She was the happiest thing in the world. And she was happy because she was enlarging her horizon. She came to know all sorts and conditions of men. Charley O'Brien, the traffic cop, was one of her best friends. W. L. Holtz, the Latin teacher, was another. Tom O'Connor, farmer-politician, and Rev. J. H. J. Rice, preacher and police judge, and Frank Beach, music master, were her special friends, and all the girls, black and white, above the track and below the track, in Pepville and Stringtown, were among her acquaintances. And she brought home riotous stories of her adventures. She loved to rollick; persiflage was her natural expression at home. Her humor was a continual bubble of joy. She seemed to think in hyperbole and metaphor. She was mischievous without malice, as full of faults as an old shoe. No angel was Mary White, but an easy girl to live with, for she never nursed a grouch five minutes in her life.

With all her eagerness for the out-of-doors, she loved books. On her table when she left her room were a book by Conrad, one by Galsworthy, *Creative Chemistry* by E. E. Slosson, and a Kipling book. She read Mark Twain, Dickens, and Kipling before she was ten — all of their writings. Wells and Arnold Bennett particularly amused and diverted her. She was entered as a student in Wellesley in 1922; was assist-ant editor of the High School Annual this year, and in line for election to the editorship of the Annual next year. She was a member of the executive committee of the High School Y. W. C. A.

Within the last two years she had begun to be moved by an ambition to draw. She began as most children do by scribbling in her school books, funny pictures. She bought cartoon magazines and took a course — rather casually, naturally, for she was, after all, a child, with no strong purposes — and this year she tasted the first fruits of success by having her pictures accepted by the High School Annual. But the thrill of delight she got when Mr. Ecord, of the Normal Annual, asked her to do the cartooning for that book this spring was too beautiful for words. She fell to her work with all her enthusiastic heart. Her drawings were accepted, and her pride — always repressed by a lively sense of the ridiculousness of the figure she was cutting — was a really gorgeous thing to see. No successful artist ever drank a deeper draft of satisfaction than she took from the little fame her work was getting among her schoolfellows. In her glory, she almost forgot her horse — but never her car.

For she used the car as a jitney bus. It was her social life. She never had a " party " in all her nearly seventeen years — wouldn't have one; but she never drove a block in the car in her life that she didn't begin to fill the car with pick-ups! Everybody rode with Mary White — white and black, old and young, rich and poor, men and women. She liked nothing better than to fill the car full of long-legged high-school boys and an occasional girl, and parade the town. She never had a " date," nor went to a dance, except once with her brother, Bill, and the " boy proposition " didn't interest her — yet. But young people — great, spring-breaking, varnish-cracking, fender-bending, door-sagging carloads of " kids " — gave her great pleasure. Her zests were keen. But the most fun she ever had in her life was acting as chairman of the committee that got up the big turkey dinner for the poor folks at the county home; scores of pies, gallons of slaw, jam, cakes, preserves, oranges, and a wilderness of turkey were loaded in the car and taken to the county home. And, being of a practical turn of mind, she risked her own Christmas dinner by staying to see that the poor folks actually got it all. Not that she was a cynic; she just disliked to tempt folks. While there she found a blind colored uncle, very old, who could do nothing but make rag rugs, and she rustled up from her school friends rags enough to keep him busy for a season. The last engagement she tried to make was to take the guests at the county home out for a car ride. And the last endeavor of her life was to try to get a rest room for colored girls in the high school. She found one girl reading in the toilet, because there was no better place for a colored girl to loaf, and it inflamed her sense of injustice and she became a nagging harpy to those who she thought could remedy the evil.

The poor she had always with her, and was glad of it. She hungered and thirsted for righteousness; and was the most impious creature in the world. She joined the Congregational Church without consulting her parents; not particularly for her soul's good. She never had a thrill of piety in her life, and would have hooted at a " testimony." But even as a little child she felt the church was an agency for helping people to more of life's abundance, and she wanted to help. She never wanted help for herself. Clothes meant little to her. It was a fight to get a new rig on her; but eventually a harder fight to get it off. She never wore a jewel and had no ring but her high-school class ring, and never asked for anything but a wrist watch. She refused to have her hair up, though she was nearly seventeen. " Mother," she protested, " you don't know how much I get by with, in my braided pigtails, that I could not with my hair up." Above every other passion of her life was her passion not to grow up, to be a child. The tomboy in her, which was big, seemed to loathe to be put away forever in skirts. She was a Peter Pan, who refused to grow up.

Her funeral yesterday at the Congregational Church was as she would have wished it; no singing, no flowers save the big bunch of red roses from her Brother Bill's Harvard classmen — Heavens, how proud that would have made her! and the red roses from the *Gazette* force — in vases at her head and feet. A short prayer, Paul's beautiful essay on "Love," from the thirteenth chapter of First Corinthians, some remarks about her democratic spirit by her friend, John H. J. Rice, pastor and police judge, which she would have deprecated if she could, a prayer sent down for her by her friend, Carl Nau, and opening the service the slow, poignant movement from Beethoven's Moonlight Sonata, which she loved, and closing the service a cutting from the joyously melancholy first movement of Tschaikowski's *Symphonie Pathétique,* which she liked to hear in certain moods on the phonograph; then the Lord's Prayer by her friends in the high school.

That was all.

For her pallbearers only her friends were chosen: her Latin teacher, W. L. Holtz; her high-school principal, Rice Brown; her doctor, Frank Foncannon; her friend, W. W. Finney; her pal at the *Gazette* office, Walter Hughes; and her brother Bill. It would have made her smile to know that her friend, Charley O'Brien, the traffic cop, had been transferred from Sixth and Commercial to the corner near the church to direct her friends who came to bid her good-by.

A rift in the clouds in a gray day threw a shaft of sunlight upon her coffin as her nervous, energetic little body sank to its last sleep. But the soul of her, the glowing, gorgeous, fervent soul of her, surely was flaming in eager joy upon some other dawn.

APPRECIATION HELPS

1. In what ways is Mary White representative of the best type of high-school girl?
2. Point out instances which reveal her democratic spirit.
3. What rank would you give Mary White on service, leadership, and character, were she a candidate for the national honor society?
4. Discuss her tastes in reading. With which authors are you familiar?
5. What in the essay tells you that her father, William Allen White, understood young people?

6. Literature has many poems written in honor of the dead: Milton's "Lycidas"; Shelley's "Adonais"; Tennyson's "In Memoriam." Which ones have you read?
7. Emerson's "Threnody" is the tribute of a father for his child. Read it.
8. Discuss the essay as a memorial for a daughter written by her father. Point out intensely human details.

COMPOSITION HINTS

1. When Clothes Meant Little to Me
2. When We Delivered a Christmas Dinner
3. The Most Generous Person I Know
4. Reforms Needed in My School
5. A Peter Pan of My Acquaintance
6. What I Have Learned from Mary White

RALPH WALDO EMERSON

The following essay on " Self-Reliance " is a plea for each man to be as original as he can, yet its author, Ralph Waldo Emerson (1803–1882), had little or no originality in him. Some of his opinions differed from those held by the people among whom he was living, and he was self-reliant enough to sacrifice himself for those opinions, retiring from the ministry of the Second Unitarian Church of Boston. But that brave action and the heretical view which prompted it are forgotten now, whereas his writings, which are free of anything so defiant, live on. What is the reason for their immortality?

The world certainly needs original thinkers, but it also needs equally writers who will point out what is good and why it is so. Emerson was this latter kind of writer, and a most excellent one too. He had conventional literary taste and a steady charm and serenity of mind.

He set his hand to many other tasks before he wrote his best essays, *English Traits,* which were published in 1856. The son of a Unitarian minister and a graduate of Harvard, he taught for three years in his brother's school. Then he studied for the Unitarian ministry, but his studies were philosophical and literary rather than theological. Next he took several trips abroad for his health.

After his retirement from the church at Boston, he continued to preach, and again visited England and the Mediterranean, meeting the English authors Landor, Coleridge, Carlyle, and Wordsworth. On his return to America he became a lecturer and met with tremendous success. The essayist is only a condensation of the lecturer. In his essays Emerson's style is clear in sentences, but obscure in paragraphs.

From 1835, in which year he remarried, his first wife having died, he lived at Concord in Massachusetts, the native town of his second wife, and thus he grew to be called the Sage of Concord. It is his sagacity that is still valued today.

The *Essays* are published in two series, and " Self-Reliance " is in the first of these. The first part of it — not quite half — is given here.

SELF–RELIANCE

I READ the other day some verses written by an eminent painter which were original and not conventional. The soul always hears an admonition in such lines, let the subject be what it may. The sentiment they instill is of more value than any thought they may contain. To believe your own thought, to believe that what is true for you in your private heart is true for all men — that is genius. Speak your latent conviction, and it shall be the universal sense; for the inmost in due time becomes the outmost, — and our first thought is rendered back to us by trumpets of the Last Judgment. Familiar as the voice of the mind is to each, the highest merit we ascribe to Moses, Plato, and Milton is, that they set at naught books and traditions, and spoke not what men, but what they thought. A man should learn to detect and watch that gleam of light which flashes across his mind from within, more than the luster of the firmament of bards and sages. Yet he dismisses without notice his thought, because it is his. In every work of genius we recognize our rejected thoughts; they come back to us with a certain alienated majesty. Great works of art have no more affecting lesson for us than this. They teach us to abide by our spontaneous impression with good-humored inflexibility then most when the whole cry of voices is on the other side. Else, tomorrow a stranger will say with masterly good sense precisely what we have thought and felt all the time, and we shall be forced to take with shame our own opinion from another.

There is a time in every man's education when he arrives at the conviction that envy is ignorance; that imitation is suicide; that he must take himself for better, for worse, as his portion; that, though the wide universe is full of good, no kernel of nourishing corn can come to him but through his toil bestowed on that plot of ground which is given to him to till. The power which resides in him is new in nature, and none but he knows what that is which he can do, nor does he know until he has tried. Not for nothing one face, one character, one fact, makes much impression on him, and another none. This sculpture in the memory is not without preëstablished harmony. The eye was placed where one ray should fall, that it might testify of that particular ray. We but half express ourselves, and are ashamed of that divine idea which each of us represents. It may be safely trusted as proportionate and of good issues, so it be faithfully imparted, but God will not have his work made manifest by cowards. A man is relieved and gay when he has put his heart into his work and done his best; but what he has said or done otherwise, shall give him no peace. It is a deliverance which does not deliver. In the attempt his genius deserts him; no muse befriends; no invention, no hope.

Trust thyself: every heart vibrates to that iron string. Accept the place the divine providence has found for you, the society of your contemporaries, the connection of events. Great men have always done so, and confided themselves child-like to the genius of their age, betraying their perception that the absolutely trustworthy was seated at their heart, working through their hands, predominating in all their being. And we are now men, and must accept in the highest mind the same transcendent destiny; and not minors and invalids in a protected corner, not cowards fleeing before a revolution, but guides, redeemers, and benefactors, obeying the Almighty effort, and advancing on Chaos and the Dark.

What pretty oracles nature yields us on this text in the face and behavior of children, babes, and even brutes! That divided and rebel mind, that distrust of a sentiment because our arithmetic has computed the strength and means opposed to our purpose, these have not. Their mind being whole, their eye is as yet unconquered, and when we look in their faces, we are disconcerted. Infancy conforms to nobody: all conform to it, so that one babe commonly makes four or five out of the adults who prattle and play to it. So God has armed youth and puberty and manhood no less with its own piquancy and charm, and made it enviable and gracious and its claims not to be put by, if it will stand by itself. Do not think the youth has no force, because he cannot speak to you and me. Hark! in the next room his voice is sufficiently clear and emphatic. It seems he knows how to speak to his contemporaries. Bashful or bold, then, he will know how to make us seniors very unnecessary.

The nonchalance of boys who are sure of a dinner, and would disdain as much as a lord to do or say aught to conciliate one, is the healthy attitude of human nature. A boy is in the parlor what the pit is in the playhouse; independent, irresponsible, looking out from his corner on such people and facts as pass by, he tries and sentences them on their merits, in the swift, summary way of boys, as good, bad, interesting, silly, eloquent, troublesome. He cumbers himself never about consequences, about interests; he gives an independent, genuine verdict. You must court him: he does not court you. But the man is, as it were, clapped into jail by his consciousness. As soon as he has once acted or spoken with éclat, he is a committed person, watched by the sympathy or the hatred of hundreds, whose affections must now enter into his account. There is no Lethe for this. Ah, that he could pass again into his neutrality! Who can thus avoid all pledges and, having observed, observe again from the same unaffected, unbiased, unbribable, unaffrighted innocence, must always be formidable. He would utter opinions on all passing affairs, which being seen to be not private, but necessary, would sink like darts into the ear of men, and put them in fear.

These are the voices which we hear in solitude, but they grow faint and inaudible as we enter into the world. Society everywhere is in conspiracy against the manhood of every one of its members. Society is a joint-stock company, in which the members agree, for the better securing of his bread to each shareholder, to surrender the liberty and culture of the eater. The virtue in most request is conformity. Self-reliance is its aversion. It loves not realities and creators, but names and customs.

Whoso would be a man must be a nonconformist. He who would gather immortal palms must not be hindered by the name of goodness, but must explore if it be goodness. Nothing is at last sacred but the integrity of your own mind. Absolve you to yourself, and you shall have the suffrage of the world. I remember an answer which when quite young I was prompted to make to a valued adviser, who was wont to importune me with the dear old doctrines of the church. On my saying, What have I to do with the sacredness of traditions, if I live wholly from within? my friend suggested: " But these impulses may be from below, not from above." I replied: " They do not seem to me to be such; but if I am the Devil's child, I will live then from the Devil." No law can be sacred to me but that of my nature. Good and bad are but names very readily transferable to that or this; the only right is what is after my constitution, the only wrong is against it. A man is to carry himself in the presence of all opposition, as if everything were titular and ephemeral but he. I am ashamed to think how easily we capitulate to badges and names, to large societies and dead institutions. Every decent and well-spoken individual affects and sways me more than is right. I ought to go upright and vital, and speak the rude truth in all ways. If malice and vanity wear the coat of philanthropy, shall that pass? If an angry bigot assumes this bountiful cause of Abolition, and comes to me with his last news from Barbados, why should I not say to him: " Go love thy infant; love thy woodchopper; be good-natured and modest: have that grace, and never varnish your hard, uncharitable ambition with this incredible tenderness for black folk a thousand miles off. Thy love afar is spite at home." Rough and graceless would be such greeting, but truth is handsomer than the affectation of love. Your goodness must have some edge to it, — else it is none. The doctrine of hatred must be preached as the counteraction of the doctrine of love when that pules and whines. I shun father and mother and wife and brother, when my genius calls me. I

would write on the lintels of the doorpost, *Whim*. I hope
it is somewhat better than whim at last, but we cannot spend
the day in explanation. Expect me not to show cause why I
seek or why I exclude company. Then, again, do not tell me,
as a good man did today, of my obligation to put all poor men
in good situations. Are they *my* poor? I tell thee, thou foolish
philanthropist, that I grudge the dollar, the dime, the cent, I
give to such men as do not belong to me and to whom I do not
belong. There is a class of persons to whom by all spiritual
affinity I am bought and sold; for them I will go to prison,
if need be; but your miscellaneous popular charities; the education at college of fools; the building of meeting-houses to
the vain end to which many now stand; alms to sots, and the
thousandfold relief societies; — though I confess with shame
I sometimes succumb and give the dollar, it is a wicked dollar
which by and by I shall have the manhood to withhold.

Virtues are, in the popular estimate, rather the exception
than the rule. There is the man *and* his virtues. Men do
what is called a good action, as some piece of courage or
charity, much as they would pay a fine in expiation of daily
nonappearance on parade. Their works are done as an apology or extenuation of their living in the world, — as invalids
and the insane pay a high board. Their virtues are penances.
I do not wish to expiate, but to live. My life is for itself and
not for a spectacle. I much prefer that it should be of a lower
strain, so it be genuine and equal, than that it should be glittering and unsteady. I wish it to be sound and sweet, and not
to need diet and bleeding. I ask primary evidence that you
are a man, and refuse this appeal from the man to his actions.
I know that for myself it makes no difference whether I do or
forbear those actions which are reckoned excellent. I cannot
consent to pay for a privilege where I have intrinsic right.
Few and mean as my gifts may be, I actually am, and do not
need for my own assurance or the assurance of my fellows any
secondary testimony.

What I must do is all that concerns me, not what the people
think. This rule, equally arduous in actual and in intellectual

life, may serve for the whole distinction between greatness and meanness. It is the harder, because you will always find those who think they know what is your duty better than you know it. It is easy in the world to live after the world's opinion; it is easy in solitude to live after our own; but the great man is he who in the midst of the crowd keeps with perfect sweetness the independence of solitude.

The objection to conforming to usages that have become dead to you is, that it scatters your force. It loses your time and blurs the impression of your character. If you maintain a dead church, contribute to a dead Bible society, vote with a great party either for the government or against it, spread your table like base housekeepers, — under all these screens I have difficulty to detect the precise man you are. And, of course, so much force is withdrawn from your proper life. But do your work, and I shall know you. Do your work, and you shall reinforce yourself. A man must consider what a blindman's-buff is this game of conformity. If I know your sect, I anticipate your argument. I hear a preacher announce for his text and topic the expediency of one of the institutions of his church. Do I not know beforehand that not possibly can he say a new and spontaneous word? Do I not know that, with all this ostentation of examining the grounds of the institution, he will do no such thing? Do I not know that he is pledged to himself not to look but at one side, — the permitted side, not as a man, but as a parish minister? He is a retained attorney, and these airs of the bench are the emptiest affectation. Well, most men have bound their eyes with one or another handkerchief, and attached themselves to some one of these communities of opinion. This conformity makes them not false in a few particulars, authors of a few lies, but false in all particulars. Their every truth is not quite true. Their two is not the real two, their four not the real four; so that every word they say chagrins us, and we know not where to begin to set them right. Meantime nature is not slow to equip us in the prison uniform of the party to which we adhere. We come to wear one cut of face and figure, and acquire by degrees the

gentlest asinine expression. There is a mortifying experience
in particular, which does not fail to wreak itself also in the
general history; I mean " the foolish face of praise," the forced
smile which we put on in company where we do not feel at
ease in answer to conversation which does not interest us. The
muscles, not spontaneously moved, but moved by a low usurp-
ing wilfulness, grow tight about the outline of the face with
the most disagreeable sensation.

For nonconformity the world whips you with its displeasure.
And therefore a man must know how to estimate a sour face.
The bystanders look askance on him in the public street or in
the friend's parlor. If this aversion had its origin in contempt and resistance like his own, he might well go home
with a sad countenance; but the sour faces of the multitude,
like their sweet faces, have no deep cause, but are put on and
off as the wind blows and a newspaper directs. Yet is the discontent of the multitude more formidable than that of the
senate and the college. It is easy enough for a firm man who
knows the world to brook the rage of the cultivated classes.
Their rage is decorous and prudent, for they are timid as being
very vulnerable themselves. But when to their feminine rage
the indignation of the people is added, when the ignorant and
the poor are aroused, when the unintelligent brute force that
lies at the bottom of society is made to growl and mow, it needs
the habit of magnanimity and religion to treat it godlike as a
trifle of no concernment.

The other terror that scares us from self-trust is our consistency, a reverence for our past act or word, because the
eyes of others have no other data for computing our orbit than
our past acts, and we are loath to disappoint them.

But why should you keep your head over your shoulder?
Why drag about this corpse of your memory, lest you contradict somewhat you have stated in this or that public place?
Suppose you should contradict yourself; what then? It seems
to be a rule of wisdom never to rely on your memory alone,
scarcely even in acts of pure memory, but to bring the past
for judgment into the thousand-eyed present, and live ever in

a new day. In your metaphysics you have denied personality to the Deity: yet when the devout motions of the soul come, yield to them heart and life, though they should clothe God with shape and color. Leave your theory, as Joseph his coat in the hand of the harlot, and flee.

A foolish consistency is the hobgoblin of little minds, adored by little statesmen and philosophers and divines. With consistency a great soul has simply nothing to do. He may as well concern himself with his shadow on the wall. Speak what you think now in hard words, and tomorrow speak what tomorrow thinks in hard words again, though it contradict everything you said today. " Ah, so you shall be sure to be misunderstood." Is it so bad, then, to be misunderstood? Pythagoras was misunderstood, and Socrates, and Jesus, and Luther, and Copernicus, and Galileo, and Newton, and every pure and wise spirit that ever took flesh. To be great is to be misunderstood.

I suppose no man can violate his nature. All the sallies of his will are rounded in by the law of his being, as the inequalities of Andes and Himmaleh are insignificant in the curve of the sphere. Nor does it matter how you gauge and try him. A character is like an acrostic or Alexandrian stanza; — read it forward, backward, or across, it still spells the same thing. In this pleasing contrite wood-life, which God allows me, let me record day by day my honest thought without prospect or retrospect, and, I cannot doubt, it will be found symmetrical, though I mean it not and see it not. My book should smell of pines and resound with the hum of insects. The swallow over my window should interweave that thread or straw he carries in his bill into my web also. We pass for what we are. Character teaches above our wills. Men imagine that they communicate their virtue or vice only by overt actions, and do not see that virtue or vice emits a breath every moment.

There will be an agreement in whatever variety of actions, so they be each honest and natural in their hour. For of one will, the actions will be harmonious, however unlike they seem.

These varieties are lost sight of at a little distance, at a little
height of thought. One tendency unites them all. The voyage
of the best ship is a zigzag line of a hundred tacks. See the
line from a sufficient distance, and it straightens itself to the
average tendency. Your genuine action will explain itself, and
will explain your other genuine actions. Your conformity explains nothing. Act singly, and what you have already done
singly will justify you now. Greatness appeals to the future.
If I can be firm enough today to do right, and scorn eyes, I
must have done so much right before as to defend me now.
Be it how it will, do right now. Always scorn appearances, and
you always may. The force of character is cumulative. All
the foregone days of virtue work their health into this. What
makes the majesty of the heroes of the senate and the field,
which so fills the imagination? The consciousness of a train of
great days and victories behind. They shed a united light
on the advancing actor. He is attended as by a visible escort
of angels. That is it which throws thunder into Chatham's
voice, and dignity into Washington's port, and America into
Adams's eye. Honor is venerable to us because it is no
ephemeris. It is always ancient virtue. We worship it today
because it is not of today. We love it and pay it homage, because it is not a trap for our love and homage, but is self-
dependent, self-derived, and therefore of an old immaculate
pedigree, even if shown in a young person.

I hope in these days we have heard the last of conformity
and consistency. Let the words be gazetted and ridiculous
henceforward. Instead of the gong for dinner, let us hear a
whistle from the Spartan fife. Let us never bow and apologize
more. A great man is coming to eat at my house. I do not
wish to please him; I wish that he should wish to please me.
I will stand here for humanity, and though I would make it
kind, I would make it true. Let us affront and reprimand the
smooth mediocrity and squalid contentment of the times, and
hurl in the face of custom, and trade, and office, the fact which
is the upshot of all history, that there is a great responsible
Thinker and Actor working wherever a man works; that a true

man belongs to no other time or place, but is the center of things. Where he is, there is nature. He measures you, and all men, and all events. Ordinarily, everybody in society reminds us of somewhat else, or of some other person. Character, reality, reminds you of nothing else; it takes place of the whole creation. The man must be so much, that he must make all circumstances indifferent. Every true man is a cause, a country, and an age; requires infinite spaces and numbers and time fully to accomplish his design; — and posterity seems to follow his steps as a train of clients. A man Caesar is born, and for ages after we have a Roman Empire. Christ is born, and millions of minds so grow and cleave to his genius, that he is confounded with virtue and the possible of man. An institution is the lengthened shadow of one man; as Monachism, of the Hermit Antony; the Reformation, of Luther; Quakerism, of Fox; Methodism, of Wesley; Abolition, of Clarkson. Scipio, Milton called "the height of Rome"; and all history resolves itself very easily into the biography of a few stout and earnest persons.

Let a man then know his worth, and keep things under his feet. Let him not peep or steal, or skulk up and down with the air of a charity-boy, a bastard, or an interloper, in the world which exists for him. But the man in the street, finding no worth in himself which corresponds to the force which built a tower or sculptured a marble god, feels poor when he looks on these. To him a palace, a statue, or a costly book has an alien and forbidding air, much like a gay equipage, and seems to say like that, "Who are you, sir?" Yet they all are his suitors for his notice, petitioners to his faculties that they will come out and take possession. The picture waits for my verdict: it is not to command me, but I am to settle its claims to praise. That popular fable of the sot who was picked up dead drunk in the street, carried to the duke's house, washed and dressed and laid in the duke's bed, and, on his waking, treated with all obsequious ceremony like the duke, and assured that he had been insane, owes its popularity to the fact, that it symbolizes so well the state of man who is in the world a sort of sot, but now and then wakes up, exercises his reason and finds himself a true prince.

Our reading is mendicant and sycophantic. In history our imagination plays us false. Kingdom and lordship, power and estate, are a gaudier vocabulary than private John and Edward in a small house and common day's work; but the things of life are the same to both; the sum total of both is the same. Why all this deference to Alfred and Scanderbeg and Gustavus? Suppose they were virtuous; did they wear out virtue? As great a stake depends on your private act today, as followed their public and renowned steps. When private men shall act with original views the luster will be transferred from the actions of kings to those of gentlemen.

The world has been instructed by its kings, who have so magnetized the eyes of nations. It has been taught by this colossal symbol the mutual reverence that is due from man to man. The joyful loyalty with which men have everywhere suffered the king, the noble, or the great proprietor to walk among them by a law of his own, make his own scale of men and things and reverse theirs, pay for benefits not with money but with honor, and represent the law in his person, was the hieroglyphic by which they obscurely signified their consciousness of their own right and comeliness, the right of every man.

APPRECIATION HELPS

1. Give examples from the essay of what Emerson means by self-reliance.
2. From your own experience give examples of self-reliance.
3. What makes this an imperative message to young people?
4. What things destroy self-reliance?
5. Discuss Emerson's ideas on nonconformity.
6. Discuss his ideas on consistency.
7. Illustrate five great truths of the essay with examples from your own experience and observation.
8. Select ten terse sayings from the essay which you enjoyed.
9. Explain: " Whoso would be a man must be a nonconformist." " What I must do is all that concerns me, not what the people

think."   "If I know your sect, I anticipate your argument."
"A foolish consistency is the hobgoblin of little minds."   "Our
reading is mendicant and sycophantic."

10. Do you agree with most of what Emerson has said?   Is it
necessary to agree with an author?   Does Emerson constantly
challenge your thought?

COMPOSITION HINTS

1. When I Was a Nonconformist
2. Why I Dislike Conformity
3. Foolish Consistencies I Have Observed
4. Do We Surrender Our Liberty to Society?
5. Emerson's Challenge to My Thinking

WILLIAM LYON PHELPS

Professor William Lyon Phelps is one of the few men surviving in the United States with the courage to ride a bicycle. That is probably one reason why Yale men (he was until he retired recently Lampson professor of English at Yale) affectionately call him Billy behind his back. Other reasons may be that he is a crack tennis-player and not such a crack (as he himself would admit) short-stop on the faculty baseball team. The strongest evidence of his endearing boyishness — Billiness, one might say — is that he is not only short-stop, but the star reporter of the baseball games. One typical comment of his in a report has become immortal: "Our team was greatly strengthened by the loss of our stand-by, Nettleton, from center field."

He is indeed a man of superabundant energy. His classes are large, but they leave him free not only for cycling, tennis, baseball, reporting, but also for music and for writing and editing. He is the president of the New Haven Symphony Orchestra, has written a score of books himself, and edited perhaps another thirty. Among those from his own pen are: *The Advance of the English Novel* (1916), *Reading the Bible* (1919), *Human Nature in the Bible* (1922). He has edited an edition of Richardson's novels in twenty volumes and recently he produced a volume of *Selected Stories from Kipling*. He conducts a department of comment in *Scribner's,* "As I Like It." *What I Like* (1933) is a delightful collection of prose writings Mr. Phelps likes and has compiled. He likes the selections of Hudson, Santayana, and Franklin included in *Essays Old and New.*

Almost his whole life has been passed in New Haven, for he was born there in 1865, graduated there in 1887, and was on the faculty there from 1891 to 1933.

The following essay reveals the ability of a famous scholar to talk about baseball in a way every boy will enjoy.

THE GREAT AMERICAN GAME[1]

BASEBALL is truly an American game. It is native and has never really flourished elsewhere. In its speed, skill, and brevity it seems particularly adapted to our high nervous tension. It lasts about as long as a theatre play and resembles that form of entertainment in more ways than one. The mystery of hero and villain is discovered in about two hours, sometimes at the rate of a thrill a minute. Frequently the unexpected happens. Victory suddenly emerges from the very core of defeat.

A DRAMATIC ENDING

In one of his poems Browning says, " Sudden the worst turns the best to the brave." No player should ever give up until the last man is out and the score is history. I remember a game between Yale and Princeton where in the ninth inning with Princeton two runs ahead and Yale at bat, two men out and one runner on first base a freshman, Arthur Camp, stepped to the plate. He obtained two strikes. The grand stand reverberated with thousands of retreating feet, for many people apparently attend a game or a drama in order to see how speedily they may escape. What do you suppose these " quitters " do with the time they have saved by beating the crowd to the exits? They seem so pathetically anxious to save it that they ought to employ it in some high and noble public service.

Well, as I was saying, young Camp stepped to the bat to the accompaniment of marching feet, all marching away from the game. With two strikes and the Princeton substitutes packing up the bats, he knocked a home run; the score was tied, for he brought in Fincke ahead of him, who had had the good sense to wait for a base on balls and thus play the game even in the face of almost certain defeat.

[1] From *Essays on Things*, published by the Macmillan Company, 1930.

This drive by Camp changed the aspect of the universe; we traveled with incredible speed from the other place to Paradise; and Princeton, who were already "Fletcherizing" the sweet morsel of victory, found in Scriptural language that they had filled their belly with the east wind. The game went to the tenth inning; but what a difference! Princeton's bright confidence was sicklied o'er with the pale cast of thought, whereas the sons of Eli, who a moment before had felt that the bitterness of death was past and were resigned to their fate, were now yelling like timber wolves that smell blood. In the extra innings Princeton got nothing; each batsman fought as one who beats the air. Yale came to the plate, and a boy named Letton knocked out another home run, having learned from a freshman that it was a simple thing to do.

Just before Camp hit the ball a girl sitting next to me soliloquized sadly, "I have never seen Yale beaten before." I replied, "But you are going to now." Camp's bat made the fitting comment on my inaccuracy. His home run was like one of those delightful footnotes in Wells's "Outline of History" where the expert who really knows what he is talking about emphatically contradicts the statement in the text.

I remember another occasion, when Yale and Princeton were playing the third game for the championship in New York, the Tigers went to bat in the ninth inning, five runs behind. Two men went out, one of them being caught at the plate. The air resounded with the noise of false prophets hurrying away from the stands. But by a combination of steady hits from Princeton, assisted by the most weird errors of the Yale infield (Frank, I know you will never be able to forget), the Jerseymen made six runs, and Yale went to bat in the last half of the ninth, knowing their task was hopeless. And it was.

There were thousands of persons who thought they had been present at a Yale victory, and they did not find out the truth until the Sunday paper contained what seemed to their disordered minds an account of some other game. That particular ninth inning gives me a slight nausea even now; yet it is one of the imperishable stars in Princeton's crown.

It is often said that college students take athletic contests too seriously; my own feeling in the matter is that they do not take them seriously enough. If you play a game with all your might, determined by every honorable means to win, then not only do you enjoy the game by self-effacement but the struggle is good discipline; in later life you will play hard to win some game where the stakes are of more lasting importance. But if you take the attitude that it is "only a game" and are neither elated by victory nor depressed by defeat, there is something wrong in you, something fundamentally wrong that is bound in maturer years to develop into a fatal illness of the spirit.

Of course I know that I shall probably be misunderstood for writing the preceding paragraph. I will risk that, however, for no player except a cheater is worse than one who is indifferent. In defeat congratulate your opponent heartily and never in any circumstance make any excuses; but please suffer inwardly. Outwardly look and inwardly feel like Esther in the Apocrypha: "Her countenance was cheerful and very amiable; but her heart was in anguish."

I remember when I was an undergraduate the professor of physics called on one of my classmates to recite. The young man said, "I don't know," took his zero and sat down. Feeling that nothing worse could happen to him, he glanced idly out of the window. "But don't dismiss the subject from your mind!" cried the professor.

If baseball is worth playing, it is worth training for. And the very sacrifices demanded in training are not only wholesomely beneficial; they ought to be actually delightful to those who really love baseball. One of the greatest athletic leaders Harvard ever had was Captain Winslow, in 1885. He announced at the beginning of the season that faithfulness in discipline would be demanded of every candidate. It so happened that a veteran on the team and one who was regarded as the best player in college had a gay evening. He was informed by Captain Winslow that his services would not be required at all that year. The offender and his friends were thunderstruck; they could not believe that the captain really meant it; many declared that without the veteran victory could not be won. "Then we shall lose," said Captain Winslow. The star did not play in a single game. But the nine not only won the championship; they were never once defeated!

Alonzo Stagg of Yale was a severe disciplinarian. A veteran player broke training on the Easter trip. The experience did not hurt him, but to his amazement he was not permitted to play till the last game of the season toward the end of June. He was then so "sharp-set" that he made a home run and helped to win the championship for Yale.

It is often said that the British do not care whether they win or lose, that they play only for the sake of the sport. Do not believe such nonsense for a moment; there are no people in the world who feel worse under defeat than Englishmen, which is one reason why they are such good sports. They fight hard and hate to be beaten.

The successful professional baseball player is almost always high-strung, eager, with nerves on edge; and, though it is necessary that he should be punished for losing his temper in public, it should be remembered that he would not lose his temper at all if he were not so keen to win. He should therefore be fined and forgiven. The unpardonable sin is not to care; to look upon playing as most failures regard their daily work; namely, as a disagreeable job that must be endured for the money and the leisure hours it brings, both of which can be spent in pleasure. This is the highway to failure in all undertakings; to believe that there is no pleasure in the work itself but only in the time spent away from it.

LOVE OF THE GAME

I remember years ago that a reporter interviewed a number of professional ball players, and asked them all this question: Do you enjoy playing? One after another answered in the negative. "How do you expect a man is going to enjoy himself sweating under a broiling sun?" "Think what rotten treatment we get from spectators when we make an error! " " The whole thing is just one hard grind with no fun in it! " Then the reporter reached old McGuire, a seasoned veteran; he said, " Like it? I love it! I love everything about it. I love the morning practice. I love going out to the game with the other boys in the bus. I love the warming-up. I love the game itself, and I love to talk it over in the evening." I admired McGuire after reading that.

The greatest ball player of all time is undoubtedly Tyrus Raymond Cobb of Detroit. He has played in the major league eighteen consecutive years and is the most valuable asset a nine ever had. Even now as I write this article, late in August, he and Sisler are fighting for the premier honors in batting. He is a great outfielder, a base runner of positive genius, and a man who in every game for eighteen years has done his utmost to win. He has never spared himself, but has thrown his body and soul into every contest. He once told me that toward the end of a season, if the championship was within reach and yet doubtful, he could not sleep, but sat up in bed night after night, thinking out plays. His mind in a game is as active as his body, and his successful batting, which often means that he makes a two-base hit where another would make a single, comes from outguessing his opponents. He knows when to pretend to run and when to run. The other day he said something that ought to be remembered. Detroit had won the game, but he had failed to hit once. Knowing how eager he was to lead the league in batting, a reporter said to him, " Too bad, Ty, you didn't get a hit today." Cobb instantly replied, " But we won the game. That's all that counts." It is his unquenchable zest as well as his bodily skill and activity that has helped to place him on an eminence in the national game where no rival, living or dead, can hope to stand.

I think the following all-professional nine would be hard to beat: Radbourn, Mathewson, Alexander, pitchers; Ewing, Kelley, Bennett, catchers; Anson, Tenney, Sisler, first base; Lajoie, E. Collins, Young, second base; Wagner, Scott, O. Bush, shortstop; Groh, Latham, White, third base; Cobb, Speaker,

Ruth, Hornsby, Tiernan, Hines, Hanlon, Crawford, Donlin, Williams, outfield. I do not say that this is the finest group of players imaginable, for I don't know that, but simply that they would be hard to beat. Every man was or is an artist.

But I think I know for certain who was the greatest pitcher of all time. His name is Radbourn. When I remember that in 1884 he won the championship for Providence by *pitching every day* toward the end of the season I think his record never has been and never will be equaled.

And as Radbourn is the greatest of all pitchers, so Amos Alonzo Stagg is unquestionably the first of college pitchers. Remember what he accomplished. He pitched for Yale in five successive years, 1886, 1887, 1888, 1889, 1890, and Yale won the championship over Harvard and over Princeton every one of those years. Stagg headed the batting order for most of that period, was a daring and successful base runner and fielded his position with extraordinary skill and judgment. He never had either blinding speed or remarkable curves, but he had almost perfect control and never forgot a batsman. If a batsman faced him once, Stagg discovered immediately that man's weakness, and always thereafter gave him just the ball most awkward to hit. It was nothing short of uncanny. Carter, another great college pitcher, had more speed and more deceptive curves than Stagg. But in his freshman year the captain would not allow him to pitch; in his sophomore year, when he was at his best, he was defeated in the final game by Harvard, Jack Highlands pitching against him; in his senior year his arm gave out, so that he could not pitch. The only year therefore in which he won a championship by pitching was his junior year. He was undoubtedly a great ball player and in championship contests actually played at one time or another pitcher, catcher, first base, second base, third base, and the outfield — an extraordinary record; and he became a fine batsman. But I submit that as a pitcher his career does not compare with that of Stagg.

HIS LAST GAME

Stagg's last game, in 1890, was the most thrilling. Princeton had been beaten, and Yale and Harvard had a game apiece. It was the last inning, with Harvard at the bat. Harvard was two runs behind, and two were out, but it had three men on bases and the redoubtable Dudley Dean at the plate. Stagg gave him a base on balls, forcing in one run — it excites me even now so that I find it almost as difficult to hit the right keys on the typewriter as the next Harvard batsman found it hard to hit the ball. As a matter of fact, Stagg forced him to hit weakly to Billy Dalzell at shortstop (good old Bill), who threw him out at first. The game was over; Yale had won for the fifth successive year, and Stagg retired like a glorious sunset.

It is curious how much more one man can make out of a position than another can. Right field always used to be regarded as the least important of the nine places. But Alfred Ripley, now president of the Merchants National Bank in Boston and a member of the Yale corporation, playing that humble position for Yale in his undergraduate days, in one game threw out four men at first base on ground hits, all of which looked to the spectator perfectly safe.

Although I yield to no one in my admiration for the game of football, there is one respect in which baseball is more agreeable to watch. The spectator actually sees every play, and, whether the umpire is right or wrong, every onlooker sees exactly what happens. But in football the umpire is all important, and yet as a rule when a touchdown is disallowed or a penalty is inflicted no one in the vast concourse has the slightest idea why. Furthermore, the technique of football is so complicated that only a few people who watch the game understand and appreciate the skill or lack of it displayed in the line, whereas the footwork, handwork, and headwork in a game of baseball are instantly apparent to nearly every man among the twenty thousand who are looking on. There is perhaps nothing in the world where proficiency is so understood and appreciated as in baseball. It would be wonderful if the fine arts of music and acting could be exhibited before audiences as competent as the horde who shout their approval or disapproval at the national game.

It is unfortunate that the ethics of amateur baseball are still so deplorable — beneath comparison with the ethics of golf or tennis. What would be thought of a golf or a tennis player who should attempt to " rattle " his opponent by jeering at him just as he was about to execute a difficult stroke? Yet such is the regular and apparently approved practice in baseball. It is simply one more proof that man as an individual can be both reasonable and gentlemanly; put him in a group and he becomes one of a pack of wild beasts.

College baseball teams are inclined to depend too much on the coach. He should train them of course and give them the benefit of his knowledge, skill, and experience, but it is an unpleasant though common sight to see a college man at bat looking anxiously at the coach on the bench to see whether he should try to bunt, to hit, or should wait for a base on balls. As the coach has it in his power to raise or lower the ethics of the game so far as his pupils are concerned, he should be selected with as much reference to his character as to his ability. Here is the place where the standards of behavior on the field can best be raised, and it is pleasant to observe that already much progress has been made in that direction. The ethics of college baseball have advanced enormously over the standards of twenty-five years ago, and they should continue to rise. One of the finest things that ever happened in baseball history was when the Harvard supporters, after their team had been defeated in the final game with Yale in 1922, actually cheered Aldrich, the Yale captain. Harvard should be prouder of that than of victory.

APPRECIATION HELPS

1. In what ways is baseball truly an American game?
2. Point out touches which tell you that Mr. Phelps is interested

in English literature as well as in baseball. How many literary allusions do you find? List them.

3. How does Mr. Phelps's early experience contribute to the convincingness of this article?
4. What may be gained by the student who takes athletic contests seriously?
5. Why ought one to " suffer inwardly " in defeat?
6. Does the author convince you that " faithfulness in discipline " is necessary?
7. Why must the real player love the game? Illustrate from your personal observation.
8. Have you enjoyed this informal discussion about a familiar sport and its players?
9. Contrast football and baseball.
10. Are the " ethics of amateur baseball deplorable " today?

COMPOSITION HINTS

1. " Sudden the Worst Turns the Best to the Brave "
2. " Fletcherizing " the Sweet Morsel of Victory
3. Play the Game
4. When the Score Was Tied
5. Better than Victory
6. His Last Game
7. Are the Ethics of Amateur Baseball Deplorable?
8. What Counts in Winning the Game

LAFCADIO HEARN

A man may be failing to succeed or to attain contentment simply because he has not yet found the right thing to do or the most congenial place in which to live: that is the encouragement to be derived from a consideration of the career of Lafcadio Hearn (1850–1904). He was forty-one before he went to Japan, there at last to find peace and fame after a life of loneliness and disagreeable toil.

Lafcadio is a quaint Christian name for a fellow to bear. It is not surprising to learn that Hearn chose it for himself when he was full-grown. He took it from his birthplace, one of the Greek Islands of the Ionian Sea, Leucadia, pronounced Lefcadia. He was the son of an Irish surgeon-major in the British Army and a Greek mother. For a time he attended the Ushaw Roman Catholic College in Durham, England. At nineteen he was thrown upon his own resources and crossed from England to the United States. But he did not find it easy to come by a livelihood. He had no gift for business or for any of the activities by which money is rapidly and easily acquired. For years he drudged in Cincinnati or New Orleans in the lower grades of newspaper work. He showed talent then, but it was not appreciated at the time, and only after his death were fragments of his writings for the press rescued from oblivion. The two little essays herewith belong to that period.

One day the editor of the New Orleans *Times-Democrat* thought he would send Hearn as correspondent to the West Indies. Hearn remained there for two years, and the result was his first published book, *Two Years in the French West Indies* (1890). Twelve months after this came out, in 1891, his newspaper sent him to Japan. There at last he found his true sphere. His newspaper connection was promptly broken and he became teacher of English in the University of Tokio. The post left him leisure in which to write, and there poured from his pen a series of books revealing

243

Japanese life to Western eyes, books full of originality, power, and literary charm.

He married a Japanese, became a naturalized Japanese citizen under the name of Yakumo Koizumi, and was converted to Buddhism. He never returned to the West.

THE MISSISSIPPI[1]

I ONCE thought, when sailing up the Ohio one bright Northern summer, that the world held nothing more beautiful than the scenery of the Beautiful River, — those voluptuous hills with their sweet feminine curves, the elfin gold of that summer haze, and the pale emerald of the river's verdure-reflecting breast. But even the loveliness of the Ohio seemed faded, and the Northern sky-blue palely cold, like the tint of iceberg pinnacles, when I beheld for the first time the splendor of the Mississippi.

"You must come on deck early tomorrow," said the kind Captain of the *Thompson Dean;* "we are entering the Sugar Country."

So I saw the sun rise over the cane-fields of Louisiana.

It rose with a splendor that recalled the manner of its setting at Memphis, but of another color; — an auroral flush of pale gold and pale green bloomed over the long fringe of cottonwood and cypress trees, and broadened and lengthened halfway round the brightening world. The glow seemed tropical, with the deep green of the trees sharply cutting against it; and one naturally looked for the feathery crests of cocoanut palms. Then the day broke gently and slowly, — a day too vast for a rapid dawn, — a day that seemed deep as Space. I thought our Northern sky narrow and cramped as a vaulted church-roof beside that sky, — a sky so softly beautiful, so purely clear in its immensity, that it made one dream of the tenderness of a woman's eyes made infinite.

[1] From G. P. Gould, *Concerning Lafcadio Hearn,* 1908, used by permission of Laura P. Gould.

And the giant river broadened to a mile, — smooth as a mirror, still and profound as a mountain lake. Between the vastness of the sky and the vastness of the stream, we seemed moving suspended in the midst of day, with only a long, narrow tongue of land on either side breaking the brightness. Yet the horizon never became wholly blue. The green-golden glow lived there all through the day; it was brightest in the south. It was so tropical, that glow; — it seemed of the Pacific, a glow that forms a background to the sight of lagoons and coral reefs and " lands where it is always afternoon."

Below this glow gleamed another golden green, the glory of the waving cane-fields beyond the trees. Huge sugar mills were breathing white and black clouds into the sky, as they masticated their mighty meal; and the smell of saccharine sweetness floated to us from either shore. Then we glided by miles of cotton-fields with their fluttering white balls; and by the mouths of broad bayous; — past swamps dark with cypress gloom, where the gray alligator dwells, and the gray Spanish moss hangs in elfish festoons from ancient trees; — past orange-trees and live-oaks, pecans and cottonwoods and broad-leaved bananas; while the green of the landscape ever varied, from a green so dark that it seemed tinged with blue to an emerald so bright that it seemed shot through with gold. The magnificent old mansions of the Southern planters, built after a generous fashion unknown in the North, with broad verandas and deliciously cool porches, and all painted white or perhaps a pale yellow, looked out grandly across the water from the hearts of shadowy groves; and, like villages of a hundred cottages, the negro quarters dotted the verdant face of the plantation with far-gleaming points of snowy whiteness.

And still that wondrous glow brightened in the south, like a far-off reflection of sunlight on the Spanish Main.

" But it does not look now as it used to in the old slave days," said the pilot, as he turned the great wheel. " The swamps were drained, and the plantations were not overgrown with cottonwood; and somehow or other the banks usen't to cave in then as they do now."

I saw indeed signs of sad ruin on the face of the great plantations; there were splendid houses crumbling to decay, and whole towns of tenantless cabins; estates of immense extent were lying almost untilled, or with only a few acres under cultivation; and the vigorous cottonwood trees had shot up in whole forests over fields once made fertile by the labor of ten thousand slaves. The scene was not without its melancholy; it seemed tinged by the reflection of a glory passed away — the glory of wealth, and the magnificence of wealth; of riches and the luxury of riches.

O fair paradise of the South, if still so lovely in thy ruin, what must thou have been in the great day of thy greatest glory!

White steamboats, heavily panting under their loads of cotton, came toiling by, and called out to us wild greeting long and shrill, until the pilot opened the lips of our giant boat, and her mighty challenge awoke a thousand phantom voices along the winding shore. Red sank the sun in a sea of fire, and bronze-hued clouds piled up against the light, like fairy islands in a sea of glory, such as were seen, perhaps, by the Adelantado of the Seven Cities.

"Those are not real clouds," said the pilot, turning to the west, his face aglow with the yellow light. "Those are only smoke clouds rising from the sugar mills of Louisiana, and drifting with the evening wind."

The daylight died away and the stars came out, but that warm glow in the southern horizon only paled, so that it seemed a little farther off. The river broadened till it looked with the tropical verdure of its banks like the Ganges, until at last there loomed up a vast line of shadows, dotted with points of light, and through a forest of masts and a host of phantom-white river boats and a wilderness of chimneys the *Thompson Dean,* singing her cheery challenge, steamed up to the mighty levee of New Orleans.

APPRECIATION HELPS

1. Find several words which embody or suggest the atmosphere of this description of the Mississippi.
2. Point out colorful verbs and adjectives which make this essay charming.
3. Discuss the contrast between the Old South and the New South. What books have you read which have given you interesting pictures of the South?

COMPOSITION HINTS

1. Sunrise over My Favorite River
2. Moonlight on My Favorite Lake
3. Elfin Gold
4. Adrift on the River
5. Seen from the Window of the Train

NEW ORLEANS[1]

by Lafcadio Hearn

GOLDEN oranges piled up in bins, — apples of the Southern Hesperides; — a melody of meridional tongues, — silky Latin tongues and their silkier patois; Chinese buyers yellow as bananas, quadroons with skin like dead gold; swarthy sailors from the Antilles; sharp odors of fruit freshly disembarked; — all the semi-tropical sights and sounds of the French market. I stood beside an orange-bin; and priced the fruit. Fifty cents a hundred! While wondering how much the fruit-vender's profit could possibly be, I was insensibly attracted by something unusual in his face — a shadow of the beauty of the antique world seemed to rest upon it. " Are you not a Greek? " I asked, for there was no mistaking the metoposcopy of that head. Yes; he was from Zante — first a sailor, now a fruit-vender; some day, perhaps, he would be a merchant.

[1] See note on last essay.

It is among those who sell, not among those who buy, that the most curious studies of human nature and of the human face are to be made in the French market. These dealers are by no means usually French, but they are mostly from the Mediterranean coasts and the Levant — from Sicily and Cyprus, Corsica and Malta, the Ionian Archipelago, and a hundred cities fringing the coasts of Southern Europe. They are wanderers, who have wandered all over the face of the earth to find rest at last in this city of the South; they are sailors who have sailed all seas, and sunned themselves at a hundred tropical ports, and finally anchored their lives by the levee of New Orleans. The Neapolitan Italian, the Spaniard, the Corsican, the Levantine Greek, seek rest from storm here, in a clime akin to their own and under a sky as divinely blue, and at a port not far distant from their beloved sea. For these Levantine sailors hate dusty inland cities and the dry air of the Great West.

If you, O reader, chance to be a child of the sea; — if, in early childhood, you listened each morning and evening to that most ancient and mystic hymn-chant of the waves, which none can hear without awe, and which no musician can learn; — if you have ever watched wonderingly the far sails of the fishing-vessels turn rosy in the blush of sunset, or silver under the moon, or golden in the glow of sunrise; — if you once breathed as your native air the divine breath of the ocean, and learned the swimmer's art from the hoary breakers, and received the Ocean-god's christening, the glorious baptism of salt, — then, perhaps, you know only too well why these sailors of the Levant cannot seek homes within the heart of the land. Twenty years may have passed since your ears last caught the thunder of that mighty ode of hexameters which the sea has always sung and will sing forever, since your eyes sought the far line where the vaulted blue of heaven touches the level immensity of rolling water, — since you breathed the breath of the ocean, and felt its clear ozone living in your veins like an elixir. Have you forgotten the mighty measure of that mighty song? Have you forgotten the divine saltiness of that unfettered wind? Is not the spell of the sea strong upon you still?

So that when the long, burning summer comes, and the city roars dustily around you, and your ears are filled with the droning hum of machinery, and your heart full of the bitterness of the struggle for life, there comes to you at long intervals in the dingy office or the crowded street some memory of white breakers and vast stretches of wrinkled sand and far-fluttering breezes that seem to whisper, " Come! "

So that when the silent night comes, — you find yourself revisiting in dreams those ocean-shores thousands of miles away. The wrinkled sand, ever shifting yet ever the same, has the same old familiar patches of vari-colored weeds and shining rocks along its level expanse; and the thunder-chant of the sea which echoes round the world, eternal yet ever new, is rolling up to heaven. The glad waves leap up to embrace you; the free winds shout welcome in your ears; white sails are shining in the west; white sea-birds are flying over the gleaming swells. And from the infinite expanse of eternal sky and everlasting sea, there comes to you, with the heavenly ocean-breeze, a thrilling sense of unbounded freedom, a delicious feeling as of life renewed, an ecstasy as of life restored. And so you start into wakefulness with the thunder of that sea-dream in your ears and tears of regret in your eyes to find about you only heat and dust and toil; the awakening rumble of traffic, and " the city sickening on its own thick breath."

And I think that the Levantine sailors dare not dwell in the midst of the land, for fear lest dreams of a shadowy sea might come upon them in the night, and phantom winds call wildly to them in their sleep, and they might awake to find themselves a thousand miles beyond the voice of the breakers.

Sometimes, I doubt not, these swarthy sellers of fruit, whose black eyes sparkle with the sparkle of the sea, and whose voices own the tones of ocean winds, sicken when a glorious breeze from the Gulf enters the city, shaking the blossoms from the magnolia trees and the orange groves. Sometimes, I doubt not, they forsake their Southern home when the dream comes upon them, and take ship for the Spanish Main. Yet I think most men may wake here from the dreams of the sea, and rest again. It is true that you cannot hear the voice of the hoary breakers in the moonlight, — only the long panting of the cotton-presses, the shouting of the boats calling upon each other through the tropical night, and the ceaseless song of night-birds and crickets. But the sea-ships, with their white wings folded, are slumbering at the wharves; the sea-winds are blowing through the moonlit streets, and from the South arises a wondrous pale glow, like the far reflection of the emerald green of the ocean. So that the Greek sailor, awakening from the vision of winds and waves, may join three fingers of his right hand, after the manner of the Eastern Church, and cross himself, and sleep again in peace.

APPRECIATION HELPS

1. Do you like the first paragraph? Why?
2. " It is among those who sell, not among those who buy, that the most curious studies of human nature and of the human face are to be made in the French market." Is this true in your locality? Describe some interesting people you have known " among those who sell."
3. Name some poems and novels which have made you feel the lure of the sea.
4. Do these bits of description reveal the interests of the author? If you have enjoyed them you would find pleasure in his *Glimpses of Unfamiliar Japan, Out of the East,* or *Kokora.*

COMPOSITION HINTS

1. The Lure of the Sea
2. Buyers and Sellers I Have Known
3. A Child of the Sea
4. The Chant of Old Ocean
5. Wind and Wave
6. When I Visited the Vegetable and Fruit Market (A Study in Color)

G. K. CHESTERTON

Mr. Gilbert Keith Chesterton is the heavyweight among famous English authors. Now, at fifty-nine, he has still an immense waistline, and ten years ago it was even greater. His girth made his friend, Mr. Bernard Shaw, who had just produced *Fanny's First Play,* describe Mr. Chesterton's own maiden dramatic effort, *Magic,* as "Fatty's First Play." His big red cheeks and his spectacles almost hide his eyes. Yet those eyes should be seen, for they reveal the mental activity always going on behind them. Mr. Chesterton is a great talker, very nimble with his mind; he is always ready with a witty answer, always finding some arresting and entertaining phrase. And he can write just as if he were speaking — not an easy thing to do. He delights in making ideas turn somersaults, and it is this which has made people eager to read what he writes, for he succeeds always in being amusing and surprising. At the same time it must be realized that he is a deeply religious Roman Catholic.

He was born in 1875 in a large district of London called Kensington, not far from the palace in which Queen Victoria was awakened early one morning to be told that she must ascend the throne of Britain although she was only seventeen. He went to a famous school situated a mile farther west. It is called St. Paul's School. In those days it stood out in the country; now it is surrounded by streets of houses, yet it has preserved its playing fields in the same inclosure as the school buildings instead of being obliged, as other big London schools have been, to transfer them to a distance. When he left St. Paul's, he was going to be a painter, and he went to study at the famous London art school, the Slade, now a part of University College. While he was there he began reviewing books about art for a magazine, and presently found himself doing so much writing that he gave up all idea of painting. Since then he has produced novels, poems, short stories, plays, essays, biographies, and literary studies. He is a tremendous worker.

251

He loves the English countryside and the foaming ale found in old wayside English inns. He lives in one of the most beautiful villages in England, Beaconsfield, from which the English statesman, Disraeli, took his new name upon being made a baron. He has twice visited America on lecture tours.

THE ROMANTIC IN THE RAIN[1]

THE middle classes of modern England are quite fanatically fond of washing; and are often enthusiastic for teetotalism. I cannot, therefore, comprehend why it is that they exhibit a mysterious dislike of rain. Rain, that inspiring and delightful thing, surely combines the qualities of these two ideals with quite a curious perfection. Our philanthropists are eager to establish public baths everywhere. Rain surely is a public bath; it might almost be called mixed bathing. The appearance of persons coming fresh from this great natural lustration is not perhaps polished or dignified; but for the matter of fact, few people are dignified when coming out of a bath. But the scheme of rain in itself is one of an enormous purification. It realizes the dream of some insane hygienist; it scrubs the sky. Its giant brooms and mops seem to reach the starry rafters and starless corners of the cosmos; it is a cosmic spring-cleaning.

If the Englishman is really fond of cold baths, he ought not to grumble at the English climate for being a cold bath. In these days we are constantly told that we should leave our little special possessions and join in the enjoyment of common social institutions and a common social machinery. I offer the rain as a thoroughly Socialistic institution. It disregards that degraded delicacy which has hitherto led each gentleman to take his shower bath in private. It is a better shower bath, because it is public and communal; and, best of all, because somebody else pulls the string.

[1] From *All Things Considered,* copyright by Dodd, Mead & Company. Inc., 1908. Published in England by A. P. Watt and Son.

As for the fascination of rain for the water-drinker, it is a fact the neglect of which I simply cannot comprehend. The enthusiastic water-drinker must regard a rainstorm as a sort of universal banquet and debauch of his own favorite beverage. Think of the imaginative intoxication of the wine-drinker if the crimson clouds sent down claret or the golden clouds hock. Paint upon primitive darkness some such scenes of apocalypse, towering and gorgeous skyscapes in which champagne falls like fire from heaven or the dark skies grow purple and tawny with the terrible colors of port. All this must the wild abstainer feel, as he rolls along in the long soaking grass, kicks his ecstatic heels to heaven, and listens to the roaring rain. It is he, the water-drinker, who ought to be the true bacchanal of the forest; for all the forests are drinking water. Moreover, the forests are apparently enjoying it; the trees rave and reel to and fro like drunken giants; they clash boughs as revelers clash cups; they roar undying thirst and howl the health of the world.

All around me as I write is a noise of Nature drinking: and Nature makes a noise when she is drinking, being by no means refined. If I count it Christian mercy to give a cup of cold water to a sufferer, shall I complain of these multitudinous cups of cold water handed round to all living things; a cup of water for every shrub; a cup of water for every weed? As Sir Philip Sidney said, their need is greater than mine — especially for water.

There is a wild garment that still carries nobly the name of a wild Highland clan: a clan come from those hills where rain is not so much an incident as an atmosphere. Surely every man of imagination must feel a tempestuous flame of Celtic romance spring up within him whenever he puts on a mackintosh. I could never reconcile myself to carrying an umbrella; it is a pompous Eastern business, carried over the heads of despots in the dry, hot lands. Shut up, an umbrella is an unmanageable walking-stick; open, it is an inadequate tent. For my part, I have no taste for pretending to be a walking pavilion; I think nothing of my hat, and precious little of my head.

If I am to be protected against wet, it must be by some closer and more careless protection, something that I can forget altogether. It might be a Highland plaid. It might be that yet more Highland thing, a mackintosh.

And there is really something in the mackintosh of the military qualities of the Highlander. The proper cheap mackintosh has a blue and white sheen as of steel or iron; it gleams like armor. I like to think of it as the uniform of that ancient clan in some of its old and misty raids. I like to think of all the Mackintoshes, in their mackintoshes, descending on some doomed Lowland village, their wet waterproofs flashing in the sun or the moon. For indeed this is one of the real beauties of rainy weather, that while the amount of original and direct light is commonly lessened, the number of things that reflect light is unquestionably increased. There is less sunshine; but there are more shiny things; such beautifully shiny things as pools and puddles and mackintoshes. It is like moving in a world of mirrors.

And indeed this is the last and not the least gracious of the causal works of magic wrought by rain; that while it decreases light, yet it doubles it. If it dims the sky, it brightens the earth. It gives the road (to the sympathetic eye) something of the beauty of Venice. Shallow lakes of water reiterate every detail of earth and sky; we dwell in a double universe. Sometimes walking upon bare and lustrous pavements, wet under numerous lamps, a man seems a black blot on all that golden looking-glass, and could fancy he was flying in a yellow sky. But wherever trees and towns hang head downwards in a pigmy puddle, the sense of Celestial topsy-turvydom is the same. This bright, wet, dazzling confusion of shape and shadow, of reality and reflection, will appeal strongly to any one with the transcendental instinct about this dreamy and dual life of ours. It will always give a man the strange sense of looking down at the skies.

APPRECIATION HELPS

1. What in the title appeals to you?
2. Do you " exhibit a mysterious dislike for rain," or do you share with Mr. Chesterton an enthusiasm for it?
3. Discuss rain as a " thoroughly Socialistic institution."
4. What are the pleasures the water-drinker should have in rain?
5. What would you include in a paragraph on the mackintosh, the umbrella, rubbers, galoshes?
6. Discuss the effect of rain on the beauty of the world. Read Stevenson's " Enjoyment of Unpleasant Places " for interesting comparisons.
7. Point out suggestive words and expressions.
8. What interests you in Mr. Chesterton's style?

COMPOSITION HINTS

1. On Shower Baths
2. On the Umbrella
3. A World of Mirrors
4. On Galoshes
5. Pools and Puddles
6. A Topsy-Turvy World

ON RUNNING AFTER ONE'S HAT[1]
by G. K. Chesterton

I FEEL an almost savage envy on hearing that London has been flooded in my absence, while I am in the mere country. My own Battersea has been, I understand, particularly favored as a meeting of the waters. Battersea was already, as I need hardly say, the most beautiful of human localities. Now that it has the additional splendor of great sheets of water, there must be something quite incomparable in the landscape (or waterscape) of my romantic town. Bat-

[1] From *All Things Considered*, copyright by Dodd, Mead & Company, Inc. 1908. Published in England by A. P. Watt and Son.

tersea must be a vision of Venice. The boat that brought the meat from the butcher's must have shot along those lanes of rippling silver with the strange smoothness of the gondola. The greengrocer who brought cabbages to the corner of the Latchmere Road must have leant upon the oar with the unearthly grace of the gondolier. There is nothing so perfectly poetical as an island; and when a district is flooded it becomes an archipelago.

Some consider such romantic views of flood or fire slightly lacking in reality. But really this romantic view of such inconveniences is quite as practical as the other. The true optimist who sees in such things an opportunity for enjoyment is quite as logical and much more sensible than the ordinary "indignant Ratepayer" who sees in them an opportunity for grumbling. Real pain, as in the case of being burnt at Smithfield or having a toothache, is a positive thing; it can be supported, but scarcely enjoyed. But, after all, our toothaches are the exception, and as for being burnt at Smithfield, it only happens to us at the very longest intervals. And most of the inconveniences that make men swear or women cry are really sentimental or imaginative inconveniences — things altogether of the mind. For instance, we often hear grown-up people complaining of having to hang about a railway station and wait for a train. Did you ever hear a small boy complain of having to hang about a railway station and wait for a train? No; for to him to be inside a railway station is to be inside a cavern of wonder and a palace of poetical pleasures. Because to him the red light and the green light on the signal are like a new sun and a new moon. Because to him when the wooden arm of the signal falls down suddenly, it is as if a great king had thrown down his staff as a signal and started a shrieking tournament of trains. I myself am of little boys' habit in this matter. They also serve who only stand and wait for the two-fifteen. Their meditations may be full of rich and fruitful things. Many of the most purple hours of my life have been passed at Clapham Junction, which is now, I suppose, under water. I have been there in many moods so fixed and mystical that the water might well have come up to my waist before I noticed it particularly. But, in the case of all such annoyances, as I have said, everything depends upon the emotional point of view. You can safely apply the test to almost every one of the things that are currently talked of as the typical nuisance of daily life.

For instance, there is a current impression that it is unpleasant to have to run after one's hat. Why should it be unpleasant to the well-ordered and pious mind? Not merely because it is running, and running exhausts one. The same people run much faster in games and sports. The same people run much more eagerly after an uninteresting little leather ball than they will after a nice silk hat. There is an idea that it is humiliating to run after one's hat, and when people say it is humiliating they mean that it is comic. It certainly is comic; but man is a very comic creature, and most of the things he does are comic — eating, for instance. And the most comic things of all are exactly the things that are most worth doing — such as making love. A man running after a hat is not half so ridiculous as a man running after a wife.

Now a man could, if he felt rightly in the matter, run after his hat with the manliest ardor and the most sacred joy. He might regard himself as a jolly huntsman pursuing a wild animal, for certainly no animal could be wilder. In fact, I am inclined to believe that hat-hunting on windy days will be the sport of the upper classes in the future. There will be a meet of ladies and gentlemen on some high ground on a gusty morning. They will be told that the professional attendants have started a hat in such-and-such a thicket, or whatever be the technical term. Notice that this employment will in the fullest degree combine sport with humanitarianism. The hunters would feel that they were not inflicting pain. Nay, they would feel that they were inflicting pleasure, rich, almost riotous pleasure, upon the people who were looking on. When last I saw an old gentleman running after his hat in Hyde Park, I told him that a heart so benevolent as his ought to be filled with peace and thanks at the thought of how much unaffected pleasure his every gesture and bodily attitude were at that moment giving to the crowd.

The same principle can be applied to every other typical domestic worry. A gentleman trying to get a fly out of the milk or a piece of cork out of his glass of wine often imagines himself to be irritated. Let him think for a moment of the patience of anglers sitting by dark pools, and let his soul be immediately irradiated with gratification and repose. Again, I have known some people of very modern views driven by their distress to the use of theological terms to which they attached no doctrinal significance, merely because a drawer was jammed tight and they could not pull it out. A friend of mine was particularly afflicted in this way. Every day his drawer was jammed, and every day in consequence it was something else that rhymes to it. But I pointed out to him that this sense of wrong was really subjective and relative; it rested entirely upon the assumption that the drawer could, should, and would come out easily. "But if," I said, "you picture to yourself that you are pulling against some powerful and oppressive enemy, the struggle will become merely exciting and not exasperating. Imagine that you are roping up a fellow creature out of an Alpine crevasse. Imagine even that you are a boy again and engaged in a tug-of-war between French and English." Shortly after saying this I left him; but I have no doubt at all that my words bore the best possible fruit. I have no doubt that every day of his life he hangs on to the handle of that drawer with a flushed face and eyes bright with battle, uttering encouraging shouts to himself, and seeming to hear all round him that roar of an applauding ring.

So I do not think it altogether fanciful or incredible to suppose that even the floods in London may be accepted and enjoyed poetically. Nothing beyond inconvenience seems really to have been caused by them; and inconvenience, as I have said, is only one aspect, and that the most unimaginative and accidental aspect of a really romantic situation. An adventure is only an inconvenience rightly considered. An inconvenience is only an adventure wrongly considered. The water that girdled the houses and shops of London must, if anything, have only increased their previous witchery and wonder. For as the Roman Catholic priest in the story said: " Wine is good with everything except water," and on a similar principle, water is good with everything except wine.

APPRECIATION HELPS

1. Recall exciting things which happened in your own family or in your own town during your absence. Suggest introductory sentences for essays presenting such experiences.
2. Imagine your home town flooded and suggest the novel situations which would arise.
3. Give a " romantic view " of your town in flood time, describing your experiences in going shopping, to school, to church.
4. Discuss the attitude of a small boy towards the railway station. Where have some of the " most purple hours " of your life been spent?
5. Discuss Chesterton's distinction between an adventure and an inconvenience. Recall some inconveniences which for you became adventures.
6. Suggest some titles for essays that embody interesting experiences, such as running after one's hat.

COMPOSITION HINTS

1. If My Village Were Flooded
2. Imaginary Inconveniences
3. Seen at the Railway Station
4. On Bureau Drawers
5. Snowed-In
6. An Adventure Which Became an Inconvenience

ARNOLD BENNETT

The career of Mr. Arnold Bennett (1867–1931) offers to the ambitious young a particularly inspiring example. Only let them heed the copybook maxims, and they will get on: such is its lesson.

Ambition he had in plenty in his twenties when the career started. He had just resolved to become a great novelist. But besides ambition he could boast of little equipment for his purpose. True, he was sensitive, unusually observant perhaps, and able somewhat to write. So are thousands of fellows, and they do not grow into great novelists. Also, against those ordinary qualities had to be set serious handicaps. He was a poor lawyer's clerk in London, an awkward provincial, so shy that he stuttered. He was uncultivated, knew nothing of life or books, and was unaware of having anything vital to say. Finally, he lacked any overwhelming urge to write. And yet he succeeded beyond the wildest dreams of optimistic youth. How on earth, one asks, did he do it? The answer is in the copybook maxims: he was patient and he was industrious.

Just that. For a time once he had run a column in a county newspaper, and he had sold one article and one short story. That was why he chose writing for his career. But when he tried to sell a second article or a second story, he failed. Somewhere something was wrong. Yet he did not despair. Instead he set himself to remedy the defect. He gave up his job as a lawyer's clerk and became the assistant editor of a little London weekly called *Woman*. The salary was only three-quarters of what he had been getting, but the new post left him free for half the week. In that spare time he read systematically and practiced incessantly with his pen. After each visit to a theater, he came home and wrote a dramatic criticism, not for publication, but for experience. Each time he read a book he wrote out a note of what had most interested him in it. He taught himself French and studied the technique of French literature.

In a few years he succeeded to the full editorship of *Woman*, and, as editor, bought serials for the paper from an agent who called at the office. One day a thought flashed upon him. What this agent sold he himself had to buy. Why should the editor not sell to the agent a serial of his own? Forthwith he wrote one and the agent took it. In 1898 it came out in book form, entitled *A Man from the North*. Mr. Bennett had become an author. But he was not satisfied; greatness yet remained to be achieved, and there was no remission of either the patience or the industry.

Soon serials and book-reviewing gave him a livelihood. He was able to abandon editing and give all his time to writing. But he did not assume independence carelessly; every moment of the future he had planned elaborately. So much time was to be devoted to reading, so much to writing, so much to pleasure. He was going to write serials and book reviews for bread and butter, and serious novels for reputation. And as he planned, so did he do. He did not just make out a time-table — he followed it closely. There lies the secret of his success.

During 1908, in a house on the edge of the lovely Forest of Fontainebleau, he penned the greatest of his novels, *The Old Wives' Tale*. When it was finished, he feared that the public might not recognize how good it was. But the public did not fail him; throughout the English-speaking world Arnold Bennett was proclaimed to be a great man. Even then, though, he did not rest. He next tried plays, and two of his plays, *Milestones* (written in collaboration) and *The Great Adventure,* each brought him a small fortune. He tried painting, but that was purely for pleasure. You could not buy a Bennett water-color if you tried ever so hard. And still he continued to be an industrious writer of novels, essays, short stories, and articles. At his death, he had between seventy and eighty books to his credit. *Imperial Palace, 1930,* was his last.

From the outset the methods he devised to become cultured and to write delighted him, and he could not resist making little books about them. Every one of these small volumes repays reading, for they are compounded of sound common sense. The following essay is from one of them.

TRANSLATING LITERATURE
INTO LIFE[1]

Lo, a parable! A certain man, having bought a large, elaborate, and complete manual of carpentry, studied it daily with much diligence and regularity. Now there were no cupboards in his house; his dining-table consisted of an arrangement of orange boxes, and he had scarcely a chair that was not a menace to the existence of the person who sat upon it. When asked why he did not set to work, and, by applying the principles of the manual, endeavor to improve the conditions of his life and of the lives of his wife and children, he replied that he was a student, and he plunged more deeply than ever into the manual of carpentry. His friends at length definitely came to the conclusion that though he was an industrious student, he was also a hopeless fool.

By which I wish to indicate that there is no virtue in study by itself. Study is not an end, but a means. I should blush to write down such a platitude, did I not know by experience that the majority of readers constantly ignore it. The man who pores over a manual of carpentry and does naught with it is a fool. But every book is a manual of carpentry, and every man who pores over any book whatever and does naught else with it is — deserving of an abusive epithet. What is the object of reading unless something definite comes of it? You would be better advised to play billiards. Where is the sense of reading history unless you obtain from it a clearer insight into actual politics and render yourself less liable to be duped by the rhetoric of party propaganda? Where is the sense of reading morals unless your own are improved? Where is the sense of reading biography unless it is going to affect what people will say about *you* after your funeral? Where is the sense of reading poetry or fiction unless you see more beauty, more passion, more scope for your sympathy, than you saw before?

[1] From the first volume of *Things That Have Interested Me,* copyright, 1921, by George H. Doran Company.

If you boldly answer: "I only read for pleasure," then I retort that the man who drinks whisky might with force say: "I only drink whisky for pleasure." And I respectfully request you not to plume yourself on your reading, nor expect to acquire merit thereby.

But should you answer: "I do try to translate literature into life," then I will ask you to take down any book at random from your shelves and conduct in your own mind an honest inquiry as to what has been the effect of that particular book on your actual living. If you can put your hand on any subsequent period, or fractional moment, of your life and say: "I acted more wisely then, I wasn't such a dupe then, I perceived more clearly then, I felt more deeply then, I saw more beauty then, I was kinder then, I was more joyous then, I was happier then, than I should have been if I had not read that book" — if you can honestly say this, then your reading of that book has not been utterly futile. But if you cannot say this, then the chances are that you have been studying a manual of carpentry while continuing to sit on a three-legged chair and to dine off an orange box.

You say: "I know all that. But it is not so easy to translate literature into life. When I think of the time I have wasted in reading masterpieces, I stand aghast."

The explanation is simple. Idleness, intellectual sloth, is the explanation. Self-conceit is the explanation. If you were invited to meet a great writer, you would brace yourself to the occasion. You would say to yourself: "I must keep my ears open, and my brain wide-awake, so as to miss nothing." You would tingle with your own bracing of yourself. But you — I mean "we" — will sit down to a great book as though we were sitting down to a ham sandwich. No sense of personal inferiority in us? No mood to resolve! No "tuning up" of the intellectual apparatus! But just a casual, easy air, as if saying to the book: "Well, come along, let's have a look at you!"

What is the matter with our reading is casualness, languor, preoccupation. We don't give the book a chance. We don't put ourselves at the disposal of the book. It is impossible to read properly without using all one's engine-power. If we are not tired after reading, common sense is not in us. How should one grapple with a superior and not be out of breath?

But even if we read with the whole force of our brain, and do nothing else, common sense is still not in us, while sublime conceit is. For we are assuming that, without further trouble, we can possess, coördinate, and assimilate all the ideas and sensations rapidly offered to us by a mind greater than our own. The assumption has only to be stated in order to appear in its monstrous absurdity. Hence it follows that something remains to be done. This something is the act of reflection. Reading without subsequent reflection is ridiculous; it is equally a proof of folly and of vanity.

Further, it is a sign of undue self-esteem to suppose that we can grasp the full import of an author's message at a single reading. I would not say that every book worth reading once is worth reading twice. But I would say that no book of great and established reputation is read till it is read at least twice. You can easily test the truth of this by reading again any classic; assuredly you will discover in it excellencies which had previously escaped you.

To resume and finish: Open a great book in the braced spirit with which you would listen to a great man. Read with the whole of your brain and soul. Tire yourself (would you not tire yourself at tennis?). Reflect. After an interval, read again. By this process, and by no other, will a book enter into you, become a part of you, and reappear in your life.

I have been consulted about the practice of making notes. Well, I do not care to offer counsels of perfection. My advice is simply to keep a pencil handy and to write down on a small sheet of paper (or in the inside back-cover if the book belongs to you) the number of the page on which anything has struck you, together with the merest hint, in half a dozen words, of what it was. If you do this, by the time you have finished the book, you will have automatically constructed a table and page-index of its salient points. It is well, of course, to write on the papers the title and author of the work, the name of the edition, and the date of perusal. A collection of these small sheets of paper would constitute a souvenir of one's reading. At the end of each year one might advantageously spend a few shillings in having the year's harvest bound. Say you have read a hundred books. A hundred uniform leaves would make a respectable volume, whose interest and utility I need not insist upon. A row of such volumes would really amount to the secret history of one's life.

APPRECIATION HELPS

1. What is the central theme of the essay? What is the author's purpose in writing it?
2. What makes a good reader? Decide what type of reader you are after studying the essay.
3. What should follow the reading of a book?
4. Name some books you consider worth a second reading.
5. Compare Bacon's " On Studies " and Ruskin's *Sesame and Lilies* with this.
6. What is your system for careful reading? Compare yours with Bennett's.
7. Do you read for pleasure? Justify the practice.
8. Name some books you have " translated into life."
9 " But you — I mean ' we ' — will sit down to a great book as though we were sitting down to a ham sandwich." Discuss.

COMPOSITION HINTS

1. " Lo, a Parable "
2. Books I Have Reread
3. How to Get the Most from a Book
4. How I Translate Literature into Life
5. Mental Laziness
6. Books Which Have Influenced Me
7. My Changing Literary Tastes

E. V. LUCAS

Mr. Edward Verrall Lucas (b. 1868) may be considered to have climbed the whole gamut of the bookselling business, since he began as an assistant in a bookshop at Brighton, on the South Coast of England, and today is head of the eminent English publishing firm of Methuen and Company. But as he is the son of an architect of Hove, the town which lies cheek by jowl with Brighton, he probably started upon his career better equipped than most young clerks in bookstores. Nevertheless the climb is a notable achievement, all the more remarkable as it has not been done on orthodox lines. For when Mr. Lucas left the Brighton bookshop, he did not go to another. He went up to London and became a free-lance newspaper man. He sent in paragraphs to the *Globe,* a distinctive evening paper, now, alas! dead, and in an emergency was taken on the regular staff. Then he evolved the " turnover " articles which most readers of the paper always scanned first. The articles were called " turnovers " because they began on the last column of the front page and turned over to the second. They were twelve hundred words long, and as Mr. Lucas and a colleague found the first six hundred words invariably easy, but the second six hundred always difficult, they came to finish each other's turnovers. By the time he left the *Globe* Mr. Lucas was on his feet as a literary man. His first book was *The Hambledon Men,* being a new edition of John Nyrins' *Young Cricketer's Tutor.* Since then he has produced over seventy volumes and yet not devoted his whole time to writing, inasmuch as most of the while he has been a publisher's adviser.

He has written novels, volumes of essays, books for children, books of biography, and books of travel. He has compiled eight anthologies, made four collections of selected writings, put forth two edited works. His most scholarly book, according to Mr. Grant Overton, is *The Life of Charles Lamb.* The most popular must be *A Wanderer in London* (1906).

The *Wanderer* travel books are a special creation of his own. He calls them "humanized guidebooks." There are volumes devoted to Holland, London, Paris, Florence, and Venice. *A Wanderer among Pictures* records an informative and entertaining tour of the European art galleries.

POSSESSIONS[1]

SOMEONE has offered me a very remarkable and beautiful and valuable gift — and I don't know what to do. A few years ago I should have accepted it with rapture. Today I hesitate, because the older one grows the less does one wish to accumulate possessions.

It is said that the reason why Jews so often become fishmongers and fruiterers and dealers in precious stones is because in every child of Israel there is a subconscious conviction that at any moment he may be called upon to return to his country, and naturally wishing to lose as little as possible by a sudden departure he chooses to traffic either in a stock which he can carry on his person, such as diamonds, or in one which, being perishable and renewable day by day, such as fruit and fish, can be abandoned at any moment with almost no loss at all. Similarly the Jews are said to favor such household things as can be easily removed: rugs, for example, rather than carpets. I have not, so far as I know, any Jewish blood, but in the few years that are left me I too want to be ready to obey the impulse towards whatever Jerusalem I hear calling me, even should it be the platonically loved city itself, although that is unlikely. Without possessions one would be the readier also for the longer last journey. Naked we come into this world and naked we should go. Nor should we wilfully add to the difficulties of leaving it.

I was lately led by its owner, rebuilder, and renovator through the rooms and gardens of a Tudor house which, with infinite

[1] From *Adventures and Enthusiasms*, copyright, 1920, by George H. Doran Company.

thought and discretion, has been reclaimed from decay and made modernly debonair. At every step, indoors and out, was something charming or adequate, whether furniture or porcelain, whether flower or shrub. Within were long cool passages where through the diamond panes sunlight splashed on the white walls, and bedrooms of the gayest daintiness; without were lawns, and vistas, and arrangements of the loveliest colors. " Well," my hostess asked me, " what do you think of it all? " I thought many things, but the one which was uppermost was this: " You are making it very hard to die."

I had a grandfather who, after he had reached a certain age, used birthdays as occasions on which to give away rather than receive presents; and I am sure he was right. But I would go beyond that. The presents which he distributed were bought for the purpose. I would fix a period in life when the wise man should begin to unload his acquisitions — accumulating only up to that point and then dispersing among the young. Ah! but you say, why be so illogical? If possessions are undesirable, are they not undesirable also for the young? Well, there are answers to that. For one thing, who said anything about being logical? And then, are we not all different? Because I choose to cease accumulating, that is no reason why others, who like to increase their possessions, should cease also. And again, even I, with all my talk of renunciation, have not suggested that it should begin till a middling period has been reached; and I am for circulating *objets d'art,* too. I should like a continual progression of pictures and other beautiful things throughout the kingdom, so that the great towns could have the chance of seeing the best as well as London.

So far am I from withholding possessions from others, that as I walked down Bond Street the other day and paused at this window and that, filled with exquisite jewels and enameled boxes and other voluptuous trifles, I thought how delightful it would be to be rich enough to buy them all — not to own them, but to give them away. To women for choice; to one woman for choice. And a letter which I remember receiving from

France during the War had some bearing upon this aspect of the case, for it mentioned a variety of possessions which carried with them, in the trenches, extraordinary and constant pleasure and consolation. The writer was a lady who worked at a canteen in the big Paris terminus for the front, and she said that the soldiers returning from their leave often displayed to her the mascots and other treasures which comforted them in their vigils, and with which they were always well supplied. Sometimes these possessions were living creatures. One soldier had produced from a basket a small fox which he had found and brought up, and which this lady fed with bread and milk while its owner ate his soup. Another had a starling. A third took out of his pocket a venerable handkerchief, which, on being unrolled, revealed the person of Marguerite — a magpie whom he adored, and who apparently adored him. They were inseparable. Marguerite had accompanied him into action and while he was on *permission,* and she was now cheering him on his return to the danger zone. She was placed on the table, where she immediately fell asleep; at the end of the meal the poor fellow rolled her again in the handkerchief, popped her in his pocket, and ran for his tragic train. But for the companionship of Marguerite his heart would have been far heavier; and she was thus a possession worth having.

APPRECIATION HELPS

1. Does Mr. Lucas take the ordinary view of possessions? Discuss his hesitancy to accumulate treasures. Are his reasons sensible?
2. What do you think of the use of birthdays to give *away* presents rather than to receive them?
3. Name some of the most precious possessions of your childhood days. What do you value highly today? Does its intrinsic value decide the worth of a possession? Illustrate.

COMPOSITION HINTS

1. My Most Valued Possession
2. Things I Can Do Without
3. Mascots and Treasures

TELEPHONICS[1]
by E. V. Lucas

AFTER fighting against bondage for years I am now a slave: I have a telephone.

Although the advantages are many, it means that I have lost the purest and rarest of life's pleasures — which was to ring up from a three-pence-in-the-slot call-office (as I continually had to do) and not be asked for the money. This, in many years, has happened to me twice; and only last week I met a very rich man who is normally of a gloomy cast, across whose features played a smile brilliant with triumph, for it also had just happened to him.

On the other hand, through having a telephone of my own I now escape one of the commonest and most tiresome of life's irritations — which is to wait outside one of these call-offices while the person inside is carrying on a conversation that is not only unnecessary and frivolous, but unending. In London these offices are used both by men and women; but in the suburbs by women only, who may be thought to be romantically engaged but really are reminding their husbands not to forget the fish. The possession of a telephone of one's own, however, does not, in an imperfect world, put an end to the ordeal of waiting. If ever a fairy godmother appeared to me (but after all these years of postponement I can hardly hope for her) with the usual offer of a granted wish, I should think long before I hit upon anything better to ask for than the restoration of all the time I had spent with my own telephone at my ear waiting to be answered. The ordinary delays can be long enough, but for true foretastes of eternity you must sit at the instrument while some one is being fetched from a distant part of the building. This is a foretaste not only of eternity but of perdition, for there is nothing to do; and to have nothing to do is to be damned. If you had a book by you, you could

[1] From *Adventures and Enthusiasms,* copyright, 1920, by George H. Doran Company.

not read it, for your thoughts are not free to wander; all that you are mentally capable of is to speculate on the progress of the messenger to the person who is wanted, upstairs or down, the present occupation of the person who is wanted, and the probable stages of his journey to the receiver. In this employment, minutes, hours, days, weeks even, seem to drag their reluctant length along.

You can imagine also the attitude of the person who is sent for. For the telephone, common as it now is, is still associated with ceremonial. At any rate, I notice that men called to it by page boys in restaurants and hotels have a special gait of importance proper to the occasion.

The possession of a telephone no doubt now and then simplifies life; but its complications are too many, even if you adopt the sound rule to be more rung against than ringing. One of them is the perplexity incident to delays and misunderstandings, and, above all, as to the constitution of Exchanges. We all, I suppose, have our own idea as to what they are like; there must at one time or other have been photographs in the more informing of the magazines; but I missed them, and, therefore, decline on a vague vision of machinery and wire-eared ladies. A friend is more definite: " A large building," he describes it, " like Olympia, the roof lost in darkness, and pallid women moving about, spinning tops and blowing penny trumpets." To me, as I have suggested, there is more of Tartarus than Olympus about it. A sufficient hell, indeed, for any misspent life, to be continually calling up numbers, and continually being met with the saddest words that are known to men: " Number engaged."

I want to understand the whole telephone system. I want to know how the operators all get to speak exactly alike. Women can be very imitative, I am aware: the chorus girl's transition from Brixton to the Savoy restaurant can be as natural as the passage of dusk to dawn, and a change of accent is usually a part of it; but it is astonishing how the operators of the different Exchanges resemble each other. They cannot all be one and the same. Miraculous as is everything connected

with the telephone — talking quietly over wires that thread
the earth beneath the busiest and noisiest of pavements in the
world is sufficiently magical — it would be a shade too marvelous for one operator to be everywhere at once. Therefore,
there must be many. Is there, then, a school of elocution,
where instruction in the most refined form of speech ever
known is imparted, together with lessons in the trilling of the
letter R? Why should they all say " No replay," when they
mean " No reply "? And how do they talk at home? It must
be terrible for their relations if they don't come down a peg
or two there. The joy with which we recognize a male voice
at the Exchange is another proof that woman does not really
represent the gentler sex.

But these are by no means all the mysteries as to which I
crave enlightenment. I want to know how the odd and alarming noises are made. There is a tapping, as of a woodpecker
with delirium tremens, which at once stuns and electrifies the
ear. How do they do that, and do they know what its effect
is? And why does one sometimes hear other conversations
over other wires, and sometimes not? Rarely are they interesting; but now and then. . . . My pen falters as I record the
humiliating want of perspicacity — the tragic inability to recognize a tip — which befell me on the morning of June 4th,
1919 — in other words, on Derby Day: the day when the art
or science of vaticination experienced in England its darkest
hour, for every prophet selected The Panther. To my annoy-
ance I had to listen to a long conversation between what seemed
to be a bookmaker and his client with regard to money to
be placed on Grand Parade. This at the time only irritated me,
but afterwards, when Grand Parade had won at 33 to 1, and I
recognized the interruption as an effort of the gods on my behalf (had I but ears to hear), how against my folly did I rail!

Telephony, it is clear, both from one's own experience and
from reading the letters in the papers, is not yet an exact science. Not, that is, in real life; although on the stage and in
American detective novels it seems to be perfect. The actor
lifts the receiver, mentions the number, and begins instantly

to talk. If he is on the film his lips move like burning rubber and his mouth becomes a shifting cavern. Do the rank and file of us, I wonder, when telephoning, thus grimace? I must fix up a mirror and see.

There are many good telephone stories. The best that I know is told of a journalist with a somewhat hypertrophied bump of reverence for worldly success, whose employer is a peer. We will call the employer Lord Forthestait and the journalist Mr. Blank. A number of the staff were talking together, in one of the rooms of the newspaper, when the telephone rang.

" You're wanted at the 'phone, Mr. Blank," said the clerk.

Blank, who was just going out to lunch, came back impatiently and snatched at the instrument.

" Yes, what is it? " he snapped out.

" Is that Blank? " came back the reply. " Lord Forthestait speaking."

" Yes, my lord," said Blank, with the meekest deference, removing his hat.

APPRECIATION HELPS

1. How may one be a " slave to a telephone "? What are the advantages and the irritations connected with a telephone?
2. Where does the author come within your experience in his discussion of telephones? Point out passages which reveal that the author is an Englishman.
3. Discuss the perplexities concerning telephones which the author wishes to have made clear.
4. Describe a visit to a telephone exchange.
5. Read in Arnold Bennett's *Your United States* his discussion of the telephone as he observed it in America. In what ways is it superior to the telephone in England?

COMPOSITION HINTS

1. Slaves to the Telephone
2. The Assistance of One's Family in Telephoning
3. " Wrong Number "

4. Things Heard over Crossed Wires
5. Personality in Voices Heard over the Telephone
6. Minor Frictions in Telephoning
7. " The Line Is Busy "
8. " More Rung against than Ringing "

ELBERT HUBBARD

" A Message to Garcia " was written in an hour. Its author was proud of the fact. It was a job done well and expeditiously. It is, further, an essay about doing all jobs well and expeditiously. Nobody of course can cavil at the sentiments it expresses. Jobs should be done well and expeditiously. Nevertheless Elbert Hubbard (1856–1915), the author, was a man with a bee in his bonnet. Unlike Thoreau, who has already been discussed, the man who considered that nearly all work was a mistake, Hubbard believed that nearly all idleness was a mistake. He was a glutton for work, not only for himself, but for others. He pushed his beliefs a long way: he held not only that a man should work hard at what he liked doing, but also that a man should do everything he needed himself. In 1892 he had visited England and met William Morris, the English poet, painter, and prose-writer, who advocated the revival of craftsmanship and gave the example by becoming a craftsman himself. Hubbard became a disciple of Morris, and founded at East Aurora, in New York, the Utopian village of Roycroft, named after another Morris disciple, the English painter, Thomas Roycroft. He ran a hand press there and made the shops attractive, took in former convicts, and let everyone choose or change his occupation. Roycroft still exists, but the other cities, towns, and villages of the United States have not grown like it.

Hubbard acquired his appetite for work in youth. He was born in Illinois and spent there a semi-pioneer-like childhood. He learned to break in a horse, to sow, plow, and reap. But he didn't like farm work, and peddled soap in Chicago instead. By the age of twenty-four he had become manager of a soap factory. Twelve years later he sold out his share in the business for $75,000. Later he reared trotting horses. He was drowned in the *Lusitania,* the liner the Germans torpedoed off the coast of Ireland in 1915.

A MESSAGE TO GARCIA[1]

Iⁿ all this Cuban business there is one man stands out on the horizon of my memory like Mars at perihelion.

When war broke out between Spain and the United States, it was very necessary to communicate quickly with the leader of the Insurgents. Garcia was somewhere in the mountain fastnesses of Cuba — no one knew where. No mail or telegraph message could reach him. The President must secure his coöperation, and quickly.

What to do!

Someone said to the President, "There is a fellow by the name of Rowan will find Garcia for you, if anybody can."

Rowan was sent for and given a letter to be delivered to Garcia. How the "fellow by the name of Rowan" took the letter, sealed it up in an oilskin pouch, strapped it over his heart, in four days landed by night off the coast of Cuba from an open boat, disappeared into the jungle, and in three weeks came out on the other side of the Island, having traversed a hostile country on foot, and delivered his letter to Garcia — are things I have no special desire now to tell in detail. The point that I wish to make is this: McKinley gave Rowan a letter to be delivered to Garcia; Rowan took the letter and did not ask, "Where is he at?"

By the Eternal! there is a man whose form should be cast in deathless bronze and the statue placed in every college of the land. It is not book-learning young men need, nor instruction about this and that, but a stiffening of the vertebrae which will cause them to be loyal to a trust, to act promptly, concentrate their energies: do the thing — "Carry a message to Garcia."

General Garcia is dead now, but there are other Garcias. No man who has endeavored to carry out an enterprise where many hands were needed, but has been well-nigh appalled at

[1] Published by the Roycroft Press and used by permission of Elbert Hubbard II.

times by the imbecility of the average man — the inability or unwillingness to concentrate on a thing and do it.

Slipshod assistance, foolish inattention, dowdy indifference, and half-hearted work seem the rule; and no man succeeds, unless by hook or crook or threat he forces or bribes other men to assist him; or mayhap, God in His goodness performs a miracle, and sends him an Angel of Light for an assistant.

You, reader, put this matter to a test: You are sitting now in your office — six clerks are within call. Summon any one and make this request: " Please look in the encyclopedia and make a brief memorandum for me concerning the life of Correggio." Will the clerk quietly say, " Yes, sir," and go do the task?

On your life he will not. He will look at you out of a fishy eye and ask one or more of the following questions:

Who was he?

Which encyclopedia?

Where is the encyclopedia?

Was I hired for that?

Don't you mean Bismarck?

What's the matter with Charlie doing it?

Is he dead?

Is there any hurry?

Shan't I bring you the book and let you look it up yourself?

What do you want to know for?

And I will lay you ten to one that after you have answered the questions, and explained how to find the information, and why you want it, the clerk will go off and get one of the other clerks to help him try to find Garcia — and then come back and tell you there is no such man. Of course I may lose my bet, but according to the Law of Average I will not. Now, if you are wise, you will not bother to explain to your " assistant " that Correggio is indexed under the C's, not in the K's, but you will smile very sweetly and say, " Never mind," and go look it up yourself. And this incapacity for independent action, this moral stupidity, this infirmity of the will, this unwillingness to cheerfully catch hold and lift — these are the things that put pure Socialism so far into the future. If men will not act for themselves, what will they do when the benefit of their effort is for all?

A first mate with knotted club seems necessary; and the dread of getting " the bounce " Saturday night holds many a worker to his place. Advertise for a stenographer, and nine out of ten who apply can neither spell nor punctuate — and do not think it necessary to.

Can such a one write a letter to Garcia?

" You see that bookkeeper," said the foreman to me in a large factory.

" Yes; what about him? "

" Well, he's a fine accountant, but if I'd send him up town on an errand, he might accomplish the errand all right, and on the other hand, might stop at four saloons on the way, and when he got to Main Street would forget what he had been sent for."

Can such a man be entrusted to carry a message to Garcia?

We have recently been hearing much maudlin sympathy expressed for the " downtrodden denizens of the sweatshop " and the " homeless wanderer searching for honest employment," and with it all often go many hard words for the men in power.

Nothing is said about the employer who grows old before his time in a vain attempt to get frowsy ne'er-do-wells to do intelligent work; and his long, patient striving after " help " that does nothing but loaf when his back is turned. In every store and factory there is a constant weeding-out process going on. The employer is constantly sending away " help " that have shown their incapacity to further the interests of the business, and others are being taken on. No matter how good times are, this sorting continues: only, if times are hard and work is scarce, the sorting is done finer — but out and forever out the incompetent and unworthy go. It is the survival of the fittest. Self-interest prompts every employer to keep the best — those who can carry a message to Garcia.

I know one man of really brilliant parts who has not the ability to manage a business of his own, and yet who is absolutely worthless to any one else, because he carries with him constantly the insane suspicion that his employer is oppressing, or intending to oppress, him. He cannot give orders, and he will not receive them. Should a message be given him to take to Garcia, his answer would probably be, " Take it yourself! "

Tonight this man walks the streets looking for work, the wind whistling through his threadbare coat. No one who knows him dare employ him, for he is a regular firebrand of discontent. He is impervious to reason, and the only thing that can impress him is the toe of a thick-soled Number Nine boot.

Of course I know that one so morally deformed is no less to be pitied than a physical cripple; but in our pitying let us drop a tear, too, for the men who are striving to carry on a great enterprise, whose working hours are not limited by the whistle, and whose hair is fast turning white through the struggle to hold in line dowdy indifference, slipshod imbecility, and the heartless ingratitude which, but for their enterprise, would be both hungry and homeless.

Have I put the matter too strongly? Possibly I have; but when all the world has gone a-slumming I wish to speak a word of sympathy for the man who succeeds — the man who, against great odds, has directed the efforts of others, and having succeeded, finds there's nothing in it: nothing but bare board and clothes. I have carried a dinner-pail and worked for day's wages, and I have also been an employer of labor, and I know there is something to be said on both sides. There is no excellence, *per se,* in poverty; rags are no recommendation; and all employers are not rapacious and high-handed, any more than all poor men are virtuous. My heart goes out to the man who does his work when the " boss " is away, as well as when he is at home. And the man who, when given a letter for Garcia, quietly takes the missive, without asking any idiotic questions, and with no lurking intention of chucking it into the nearest sewer, or of doing aught else but deliver it, never gets " laid off," nor has to go on a strike for higher wages. Civilization is one long, anxious search for just such individuals. Anything such a man asks shall be granted. He is wanted in every city, town and village — in every office, shop, store and factory. The world cries out for such; he is needed and needed badly — the man who can " Carry a Message to Garcia."

APPRECIATION HELPS

1. This " literary trifle " was written in a single hour, states the author in his *Apologia*. Point out places which reveal intensity of thought.
2. What is the central thought of the essay?
3. In 1913, over forty million copies of " A Message to Garcia " had been printed. Explain the popularity of the " literary trifle."
4. If you were a director of railways or a general of an army, why would you wish all men under you to read this essay?
5. What essential qualities do many workers lack? What qualities are essential for the good worker?
6. What is your school doing to develop men and women who can carry a " message to Garcia "?

COMPOSITION HINTS

1. A Garcia of My Acquaintance
2. " Was I Hired for That? "
3. " When the Cat's Away "
4. Loyal to a Trust
5. Does School Train for Later Responsibilities?

JOSEPH CONRAD

Imagine that America had no seaboard and no ships, and that as you grew up you had a longing to become a sailor. That this longing became so strong that when you reached manhood you left America and went away to France, and became an apprentice in a French ship, taught yourself the French language, took your successive examinations in French, and became the captain of a French ship. That, after sailing the seas for twenty years, you retired on land in France, though still visiting America from time to time, and began to write tales in this French which you had acquired instead of in your own more familiar tongue.

Well, that was what Joseph Conrad (1857–1924), one of the greatest of modern novelists, did. Only, of course, he was not an American, for in America there is no difficulty about going to sea. He was a Pole, and, as Poland has no seaboard, he became an English sailor. His real name was Teodor Josef Konrad Korzeniowski. The district of Poland in which he was born was then an inland province of Russia. He grew up speaking Polish and Russian, and of course, like all educated Russians, French, but no English. As a child, though, he had the irresistible yearning to be a sailor. He had heard that English seamen and English ships were the best in the world, and so he decided that he would become an English sailor. At the price of great determination and much hardship he succeeded. In the silent watches of the night, as the ship, with her great spread of creaking and flapping canvas, swung under the stars — for he passed all his early years at sea in sailing vessels — the Polish apprentice taught himself both English and navigation. He became a captain and cruised in the China seas, in the Indian Ocean, in the West Indies, all over the world. One year he might be in the Malay Straits. Another he might have charge of a steamer which went up from the English Channel to the French river port of Rouen, which he must have found a curious contrast.

It was on board this latter steamer that he completed the manuscript of a novel over which he had lavished the care of years. A novel in English — that alien language he had picked up in order to pass his examinations and gain command of a ship. He was nearly forty by now, and his health compelled him to take a holiday from the sea. He submitted the manuscript to a London publisher, with the private determination never to write any more if it should be rejected. Fortunately for the world it was accepted, and the publisher's reader, Mr. Edward Garnett (who became his close friend), said to him, " Why not try another? " The same evening Conrad went home and began his second novel. Thus he abandoned seafaring and settled down in a little farmhouse among the hopfields of the Garden of England (as the county of Kent, southeast of London, is well described), all his time devoted to writing.

It turned out not only that he could write English, but that he could write it supremely well. The critics all praised his books, and the leading English novelists acclaimed him as a master. But the public was slow to recognize him, his books did not sell, and Conrad, when over fifty, and with a wife and children to support, was enduring years of poverty on land after braving for so long the perils of the sea. Then, in 1913, appeared his novel *Chance*. And chance smiled on him. People talked about the book, recommended it one to another, and soon the whole public of England and America was reading it. Conrad at last had come into his own. Thereafter all his books were in demand, all the new ones and those he had written in the long, lean years of his comparative obscurity.

In addition to his novels there are two volumes of his reminiscences. It is from one of these that the following essay is taken.

LANDFALLS AND DEPARTURES[1]

> And shippes by the brinke comen and gon,
> And in swich forme endure a day or two.
> —*The Frankeleyns Tale.*

LANDFALL and Departure mark the rhythmical swing of a seaman's life and of a ship's career. From land to land is the most concise definition of a ship's earthly fate. A " Departure " is not what a vain people of landsmen may think. The term " Landfall " is more easily understood; you fall in with the land, and it is a matter of a quick eye and of a clear atmosphere. The Departure is not the ship's going away from her port any more than the Landfall can be looked upon as the synonym of arrival. But there is this difference in the Departure: that the term does not imply so much a sea event as a definite act entailing a process — the precise observation of certain landmarks by means of the compass card.

Your Landfall, be it a peculiarly shaped mountain, a rocky headland, or a stretch of sand-dunes, you meet at first with a single glance. Further recognition will follow in due course; but essentially a Landfall, good or bad, is made and done with at the first cry of " Land ho! " The Departure is distinctly a ceremony of navigation. A ship may have left her port some time before; she may have been at sea, in the fullest sense of the phrase, for days; but, for all that, as long as the coast she was about to leave remained in sight, a southern-going ship of yesterday had not in the sailor's sense begun the enterprise of a passage.

The taking of Departure, if not the last sight of the land, is, perhaps, the last professional recognition of the land on the part of a sailor. It is the technical, as distinguished from the sentimental, " good-bye." Henceforth he has done with the coast astern of his ship. It is a matter personal to the man. It is not the ship that takes her Departure; the seaman takes

[1] From *The Mirror of the Sea,* copyright by Doubleday, Page and Company, 1926.

his Departure by means of cross-bearings which fix the place of the first tiny pencil-cross on the white expanse of the track-chart, where the ship's position at noon shall be marked by just such another tiny pencil-cross for every day of her passage. And there may be sixty, eighty, any number of these crosses on the ship's track from land to land. The greatest number in my experience was a hundred and thirty of such crosses from the pilot station at the Sand Heads in the Bay of Bengal to the Scilly's light. A bad passage. . . .

A Departure, the last professional sight of land, is always good, or at least good enough. For even, if the weather is thick, it does not matter much to a ship having all the open sea before her bows. A Landfall may be good or bad. You encompass the earth with one particular spot of it in your eye. In all the devious tracings the course of a sailing-ship leaves upon the white paper of a chart she is always aiming for that one little spot — maybe a small island in the ocean, a single headland upon the long coast of a continent, a light-house on a bluff, or simply the peaked form of a mountain like an ant heap afloat upon the waters. But if you have sighted it on the expected bearing, then that Landfall is good. Fogs, snow-storms, gales thick with clouds and rain — those are the enemies of good Landfalls.

II

Some commanders of ships take their Departure from the home coast sadly, in a spirit of grief and discontent. They have a wife, children perhaps, some affection at any rate, or perhaps only some pet vice; they must be left behind for a year or more. I remember only one man who walked his deck with a springy step, and gave the first course of the passage in an elated voice. But he, as I learned afterwards, was leaving nothing behind him, except a welter of debts and threats of legal proceedings.

On the other hand, I have known many captains who, directly their ship had left the narrow waters of the Channel,

would disappear from the sight of their ship's company altogether for some three days or more. They would take a long
dive, as it were, into their state-room, only to emerge a few
days afterwards with a more or less serene brow. Those were
the men easy to get on with. Besides, such a complete retirement seemed to imply a satisfactory amount of trust in their
officers, and to be trusted displeases no seaman worthy of the
name.

On my first voyage, as chief mate with good Captain
MacW—— I remember that I felt quite flattered, and went
blithely about my duties, myself a commander for all practical
purposes. Still, whatever the greatness of my illusion, the fact
remained that the real commander was there, backing up my
self-confidence, though invisible to my eyes behind a maple-
wood veneered cabin-door with a white china handle.

That is the time, after your Departure is taken, when the
spirit of your commander communes with you in a muffled
voice, as if from the sanctum sanctorum of a temple; because,
call her a temple or a " hell afloat " — as some ships have been
called — the captain's state-room is surely the august place in
every vessel.

The good MacW—— would not even come out to his meals,
and fed solitarily in his holy of holies from a tray covered
with a white napkin. Our steward used to bend an ironic
glance at the perfectly empty plates he was bringing out from
there. This grief for his home, which overcomes so many
married seamen, did not deprive Captain MacW—— of his
legitimate appetite. In fact, the steward would almost invariably come up to me, sitting in the captain's chair at the
head of the table, to say in a grave murmur, " The captain
asks for one more slice of meat and two potatoes." We, his
officers, could hear him moving about in his berth, or lightly
snoring, or fetching deep sighs, or splashing and blowing in his
bathroom; and we made our reports to him through the key-
hole, as it were. It was the crowning achievement of his
amiable character that the answers we got were given in a quite
mild and friendly tone. Some commanders in their periods of

seclusion are constantly grumpy, and seem to resent the mere sound of your voice as an injury and an insult.

But a grumpy recluse cannot worry his subordinates, whereas the man in whom the sense of duty is strong (or, perhaps, only the sense of self-importance), and who persists in airing on deck his moroseness all day — and perhaps half the night — becomes a grievous infliction. He walks the poop darting gloomy glances as though he wished to poison the sea, and snaps your head off savagely whenever you happen to blunder within ear-shot. And these vagaries are the harder to bear patiently, as becomes a man and an officer, because no sailor is really good-tempered during the first few days of a voyage. There are regrets, memories, the instinctive longing for the departed idleness, the instinctive hate of all work. Besides, things have a knack of going wrong at the start, especially in the matter of irritating trifles. And there is the abiding thought of a whole year of more or less hard life before one, because there was hardly a southern-going voyage in the yesterday of the sea which meant anything less than a twelvemonth. Yes; it needed a few days after the taking of your departure for a ship's company to shake down into their places, and for the soothing deep-water ship routine to establish its beneficent sway.

It is a great doctor for sore hearts and sore heads, too, your ship's routine, which I have seen soothe — at least for a time — the most turbulent of spirits. There is health in it, and peace, and satisfaction of the accomplished round; for each day of the ship's life seems to close a circle within the wide ring of the sea horizon. It borrows a certain dignity of sameness from the majestic monotony of the sea. He who loves the sea loves also the ship's routine.

Nowhere else than upon the sea do the days, weeks, and months fall away quicker into the past. They seem to be left astern as easily as the light air-bubbles in the swirls of the ship's wake, and vanish into a great silence in which your ship moves on with a sort of magical effect. They pass away, the days, the weeks, the months. Nothing but a gale can disturb the orderly life of the ship; and the spell of unshaken monotony that seems to have fallen upon the very voices of her men is broken only by the near prospect of a Landfall.

Then is the spirit of the ship's commander stirred strongly again. But it is not moved to seek seclusion and to remain, hidden and inert, shut up in a small cabin with the solace of a good bodily appetite. When about to make the land, the spirit of the ship's commander is tormented by an unconquerable restlessness. It seems unable to abide for many seconds together in the holy of holies of the captain's state-room; it will go out on deck and gaze ahead, through straining eyes, as the appointed moment comes nearer. It is kept vigorously upon the stretch of excessive vigilance. Meantime, the body of the ship's commander is being enfeebled by want of appetite; at least, such is my experience, though "enfeebled" is perhaps not exactly the word. I might say, rather, that it is spiritualized by a disregard for food, sleep, and all the ordinary comforts, such as they are, of sea life. In one or two cases I have known that detachment from the grosser needs of existence remain regrettably incomplete in the matter of drink.

But these two cases were, properly speaking, pathological cases, and the only two in all my sea experience. In one of these two instances of a craving for stimulants, developed from sheer anxiety, I cannot assert that the man's seaman-like qualities were impaired in the least. It was a very anxious case, too, the land being made suddenly, close-to, on a wrong bearing, in thick weather, and during a fresh on-shore gale. Going below to speak to him soon after, I was unlucky enough to catch my captain in the very act of hasty cork-drawing. The sight, I may say, gave me an awful scare. I was well aware of the morbidly sensitive nature of the man. Fortunately, I managed to draw back unseen, and taking care to stamp heavily with my sea-boots at the foot of the cabin stairs, I made my second entry. But for this unexpected glimpse, no act of his during the next twenty-four hours could have given me the slightest suspicion that all was not well with his nerve.

Quite another case, and having nothing to do with drink, was that of poor Captain B——. He used to suffer from sick headaches, in his young days, every time he was approaching a coast. Well over fifty years of age when I knew him, short, stout, dignified, perhaps a little pompous, he was a man of a singularly well-informed mind, the least sailor-like in outward aspect, but certainly one of the best seamen whom it has been my good luck to serve under. He was a Plymouth man, I think, the son of a country doctor, and both his elder boys were studying medicine. He commanded a big London ship, fairly well known in her day. I thought no end of him, and that is why I remember with a peculiar satisfaction the last words he spoke to me on board his ship after an eighteen months' voyage. It was in the dock in Dundee, where we had brought a full cargo of jute from Calcutta. We had been paid off that morning, and I had come on board to take my sea chest away and to say good-by. In his slightly lofty but courteous way he inquired what were my plans. I replied that I intended leaving for London by the afternoon train, and thought of going up for examination to get my master's certificate. I had just enough service for that. He recommended me for not wasting my time, with such an evident interest in my case that I was quite surprised; then, rising from his chair, he said:

"Have you a ship in view after you have passed?"

I answered that I had nothing whatever in view.

He shook hands with me and pronounced the memorable words:

"If you happen to be in want of employment, remember that as long as I have a ship you have a ship, too."

In the way of compliment there is nothing to beat this from a ship's captain to his second mate at the end of a voyage, when the work is over and the subordinate is done with. And there is a pathos in that memory, for the poor fellow never went to sea again after all. He was already ailing when we

passed St. Helena; was laid up for a time when we were off
the Western Islands, but got out of bed to make his Landfall.
He managed to keep up on deck as far as the Downs, where,
giving his orders in an exhausted voice, he anchored for a few
hours to send a wire to his wife and take aboard a North Sea
pilot to help him sail the ship up the east coast. He had not
felt equal to the task by himself, for it is the sort of thing that
keeps a deep-water man on his feet pretty well night and day.

When we arrived in Dundee, Mrs. B—— was already there,
waiting to take him home. We traveled up to London by the
same train; but by the time I had managed to get through with
my examination the ship had sailed on her next voyage without
him, and, instead of joining her again, I went by request to see
my old commander in his home. This is the only one of my
captains I have ever visited in that way. He was out of bed
by then, " quite convalescent," as he declared, making a few
tottering steps to meet me at the sitting-room door. Evidently
he was reluctant to take his final cross-bearings of this earth
for a Departure on the only voyage to an unknown destination
a sailor ever undertakes. And it was all very nice — the large,
sunny room; his deep easy-chair in a bow window, with pillows and a footstool; the quiet, watchful care of the elderly,
gentle woman who had borne him five children, and had not,
perhaps, lived with him more than five full years out of the
thirty or so of their married life. There was also another
woman there in a plain black dress, quite grey-haired, sitting
very erect on her chair with some sewing, from which she
snatched side-glances in his direction, and uttering not a single
word during all the time of my call. Even when, in due
course, I carried over to her a cup of tea, she only nodded at
me silently, with the faintest ghost of a smile, on her tight-set
lips. I imagine she must have been a maiden sister of Mrs.
B—— come to help nurse her brother-in-law. His youngest
boy, a late-comer, a great cricketer it seemed, twelve years old
or thereabouts, chattered enthusiastically of the exploits of
W. G. Grace. And I remember his eldest son, too, a newly-
fledged doctor, who took me out to smoke in the garden, and,

shaking his head with professional gravity, but with genuine concern, muttered: "Yes, but he doesn't get back his appetite. I don't like that — I don't like that at all." The last sight of Captain B——— I had was as he nodded his head to me out of the bow window when I turned round to close the front gate.

It was a distinct and complete impression, something that I don't know whether to call a Landfall or a Departure. Certainly he had gazed at times very fixedly before him with the Landfall's vigilant look, this sea-captain seated incongruously in a deep-backed chair. He had not then talked to me of employment, of ships, of being ready to take another command; but he had discoursed of his early days, in the abundant but thin flow of a wilful invalid's talk. The women looked worried, but sat still, and I learned more of him in that interview than in the whole eighteen months we had sailed together. It appeared he had "served his time" in the copper-ore trade, of old days between Swansea and the Chilean coast, coal out and ore in, deep-loaded both ways, as if in wanton defiance of the great Cape Horn seas — a work, this, for staunch ships, and a great school of staunchness for West-Country seamen. A whole fleet of copper-bottomed barques, as strong in rib and planking, as well-found in gear, as ever was sent upon the seas, manned by hardy crews and commanded by young masters, was engaged in that now long-defunct trade. "That was the school I was trained in," he said to me almost boastfully, lying back amongst his pillows with a rug over his legs. And it was in that trade that he obtained his first command at a very early age. It was then that he mentioned to me how, as a young commander, he was always ill for a few days before making land after a long passage. But this sort of sickness used to pass off with the first sight of a familiar landmark. Afterwards, he added, as he grew older, all that nervousness wore off completely; and I observed his weary eyes gaze steadily ahead, as if there had been nothing between him and the straight line of sea and sky, where whatever a seaman is looking for is first bound to appear. But I have also seen his eyes rest fondly upon the faces in the room, upon the pictures on the wall, upon all the familiar objects of that home, whose abiding and clear image must have flashed often on his memory in times of stress and anxiety at sea. Was he looking out for a strange Landfall, or taking with an untroubled mind the bearings for his last Departure?

It is hard to say; for in that voyage from which no man returns Landfall and Departure are instantaneous, merging together into one moment of supreme and final attention. Certainly I do not remember observing any sign of faltering in the set expression of his wasted face, no hint of the nervous anxiety of a young commander about to make land on an uncharted shore. He had had too much experience of Departures and Landfalls! And had he not " served his time " in the famous copper-ore trade out of the Bristol Channel, the work of the staunchest ships afloat, and the school of staunch seamen?

APPRECIATION HELPS

1. What distinction is drawn between Landfall and Departure?
2. What interested you in the different spirit with which commanders take their departure?
3. Discuss routine as a " great doctor for sore hearts and for sore heads." Read " Routine and Ideals," by LeBaron Russell Briggs.
4. Discuss the passage of time aboard ship.
5. How has Conrad succeeded in giving you a taste of the sea?
6. Point out examples of his fine sense for the nice, the exact, word in which to clothe his thought.
7. Name other men whose native tongue was not English who became masters in its use.
8. Read his *Mirror of the Sea* if you enjoyed this sketch of sea life.

COMPOSITION HINTS

1. " Land Ho! "
2. A Bad Passage
3. When My Superior Officer Was Grumpy
4. Irritating Trifles
5. Advantages of Living on the Seacoast
6. Advantages of an Inland Home

FRANCIS BACON

In China it is the wont for any youth desirous of entering a government department to journey to Peking upon passing his examinations and there to wait, perchance many years, until the post for which he has applied falls vacant. The actual incumbent of the office may be hale and hearty, a previous applicant may have first to reap the fruits of patience before the youth himself can enter into what he has marked down as his own; these considerations have not affected the scrupulousness with which the custom is uniformly observed. Thus a large proportion of the population of Peking (or as we must now say Peiping) consists of future officials. During their years of waiting these slaves of hope have of course to subsist, and to subsist they usually fall into debt. Hence it is not surprising that once the youth who now is no longer a youth has reached the goal of his desires, he should thereafter accept bribes in the light of legitimate emoluments and devote such additional income to the pacification of creditors who with the lapse of time have grown both impatient and voracious. So is China known as the land of *squeeze,* a land where none is too humble or too exalted to sweep the clandestine gift of cash into the mystery of his capacious sleeve.

The career of Francis Bacon (1561–1626), who in greatness towers far above all others whose work is sampled in this volume, closely resembles that of a Chinese official. In his early years he was led to expect that the powerful aid of influential relatives would be exercised in his favor, but again and again he was disappointed. This constant deferring of hope affected him ill; his life was harassed by want of means. At last, when he was fifty-seven, luck changed. He became Lord High Chancellor of England, and other honors showered upon him: he was made Sir Francis Bacon, then Baron Verulam, and finally, in 1621, Viscount St. Albans. But these good things came too late. Like the Chinaman, he had now to satisfy the creditors of his impecunious years. And a few months after he was made a viscount, he was accused of receiving gifts from those whose suits were before him as Lord Chancellor. In England *squeeze* has never been revered as in China; Bacon, the highest judge in the kingdom, was brought to trial. He confessed his guilt and, being convicted of bribery, was fined £40,000 and deposed from office. Well could he write "Of Riches" and "Of Friendship," two of his famous Essays given here.

It is a sad story, yet there is an important lesson in it if a lesson is sought: a man may wait long for the well-paid position he yearns to hold, and in the end he may fail to retain it, yet nevertheless he may be great. For Bacon, as has been indicated, was a very great man indeed. He was a learned as well as a dishonest judge. He was great as a writer: perhaps you will not appreciate fully now, but you may some day, the majesty and profundity of his sentences; and he wrote as well in Latin as he did in English. Still, it is not in his jurisprudence nor in his writing that his chief greatness lies, but in something more wonderful, maybe, than either. It is not too much to say that if you awaken each morning in a room centrally heated, wash in warm water, eat a breakfast cooked by gas, travel to school in an electric trolley-car, have electric light to read by at evening, use the telephone or a motorcar, Bacon is the first man you have to thank for all these blessings. He is the father of modern science.

Well could he write "Of Studies" and "Of Truth," two more essays you can read presently. His whole life was devoted to the study of how to discover truth. Before him and while he lived people employed the most fantastic and ludicrous means for obtaining absurd explanations of the great problems of the universe, usually explanations that satisfied the pet theories they nourished before ever they began study. Such alleged investigations make one explode in laughter today, but until Bacon came on the scene they were taken with the greatest seriousness. He it was who discredited such tomfoolery forever. During seventeen years he labored at "the exposition of a new method by which the human mind might proceed with security and certainty towards the true end of all human thought and action." In this Latin treatise he showed that if one really wanted to find out anything, and not just amuse oneself, the only way was by trial and error: the experimental method. And that experiments might lead to momentous discoveries he revealed a powerful help of which he was the inventor: induction.

In finding out about things there are just two ways of setting to work: by deduction or by induction. Sherlock Holmes has made everyone familiar with deduction. What it is and what is induction and how they differ can be made clear very easily. Your mother and father notice that all boys and girls go to school. You are a boy or girl. They conclude that you ought to go to school too. That is deduction: it is pretty easy and safe. Induction is harder and more dangerous. You go to school, and you are a boy or girl. You conclude that all boys and girls go to school. That is induction. Deduction is from the general to the particular; induction from the particular to the general. It is usually by induction that all great scientific discoveries have been made, and as Bacon originated induction, so are these great discoveries owed to him. It matters little that the inductive method, as he worked it out, was not quite right, that later men had to come along and perfect it. Bacon led the way: this man, who was fined and shamed for accepting bribes, changed the whole course of human thought and of human endeavor.

OF RICHES

I CANNOT call riches better than the baggage of virtue. The Roman word is better, *impedimenta;* for as the baggage is to an army, so is riches to virtue; it cannot be spared nor left behind, but it hindereth the march; yea, and the care of it sometimes loseth or disturbeth the victory. Of great riches there is no real use, except it be in the distribution; the rest is but conceit. So saith Salomon: *Where much is, there are many to consume it; and what hath the owner but the sight of it with his eyes?* The personal fruition in any man cannot reach to feel great riches: there is a custody of them; or a power of dole and donative of them; or a fame of them; but no solid use to the owner. Do you not see what feigned prices are set upon little stones and rarities? and what works of ostentation are undertaken, because there might seem to be some use of great riches? But then you will say, they may be of use to buy men out of dangers or trouble. Salomon saith: *Riches are as a stronghold in the imagination of the rich man.* But this is excellently expressed, that it is in imagination, and not always in fact. For certainly great riches have sold more men than they have brought out. Seek not proud riches, but such as thou mayest get justly, use soberly, distribute cheerfully, and leave contentedly. Yet have no abstract nor friarly contempt of them. But distinguish, as Cicero saith well of Rabirius Posthumus: *In studio rei amplificandæ apparebat non avaritiæ prædam sed instrumentum bonitati quæri.* Hearken also to Salomon, and beware of hasty gathering of riches: *Qui festinat ad divitias non erit insons.* The poets feign that when Plutus (which is Riches) is sent from Jupiter, he limps and goes slowly; but when he is sent from Pluto, he runs and is swift of foot; meaning, that riches gotten by good means and just labor pace slowly; but when they come by the death of others (as by the course of inheritance, testaments, and the like), they come tumbling upon a man. But it might be applied likewise to Pluto, taking him for the devil. For when riches come from the devil (as by fraud and oppression and unjust means), they come upon speed. The ways to enrich are many, and most of them foul. Parsimony is one of the best, and yet is not innocent; for it withholdeth men from works of liberality and charity. The improvement of the ground is the most natural obtaining of riches; for it is our great mother's blessing, the earth's; but it is slow. And yet, where men of great wealth do stoop to husbandry, it multiplieth riches exceedingly. I knew a nobleman in England, that had the greatest audits of any man in my time; a great grazier, a great sheep-master, a great timber man, a great collier, a great corn-master, a great lead-man, and so of iron, and a number of the like points of husbandry: so as the earth seemed a sea to him, in respect of the perpetual importation. It was truly observed by one, that himself came very hardly to a little riches, and very easily to great riches. For when a man's stock is come to that, that he can expect the prime of markets, and overcome those bargains which for their greatness are few men's money, and be partner in the industries of younger men, he cannot but increase mainly. The gains of ordinary trades and vocations are honest, and furthered by two things chiefly: by diligence, and by a good name for good and fair dealing. But the gains of bargains are of a more doubtful nature; when men shall wait upon others' necessity, broke by servants and instruments to draw them on, put off others cunningly that would be better chapmen, and the like practices, which are crafty and naught. As for the chopping of bargains, when a man buys, not to hold, but to sell over again, that commonly grindeth double, both upon the seller and upon the buyer. Sharings do greatly enrich, if the hands be well chosen that are trusted. Usury is the certainest means of gain, though one of the worst; as that whereby a man doth eat his bread *in sudore vultûs alieni,* and besides, doth plow upon Sundays. But yet, certain though it be, it hath flaws; for that the scriveners and brokers do value unsound men, to serve their own turn. The fortune in being the first in an invention, or in a privilege, doth cause sometimes a wonderful overgrowth in riches; as it was with the first sugar man in the Canaries: therefore if a man can play the true logician, to have as well judgment as invention, he may do great matters; especially if the times be fit. He that resteth upon gains certain, shall hardly grow to great riches: and he that puts all upon adventures, doth oftentimes break and come to poverty: it is good therefore to guard adventures with certainties that may uphold losses. Monopolies, and coemption of wares for re-sale, where they are not restrained, are great means to enrich; especially if the party have intelligence what things are like to come into request, and so store himself beforehand. Riches gotten by service, though it be of the best rise, yet when they are gotten by flattery, feeding humors, and other servile conditions, they may be placed amongst the worst. As for fishing for testaments and executorships (as Tacitus saith of Seneca, *testamenta et orbos tanquam indagine capi*), it is yet worse; by how much men submit themselves to meaner persons than in service. Believe not much them that seem to despise riches: for they despise them that despair of them; and none worse, when they come to them. Be not penny-wise; riches have wings, and sometimes they fly away of themselves, sometimes they must be set flying to bring in more. Men leave their riches either to their kindred, or to the public; and moderate portions prosper best in both. A great state left to an heir is as a lure to all the birds of prey round about to seize on him, if he be not the better stablished in years and judgment. Likewise glorious gifts and foundations are like *sacrifices without salt;* and but the painted sepulchers of alms, which soon will putrefy and corrupt inwardly. Therefore measure not thine advancements by quantity, but frame them by measure: and defer not charities till death; for certainly, if a man weigh it rightly, he that doth so is rather liberal of another man's than of his own.

APPRECIATION HELPS

1. List the advantages and the disadvantages Bacon recognizes in riches. Are these as potent now as in his time?
2. What are the uses to which money should be put?
3. Discuss examples of men who have used riches wisely.
4. What changes in the world's attitude toward wealth have come within the lifetime of your father? Illustrate.
5. Name characters in literature influenced for evil by riches. Name some who have done great good with riches.
6. Explain: " Gains of bargains are of a doubtful nature."

COMPOSITION HINTS

1. " Where Much Is, There Are Many to Consume It "
2. Little Stones and Rarities I Prize
3. When My Bargain Was Costly
4. Penny-Wise and Pound-Foolish
5. When My Riches Had Wings
6. Advantages of Riches

OF STUDIES

by Francis Bacon

STUDIES serve for delight, for ornament, and for ability. Their chief use for delight is in privateness and retiring; for ornament, is in discourse; and for ability, is in the judgment and disposition of business. For expert men can execute and perhaps judge of particulars, one by one; but the general counsels, and the plots and marshaling of affairs, come best from those that are learned. To spend too much time in studies is sloth; to use them too much for ornament is affectation; to make judgment wholly by their rules is the humor of a scholar. They perfect nature, and are perfected by experience; for natural abilities are like natural plants, that need proyning by study; and studies themselves do give forth directions too much at large, except they be bounded in by experience. Crafty men contemn studies; simple men admire them; and wise men use them: for they teach not their own use; but that is a wisdom without them and above them, won by observation. Read not to contradict and confute; nor to believe and take for granted; nor to find talk and discourse; but to weigh and consider. Some books are to be tasted, others to be swallowed, and some few to be chewed and digested: that is, some books are to be read only in parts; others to be read, but not curiously; and some few to be read wholly, and with diligence and attention. Some books also may be read by deputy, and extracts made of them by others; but that would be only in the less important arguments, and the meaner sort of books; else distilled books are like common distilled waters, flashy things. Reading maketh a full man; conference a ready man; and writing an exact man. And therefore, if a man write little, he had need have a great memory; if he confer little, he had need have a present wit; and if he read little, he had need have much cunning, to seem to know that he doth not. Histories make men wise; poets witty; the mathematics subtile; natural philosophy deep; moral grave; logic and rhetoric able to contend. *Abeunt studia in mores.* Nay, there is no stond or impediment in the wit, but may be wrought out by fit studies: like as diseases of the body may have appropriate exercises. Bowling is good for the stone and reins; shooting for the lungs and breast; gentle walking for the stomach; riding for the head; and the like. So if a man's wit be wandering, let him study the mathematics; for a demonstration, if his wit be called away never so little, he must begin again: if his wit be not apt to distinguish or find differences, let him study the schoolmen; for they are *cymini sectores:* if he be not apt to beat over matters, and to call one thing to prove and illustrate another, let him study the lawyers' case: so every defect of the mind may have a special receipt.

APPRECIATION HELPS

1. Discuss Bacon's ability to pack his thought in brief statements. Select any sentence or section and try to express completely in your own words Bacon's thought.
2. Discuss the purpose of reading.
3. Give examples of books suited to each one of the following purposes of reading: " Studies serve for delight, for ornament, and for ability."
4. What books are " to be tasted, swallowed, chewed "?
5. Think of several of the best-read persons you know; and decide whether their reading has been worth the time.
6. Why is this essay considered by many to be Bacon's most perfect piece of writing?

COMPOSITION HINTS

1. Studies Serve for Delight
2. Spending too Much Time in Studies
3. Wise Men Use Studies
4. Books to Be Tasted
5. Books to Be Digested
6. When I Read by Deputy
7. When My Wits Went Wandering

OF FRIENDSHIP

by Francis Bacon

IT had been hard for him that spake it to have put more truth than untruth together in a few words, than in that speech, *Whosoever is delighted in solitude is either a wild beast or a god*. For it is most true that a natural and secret hatred and aversation towards society, in any man, hath somewhat of the savage beast; but it is most untrue that it should have any character at all of the divine nature; except it proceed, not out of a pleasure in solitude, but out of a love and desire to sequester a man's self for a higher conversation: such as is found to have been falsely and feignedly in some of the heathen; as Epimenides the Candian, Numa the Roman, Empedocles the Sicilian, and Apollonius of Tyana; and truly and really in divers of the ancient hermits and holy fathers of the church. But little do men perceive what solitude is, and how far it extendeth. For a crowd is not company, and faces are but a gallery of pictures, and talk but a tinkling cymbal, where there is no love. The Latin adage meeteth with it a little. *Magna civitas, magna solitudo;* because in a great town friends are scattered; so that there is not that fellowship, for the most part, which is in less neighborhoods. But we may go farther, and affirm most truly that it is a mere and miserable solitude to want true friends, without which the world is but a wilderness; and even in this sense also of solitude, whosoever in the frame of his nature and affections is unfit for friendship, he taketh it of the beast, and not from humanity.

A principal fruit of friendship is the ease and discharge of the fullness and swellings of the heart, which passions of all kind do cause and induce. We know diseases of stoppings and suffocations are the most dangerous in the body; and it is not much otherwise in the mind; you may take sarza to open the liver, steel to open the spleen, flowers of sulphur for the lungs, castoreum for the brain; but no receipt openeth the heart, but a true friend, to whom you may impart griefs, joys, fears, hopes, suspicions, counsels, and whatsoever lieth upon the heart to oppress it, in a kind of civil shrift or confession.

It is a strange thing to observe how high a rate great kings and monarchs do set upon this fruit of friendship whereof we speak: so great, as they purchase it many times at the hazard of their own safety and greatness. For princes, in regard of the distance of their fortune from that of their subjects and servants, cannot gather this fruit, except (to make themselves capable thereof) they raise some persons to be as it were companions and almost equals to themselves, which many times sorteth to inconvenience. The modern languages give unto such persons the name of *favorites,* or *privadoes;* as if it were matter of grace, or conversation. But the Roman name attaineth the true use and cause thereof, naming them *participes curarum;* for it is that which tieth the knot. And we see plainly that this hath been done, not by weak and passionate princes only, but by the wisest and most politic that ever reigned; who have oftentimes joined to themselves some of their servants, whom both themselves have called *friends,* and allowed others likewise to call them in the same manner, using the word which is received between private men.

L. Sylla, when he commanded Rome, raised Pompey (after surnamed the Great) to that height, that Pompey vaunted himself for Sylla's overmatch. For when he had carried the consulship for a friend of his, against the pursuit of Sylla, and that Sylla did a little resent thereat, and began to speak great, Pompey turned upon him again, and in effect bade him be quiet; *for that more men adored the sun rising than the sun setting.* With Julius Cæsar, Decimus Brutus had obtained that interest, as he set him down in his testament for heir in remainder after his nephew; and this was the man that had power with him to draw him forth to his death. For when Cæsar would have discharged the senate, in regard of some ill presages, and specially a dream of Calpurnia, this man lifted him gently by the arm out of his chair, telling him he hoped he would not dismiss the senate till his wife had dreamt a better dream. And it seemeth his favor was so great, as Antonius, in a letter which is recited *verbatim* in one of Cicero's *Philippics,* calleth him *venefica,* " witch "; as if he had enchanted Cæsar. Augustus raised Agrippa (though of mean birth) to that height, as, when he consulted with Mæcenas about the marriage of his daughter Julia, Mæcenas took the liberty to tell him, *that he must either marry his daughter to Agrippa, or take away his life; there was no third way, he had made him so great.* With Tiberius Cæsar, Sejanus had ascended to that height, as they two were termed and reckoned as a pair of friends. Tiberius in a letter to him saith, *Hæc pro amicitiâ nostrâ non occultavi;* and the whole senate dedicated an altar to Friendship, as to a goddess, in respect of the great dearness of friendship between them two. The like or more was between Septimius Severus and Plautianus. For he forced his eldest son to marry the daughter of Plautianus; and would often maintain Plautianus in doing affronts to his son; and did write also in a letter to the senate by these words: *I love the man so well, as I wish he may over-live me.* Now if these princes had been as a Trajan, or a Marcus Aurelius, a man might have thought that this had proceeded of an abundant goodness of nature; but being men so wise, of such strength and severity of mind, and so extreme lovers of themselves, as all these were, it proveth most plainly that they found their own felicity (though as great as ever happened to mortal men) but as an half piece, except they might have a friend to make it entire: and yet, which is more, they were princes that had wives, sons, nephews; and yet all these could not supply the comfort of friendship.

It is not to be forgotten, what Comineus observeth of his first master, Duke Charles the Hardy; namely, that he would communicate his secrets with none; and least of all, those secrets which troubled him most. Whereupon he goeth on and saith that towards his latter time *that closeness did impair and a little perish his understanding.* Surely Comineus might have made the same judgment also, if it had pleased him, of his second master. Lewis the Eleventh, whose closeness was indeed his tormentor. The parable of Pythagoras is dark, but true; *Cor ne edito,* " Eat not the heart." Certainly, if a man would give it a hard phrase, those that want friends to open themselves unto are cannibals of their own hearts. But one thing is most admirable (wherewith I will conclude this first fruit of friendship), which is, that this communicating of a man's self to his friends works two contrary effects; for it redoubleth joys, and cutteth griefs in halves. For there is no man that imparteth his joys to his friend, but he joyeth the more; and no man that imparteth his griefs to his friend, but he grieveth the less. So that it is, in truth of operation upon a man's mind, of like virtue as the alchemists use to attribute to their stone for man's body; that it worketh all contrary effects, but still to the good and benefit of nature. But yet, without praying in aid of alchemists, there is a manifest image of this in the ordinary course of nature. For in bodies, union strengtheneth and cherisheth any natural action; and, on the other side, weakeneth and dulleth any violent impression: and even so is it of minds.

The second fruit of friendship is healthful and sovereign for the understanding, as the first is for the affections. For friendship maketh indeed a fair day in the affections, from storm and tempests; but it maketh daylight in the understanding, out of darkness and confusion of thoughts. Neither is this to be understood only of faithful counsel, which a man receiveth from his friend; but before you come to that, certain it is that whosoever hath his mind fraught with many thoughts, his wits and understanding do clarify and break up, in the communicating and discoursing with another: he tosseth his thoughts more easily; he marshaleth them more orderly; he seeth how they look when they are turned into words; finally, he waxeth wiser than himself; and that more by an hour's discourse than by a day's meditation. It was well said by Themistocles to the king of Persia, *that speech was like cloth of Arras, opened and put abroad; whereby the imagery doth appear in figure; whereas in thoughts they lie but as in packs.* Neither is this second fruit of friendship, in opening the understanding, restrained only to such friends as are able to give a man counsel (they indeed are best); but even without that, a man learneth of himself, and bringeth his own thoughts to light, and whetteth his wits as against a stone, which itself cuts not. In a word, a man were better relate himself to a statua or picture, than to suffer his thoughts to pass in smother.

Add now, to make this second fruit of friendship complete, that other point, which lieth more open, and falleth within vulgar observation; which is faithful counsel from a friend. Heraclitus saith well in one of his enigmas, *Dry light is ever the best*. And certain it is that the light that a man receiveth by counsel from another is drier and purer than that which cometh from his own understanding and judgment; which is ever infused and drenched in his affections and customs. So as there is as much difference between the counsel that a friend giveth, and that a man giveth himself, as there is between the counsel of a friend and of a flatterer. For there is no such flatterer as is a man's self; and there is no such remedy against flattery of a man's self as the liberty of a friend. Counsel is of two sorts; the one concerning manners, the other concerning business. For the first; the best preservative to keep the mind in health is the faithful admonition of a friend. The calling of a man's self to a strict account is a medicine, sometime, too piercing and corrosive. Reading good books of morality is a little flat and dead. Observing our faults in others is sometimes unproper for our case. But the best receipt (best, I say, to work, and best to take) is the admonition of a friend. It is a strange thing to behold what gross errors and extreme absurdities many (especially of the greater sort) do commit, for want of a friend to tell them of them, to the great damage both of fame and fortune. For, as S. James saith, they are as men *that look sometimes into a glass, and presently forget their own shape and favor*. As for business, a man may think, if he will, that two eyes see no more than one; or that a gamester seeth always more than a looker-on; or that a man in anger is as wise as he that hath said over the four-and-twenty letters; or that a musket may be shot off as well upon the arm as upon a rest; and such other fond and high imaginations, to think himself all in all. But when all is done, the help of good counsel is that which setteth business straight. And if any man think that he will take counsel, but it shall be by pieces, asking counsel in one business of one man, and in another business of another man; it is well (that is to say, better perhaps than if he asked none at all); but he runneth two dangers. One, that he shall not be faithfully counseled; for it is a rare thing, except it be from a perfect and entire friend, to have counsel given, but such as shall be bowed and crooked to some ends which he hath that giveth it. The other, that he shall have counsel given, hurtful and unsafe (though with good meaning), and mixed partly of mischief and partly of remedy; even as if you would call a physician, that is thought good for the cure of the disease you complain of, but is unacquainted with your body; and therefore may put you in way for a present cure, but overthroweth your health in some other kind; and so cure the disease and kill the patient. But a friend that is wholly acquainted with a man's estate will beware, by furthering any present business, how he dasheth upon other inconvenience. And therefore rest not upon scattered counsels; they will rather distract and mislead than settle and direct.

After these two noble fruits of friendship (peace in the affections, and support of the judgment) followeth the last fruit, which is like the pomegranate, full of many kernels; I mean aid and bearing a part in all actions and occasions. Here the best way to represent to life the manifold use of friendship is to cast and see how many things there are which a man cannot do himself; and then it will appear that it was a sparing speech of the ancients, to say *that a friend is another himself:* for that a friend is far more than himself. Men have their time, and die many times in desire of some things which they principally take to heart; the bestowing of a child, the finishing of a work, or the like. If a man have a true friend, he may rest almost secure that the care of those things will continue after him. So that a man hath as it were two lives in his desires. A man hath a body, and that body is confined to a place; but where friendship is, all offices of life are as it were granted to him and his deputy; for he may exercise them by his friend. How many things are there which a man cannot, with any face or comeliness, say or do himself! A man can scarce allege his own merits with modesty, much less extol them; a man cannot sometimes brook to supplicate or beg; and a number of the like. But all these are graceful in a friend's mouth, which are blushing in a man's own. So again, a man's person hath many proper relations which he cannot put off. A man cannot speak to his son but as a father; to his wife but as a husband; to his enemy but upon terms: whereas a friend may speak as the case requires, and not as it sorteth with the person. But to enumerate these things were endless: I have given the rule, where a man cannot fitly play his own part: if he have not a friend, he may quit the stage.

APPRECIATION HELPS

1. What estimate does Bacon place upon friendship?
2. What are the " fruits of friendship "?
3. List the qualities you demand in your good friends.
4. Study Bacon's literary and historical references. In what literature was he especially interested? Why?
5. Do you feel that Bacon knew men and human nature intimately? Do these essays reveal the kind of ability it would require to write the works of Shakespeare?

COMPOSITION HINTS

1. Bypaths of Friendship
2. When I Heeded a Friendly Admonition
3. A Father Who Is a Friend
4. When a Crowd Was not Company
5. " Friendship Redoubles Joy and Cuts Griefs in Half "

OF TRUTH

by Francis Bacon

WHAT *is truth?* said jesting Pilate, and would not stay for an answer. Certainly there be that delight in giddiness, and count it a bondage to fix a belief; affecting free-will in thinking, as well as in acting. And though the sects of philosophers of that kind be gone, yet there remain certain discoursing wits which are of the same veins, though there be not so much blood in them as was in those of the ancients. But it is not only the difficulty and labor which men take in finding out of truth, nor again that when it is found it imposeth upon men's thoughts, that doth bring lies in favor; but a natural though corrupt love of the lie itself. One of the later schools of the Grecians examineth the matter, and is at a stand to think what should be in it, that men should love lies; where neither they make for pleasure, as with poets; nor for advantage, as with the merchant; but for the lie's sake. But I cannot tell: this same truth is a naked and open daylight, that doth not show the masques and mummeries and triumphs of the world, half so stately and daintily as candlelights. Truth may perhaps come to the price of a pearl, that showeth best by day; but it will not rise to the price of a diamond or carbuncle, that showeth best in varied lights. A mixture of a lie doth ever add pleasure. Doth any man doubt, that if there were taken out of men's minds vain opinions, flattering hopes, false valuations, imaginations as one would, and the like, but it would leave the minds of a number of men poor shrunken things, full of melancholy and indisposition, and unpleasing to themselves? One of the fathers, in great severity, called poesy *vinum dæmonum,* because it filleth the imagination, and yet it is but with the shadow of a lie. But it is not the lie that passeth through the mind, but the lie that sinketh in and settleth in it, that doth the hurt such as we spake of before. But howsoever these things are thus in men's depraved judgments and affections, yet truth, which only doth judge itself, teacheth that the inquiry of truth, which is the love-making or wooing of it, the knowledge of truth, which is the presence of it, and the belief of truth, which is the enjoying of it, is the sovereign good of human nature. The first creature of God, in the works of the days, was the light of the sense; the last was the light of reason; and his sabbath work, ever since, is the illumination of his Spirit. First he breathed light upon the face of the matter or chaos; then he breathed light into the face of man; and still he breatheth and inspireth light into the face of his chosen. The poet that beautified the sect that was otherwise inferior to the rest, saith yet excellently well: *It is a pleasure to stand upon the shore, and to see ships tossed upon the sea: a pleasure to stand in the window of a castle, and to see a battle and the adventures thereof below: but no pleasure is comparable to the standing upon the vantage ground of truth* (a hill not to be commanded, and where the air is always clear and serene), *and to see the errors, and wanderings, and mists, and tempests, in the vale below:* so always that this prospect be with pity, and not with swelling or pride. Certainly, it is heaven upon earth, to have a man's mind move in charity, rest in providence, and turn upon the poles of truth.

To pass from theological and philosophical truth, to the truth of civil business: it will be acknowledged, even by those that practice it not, that clear and round dealing is the honor of man's nature; and that mixture of falsehood is like alloy in coin of gold and silver; which may make the metal work the better, but it embaseth it. For these winding and crooked courses are the goings of the serpent; which goeth basely upon the belly, and not upon the feet. There is no vice that doth so cover a man with shame as to be found false and perfidious. And therefore Montaigne saith prettily, when he inquired the reason, why the word of the lie should be such a disgrace and such an odious charge; saith he, *If it be well weighed, to say that a man lieth is as much to say as that he is brave towards God and a coward towards men.* For a lie faces God, and shrinks from man. Surely the wickedness of falsehood and breach of faith cannot possibly be so highly expressed, as in that it shall be the last peal to call the judgments of God upon the generations of men; it being foretold that, when Christ cometh, *he shall not find faith upon the earth.*

APPRECIATION HELPS

1. What is meant by " free-will in thinking "?
2. What are the motives which lead men to untruth today?
3. Explain: " A mixture of a lie doth ever add pleasure."
4. List five ideas Bacon develops on truth.
5. Discuss Montaigne's quotation in the last paragraph.
6. Compare Bacon on truth with Kipling on the same theme (" Independence ").

COMPOSITION HINTS

1. On Truth
2. On Dishonesty
3. Caught in an Untruth
4. " The Soul of Honor "
5. Are Untruths Ever Justifiable?

HEYWOOD BROUN

Mr. Heywood Broun looks lazy. A bulky man whose fat suggests a distaste of exertion, he can scarcely be called a beau in dress; indeed, one might suspect him of lying abed until just after the very last second. He is black-haired, too, like those animals that sleep through the whole winter, and in his large pale face are drowsy eyes. If ever he goes anywhere on foot, he shambles rather than walks, and usually he sits rather than shambles. Yet all that is make-believe. In reality he is of the breed of Titans. Wet or fine, winter and summer, all the year round except for a hard-won and brief vacation, he writes fourteen hundred words each day seven days a week, fourteen hundred words for which he has to find the subjects, and next morning, fresh, whimsical, and entertaining, there they are in the New York *World-Telegram* under the heading, " It Seems to Me." Thousands of men and women would rather omit at least the dinner dessert than the perusal of that column. But how few give a thought to the miracle of its production! The novelist thinks his bread well earned if he achieves a thousand words a day of the book he has all planned out; other writers, it is true, have spurts of three thousand words and more at a time, but they rest three days out of seven. Mr. Broun apparently never rests: each morning he must get to his typewriter and somehow fill the blank page with reflections, not any reflections — that would be easier — but reflections on matters that are being discussed and thought over that very day. And his success proves that he fills the page well. It is a wonderful performance. The motorcar's engine, the marvels of wireless, the fur-trapper's frosty quest, the pearl-fisher's patient diving, all dwindle to the commonplace beside this prodigy; yet the air mail between New York and Chicago each night is not more regular.

One pictures Mr. Broun bowed down and careworn with such a task. On the contrary, he seems to thrive upon it. He finds time to write novels as well, and excellent novels they are. A few years

ago he was also a dramatic critic, not just for one publication, but for a daily, a monthly, and probably a couple of weeklies. And the big ball games bring him forth as a reporter. There simply is no limit to his capacity for work.

It was as a baseball reporter that he began. He was born in Brooklyn in 1888; he went to Harvard Law School. Then he got a job on the *Morning Telegraph* back in 1908, and thence in a few years he went to the New York *Tribune*. He was such a good baseball reporter that the *Tribune* thought it would be interesting to have him report on books and plays as he did on baseball. The experiment was so successful that the *World* invited him to come to them. So started " It Seems to Me." (When the *World* was merged with the *Evening Telegram,* Mr. Broun followed it.) This gave Messrs. Putnam the belief that he would be a good novelist; he agreed, and in the fall of 1922 came *The Boy Grew Older.* In 1917 he went to France as a war correspondent with the A. E. F. Essays, like " The Fifty-First Dragon " that follows, he has just taken in his stride. One wonders what he will add to his occupations next.

THE FIFTY-FIRST DRAGON[1]

OF all the pupils at the knight school Gawaine le Cœur-Hardy was among the least promising. He was tall and sturdy, but his instructors soon discovered that he lacked spirit. He would hide in the woods when the jousting class was called, although his companions and members of the faculty sought to appeal to his better nature by shouting to him to come out and break his neck like a man. Even when they told him that the lances were padded, the horses no more than ponies and the field unusually soft for late autumn, Gawaine refused to grow enthusiastic. The Headmaster and the Assistant Professor of Pleasaunce were discussing the case one spring afternoon and the Assistant Professor could see no remedy but expulsion.

" No," said the Headmaster, as he looked out at the purple

[1] From *Seeing Things at Night,* published by Harcourt, Brace and Company, 1921.

hills which ringed the school, "I think I'll train him to slay dragons."

"He might be killed," objected the Assistant Professor.

"So he might," replied the Headmaster brightly, but he added, more soberly, "we must consider the greater good. We are responsible for the formation of this lad's character."

"Are the dragons particularly bad this year?" interrupted the Assistant Professor. This was characteristic. He always seemed restive when the head of the school began to talk ethics and the ideals of the institution.

"I've never known them worse," replied the Headmaster. "Up in the hills to the south last week they killed a number of peasants, two cows and a prize pig. And if this dry spell holds there's no telling when they may start a forest fire simply by breathing around indiscriminately."

"Would any refund on the tuition fee be necessary in case of an accident to young Cœur-Hardy?"

"No," the principal answered, judicially, "that's all covered in the contract. But as a matter of fact he won't be killed. Before I send him up in the hills I'm going to give him a magic word."

"That's a good idea," said the Professor. "Sometimes they work wonders."

From that day on Gawaine specialized in dragons. His course included both theory and practice. In the morning there were long lectures on the history, anatomy, manners and customs of dragons. Gawaine did not distinguish himself in these studies. He had a marvelously versatile gift for forgetting things. In the afternoon he showed to better advantage, for then he would go down to the South Meadow and practice with a battle-ax. In this exercise he was truly impressive, for he had enormous strength as well as speed and grace. He even developed a deceptive display of ferocity. Old alumni say that it was a thrilling sight to see Gawaine charging across the field toward the dummy paper dragon which had been set up for his practice. As he ran he would brandish his ax and shout "A murrain on thee!" or some other vivid bit of campus slang. It never took him more than one stroke to behead the dummy dragon.

Gradually his task was made more difficult. Paper gave way to papier-mâché and finally to wood, but even the toughest of these dummy dragons had no terrors for Gawaine. One sweep of the ax always did the business. There were those who said that when the practice was protracted until dusk and the dragons threw long, fantastic shadows across the meadow Gawaine did not charge so impetuously nor shout so loudly. It is possible there was malice in this charge. At any rate, the Headmaster decided by the end of June that it was time for the test. Only the night before a dragon had come close to the school grounds and had eaten some of the lettuce from the garden. The faculty decided that Gawaine was ready. They gave him a diploma and a new battle-ax and the Headmaster summoned him to a private conference.

" Sit down," said the Headmaster. " Have a cigarette."

Gawaine hesitated.

" Oh, I know it's against the rules," said the Headmaster. " But after all, you have received your preliminary degree. You are no longer a boy. You are a man. Tomorrow you will go out into the world, the great world of achievement."

Gawaine took a cigarette. The Headmaster offered him a match, but he produced one of his own and began to puff away with a dexterity which quite amazed the principal.

" Here you have learned the theories of life," continued the Headmaster, resuming the thread of his discourse, " but after all, life is not a matter of theories. Life is a matter of facts. It calls on the young and the old alike to face these facts, even though they are hard and sometimes unpleasant. Your problem, for example, is to slay dragons."

" They say that those dragons down in the south wood are five hundred feet long," ventured Gawaine, timorously.

" Stuff and nonsense! " said the Headmaster. " The curate saw one last week from the top of Arthur's Hill. The dragon was sunning himself down in the valley. The curate didn't have an opportunity to look at him very long because he felt it was his duty to hurry back to make a report to me. He said the monster, or shall I say, the big lizard? — wasn't an inch over two hundred feet. But the size has nothing at all to do with it. You'll find the big ones even easier than the little ones. They're far slower on their feet and less aggressive, I'm told. Besides, before you go I'm going to equip you in such fashion that you need have no fear of all the dragons in the world."

" I'd like an enchanted cap," said Gawaine.

" What's that? " answered the Headmaster, testily.

" A cap to make me disappear," explained Gawaine.

The Headmaster laughed indulgently. " You mustn't believe all those old wives' stories," he said. " There isn't any such thing. A cap to make you disappear, indeed! What would you do with it? You haven't even appeared yet. Why, my boy, you could walk from here to London, and nobody would so much as look at you. You're nobody. You couldn't be more invisible than that."

Gawaine seemed dangerously close to a relapse into his old habit of whimpering. The Headmaster reassured him: " Don't worry; I'll give you something much better than an enchanted cap. I'm going to give you a magic word. All you have to do is to repeat this magic charm once and no dragon can possibly harm a hair of your head. You can cut off his head at your leisure."

He took a heavy book from the shelf behind his desk and began to run through it. " Sometimes," he said, " the charm is a whole phrase or even a sentence. I might, for instance, give you ' To make the ' — No, that might not do. I think a single word would be best for dragons."

" A short word," suggested Gawaine.

" It can't be too short or it wouldn't be potent. There isn't so much hurry as all that. Here's a splendid magic word: ' Rumplesnitz.' Do you think you can learn that? "

Gawaine tried and in an hour or so he seemed to have the word well in hand. Again and again he interrupted the lesson to inquire, " And if I say ' Rumplesnitz ' the dragon can't possibly hurt me?" And always the Headmaster replied, "If you only say 'Rumplesnitz,' you are perfectly safe."

Toward morning Gawaine seemed resigned to his career. At daybreak the Headmaster saw him to the edge of the forest and pointed him to the direction in which he should proceed. About a mile away to the southwest a cloud of steam hovered over an open meadow in the woods and the Headmaster assured Gawaine that under the steam he would find a dragon. Gawaine went forward slowly. He wondered whether it would be best to approach the dragon on the run as he did in his practice in the South Meadow or to walk slowly toward him, shouting "Rumplesnitz" all the way.

The problem was decided for him. No sooner had he come to the fringe of the meadow than the dragon spied him and began to charge. It was a large dragon and yet it seemed decidedly aggressive in spite of the Headmaster's statement to the contrary. As the dragon charged it released huge clouds of hissing steam through its nostrils. It was almost as if a gigantic teapot had gone mad. The dragon came forward so fast and Gawaine was so frightened that he had time to say "Rumplesnitz" only once. As he said it, he swung his battle-ax and off popped the head of the dragon. Gawaine had to admit that it was even easier to kill a real dragon than a wooden one if only you said "Rumplesnitz."

Gawaine brought the ears home and a small section of the tail. His schoolmates and the faculty made much of him, but the Headmaster wisely kept him from being spoiled by insisting that he go on with his work. Every clear day Gawaine rose at dawn and went out to kill dragons. The Headmaster kept him at home when it rained, because he said the woods were damp and unhealthy at such times and that he didn't want the boy to run needless risks. Few good days passed in which Gawaine failed to get a dragon. On one particularly fortunate day he killed three, a husband and wife and a visiting relative. Gradually he developed a technique. Pupils who sometimes watched him from the hilltops a long way off said that he often allowed the dragon to come within a few feet before he said "Rumplesnitz." He came to say it with a mocking sneer. Occasionally he did stunts. Once when an excursion party from London was watching him he went into action with his right hand tied behind his back. The dragon's head came off just as easily.

As Gawaine's record of killings mounted higher the Headmaster found it impossible to keep him completely in hand. He fell into the habit of stealing out at night and engaging in long drinking bouts at the village tavern. It was after such a debauch that he rose a little before dawn one fine August morning and started out after his fiftieth dragon. His head was heavy and his mind sluggish. He was heavy in other respects as well, for he had adopted the somewhat vulgar practice of wearing his medals, ribbons and all, when he went out dragon hunting. The decorations began on his chest and ran all the way down to his abdomen. They must have weighed at least eight pounds.

Gawaine found a dragon in the same meadow where he had killed the first one. It was a fair-sized dragon, but evidently an old one. Its face was wrinkled and Gawaine thought he had never seen so hideous a countenance. Much to the lad's disgust, the monster refused to charge and Gawaine was obliged to walk toward him. He whistled as he went. The dragon regarded him hopelessly, but craftily. Of course it had heard of Gawaine. Even when the lad raised his battle-ax the dragon made no move. It knew that there was no salvation in the quickest thrust of the head, for it had been informed that this hunter was protected by an enchantment. It merely waited, hoping something would turn up. Gawaine raised the battle-ax and suddenly lowered it again. He had grown very pale and he trembled violently. The dragon suspected a trick. "What's the matter?" it asked, with false solicitude.

"I've forgotten the magic word," stammered Gawaine.

"What a pity," said the dragon. "So that was the secret. It doesn't seem quite sporting to me, all this magic stuff, you know. Not cricket, as we used to say when I was a little dragon; but after all, that's a matter of opinion."

Gawaine was so helpless with terror that the dragon's confidence rose immeasurably and it could not resist the temptation to show off a bit.

"Could I possibly be of any assistance?" it asked. "What's the first letter of the magic word?"

"It begins with an 'r,'" said Gawaine weakly.

"Let's see," mused the dragon, "that doesn't tell us much, does it? What sort of a word is this? Is it an epithet, do you think?"

Gawaine could do no more than nod.

"Why, of course," exclaimed the dragon, "reactionary Republican."

Gawaine shook his head.

"Well, then," said the dragon, "we'd better get down to business. Will you surrender?"

With the suggestion of a compromise Gawaine mustered up enough courage to speak.

"What will you do if I surrender?" he asked.

"Why, I'll eat you," said the dragon.

"And if I don't surrender?"

"I'll eat you just the same."

"Then it doesn't make any difference, does it?" moaned Gawaine.

"It does to me," said the dragon with a smile. "I'd rather you didn't surrender. You'd taste much better if you didn't."

The dragon waited for a long time for Gawaine to ask "Why?" but the boy was too frightened to speak. At last the dragon had to give the explanation without his cue line. "You see," he said, "if you don't surrender you'll taste better because you'll die game."

This was an old and ancient trick of the dragon's. By means of some such quip he was accustomed to paralyze his victims with laughter and then to destroy them. Gawaine was sufficiently paralyzed as it was, but laughter had no part in his helplessness. With the last word of the joke the dragon drew back his head and struck. In that second there flashed into the mind of Gawaine the magic word "Rumplesnitz," but there was no time to say it. There was time only to strike and, without a word, Gawaine met the onrush of the dragon with a full swing. He put all his back and shoulders into it. The impact was terrific and the head of the dragon flew away almost a hundred yards and landed in a thicket.

Gawaine did not remain frightened very long after the death of the dragon. His mood was one of wonder. He was enormously puzzled. He cut off the ears of the monster almost in a trance. Again and again he thought to himself, " I didn't say 'Rumplesnitz'! " He was sure of that and yet there was no question that he had killed the dragon. In fact, he had never killed one so utterly. Never before had he driven a head for anything like the same distance. Twenty-five yards was perhaps his best previous record. All the way back to the knight school he kept rumbling about in his mind seeking an explanation for what had occurred. He went to the Headmaster immediately and after closing the door told him what had happened. " I didn't say 'Rumplesnitz,'" he explained with great earnestness.

The Headmaster laughed. " I'm glad you've found out," he said. " It makes you ever so much more of a hero. Don't you see that? Now you know that it was you who killed all these dragons and not that foolish little word 'Rumplesnitz.'"

Gawaine frowned. " Then it wasn't a magic word after all? " he asked.

" Of course not," said the Headmaster, " you ought to be too old for such foolishness. There isn't any such thing as a magic word."

" But you told me it was magic," protested Gawaine. " You said it was magic and now you say it isn't."

" It wasn't magic in a literal sense," answered the Headmaster, " but it was much more wonderful than that. The word gave you confidence. It took away your fears. If I hadn't told you that you might have been killed the very first time. It was your battle-ax did the trick."

Gawaine surprised the Headmaster by his attitude. He was obviously distressed by the explanation. He interrupted a long philosophic and ethical discourse by the Headmaster with, " If I hadn't of hit 'em all mighty hard and fast any one of 'em might have crushed me like a, like a — " He fumbled for a word.

" Egg shell," suggested the Headmaster.

" Like a egg shell," assented Gawaine, and he said it many times. All through the evening meal people who sat near him heard him muttering, " Like a egg shell, like a egg shell."

The next day was clear, but Gawaine did not get up at dawn. Indeed, it was almost noon when the Headmaster found him cowering in bed, with the clothes pulled over his head. The principal called the Assistant Professor of Pleasaunce, and together they dragged the boy toward the forest.

" He'll be all right as soon as he gets a couple more dragons under his belt," explained the Headmaster.

The Assistant Professor of Pleasaunce agreed. " It would be a shame to stop such a fine run," he said. " Why, counting that one yesterday, he's killed fifty dragons."

They pushed the boy into a thicket above which hung a meager cloud of steam. It was obviously quite a small dragon. But Gawaine did not come back that night or the next. In fact, he never came back. Some weeks afterward brave spirits from the school explored the thicket, but they could find nothing to remind them of Gawaine except the metal part of his medals. Even the ribbons had been devoured.

The Headmaster and the Assistant Professor of Pleasaunce agreed that it would be just as well not to tell the school how Gawaine had achieved his record and still less how he came to die. They held that it might have a bad effect on school spirit. Accordingly, Gawaine has lived in the memory of the school as its greatest hero. No visitor succeeds in leaving the building today without seeing a great shield which hangs on the wall of the dining hall. Fifty pairs of dragons' ears are mounted upon the shield and underneath in gilt letters is " Gawaine le Cœur-Hardy," followed by the simple inscription, " He killed fifty dragons." The record has never been equaled.

APPRECIATION HELPS

1. What is Broun's purpose in writing the essay?
2. What truth underlies this fable, or allegorical essay?
3. Why did the principal give Gawaine a " magic word "?   What was its real value to Gawaine?
4. Why was his conquest greater when he forgot the word?
5. Explain the title.
6. Write an allegory setting forth some truth of your school life.

COMPOSITION HINTS

1. When to Say " Rumplesnitz " in School
2. My Fifty-first Dragon
3. When I Employ Magic Words

DAVID GRAYSON

Who David Grayson is might still be unanswered had there not been so many David Graysons. The first original one attained a sudden popularity as the unknown author of a series entitled *Adventures in Contentment* which appeared in the *American Magazine* about two decades ago. They were republished in book form by Messrs. Doubleday, Page, and still the secret of authorship was kept. Then the other David Graysons came on the scene. They turned up on various lecture platforms all over the country, and on some nights there would be a dozen men addressing audiences at the same time in different states of the Union and all calling themselves David Grayson. That could not go on. So it was revealed that *the* David Grayson was Mr. Ray Stannard Baker (b. 1870) and that therefore anyone calling himself David Grayson and not resembling Mr. Baker was an impostor. The impositions ceased.

The following paper is from that famous book which came to be written as the result of a walking tour through Michigan and Wisconsin that Mr. Baker took as a change from the hurly-burly of New York life and the hectic character of much European travel. Originally in Chicago he was interested in the under-dog and so became a crusader of the pen. When it was suggested by Mr. John S. Phillips that he should publish his notebooks of wanderings afoot, he realized that he could not put forth these reflections of a dreamer under the same name as that with which he had signed his crusading articles. Thus did he take to the pseudonym which was to create so much trouble on the lecture platform.

Mr. Baker was director of the American Press Bureau in Paris during the Peace Conference, and in that capacity became a close friend of the late President Wilson. Hence he was well equipped to write *What Wilson Did in Paris* (1919) and *Woodrow Wilson* (1923).

I ENTERTAIN AN AGENT UNAWARES[1]

WITH the coming of winter I thought the life of a farmer might lose something of its charm. So much interest lies in the growth not only of crops but of trees, vines, flowers, sentiments and emotions. In the summer the world is busy, concerned with many things and full of gossip: in the winter I anticipated a cessation of many active interests and enthusiasms. I looked forward to having time for my books and for the quiet contemplation of the life around me. Summer indeed is for activity, winter for reflection. But when winter really came every day discovered some new work to do or some new adventure to enjoy. It is surprising how many things happen on a small farm. Examining the book which accounts for that winter, I find the history of part of a forenoon, which will illustrate one of the curious adventures of a farmer's life. It is dated January 5.

I went out this morning with my ax and hammer to mend the fence along the public road. A heavy frost fell last night and the brown grass and the dry ruts of the roads were powdered white. Even the air, which was perfectly still, seemed full of frost crystals, so that when the sun came up one seemed to walk in a magic world. I drew in a long breath and looked out across the wonderful shining country and I said to myself:

"Surely, there is nowhere I would rather be than here." For I could have traveled nowhere to find greater beauty or a better enjoyment of it than I had here at home.

As I worked with my ax and hammer, I heard a light wagon come rattling up the road. Across the valley a man had begun to chop a tree. I could see the ax steel flash brilliantly in the sunshine before I heard the sound of the blow.

The man in the wagon had a round face and a sharp blue eye. I thought he seemed a businesslike young man.

"Say, there," he shouted, drawing up at my gate, "would

[1] From *Adventures in Contentment,* published by Doubleday, Page and Company, 1907.

you mind holding my horse a minute? It's a cold morning and he's restless."

"Certainly not," I said, and I put down my tools and held his horse.

He walked up to my door with a brisk step and a certain jaunty poise of the head.

"He is well contented with himself," I said. "It is a great blessing for any man to be satisfied with what he has got."

I heard Harriet open the door — how every sound rang through the still morning air!

The young man asked some question and I distinctly heard Harriet's answer:

"He's down there."

The young man came back: his hat was tipped up, his quick eye darted over my grounds as though in a single instant he had appraised everything and passed judgment upon the cash value of the inhabitants. He whistled a lively little tune.

"Say," he said, when he reached the gate, not at all disconcerted, "I thought you was the hired man. Your name's Grayson, ain't it? Well, I want to talk with you."

After tying and blanketing his horse and taking a black satchel from his buggy he led me up to my house. I had a pleasurable sense of excitement and adventure. Here was a new character come to my farm. Who knows, I thought, what he may bring with him: who knows what I may send away by him? Here in the country we must set our little ships afloat on small streams, hoping that somehow, some day, they will reach the sea.

It was interesting to see the busy young man sit down so confidently in our best chair. He said his name was Dixon, and he took out from his satchel a book with a fine showy cover. He said it was called *Living Selections from Poet, Sage and Humourist.*

"This," he told me, "is only the first of the series. We publish six volumes full of literchoor. You see what a heavy book this is?"

I tested it in my hand: it was a heavy book.

"The entire set," he said, "weighs over ten pounds. There are 1,162 pages, enough paper if laid down flat, end to end, to reach half a mile."

I cannot quote his exact language: there was too much of it, but he made an impressive showing of the amount of literature that could be had at a very low price per pound. Mr. Dixon was a hypnotist. He fixed me with his glittering eye, and he talked so fast, and his ideas upon the subject were so original that he held me spellbound. At first I was inclined to be provoked: one does not like to be forcibly hypnotized, but gradually the situation began to amuse me, the more so when Harriet came in.

"Did you ever see a more beautiful binding?" asked the agent, holding his book admiringly at arm's length. "This up here," he said, pointing to the illuminated cover, "is the Muse of Poetry. She is scattering flowers — poems, you know. Fine idea, ain't it? Coloring fine, too."

He jumped up quickly and laid the book on my table, to the evident distress of Harriet.

"Trims up the room, don't it?" he exclaimed, turning his head a little to one side and observing the effect with an expression of affectionate admiration.

"How much," I asked, "will you sell the covers for without the insides?"

"Without the insides?"

"Yes," I said, "the binding will trim up my table just as well without the insides."

I thought he looked at me a little suspiciously, but he was evidently satisfied by my expression of countenance, for he answered promptly:

"Oh, but you want the insides. That's what the books are for. The bindings are never sold alone."

He then went on to tell me the prices and terms of payment, until it really seemed that it would be cheaper to buy the books than to let him carry them away again. Harriet stood in the doorway behind him frowning and evidently trying to catch my eye. But I kept my face turned aside so that I could not see her signal of distress and my eyes fixed on the young man Dixon. It was as good as a play. Harriet there, serious-minded, thinking I was being befooled, and the agent thinking he was befooling me, and I, thinking I was befooling both of them — and all of us wrong. It was very like life wherever you find it.

Finally, I took the book which he had been urging upon me, at which Harriet coughed meaningly to attract my attention. She knew the danger when I really got my hands on a book. But I made up as innocent as a child. I opened the book almost at random — and it was as though, walking down a strange road, I had come upon an old tried friend not seen before in years. For there on the page before me I read:

> The world is too much with us; late and soon,
> Getting and spending, we lay waste our powers:
> Little we see in Nature that is ours;
> We have given our hearts away, a sordid boon!
> The sea that bares her bosom to the moon;
> The wind that will be howling at all hours,
> But are up-gathered now like sleeping flowers;
> For this, for everything, we are out of tune;

And as I read it came back to me — a scene like a picture — the place, the time, the very feel of the hour when I first saw those lines. Who shall say that the past does not live! An odor will sometimes set the blood coursing in an old emotion, and a line of poetry is the resurrection and the life. For a moment I forgot Harriet and the agent, I forgot myself, I even forgot the book on my knee — everything but that hour in the past — a view of shimmering hot housetops, the heat and dust and noise of an August evening in the city, the dumb weariness of it all, the loneliness, the longing for green fields; and then these great lines of Wordsworth, read for the first time, flooding in upon me:

> " Great God! I'd rather be
> A pagan suckled in a creed outworn:
> So might I, standing on this pleasant lea,

Have glimpses that would make me less forlorn;
Have sight of Proteus rising from the sea;
Or hear old Triton blow his wreathèd horn."

When I had finished I found myself standing in my own
room with one arm raised, and, I suspect, a trace of tears in
my eyes — there before the agent and Harriet. I saw Harriet
lift one hand and drop it hopelessly. She thought I was captured at last. I was past saving. And as I looked at the
agent I saw "grim conquest glowing in his eye!" So I sat
down not a little embarrassed by my exhibition — when I had
intended to be self-poised.

"You like it, don't you?" said Mr. Dixon unctuously.

"I don't see," I said earnestly, "how you can afford to sell
such things as this so cheap."

"They *are* cheap," he admitted regretfully. I suppose he
wished he had tried me with the half-morocco.

"They are priceless," I said, "absolutely priceless. If you
were the only man in the world who had that poem, I think
I would deed you my farm for it."

Mr. Dixon proceeded, as though it were all settled, to get
out his black order book and open it briskly for business. He
drew his fountain pen, capped it, and looked up at me ex-
pectantly. My feet actually seemed slipping into some irresistible whirlpool. How well he understood practical psychology! I struggled within myself, fearing engulfment: I was
all but lost.

"Shall I deliver the set at once," he said, "or can you wait
until the first of February?"

At that critical moment a floating spar of an idea swept my
way and I seized upon it as the last hope of the lost.

"I don't understand," I said, as though I had not heard his
last question, "how you dare go about with all this treasure
upon you. Are you not afraid of being stopped in the road
and robbed? Why, I've seen the time when, if I had known
you carried such things as these, such cures for sick hearts,
I think I should have stopped you myself!"

"Say, you *are* an odd one," said Mr. Dixon.

" Why do you sell such priceless things as these? " I asked, looking at him sharply.

" Why do I sell them? " and he looked still more perplexed. " To make money, of course; same reason you raise corn."

" But here is wealth," I said, pursuing my advantage. " If you have these you have something more valuable than money."

Mr. Dixon politely said nothing. Like a wise angler, having failed to land me at the first rush, he let me have line. Then I thought of Ruskin's words, " Nor can any noble thing be wealth except to a noble person." And that prompted me to say to Mr. Dixon:

" These things are not yours; they are mine. You never owned them; but I will sell them to you."

He looked at me in amazement, and then glanced around — evidently to discover if there were a convenient way of escape.

" You're all straight, are you? " he asked, tapping his forehead; " didn't anybody ever try to take you up? "

" The covers are yours," I continued as though I had not heard him, " the insides are mine and have been for a long time: that is why I proposed buying the covers separately."

I opened his book again. I thought I would see what had been chosen for its pages. And I found there many fine and great things.

" Let me read you this," I said to Mr. Dixon; " it has been mine for a long time. I will not sell it to you. I will give it to you outright. The best things are always given."

Having some gift in imitating the Scotch dialect, I read:

> November chill blaws loud wi' angry sugh;
>   The short'ning winter day is near a close;
> The miry beasts retreating frae the pleugh;
>   The black'ning trains o' craws to their repose:
> The toil-worn Cotter frae his labour goes,
>   This night his weekly moil is at an end,
> Collects his spades, his mattocks and his hoes,
>   Hoping the morn in ease and rest to spend,
> And weary, o'er the moor, his course does
>   Hameward bend.

So I read " The Cotter's Saturday Night." I love the poem very much myself, sometimes reading it aloud, not so much for the tenderness of its message, though I prize that, too, as for the wonder of its music.

> Compar'd with these, Italian trills are tame;
> The tickl'd ear no heart-felt raptures raise.

I suppose I showed my feeling in my voice. As I glanced up from time to time I saw the agent's face change, and his look deepen and the lips, usually so energetically tense, loosen with emotion. Surely no poem in all the language conveys so perfectly the simple love of the home, the quiet joys, hopes, pathos of those who live close to the soil.

When I had finished — I stopped with the stanza beginning:

> Then homeward all take off their sev'ral way;

the agent turned away his head trying to brave out his emotion. Most of us, Anglo-Saxons, tremble before a tear when we might fearlessly beard a tiger.

I moved up nearer to the agent and put my hand on his knee; then I read two or three of the other things I found in his wonderful book. And once I had him laughing and once again I had the tears in his eyes. Oh, a simple young man, a little crusty without, but soft inside — like the rest of us.

Well, it was amazing, once we began talking not of books but of life, how really eloquent and human he became. From being a distant and uncomfortable person, he became at once like a near neighbor and friend. It was strange to me — as I have thought since — how he conveyed to us in few words the essential emotional note of his life. It was no violin tone, beautifully complex with harmonics, but the clear simple voice of the flute. It spoke of his wife and his baby girl and his home. The very incongruity of detail — he told us how he grew onions in his back yard — added somehow to the homely glamour of the vision which he gave us. The number of his house, the fact that he had a new cottage organ, and that the baby ran away and lost herself in Seventeenth Street — were all, curiously, fabrics of his emotion.

·

It was beautiful to see commonplace facts grow phosphorescent in the heat of true feeling. How little we may come to know Romance by the cloak she wears and how humble must be he who would surprise the heart of her!

It was, indeed, with an indescribable thrill that I heard him add the details, one by one — the mortgage on his place, now rapidly being paid off, the brother who was a plumber, the mother-in-law who was not a mother-in-law of the comic papers. And finally he showed us the picture of the wife and baby that he had in the cover of his watch; a fat baby with its head resting on its mother's shoulder.

" Mister," he said, " p'r'aps you think it's fun to ride around the country like I do, and be away from home most of the time. But it ain't. When I think of Minnie and the kid — "

He broke off sharply, as if he had suddenly remembered the shame of such confidences.

" Say," he asked, " what page is that poem on? "

I told him.

" One forty-six," he said. " When I get home I'm going to read that to Minnie. She likes poetry and all such things. And where's that other piece that tells how a man feels when he's lonesome? Say, that fellow knew! "

We had a genuinely good time, the agent and I, and when he finally rose to go, I said:

" Well, I've sold you a new book."

" I see now, mister, what you mean."

I went down the path with him and began to unhitch his horse.

" Let me, let me," he said eagerly.

Then he shook hands, paused a moment awkwardly as if about to say something, then sprang into his buggy without saying it.

When he had taken up his reins he remarked:

" Say! but you'd make an agent! You'd hypnotize 'em."

I recognized it as the greatest compliment he could pay me: the craft compliment.

Then he drove off, but pulled up before he had gone five

yards. He turned in his seat, one hand on the back of it, his whip raised.

" Say! " he shouted, and when I walked up he looked at me with fine embarrassment.

" Mister, perhaps you'd accept one of these sets from Dixon free gratis, for nothing."

" I understand," I said, " but you know I'm giving the books to you — and I couldn't take them back again."

" Well," he said, " you're a good one, anyhow. Good-by again," and then, suddenly, business naturally coming uppermost, he remarked with great enthusiasm:

" You've given me a new idea. *Say,* I'll sell 'em."

" Carry them carefully, man," I called after him; " they are precious."

So I went back to my work, thinking how many fine people there are in this world — if you scratch 'em deep enough.

APPRECIATION HELPS

1. How has David Grayson made the life of a farmer seem attractive?
2. What do we like or dislike in the agent when he is first introduced?   Is his attitude towards " literchoor " overdrawn?
3. In what sense were the books " owned " by David Grayson?
4. Name some books you own in that sense of the word.   Name some you have been made to read that you do not own.
5. What fine qualities did David Grayson discover in the agent when he had " scratched deep enough "?
6. Read *Adventures in Contentment, Adventures in Friendship,* and *Great Possessions.*

COMPOSITION HINTS

1. Frost Magic
2. My Adventure as a Salesman
3. I Entertain an Agent Unawares
4. The Lure of the Farm
5. When I Was Lonely
6. Queer Characters I Have Met

STEWART EDWARD WHITE

As a preface to this paper one cannot do better than quote the introduction Mr. Christopher Morley wrote to an extract from *The Forest* in the first series of his *Modern Essays* (Harcourt, Brace and Company):

" This is from *The Forest* — one of Stewart Edward White's many delightful volumes. A very large public has enjoyed Mr. White's writings — many of his readers, perhaps, without accurately realizing how extraordinarily good they are.

" Mr. White was born in Grand Rapids, Michigan, 1873; studied at the University of Michigan; has hunted big game in Africa; served as major of field artillery, 1917–18; and is a Fellow of the Royal Geographical Society. His first book, *The Westerners,* was published in 1901, since when they have followed regularly."

One might add that Mr. White's home is now in Burlingame, California.

ON MAKING CAMP[1]

Who hath smelt wood-smoke at twilight? Who hath heard the
    birch log burning?
Who is quick to read the noises of the night?
Let him follow with the others, for the young men's feet are
    turning
To the camps of proved desire and known delight.

In the Ojibway language *wigwam* means a good spot for camping, a place cleared for a camp, a camp as an abstract proposition, and a camp in the concrete as represented by a tent, a thatched shelter, or a conical tepee. In like manner, the English word *camp* lends itself to a variety of concepts.

[1] From *The Forest,* published by Doubleday, Page and Company, 1903.

I once slept in a four-poster bed over a polished floor in an elaborate servant-haunted structure which, mainly because it was built of logs and overlooked a lake, the owner always spoke of as his camp. Again, I once slept on a bed of prairie grass, before a fire of dried buffalo chips and mesquite, wrapped in a single light blanket, while a good vigorous rainstorm made new cold places on me and under me all night. In the morning the cowboy with whom I was traveling remarked that this was "sure a lonesome proposition as a camp."

Between these two extremes is infinite variety, grading upwards through the divers bivouacs of snow, plains, pines, or hills, to the bark shelter; past the dog-tent, the A-tent, the wall-tent, to the elaborate permanent canvas cottage of the luxurious camper, the dugout winter retreat of the range cowboy, the trapper's cabin, the great log-built lumber-jack communities, and the last refinements of sybaritic summer homes in the Adirondacks. All these are camps. And when you talk of making camp you must know whether that process is to mean only a search for rattlesnakes and enough acrid-smoked fuel to boil tea, or a winter's consultation with an expert architect; whether your camp is to be made on the principle of Omar's one-night Sultan, or whether it is intended to accommodate the full days of an entire summer.

But to those who tread the Long Trail the making of camp resolves itself into an algebraical formula. After a man has traveled all day through the Northern wilderness he wants to rest, and anything that stands between himself and his repose he must get rid of in as few motions as is consistent with reasonable thoroughness. The end in view is a hot meal and a comfortable dry place to sleep. The straighter he can draw the line to those two points the happier he is.

Early in his woods experience Dick became possessed with the desire to do everything for himself. As this was a laudable striving for self-sufficiency, I called a halt at about three o'clock one afternoon in order to give him plenty of time.

Now Dick is a good, active, able-bodied boy, possessed of

average intelligence and rather more than average zeal. He even had theory of a sort, for he had read various *Boy Campers, or the Trapper's Guide, How to Camp Out, The Science of Woodcraft,* and other able works. He certainly had ideas enough, and confidence enough. I sat down on a log.

At the end of three hours' flustration, heat, worry, and good hard work, he had accomplished the following results: A tent, very saggy, very askew, covered a four-sided area — it was not a rectangle — of very bumpy ground. A hodge-podge bonfire, in the center of which an inaccessible coffee-pot toppled menacingly, alternately threatened to ignite the entire surrounding forest or to go out altogether through lack of fuel. Personal belongings strewed the ground near the fire, and provisions cumbered the entrance to the tent. Dick was anxiously mixing batter for the cakes, attempting to stir a pot of rice often enough to prevent it from burning, and trying to rustle sufficient dry wood to keep the fire going. This diversity of interests certainly made him sit up and pay attention. At each instant he had to desert his flour-sack to rescue the coffee-pot, or to shift the kettle, or to dab hastily at the rice, or to stamp out the small brush, or to pile on more dry twigs. His movements were not graceful. They raised a scurry of dry bark, ashes, wood dust, twigs, leaves, and pine needles, a certain proportion of which found their way into the coffee, the rice, and the sticky batter, while the smaller articles of personal belongings, hastily dumped from the duffel-bag, gradually disappeared from view in the manner of Pompeii and ancient Vesuvius. Dick burned his fingers and stumbled about and swore, and looked so comically-pathetically red-faced through the smoke that I, seated on the log, at the same time laughed and pitied. And in the end, when he needed a continuous steady fire to fry his cakes, he suddenly discovered that dry twigs do not make coals, and that his previous operations had used up all the fuel within easy circle of the camp.

So he had to drop everything for the purpose of rustling wood, while the coffee chilled, the rice cooled, the bacon congealed, and all the provisions, cooked and uncooked, gathered entomological specimens. At the last, the poor bedeviled theorist made a hasty meal of scorched food, brazenly postponed the washing of dishes until the morrow, and coiled about his hummocky couch to dream the nightmares of complete exhaustion.

Poor Dick! I knew exactly how he felt, how the low afternoon sun scorched, how the fire darted out at unexpected places, how the smoke followed him around, no matter on which side of the fire he placed himself, how the flies all took to biting when both hands were occupied, and how they all miraculously disappeared when he had set down the frying-pan and knife to fight them. I could sympathize, too, with the lonely, forlorn, lost-dog feeling that clutched him after it was all over. I could remember how big and forbidding and unfriendly the forest had once looked to me in like circumstances, so that I had felt suddenly thrust outside into empty spaces. Almost was I tempted to intervene; but I liked Dick, and I wanted to do him good. This experience was harrowing, but it prepared his mind for the seeds of wisdom. By the following morning he had chastened his spirit, forgotten the assurance breathed from the windy pages of the Boy Trapper Library, and was ready to learn.

Have you ever watched a competent portraitist at work? The infinite pains a skilled man spends on the preliminaries before he takes one step towards a likeness nearly always wears down the patience of the sitter. He measures with his eye, he plumbs, he sketches tentatively, he places in here a dab, there a blotch, he puts behind him apparently unproductive hours —and then all at once he is ready to begin something that will not have to be done over again. An amateur, however, is carried away by his desire for results. He dashes in a hit-or-miss early effect, which grows into an approximate likeness almost immediately, but which will require infinite labor, alteration, and anxiety to beat into finished shape.

The case of the artist in making camps is exactly similar, and the philosophical reasons for his failure are exactly the same. To the superficial mind a camp is a shelter, a bright fire, and a smell of cooking. So when a man is very tired he cuts across lots to those three results. He pitches his tent, lights his fire, puts over his food — and finds himself drowned in detail, like my friend Dick.

The following is, in brief, what during the next six weeks I told that youth, by precept, by homily, and by making the solution so obvious that he could work it out for himself.

When five or six o'clock draws near, begin to look about you for a good level dry place, elevated some few feet above the surroundings. Drop your pack or beach your canoe. Examine the location carefully. You will want two trees about ten feet apart, from which to suspend your tent, and a bit of flat ground underneath them. Of course the flat ground need not be particularly unencumbered by brush or saplings, so the combination ought not to be hard to discover. Now return to your canoe. Do not unpack the tent.

With the little ax clear the ground thoroughly. By bending a sapling over strongly with the left hand, clipping sharply at the strained fibers, and then bending it as strongly the other way to repeat the ax stroke on the other side, you will find that treelets of even two or three inches diameter can be felled by two blows. In a very few moments you will have accomplished a hole in the forest, and your two supporting trees will stand sentinel at either end of a most respectable-looking clearing. Do not unpack the tent.

Now, although the ground seems free of all but unimportant growths, go over it thoroughly for little shrubs and leaves. They look soft and yielding, but are often possessed of unexpectedly abrasive roots. Besides, they mask the face of the ground. When you have finished pulling them up by the roots, you will find that your supposedly level plot is knobby with hummocks. Stand directly over each little mound; swing the back of your ax vigorously against it, adze-wise, between your legs. Nine times out of ten it will crumble, and the tenth time means merely a root to cut or a stone to pry out. At length you are possessed of a plot of clean, fresh earth, level and soft, free from projections. But do not unpack your tent.

Lay a young birch or maple an inch or so in diameter across a log. Two clips will produce you a tent-peg. If you are inexperienced, and cherish memories of striped lawn marquees, you will cut them about six inches long. If you are wise and old and gray in woods experience, you will multiply that length by four. Then your loops will not slip off, and you will have a real grip on mother earth, than which nothing can be more desirable in the event of a heavy rain and wind squall about midnight. If your ax is as sharp as it ought to be, you can point them more neatly by holding them suspended in front of you while you snip at their ends with the ax, rather than by resting them against a solid base. Pile them together at the edge of the clearing. Cut a crotched sapling eight or ten feet long. Now unpack your tent.

In a wooded country you will not take the time to fool with tent-poles. A stout line run through the eyelets and along the apex will string it successfully between your two trees. Draw the line as tight as possible, but do not be too unhappy if, after your best efforts, it still sags a little. That is what your long crotched stick is for. Stake out your four corners. If you get them in a good rectangle and in such relation to the apex as to form two isosceles triangles of the ends, your tent will stand smoothly. Therefore, be an artist and do it right. Once the four corners are well placed, the rest follows naturally. Occasionally in the North Country it will be found that the soil is too thin, over the rocks, to grip the tent-pegs. In that case drive them at a sharp angle as deep as they will go, and then lay a large flat stone across the slant of them. Thus anchored, you will ride out a gale. Finally, wedge your long sapling crotch under the line — outside the tent, of course — to tighten it. Your shelter is up. If you are a woodsman, ten or fifteen minutes has sufficed to accomplish all this.

There remains the question of a bed, and you'd better attend to it now, while your mind is still occupied with the shelter problem. Fell a good thrifty young balsam and set to work pulling off the fans. Those you cannot strip off easily with your hands are too tough for your purpose. Lay them carelessly crisscross against the blade of your ax and up the handle. They will not drop off, and when you shoulder that ax you will resemble a walking haystack, and will probably experience a genuine emotion of surprise at the amount of balsam that can be thus transported. In the tent lay smoothly one layer of fans, convex side up, butts toward the foot. Now thatch the rest on top of this, thrusting the butt ends underneath the layer already placed in such a manner as to leave the fan ends curving up and down toward the foot of your bed. Your second emotion of surprise will assail you as you realize how much spring inheres in but two or three layers thus arranged. When you have spread your rubber blanket, you will be possessed of a bed as soft, and a great deal more aromatic and luxurious than any you would be able to buy in town.

Your next care is to clear a living space in front of the tent. This will take you about twenty seconds, for you need not be particular as to stumps, hummocks, or small brush. All you want is room for cooking, and suitable space for spreading out your provisions. But do not unpack anything yet.

Your fireplace you will build of two green logs laid side by side. The fire is to be made between them. They should converge slightly, in order that the utensils to be rested across them may be of various sizes. If your vicinity yields flat stones, they build up even better than the logs — unless they happen to be of granite. Granite explodes most disconcertingly. Poles sharpened, driven upright into the ground, and then pressed down to slant over the fireplace, will hold your kettles a suitable height above the blaze.

Fuel should be your next thought. A roll of birch bark first of all. Then some of the small, dry, resinous branches that stick out from the trunks of medium-sized pines, living or dead. Finally, the wood itself. If you are merely cooking supper, and have no thought for a warmth-fire or a friendship-fire, I should advise you to stick to the dry pine branches, helped out, in the interest of coals for frying, by a little dry maple or birch. If you need more of a blaze, you will have to search out, fell, and split a standing dead tree. This is not at all necessary. I have traveled many weeks in the woods without using a more formidable implement than a one-pound hatchet. Pile your fuel — a complete supply, all you are going to need — by the side of your already improvised fireplace. But, as you value your peace of mind, do not fool with matches.

It will be a little difficult to turn your mind from the concept of fire, to which all these preparations have compellingly led it, — especially as a fire is the one cheerful thing your weariness needs the most at this time of day, — but you must do so. Leave everything just as it is, and unpack your provisions.

First of all, rinse your utensils. Hang your tea-pail, with the proper quantity of water, from one slanting pole, and your kettle from the other. Salt the water in the latter receptacle. Peel your potatoes, if you have any; open your little provision sacks; puncture your tin cans, if you have any; slice your bacon; clean your fish; pluck your birds; mix your dough or batter; spread your table tinware on your tarpaulin or a sheet of birch bark; cut a kettle-lifter; see that everything you are going to need is within direct reach of your hand as you squat on your heels before the fireplace. Now light your fire.

The civilized method is to build a fire and then to touch a match to the completed structure. If well done and in a grate or stove, this works beautifully. Only in the woods you have no grate. The only sure way is as follows: Hold a piece of birch bark in your hand. Shelter your match all you know how. When the bark has caught, lay it in your fireplace, assist it with more bark, and gradually build up, twig by twig, stick by stick, from the first pin-point of flame, all the fire you are going to need. It will not be much. The little hot blaze rising between the parallel logs directly against the aluminum of your utensils will do the business in very short order. In fifteen minutes at most your meal is ready. And you have been able to attain to hot food thus quickly because you were prepared.

In case of very wet weather the affair is altered somewhat. If the rain has just commenced, do not stop to clear out very thoroughly, but get your tent up as quickly as possible, in order to preserve an area of comparatively dry ground. But if the earth is already soaked, you had best build a bonfire to dry out by, while you cook over a smaller fire a little distance removed, leaving the tent until later. Or it may be well not to pitch the tent at all, but to lay it across slanting supports at an angle to reflect the heat against the ground.

It is no joke to light a fire in the rain. An Indian can do it more easily than a white man, but even an Indian has more trouble than the story-books acknowledge. You will need a greater quantity of birch bark, a bigger pile of resinous dead limbs from the pine-trees, and perhaps the heart of a dead pine stub or stump. Then, with infinite patience, you may be able to tease the flame. Sometimes a small dead birch contains in the waterproof envelope of its bark a species of powdery, dry touchwood that takes the flame readily. Still, it is easy enough to start a blaze — a very fine-looking, cheerful, healthy blaze; the difficulty is to prevent its petering out the moment your back is turned.

But the depths of woe are sounded and the limit of patience reached when you are forced to get breakfast in the dripping forest. After the chill of early dawn you are always reluctant in the best of circumstances to leave your blankets, to fumble with numbed fingers for matches, to handle cold steel and slippery fish. But when every leaf, twig, sapling, and tree contains a douche of cold water; when the wetness oozes about your moccasins from the soggy earth with every step you take; when you look about you and realize that somehow, before you can get a mouthful to banish that before-breakfast ill-humor, you must brave cold water in an attempt to find enough fuel to cook with, then your philosophy and early religious training avail you little. The first ninety-nine times you are forced to do this you will probably squirm circumspectly through the brush in a vain attempt to avoid shaking water down on yourself; you will resent each failure to do so, and at the end your rage will personify the wilderness for the purpose of one sweeping anathema. The hundredth time will bring you wisdom. You will do the anathema — rueful rather than enraged —

from the tent opening. Then you will plunge boldly in and get wet. It is not pleasant, but it has to be done, and you will save much temper, not to speak of time.

Dick and I earned our diplomas at this sort of work. It rained twelve of the first fourteen days we were out. Toward the end of that two weeks I doubt if even an Indian could have discovered a dry stick of wood in the entire country. The land was of Laurentian rock formation, running in parallel ridges of bare stone separated by hollows carpeted with a thin layer of earth. The ridges were naturally ill adapted to camping, and the cup hollows speedily filled up with water until they became most creditable little marshes. Often we hunted for an hour or so before we could find any sort of a spot to pitch our tent. As for a fire, it was a matter of chopping down dead trees large enough to have remained dry inside, of armfuls of birch bark, and of the patient drying out, by repeated ignition, of enough fuel to cook very simple meals. Of course we could have kept a big fire going easily enough, but we were traveling steadily and had not the time for that. In these trying circumstances Dick showed that, no matter how much of a tenderfoot he might be, he was game enough under stress.

But to return to our pleasant afternoon. While you are consuming the supper you will hang over some water to heat for the dish-washing, and the dish-washing you will attend to the moment you have finished eating. Do not commit the fallacy of sitting down for a little rest. Better finish the job completely while you are about it. You will appreciate leisure so much more later. In lack of a wash-rag you will find that a bunch of tall grass bent double makes an ideal swab.

Now brush the flies from your tent, drop the mosquito-proof lining, and enjoy yourself. The whole task, from first to last, has consumed but a little over an hour. And you are through for the day. In the woods, as nowhere else, you will earn your leisure only by forethought. Make no move until you know it follows the line of greatest economy. To putter is to wallow in endless desolation. If you cannot move directly and swiftly and certainly along the line of least resistance in everything you do, take a guide with you; you are not of the woods people. You will never enjoy doing for yourself, for your days will be crammed with unending labor.

It is but a little after seven. The long crimson shadows of the North Country are lifting across the aisles of the forest. You sit on a log, or lie on your back, and blow contented clouds straight up into the air. Nothing can disturb you now. The wilderness is yours, for you have taken from it the essentials of primitive civilization, — shelter, warmth, and food. An hour ago a rainstorm would have been a minor catastrophe. Now you do not care. Blow high, blow low, you have made for yourself an abiding-place, so that the signs of the sky are less important to you than to the city dweller who wonders if he should take an umbrella. From your doorstep you can look placidly out on the great unknown. The noises of the forest draw close about you their circle of mystery, but the circle cannot break upon you, for here you have conjured the homely sounds of kettle and crackling flame to keep ward. Thronging down through the twilight steal the jealous woodland shadows, awful in the sublimity of the Silent Places, but at the sentry outposts of your fire-lit trees they pause like wild animals, hesitating to advance. The wilderness, untamed, dreadful at night, is all about; but this one little spot you have reclaimed. Here is something before unknown to the eerie spirits of the woods. As you sleepily knock the ashes from the pipe, you look about on the familiar scene with accustomed satisfaction. You are at home.

APPRECIATION HELPS

1. Mention the various meanings the word *camp* connotes.
2. Describe the habits of the most skilled camper you know.
3. What amusing or distressing experiences have you had because you were ignorant of the ways of camping?
4. What values do you attach to a knowledge of woodcraft?
5. What qualities were developed in your ancestors by their pioneering experiences? Where in America may one live the

life of a pioneer? How many boys of your acquaintance are resourceful enough to maintain existence if pioneering life were forced upon them?

6. What out-of-door experiences of your own have been recalled by this essay?

7. Name ten books dealing with nature and life away from civilization which you have enjoyed.

8. How has the author " put you there " in his closing paragraph?

COMPOSITION HINTS

1. Wood Smoke at Twilight
2. Noises of the Night
3. Some Camps I Have Known
4. Sleeping out of Doors
5. " Do not Unpack Your Tent "
6. A Tenderfoot in the Woods
7. Preparing a Dinner in the Open
8. A Harrowing Camping Experience
9. Before-Breakfast Ill Humors

ROBERT CORTES HOLLIDAY

A champion bicycle rider at sixteen in his native Indianapolis —
such was the early triumph of Mr. Robert Cortes Holliday
(b. 1880). For the rest of his career one may well quote Mr.
Christopher Morley: "That triumph, however, was not permanently satisfying, for he came to New York in 1899 to study
art; lived for a while, precariously, as an illustrator; worked for
several years as a bookseller in Charles Scribner's retail store, and
passed through all sorts of curious jobs on Grub Street, among
others book-reviewer on the *Tribune* and *Times*. He was editor
of the *Bookman* after that magazine was taken over by the George
H. Doran Company, and retired to the genteel dignity of 'contributing editor' in 1920, to obtain leisure for more writing of
his own.

"Mr. Holliday," adds Mr. Morley, "has the genuine gift of
the personal essay, mellow, fluent, and pleasantly eccentric. His
Walking-Stick Papers, Broome Street Straws, Turns about Towns,
and *Peeps at People* have that charming rambling humor that
descends to him from his masters in this art, Hazlitt and Thackeray."

ON CARRYING A CANE[1]

SOME people, without doubt, are born with a deep instinct
for carrying a cane; some consciously acquire the habit of
carrying a cane; and some find themselves in a position
where the matter of carrying a cane is thrust upon them.

Canes are carried in all parts of the world, and have been
carried — or that which was the forefather of them has been
carried — since human history began. Indeed, a very fair ac-

[1] From *The Walking-Stick Papers,* published by George H. Doran, 1918.
Copyright by *The Bookman.*

343

count of mankind might be made by writing the story of its canes. And nothing that would readily occur to mind would more eloquently express a civilization than its evident attitude toward canes. Perhaps nothing can more subtly convey the psychology of a man than his feeling about a cane.

The prehistoric ape, we are justified in assuming, struggled upright upon a cane. The cane, so to speak, with which primitive man wooed his bride, defended his life, liberty, and pursuit of happiness, and brought down his food, was (like all canes which are in good taste) admirably chosen for the occasion. The spear, the stave, the pilgrim's staff, the sword, the scepter — always has the cane-carrying animal borne something in his hand. And, down the long vista of the past, the cane, in its various manifestations, has ever been the mark of strength, and so of dignity. Thus as a man originally became a gentleman, or a king, by force of valor, the cane in its evolution has ever been the symbol of a superior caste.

A man cannot do manual labor carrying a cane. And it would be a moral impossibility for one of servile state — a butler, for instance, or a ticket-chopper — to present himself in the rôle of his occupation ornamented with a cane. One held in custody would not be permitted to appear before a magistrate flaunting a cane. Until the stigma which attaches to his position may be erased he would be shorn of this mark of nobility, the cane.

Canes are now carried mostly by the very youthful and the very aged, the powerful, the distinguished, the patrician, the self-important, and those who fancy to exalt themselves. Some, to whom this privilege is denied during the week by their fear of adverse public opinion, carry canes only on Sundays and holidays. By this it is shown that on these days they are their own masters.

Custom as to carrying canes varies widely in different parts of the world; but it may be taken as a general maxim that the farther west you go the less you see of canes. The instinct for carrying a cane is more natural in old civilizations, where the tradition is of ancient growth, than in newer ones, where frequently a cane is regarded as the sign of an effete character. As we have been saying, canes, we all feel, have an affinity with the idea of an aristocracy. If you do not admit that the idea of an aristocracy is a good one, then doubtless you are down on canes. It is interesting to observe that canes have flourished at all especially chivalrous periods and in all especially chivalrous communities. No illustrator would portray a young planter of the Old South without his cane; and that fragrant old-school figure, a southern " Colonel," without his cane is inconceivable. Canes connote more or less leisure. They convey a subtle insinuation of some degree of culture.

Our distinguished grandfathers carried canes, frequently handsome gold-headed ones, especially if they were ministers, Bishops, or " Presiding Elders "; when, in those mellow times, it was the custom for a congregation to present its minister with a gold-headed cane duly inscribed. Our fathers of some consequence carried canes of a gentlemanly pattern, often ones with ivory handles. Though in the days when those of us now sometime grown were small one had to have arrived at the dignity of at least middle-age before it was seemly for one to carry a cane. In England, however, and particularly at Eton, it has long been a common practice for small aristocrats to affect canes.

The dandies, fops, exquisites, and beaux of picturesque and courtly ages were, of course, very partial to canes, and sometimes wore them attached to the wrist by a thong. It has been the custom of the Surgeon of the King of England to carry a " Gold Headed Cane." This cane has been handed down to the various incumbents of this office since the days of Dr. John Radcliffe, who was the first holder of the cane. It has been used for two hundred years or more by the greatest physicians and surgeons in the world, who succeeded to it. " The Gold Headed Cane " was adorned by a cross-bar at the top instead of a knob. The fact is explained by Munk, in that Radcliffe, the first owner, was a rule unto himself and possibly preferred this device as a mark of distinction beyond the knob used by physicians in general. Men of genius now and then have found in their choice of a cane an opportunity for the play of their eccentricity, such a celebrated cane being the tall wand of Whistler. Among the relics of great men preserved in museums for the inspiration of the people canes generally are to be found. We have all looked upon the cane of George Washington at Mount Vernon and the walking-stick of Carlyle in Cheyne Walk. And is each not eloquent of the man who cherished it?

Freak canes are displayed here and there by persons of a pleasantly bizarre turn of mind: canes encased in the hide of an elephant's tail, canes that have been intricately carven by some Robinson Crusoe, or canes of various other such species of curiosity. There is a veteran New York journalist who will be glad to show any student of canes one which he prizes highly that was made from the limb of a tree upon which a friend of his was hanged. In our age of handy inventions a type of cane is manufactured in combination with an umbrella.

Canes are among the useful properties of the theater. He would be a decidedly incomplete villain who did not carry a cane. Imaginative literature is rich in canes. Who ever heard of a fairy godmother without a cane? Who with any feeling for terror has not been startled by the tap, tap of the cane of old Pew in *Treasure Island*? There is an awe and a pathos in canes, too, for they are the light to blind men. And the romance of canes is further illustrated in this: they, with rags and the wallet, have been among the traditional accouterments of beggars, the insignia of the " dignity springing from the very depth of desolation; as to be naked is to be so much nearer to the being a man, than to go in livery." J. M. Barrie was so fond of an anecdote of a cane that he employed it several times in his earlier fiction. This was the story of a young man who had a cane with a loose knob, which in society he would slyly shake so that it tumbled off, when he would exclaim: " Yes, that cane is like myself; it always loses its head in the presence of ladies."

Canes have figured prominently in humor. The Irishman's shillelagh was for years a conspicuous feature of the comic press. And there will instantly come to everyone's mind that immortal passage in " Tristram Shandy." Trim is discoursing upon life and death:

" Are we not here now, continued the Corporal (striking the end of his stick perpendicularly upon the floor, so as to give an idea of health and stability) — and are we not (dropping his hat upon the ground) gone! in a moment! — 'Twas infinitely striking! Susannah burst into a flood of tears."

Canes are not absent from poetry. Into your ears already has come the refrain of " The Last Leaf ":

> And totters o'er the ground,
> With his cane.

And, doubtless, floods of instances of canes that the world will not willingly let die will occur to one upon a moment's reflection.

Canes are inseparable from art. All artists carry them; and the poorer the artist the more attached is he to his cane. Canes are indispensable to the simple vanity of the Bohemian. One of the most memorable drawings of Steinlen depicts the quaint soul of a child of the Latin Quarter: an elderly Bohemian, very much frayed, advances wreathed in the sunshine of his boutonnière and cane. Canes are invariably an accompaniment of learning. Sylvester Bonnard would of course not be without his cane; nor would any other true bookworm, as may be seen any day in the reading-room of the British Museum and of the New York Public Library. It is, indeed, indisputable that canes, more than any other article of dress, are peculiarly related to the mind. There is an old book-seller on Fourth Avenue whose clothes when he dies, like the boots of Michelangelo, probably will require to be pried loose from him, so incessantly has he worn them within the memory of man. None has ever looked upon him in the open air without his cane. And is not that emblem of omniscience and authority, the schoolmaster's ferule, directly of the cane family? So large has the cane loomed in the matter of chastisement that the word cane has become a verb, to cane.

Women as well as men play their part in the colorful story of the cane. The shepherdess's crook might be regarded as the precursor of canes for ladies. In Merrie England in the age when the May-pole flourished it was fashionable, we know from pictures, for comely misses and grande dames to sport tall canes mounted with silver or gold and knotted with a bow of ribbon. The dowager duchess of romantic story has always appeared leaning upon her cane. Do not we so see the rich aunt of Rawdon Crawley? And Mr. Walpole's Duchess of Wrexe, certainly, was supported in her domination of the old order of things by a cane. The historic old croons of our own early days smoked a clay or a corn-cob pipe and went bent upon a cane.

In England today it is swagger for women to carry sticks — in the country. And here the thoughtful spectator of the human scene notes a nice point. It is not etiquette, according to English manners, for a woman to carry a cane in town. Some American ladies who admire and would emulate English customs have not been made acquainted with this delicate nuance of taste, and so are very unfashionable when they would be ultra-fashionable.

Anybody returning from the Alps should bring back an Alpine stock with him; everyone who has visited Ireland upon his return has presented some close friend with a blackthorn stick; nobody has made a walking tour of England without an ash stick. In London all adult males above the rank of costers carry "sticks"; in New York sticks are customary with many who would be ashamed to assume them did they live in the Middle West, where the infrequent sticks to be seen upon the city streets are in many cases the sign of transient mummers. And yet it is a curious fact that in communities where the stick is conspicuously absent from the streets it is commonly displayed in show-windows, in company with cheap suits and decidedly loud gloves. Another odd circumstance is this: trashy little canes hawked by sidewalk venders generally appear with the advent of toy balloons for sale on days of big parades.

In Jamaica, Long Island, the visitor would probably see canes in the hands only of prosperous colored gentlemen. And than this fact probably nothing throws more light on the winning nature of the colored race, and on the character and function of canes. In San Francisco — but the adequate story, the Sartor Resartus — the World as Canes, remains to be written.

This, of course, is the merest essay into this vast and significant subject.

APPRECIATION HELPS

1. What is meant by the expression "a visiting mind"? Does it describe the author of this essay? Name some other essayists it might well describe.
2. What quotation underlies the first paragraph? How does it add to your pleasure in reading to recognize quotations? Find other examples in this essay.
3. "A very fair account of mankind might be made by writing the story of its canes." Discuss. Substitute other words for the word "canes" in that sentence.
4. "The cane in its evolution has ever been the symbol of a superior caste." Discuss.
5. Comment on the amount of material assembled by the author for this essay. Suggest other subjects for familiar essays.
6. Name places in literature, art, or history where you have met the cane.
7. "Temperamentally, Holliday is one with Lamb and Stevenson." Discuss.
8. Read from the author's *Walking-Stick Papers* the following: "Caun't Speak the Language," "Help Wanted — Male, Female," "On Going a Journey," "Why Men Can't Read Novels by Women," "As to People," "The Dessert of Life."

COMPOSITION HINTS

1. On Carrying Bundles
2. On Wearing New Shoes
3. On Seeing My Name in Print
4. On Second Thoughts
5. On Entertaining a Baby
6. On Family Expectations
7. Ultra-Fashionable Fads
8. Fashions Thrust upon Me

CHARLES S. BROOKS

Mr. Charles Stephen Brooks (b. 1878) is an extremely popular essayist and writer of travel books. *There's Pippins and Cheese to Come* (1917), *Chimney-Pot Papers* (1919), are titles of his collections of essays, and among his travel books are *Hints to Pilgrims* (1921) and *A Thread of English Road* (1924). His works are published either by the Yale Press or by Harcourt, Brace and Company.

He is also deeply interested in the theater, and at his own expense built a little theater in Cleveland, where he lives. It has become one of the most flourishing of its kind in the country.

For fifteen years Mr. Brooks worked in the family firm, Brooks and Company, printers, but he retired in 1915 because he wanted leisure in which to write essays. This desire to write grew in him slowly. At Yale he was an omnivorous reader, but did little writing. He was content, he says, with " eating, drinking, and being merry." He plays golf, but there are no cups on *his* mantel.

TO BE READ ONLY BY SERIOUS STUPID PERSONS[1]

NOTHING, I repeat, can exceed my astonishment of a month ago when, on a visit by invitation to a college president at his office, I was asked to conduct a class in composition — essays, stories, the carpentry of plays, things like that.

I am still young enough to be afraid of a college president, who seems in general to be rather a cold storage for the icy

[1] From *A Thread of English Road,* copyright by Harcourt, Brace and Company, Inc.

fruits of culture. Nor have I forgotten a certain occasion of alarm in my student days at such a summons. As I rung the doorbell last month a dim fancy flashed upon me that again my marks were down. Was I warned in French, or had Algebra risen as of old to plague me? Perhaps I was to lose my room on the campus for some misdemeanor. Time was when such a disgrace lay on me. I must betray the almost forgotten sins of youth.

Fancy, then, my relief and astonishment when I was invited to conduct a class in the university. I, whose memory still stung with the birch, was to wield the birch myself; and I pray that I may not descend to vicarious revenge.

In what way does one go about a task of teaching and how may one prepare? Many years ago, for one day only, I was a substitute instructor in a Sunday school; but then a leaflet was handed out with the lesson set. I had only to brush up on the golden text and use a long pointer on the map, as harder matters were handled by the superintendent in his address at the end. But now, with two months before me for preparation, I do not know which way to turn. The faculty left within a few days of my appointment, and I was alone to sweat upon the problem.

I bought a book or so, but fouled myself in unnecessary rules and then escaped to Europe dragging my burden with me. Like the hag of a story-book I am bent under a sack of troubles.

It will be terrifying, when we open in September, to see a row of eager faces shining with expectation that I have a secret to make their writing easy, to see pencils poised for a word of wisdom as if I were a balloon of hottest gas and would presently loose the windy vent; still more terrifying to behold a general nodding of curly heads or snapping after flies. This last, with a rubber band, is a harmless sport for a drowsy student and tends to rid the room of pests, but I must now forget how it was once my solace and frown upon the custom. I used, also, through a sleepy hour of the English poets, to draw lines slantwise on my book, twisting them about to avoid cutting any word; and these lines to me were a railroad in a rolling country and it was a trick to choose the shortest course of easy curve. If a decasyllable rose like a mountain across a necessary path I dug a tunnel. It is nonsense, however, I shall deny my students.

Suppose I run dry before the hour is out! Here on the sands of England I can compose a speech that will last the afternoon. I can swing my arms in expressive gesture and find apt references at will. But before my class, in my hot embarrassment, my flowery periods may shrivel to fifteen minutes. How do teachers fill the gap? Do they scrawl headings on their cuffs? Do they lead a song to fill the empty portion of the dawdling hour? Or will it be possible to stir the clock to a livelier pace? "My dear young ladies," I shall say, "consult for a moment the blackboard at the rear!" And then when their backs are turned, perhaps I may lunge forward secretly to push ahead the minute hand.

And in those golden days of October when the trees are ripe with frost and the wind whistles a shrewd invitation from the north, how shall I hold their truant thoughts indoors, prisoners to my droning voice?

Will I be asked hard questions? I must look up metaphor and simile. And certainly I must thumb around my grammar to find what an anacoluthon is. It might pop out and bite me any morning. Metonymy! There's a tough old customer. And synecdoche! I had thought that I would never need that word again when I dismissed it so many years ago. And would and should are like a pair of twins who have lost their ribbons.

In my own writing I say in turn these last two words aloud and my ear makes the choice by an uninstructed instinct; just as I find a bass in a chorus by trying all the pitches until I slip to a level that doesn't hurt. To this harmonious rumble I add now and then an upward quaver that does much toward stifling the shrill and unwholesome flutings of the tenor; but can a classroom run unfettered on careless instinct?

Shall I follow Falstaff in my class and decline to give reasons on compulsion though they be as plentiful as blackberries? My students must look up these things themselves, I shall say, so that they will (or is it shall?) stick better in the memory. It will be best to scorn all definitions, to booh at these hard questions, and inform my class, thank God, that we have passed the primer.

I may as well confess at the very outset that style cannot be taught, that its best masters have taught themselves. A teacher's finger never wagged at Shakespeare. It was the hard practice of the world that laid its instructive birch across his shoulders. And how little we know of the methods of genius or even of talent! Did Lear drag word by word with continual mending, or did it brawl firsthand from a running pen? Were the "Spectator Papers" patched and polished through successive midnights or flung breathless to the printer's devil? Barchester, I have said, was written on Trollope's knee in railway carriages, and Dickens composed his "Pickwick Papers" largely to the jolting of a hackney cab; but were these bouncing sentences never set afterwards to a smoother order? Was Thackeray's writing as facile as it sounds? William Dean Howells once told me that, after his first book, he never rewrote a novel; but is his memory to be entirely trusted? Now and then there is an exquisite page that was surely whittled. It is said that easy writing makes hard reading, and with equal emphasis the polished sentence is decried for its too apparent artifice.

Stevenson has, in a measure, admitted us to his confidence. On his excursions he put a notebook in his pocket and wove the scenery into words, but it was by rewriting, as he confesses, that he learned the mastery of words. There is hardly another modern writer who has so tinkered the mosaic of a sentence, and his sedulous ape is the most familiar beast in the literary zoo. And yet, if we try to follow the detail of his confession, his answers are as baffling as the juggler's explanation when he tucks back his cuffs and tells how he took the kicking rabbit from his hat. A friend of mine who practices to write a novel never reads an author who might affect his style; yet I myself believe in the schooling of the sedulous ape if finally one escapes from imitation and takes a free diploma at the end. There are as many methods as there are writers. We can know at most that all of them served a solitary apprenticeship outside the class room. Nor are the drugs of Coleridge and De Quincey any clue. It is an old story that Steele toiled at his Christian Hero with his head bandaged against his last night's cup, but the practice seldom makes a masterpiece, and I shall not commend it to my class.

All of these fellows of the ink pot, when writing their autobiographies, would serve material for our schooling if they printed generous pages of the choicer paragraphs with marks of erasure and correction. Ripening versions of the Grecian Urn, for example, would give us a hint or so to mend our own verse. We could rummage, as it were, in Walter Pater's wastebasket and study his struggle to perfection. And to smooth out the succession of his rising triumph would be of better use than the study of any treatise on style. Crippled sentences would acquire bit by bit an easy grace and speed which, in the final reading, we might swear were of swift impromptu.

With such hope I have examined the manuscripts that lie open in museums; but they are too perfect, and I suspect that they were copied fair, ironed and smoothed for the printer with all the tangle of the margin dusted clear. Work done, they have put on a white collar for the party, when I had hoped to find them sweating in their overalls. And I therefore suggest that famous authors, when they bequeath their manuscripts to some great gallery, throw their early mangled copies in the bundle with all their blots and changes, so that students after them may learn how the cadence of their pages rose.

It is to the point that in a life of Shakespeare written lately by J. Q. Adams there is offered a page of somewhat tangled alterations as possibly in the autograph of Shakespeare — a page from a play of another author tinkered for the Globe. But the writing is so foul to a modern eye that a layman cannot read it, and so the lesson fails.

There are some things, however, that may be taught in class; and I thought I might instruct my students in a thrifty use of adjectives, inasmuch as most beginners hang them on every noun and choose to think that a very high mountain is really taller than a mountain. Perhaps I might bar them from the use of any adjectives to rouse their ingenuity to find a noun that needs no padding. After a thrifty season, an adjective now and then might be allowed them like a single pancake in convalescence.

An artificial stretching of vocabulary is not to be urged; for the number of words employed, for purposes of style, is a secondary matter. It is their quality and fine use that are needed most. Nor may students exult when they have found a hard word to express their thought. For, in the first place, hard words make hard reading. Beneath their weight a sentence staggers like a man with a bag of coal. It is usually a pattern of easy words that gives a sentence grace, and any octosyllabic explosion blows the thought quite off its track. But secondly, and of more importance, hard words have mostly been coined for a special use and their meaning is narrow and scientific. They stiffen a paragraph to a formula. They smell unpleasantly of the laboratory and the schoolroom.

But common words have grown up with the language. They have been bartered back and forth until they are loaded with experience and association. With them life has been measured for a thousand years. To them cling both joy and sadness. Each century has left a deposit on them. Their very meaning has shifted back and forth as fashions change. Democracy or despotism, city or country preference, farce or tragedy, youth or age, power or slavery, reverence or contempt, have set them to different uses. They have lived in triumph and adversity, in gutter and palace. They have been both truth and jest and have starved and feasted. Sometimes they have started life poor and out at elbow, but have come to better fortune; or, fed in youth from a golden spoon, they have sunk to poverty.

With these common words children have been taught a

lesson at their mother's knee, with them they have been sung to sleep. A million books have been made of them, and the far-off hum of cities is the thick fabric of their use. They have lulled multitudes to obedience, and rebellion has been stirred by them. At their sound Saxon and Roman set up their standards. By them London Tower was built. They have been shouted in medieval streets. Ladies have listened to their song and have confessed their love to the silly moon. With them the Magna Charta was signed and the Armada fought. They crossed the seas in the stormy *Mayflower* and set up their stockade against the Indians. Their common use has built America. These common words defy exact definition because they mean so much. They contain a hundred elusive overtones of racial experience and recollection. A secret of style is to make this overtone a servant to the thought.

Sometimes, it is true, they seem shabby at the seam, and worn and rubbed. And yet it is usually their partnership with other words that is threadbare. An adjective and noun, like a fretting family, have been hitched together until both their backs are sore. But freed from one another for a season each regains its freshness. For words themselves — old common words — do not wear out. Let but a master use them and they shine at a dozen facets. It is the base kitchen word that is the surest timber for a sonnet, but it must divorce itself from stale and spotted company. The babble of vulgar tongues can be made the trumpet of shrewd persuasion if only its art is studied.

Words must do more than fit the sense. They must, also, please the ear; for in prose as well as verse there is a kind of cadence, although of a different and more liberal sort. If this cadence falls to monotonous singsong it palls like a second spoon of honey, and prose therefore must know how to break its melody with comely discord. Verse holds like a dancer to his waltz, but the feet of prose must move in a looser measure and ignore the insistent drum. Yet a dim cadence demands an accent here and there and a word must be discarded if it does not show the necessary stress. It would be good practice to take a page of excellent prose and by the substitution of words of equal meaning and different stress see how its ease and grace depart.

In prose, also, as well as verse, the ear discriminates among the vowels and consonants. They must lie in untiring sequence without hammering on a single letter. A word, for example, that overloads a sentence with the letter " s " must be abandoned even if Webster affirms that its meaning fits precisely to the niche. In these cases the ear must sit as an equal partner with the reason.

There is a loose uncomely kind of sentence that never shoots at the mark but wanders like a sniffing dog. This is bred by our newspapers and is the offspring of haste and disordered thinking. I know of no better ridicule of this than a chapter of Quiller-Couch's Art of Writing entitled " Jargon "; and this chapter I shall ram down my students' gullets until they gag.

There is a false instruction that recommends solely an Anglo-Saxon word. For the glory of English is its rich theft from many languages, and it is a narrow democracy of letters that challenges the family of a word and inquires too closely by what steerage it came to us. And I have observed that many writers who in theory decry a word that is derived from Latin are the first to be off their guard and use it.

But chiefly I shall impress upon my students that writing reflects the brain, and that the beauty and clarity of words arise from a beauty and clarity of thought and judgment. Nor can water be pumped from an empty well. It is by the study of great books and by experience of life that they can learn to write. And then a whole world opens to their expression.

Youth is but half itself if it gropes not blindly in a maze of thought, if it stretch not to grasp the moon; and it shall be my labor to discover in its unskilled utterance this world that is too tremendous to be tied within the logic of an apprenticed sentence. On such paragraphs, however loosely they ramble to an ineffective end, I shall not lay a sacrilegious finger, because I know that the glory of the sunrise lies unexpressed sometimes behind the mist of words. Some day, when their apprenticeship is past, may these glittering peaks still remain to give color to thoughts that the years perhaps have dulled. Any practiced writer of mature age remembers his early effort; and, although the reward of his youthful labor filled only a feverish and silly page, he knows with what sharp reality he worked. He is lucky if the old fire still warms him when his schooling has progressed through twenty years. A better chapter, now, that runs in comprehensive order, is a tamer cousin to the youth that stood bewildered and ineffective on the heights. Once, under the romantic moon of Heidelberg, I wrote a story of a king's jester and of lovers that sighed upon the midnight. The manuscript, the very plot, is gone; but in my silly memory it quite tops what I have written since.

And so now, here, on the sands of Shanklin, I argue in fancy with my class and guide them by sweet persuasion. Already I see myself a person of some dignity, moving with solemn step across the campus with a black bag that contains my papers, while freshmen stand aside to courtesy. I shall converse with the president almost as an equal. And when October has burned the fruits of earth and the wind vainly whistles its invitation from the north, I shall sit snug within my class room in fearful state behind my birch. I shall commune with the masters of the past and guide my students on the flowery paths of culture.

And now perhaps my gambling friends have lost their last shilling on the metal horses that race on Shanklin's pier and we may go to lunch.

APPRECIATION HELPS

1. Where does the author show sympathy for the point of view of the student? understanding for the problems of the teacher?
2. Did his interesting enumeration of forgotten facts remind you of ones you had learned and joyfully forgotten? What?
3. How did you learn what you know about writing? Discuss the statement that " style cannot be taught." Why is this true?
4. Read Stevenson's " A College Magazine," in *Memories and Portraits,* and find his explanation of how he learned to write.
5. Does your best writing come through careful revision?

6. What suggestions would you make to the high-school student who wishes to learn to write for the school publications?
7. Discuss: " thrifty use of adjectives "; " artificial stretching of vocabulary "; " common words "; " the glory of English is its rich theft from many languages."

COMPOSITION HINTS

1. Sleepy Hours in the Class Room
2. When the Lecture Bores Me
3. Hard Questions I Have Been Asked
4. Unfettered Classrooms
5. " Beasts in the Literary Zoo "
6. Staggering Sentences
7. Jargon
8. My Maiden Effort
9. School Knowledge to Be Joyfully Forgotten
10. The Beauty of Common Words
11. When My Story Was Printed

WILLIAM HENRY HUDSON

William Henry Hudson (1841–1922) was born of American parents on the pampas of La Plata, Argentine. His father was born in Marblehead, Massachusetts, and his mother in Maine. His boyhood was spent far from the culture of Europe, in Argentina. Educated by tutors and by his mother, the boy had long hours alone, and he developed for himself the marvelous observation which made him a great naturalist. His studies were of the wild life all around him both in South America, and some thirty years later, in England, where he spent his later life. For research problems and for museums he cared nothing. Animals, birds, trees, and flowers he saw clearly in their natural locations, and he had the power to describe them accurately in his books. Sincere, exact, original, he is excelled only by Thoreau as a man of letters in the field of nature. He has a fitting memorial in the bird sanctuary in Hyde Park that bears his name.

Ill health and poverty marred much of his life. Going to London in 1874, he labored to earn a living by writing, compelled " to exist shut out from nature for long periods, sick, poor, and friendless." Fame and a reasonable independence began only just before death.

Perhaps Hudson's best book is *Far Away and Long Ago* (1924), but *Purple Land* (1885), *Green Mansions* (1904), *Tales of the Pampas* (1905), and *The Naturalist in La Plata* (1892) are charming. *A Traveler in Little Things* (1921) is one of his last books.

Although his writings were slow to win recognition, his audience has grown steadily, delighted with the perfect naturalness of his style and with the charm and truth of his material. John Galsworthy has said: " He puts down what he sees and feels, out of sheer love of the thing seen and the emotion felt; the smell of the lamp has not touched a single page that he ever wrote. . . . To use words so true and simple that they oppose no obstacle to the flow of thought and feeling from mind to mind, and yet by juxtaposition of word sounds set up in the recipient continuing emotion or gratification — this is the essence of style; and Hudson's writing has preëminently this double quality."

THE DEATH OF AN OLD DOG[1]

WHEN recalling the impressions and experiences of that most eventful sixth year, the one incident which looks biggest in memory, at all events in the last half of that year, is the death of Caesar. There is nothing in the past I can remember so well: it was indeed the most important event of my childhood — the first thing in a young life which brought the eternal note of sadness in.

It was in the early spring, about the middle of August, and I can even remember that it was windy weather and bitterly cold for the time of the year, when the old dog was approaching his end.

Caesar was an old valued dog, although of no superior breed: he was just an ordinary dog of the country, short-haired, with long legs and a blunt muzzle. The ordinary dog or native cur was about the size of a Scotch collie; Caesar was quite a third larger, and it was said of him that he was as much above all other dogs of the house, numbering about twelve or fourteen, in intelligence and courage as in size. Naturally, he was the leader and master of the whole pack, and when he got up with an awful growl, baring his big teeth, and hurled himself on the others to chastise them for quarreling or any other infringement of dog law, they took it lying down. He was a black dog, now in his old age sprinkled with white hairs all over his body, the face and legs having gone quite grey. Caesar in a rage, or on guard at night, or when driving cattle in from the plains, was a terrible being; with us children he was mild-tempered and patient, allowing us to ride on his back, just like old Pechicho the sheep-dog, described in the first chapter.

[1] From *Far Away and Long Ago,* published and copyrighted by E. P. Dutton & Co., New York, 1924.

Now, in his decline, he grew irritable and surly, and ceased to be our playmate. The last two or three months of his life were very sad, and when it troubled us to see him so gaunt, with his big ribs protruding from his sides, to watch his twitchings when he dozed, groaning and wheezing the while, and marked, too, how painfully he struggled to get up on his feet, we wanted to know why it was so — why we could not give him something to make him well. For answer they would open his great mouth to show us his teeth — the big blunt canines and old molars worn down to stumps. Old age was what ailed him — he was thirteen years old, and that did verily seem to me a great age, for I was not half that, yet it seemed to me that I had been a very, very long time in the world.

No one dreamed of such a thing as putting an end to him — no hint of such a thing was ever spoken. It was not the custom in that country to shoot an old dog because he was past work. I remember his last day, and how often we came to look at him and tried to comfort him with warm rugs and the offer of food and drink where he was lying in a sheltered place, no longer able to stand up. And that night he died: we knew it as soon as we were up in the morning. Then, after breakfast, during which we had been very solemn and quiet, our schoolmaster said: "We must bury him today — at twelve o'clock, when I am free, will be the best time; the boys can come with me, and old John can bring his spade." This announcement greatly excited us, for we had never seen a dog buried, and had never even heard of such a thing having ever been done.

About noon that day old Caesar, dead and stiff, was taken by one of the workmen to a green open spot among the old peach trees, where his grave had already been dug. We followed our schoolmaster and watched while the body was lowered and the red earth shoveled in. The grave was deep, and Mr. Trigg assisted in filling it, puffing very much over the task and stopping at intervals to mop his face with his colored cotton handkerchief.

Then, when all was done, while we were still standing silently around, it came into Mr. Trigg's mind to improve the occasion. Assuming his schoolroom expression he looked round at us and said solemnly: "That's the end. Every dog has his day and so has every man; and the end is the same for both. We die like old Caesar, and are put into the ground and have the earth shoveled over us."

Now these simple, common words affected me more than any other words I have heard in my life. They pierced me to the heart. I had heard something terrible — too terrible to think of, incredible — and yet — and yet if it was not so, why had he said it? Was it because he hated us, just because we were children and he had to teach us our lessons, and wanted to torture us? Alas! no, I could not believe that! Was this, then, the horrible fate that awaited us all? I had heard of death — I knew there was such a thing; I knew that all animals had to die, also that some men died. For how could anyone, even a child in its sixth year, overlook such a fact, especially in the country of my birth — a land of battle, murder, and sudden death? I had not forgotten the young man tied to the post in the barn who had killed someone, and would perhaps, I had been told, be killed himself as a punishment. I knew, in fact, that there was good and evil in the world, good and bad men, and the bad men — murderers, thieves, and liars — would all have to die, just like animals; but that there was any life after death I did not know. All the others, myself and my own people included, were good and would never taste death. How it came about that I had got no further in my system or philosophy of life I cannot say; I can only suppose that my mother had not yet begun to give me instruction in such matters on account of my tender years, or else that she had done so and that I had understood it in my own way. Yet, as I discovered later, she was a religious woman, and from infancy I had been taught to kneel and say a little prayer each evening: "Now I lay me down to sleep, I pray the Lord my soul to keep"; but who the Lord was or what my soul was I had no idea. It was just a pretty little way of saying in rhyme that I was going to bed. My world was a purely material one, and a most wonderful world it was, but how I came to be in

it I didn't know; I only knew (or imagined) that I would be
in it always, seeing new and strange things every day, and
never, never get tired of it. In literature it is only in Vaughan,
Traherne, and other mystics, that I find any adequate expression of that perpetual rapturous delight in nature and my own
existence which I experienced at that period.

And now these never-to-be-forgotten words spoken over the
grave of our old dog had come to awaken me from that beautiful dream of perpetual joy!

When I recall this event I am less astonished at my ignorance
than at the intensity of the feeling I experienced, the terrible
darkness it brought on so young a mind. The child's mind we
think, and in fact know, is like that of the lower animals; or
if higher than the animal mind, it is not so high as that of the
simplest savage. He cannot concentrate his thought — he cannot think at all; his consciousness is in its dawn; he revels in
colors, in odors, is thrilled by touch and taste and sound, and
is like a well-nourished pup or kitten at play on a green turf
in the sunshine. This being so, one would have thought that
the pain of the revelation I had received would have quickly
vanished — that the vivid impressions of external things would
have blotted it out and restored the harmony. But it was not
so; the pain continued and increased until it was no longer to
be borne; then I sought my mother, first watching until she
was alone in her room. Yet when with her I feared to speak
lest with a word she should confirm the dreadful tidings.
Looking down, she all at once became alarmed at the sight of
my face, and began to question me. Then, struggling against
my tears, I told her of the words which had been spoken at the
old dog's burial, and asked her if it was true, if I — if she — if
all of us had to die and be buried in the ground? She replied
that it was not wholly true; it was only true in a way, since
our bodies had to die and be buried in the earth, but we had an
immortal part which could not die. It was true that old Caesar
had been a good, faithful dog, and felt and understood things
almost like a human being, and most persons believed that
when a dog died he died wholly and had no after-life. We

could not know that; some very great, good men had thought differently; they believed that the animals, like us, would live again. That was also her belief — her strong hope; but we could not know for certain, because it had been hidden from us. For ourselves, we knew that we could not really die, because God Himself, who made us and all things, had told us so, and His promise of eternal life had been handed down to us in His Book — in the Bible.

To all this and much more I listened trembling, with a fearful interest, and when I had once grasped the idea that death when it came to me, as it must, would leave me alive after all — that, as she explained, the part of me that really mattered, the myself, the I am I, which knew and considered things, would never perish, I experienced a sudden immense relief. When I went out from her side again I wanted to run and jump for joy and cleave the air like a bird. For I had been in prison and had suffered torture, and was now free again — death would not destroy me!

There was another result of my having unburdened my heart to my mother. She had been startled at the poignancy of the feeling I had displayed, and, greatly blaming herself for having left me too long in that ignorant state, began to give me religious instruction. It was too early, since at that age it was not possible for me to rise to the conception of an immaterial world. That power, I imagine, comes later to the normal child at the age of ten or twelve. To tell him when he is five or six or seven that God is in all places at once and sees all things, only produces the idea of a wonderfully active and quick-sighted person, with eyes like a bird's, able to see what is going on all round. A short time ago I read an anecdote of a little girl who, on being put to bed by her mother, was told not to be afraid in the dark, since God would be there to watch and guard her while she slept. Then, taking the candle, the mother went down stairs; but presently her little girl came down too, in her nightdress, and, when questioned, replied, " I'm going to stay down here in the light, mummy, and you can go up to my room and sit with God." My own idea of God at that time was no higher. I would lie awake thinking of him there in the room, puzzling over the question as to how he could attend to all his numerous affairs and spend so much time looking after me. Lying with my eyes open, I could see nothing in the dark; still, I knew he was there, because I had been told so, and this troubled me. But no sooner would I close my eyes than his image would appear standing at a distance of three or four feet from the head of the bed, in the form of a column five feet high or so and about four feet in circumference. The color was blue, but varied in depth and intensity; on some nights it was sky-blue, but usually of a deeper shade, a pure, soft, beautiful blue like that of the morning-glory or wild geranium.

It would not surprise me to find that many persons have some such material image or presentment of the spiritual entities they are taught to believe in at too tender an age. Recently, in comparing childish memories with a friend, he told me that he too always saw God as a blue object, but of no definite shape.

That blue column haunted me at night for many months; I don't think it quite vanished, ceasing to be anything but a memory, until I was seven — a date far ahead of where we are now.

APPRECIATION HELPS

1. What are some vivid and eventful memories of your first six years?
2. Can you select the most important event of your childhood, as Hudson has done, and recall the very weather associated with it?
3. Select some effective concrete details in the description of Caesar which help to make him a personality.
4. In what sense is old age the worst of all diseases?
5. Do you find a common experience in Hudson's recital of a little boy's inability to understand death, and a similar confusion of mind concerning prayers to a watchful God?
6. Hudson was a famous naturalist, and always he was " seeing new and strange things every day," and never tiring of them.

Do you live or spend your summers in a place where you feel a perpetual delight in nature?

7. Try to analyze your early conceptions of Santa Claus, of God, of angels, of fairies, of ghosts, and see whether your images were *material*.

8. Discuss: " My world was a purely material one, and a most wonderful world it was."

9. If you enjoyed this sketch, you will like Hudson's *Far Away and Long Ago*.

COMPOSITION HINTS

1. Write brief sketches of several of your pets.
2. Describe the burial of some pet.
3. Write about some happenings that taught you " that there was good and evil in the world, good and bad men."
4. An Eventful Sixth Year
5. " Every Dog Has His Day "
6. " Seeing New and Strange Things "
7. From your own experience and observation discuss the limitations of a child's mind.
8. Comment on Hudson's power of close observation.

HELEN ADAMS KELLER

No reader who even pretends to follow current writing is ignorant of the facts concerning the adventurous life of Helen Keller. Left deaf and blind at nineteen months after an illness, she was also dumb, since there seemed no way to teach her to speak. But today she is known everywhere for her achievements, because Miss Anne Sullivan (Mrs. John A. Macy) made her a part of the world of people by teaching her how to communicate with the world about her. Forty-six years of devotion have earned Mrs. Macy the title of " the other half of Helen Keller." A wise aunt of Helen's said of the little girl who was blind, deaf, and dumb, " This child has more sense than all the Kellers if there is ever any way to reach her mind." In 1887, Miss Sullivan came to Tuscumbia, Alabama, where Helen Keller was born, in 1880, to take charge of the child's training. The first task was to gain Helen's love, so that she would accept her mentor's control. How the first word, " water," was learned is a thrilling story. Miss Sullivan says: " One day we went to the pump house. I made Helen hold her mug under the spout while I pumped. As the cold water gushed forth, I spelled ' w-a-t-e-r ' several times. All the way back to the house she was highly excited, and learned the name of every object she touched. In a few hours she had added thirty new words to her vocabulary."

Miss Keller's life and interests may be read in *The Story of My Life* (1902) and *The World I Live in* (1908). Certainly one agrees with Mark Twain's statement: " You are a wonderful creature — you and your other half together — Miss Sullivan, I mean, for it took the pair of you to make a complete and perfect whole."

There are many records of men and women who made physical handicaps stepping-stones to splendid strength, but none of any other who had such heavy handicaps as Helen Keller, and none of any who won to a higher intellectual and spiritual power. The essay here appeared in the *Atlantic Monthly*.

THREE DAYS TO SEE

ALL of us have read thrilling stories in which the hero had only a limited and specified time to live. Sometimes it was as long as a year; sometimes as short as twenty-four hours. But always we were interested in discovering just how the doomed man chose to spend his last days or his last hours. I speak, or course, of free men who have a choice, not condemned criminals whose sphere of activities is strictly delimited.

Such stories set us thinking, wondering what we should do under similar circumstances. What events, what experiences, what associations should we crowd into those last hours as mortal beings? What happiness should we find in reviewing the past, what regrets?

Sometimes I have thought it would be an excellent rule to live each day as if we should die tomorrow. Such an attitude would emphasize sharply the values of life. We should live each day with a gentleness, a vigor, and a keenness of appreciation which are often lost when time stretches before us in the constant panorama of more days and months and years to come. There are those, of course, who would adopt the epicurean motto of " Eat, drink, and be merry," but most people would be chastened by the certainty of impending death.

In stories, the doomed hero is usually saved at the last minute by some stroke of fortune, but almost always his sense of values is changed. He becomes more appreciative of the meaning of life and its permanent spiritual values. It has often been noted that those who live, or have lived, in the shadow of death bring a mellow sweetness to everything they do.

Most of us, however, take life for granted. We know that one day we must die, but usually we picture that day as far in the future. When we are in buoyant health, death is all but unimaginable. We seldom think of it. The days stretch out in an endless vista. So we go about our petty tasks, hardly aware of our listless attitude toward life.

The same lethargy, I am afraid, characterizes the use of all our faculties and senses. Only the deaf appreciate hearing, only the blind realize the manifold blessings that lie in sight. Particularly does this observation apply to those who have lost sight and hearing in adult life. But those who have never suffered impairment of sight or hearing seldom make the fullest use of these blessed faculties. Their eyes and ears take in all sights and sounds hazily, without concentration and with little appreciation. It is the same old story of not being grateful for what we have until we lose it, of not being conscious of health until we are ill.

I have often thought it would be a blessing if each human being were stricken blind and deaf for a few days at some time during his early adult life. Darkness would make him more appreciative of sight; silence would teach him the joys of sound.

Now and then I have tested my seeing friends to discover what they see. Recently I was visited by a very good friend who had just returned from a long walk in the woods, and I asked her what she had observed. "Nothing in particular," she replied. I might have been incredulous had I not been accustomed to such responses, for long ago I became convinced that the seeing see little.

How was it possible, I asked myself, to walk for an hour through the woods and see nothing worthy of note? I who cannot see find hundreds of things to interest me through mere touch. I feel the delicate symmetry of a leaf. I pass my hands lovingly about the smooth skin of a silver birch, or the rough shaggy bark of a pine. In spring I touch the branches of trees hopefully in search of a bud, the first sign of awakening Nature after her winter's sleep. I feel the delightful, velvety texture of a flower, and discover its remarkable convolutions; and something of the miracle of Nature is revealed to me. Occasionally, if I am very fortunate, I place my hand gently on a small tree and feel the happy quiver of a bird in full song. I am delighted to have the cool waters of a brook rush through my open fingers. To me a lush carpet of pine needles or spongy grass is more welcome than the most luxurious Persian rug. To me the pageant of seasons is a thrilling and unending drama, the action of which streams through my finger tips.

At times my heart cries out with longing to see all these things. If I can get so much pleasure from mere touch, how much more beauty must be revealed by sight. Yet, those who have eyes apparently see little. The panorama of color and action which fills the world is taken for granted. It is human, perhaps, to appreciate little that which we have and to long for that which we have not, but it is a great pity that in the world of light the gift of sight is used only as a mere convenience rather than as a means of adding fullness to life.

If I were the president of a university I should establish a compulsory course in " How to Use Your Eyes." The professor would try to show his pupils how they could add joy to their lives by really seeing what passes unnoticed before them. He would try to awake their dormant and sluggish faculties.

Perhaps I can best illustrate by imagining what I should most like to see if I were given the use of my eyes, say, for just three days. And while I am imagining, suppose you, too, set your mind to work on the problem of how you would use your own eyes if you had only three more days to see. If with the oncoming darkness of the third night you knew that the sun would never rise for you again, how would you spend those three precious intervening days? What would you most want to let your gaze rest upon?

I, naturally, should want most to see the things which have become dear to me through my years of darkness. You, too, would want to let your eyes rest long on the things that have become dear to you so that you could take the memory of them with you into the night that loomed before you.

If, by some miracle, I were granted three seeing days, to be followed by a relapse into darkness, I should divide the period into three parts.

On the first day, I should want to see the people whose kindness and gentleness and companionship have made my life worth living. First I should like to gaze long upon the face of my dear teacher, Mrs. Anne Sullivan Macy, who came to me when I was a child and opened the outer world to me. I should want not merely to see the outline of her face, so that I could cherish it in my memory, but to study that face and find in it the living evidence of the sympathetic tenderness and patience with which she accomplished the difficult task of my education. I should like to see in her eyes that strength of character which has enabled her to stand firm in the face of difficulties, and that compassion for all humanity which she has revealed to me so often.

I do not know what it is to see into the heart of a friend through that " window of the soul," the eye. I can only " see " through my finger tips the outline of a face. I can detect laughter, sorrow, and many other obvious emotions. I know my friends from the feel of their faces. But I cannot really picture their personalities by touch. I know their personalities, of course, through other means, through the thoughts they express to me, through whatever of their actions are revealed to me. But I am denied that deeper understanding of them which I am sure would come through sight of them, through watching their reactions to various expressed thoughts and circumstances, through noting the immediate and fleeting reactions of their eyes and countenance.

Friends who are near to me I know well, because through the months and years they reveal themselves to me in all their phases; but of casual friends I have only an incomplete impression, an impression gained from a handclasp, from spoken words which I take from their lips with my finger tips, or which they tap into the palm of my hand.

How much easier, how much more satisfying it is for you who can see to grasp quickly the essential qualities of another person by watching the subtleties of expression, the quiver of a muscle, the flutter of a hand. But does it ever occur to you to use your sight to see into the inner nature of a friend or acquaintance? Do not most of you seeing people grasp casually the outward features of a face and let it go at that?

For instance, can you describe accurately the faces of five

good friends? Some of you can, but many cannot. As an experiment, I have questioned husbands of long standing about the color of their wives' eyes, and often they express embarrassed confusion and admit that they do not know. And, incidentally, it is a chronic complaint of wives that their husbands do not notice new dresses, new hats, and changes in household arrangements.

The eyes of seeing persons soon become accustomed to the routine of their surroundings, and they actually see only the startling and spectacular. But even in viewing the most spectacular sights the eyes are lazy. Court records reveal every day how inaccurately "eyewitnesses" see. A given event will be "seen" in several different ways by as many witnesses. Some see more than others, but few see everything that is within the range of their vision.

Oh, the things that I should see if I had the power of sight for just three days!

The first day would be a busy one. I should call to me all my dear friends and look long into their faces, imprinting upon my mind the outward evidences of the beauty that is within them. I should let my eyes rest, too, on the face of a baby, so that I could catch a vision of the eager, innocent beauty which precedes the individual's consciousness of the conflicts which life develops.

And I should like to look into the loyal, trusting eyes of my dogs — the grave, canny little Scottie, Darkie, and the stalwart, understanding Great Dane, Helga, whose warm, tender, and playful friendships are so comforting to me.

On that busy first day I should also view the small simple things of my home. I want to see the warm colors in the rugs under my feet, the pictures on the walls, the intimate trifles that transform a house into home. My eyes would rest respectfully on the books in raised type which I have read, but they would be more eagerly interested in the printed books which seeing people can read, for during the long night of my life the books I have read and those which have been read to me have built themselves into a great shining lighthouse, revealing to me the deepest channels of human life and the human spirit.

In the afternoon of that first seeing day, I should take a long walk in the woods and intoxicate my eyes on the beauties of the world of Nature, trying desperately to absorb in a few hours the vast splendor which is constantly unfolding itself to those who can see. On the way home from my woodland jaunt my path would lie near a farm so that I might see the patient horses plowing in the field (perhaps I should see only a tractor!) and the serene content of men living close to the soil. And I should pray for the glory of a colorful sunset.

When dusk had fallen, I should experience the double delight of being able to see by artificial light, which the genius of man has created to extend the power of his sight when Nature decrees darkness.

In the night of that first day of sight, I should not be able to sleep, so full would be my mind of the memories of the day.

The next day — the second day of sight — I should arise with the dawn and see the thrilling miracle by which night is transformed into day. I should behold with awe the magnificent panorama of light with which the sun awakens the sleeping earth.

This day I should devote to a hasty glimpse of the world, past and present. I should want to see the pageant of man's progress, the kaleidoscope of the ages. How can so much be compressed into one day? Through the museums, of course. Often I have visited the New York Museum of Natural History to touch with my hands many of the objects there exhibited, but I have longed to see with my eyes the condensed history of the earth and its inhabitants displayed there — animals and the races of men pictured in their native environment; gigantic carcasses of dinosaurs and mastodons which roamed the earth long before man appeared, with his tiny stature and powerful brain, to conquer the animal kingdom; realistic presentations of the processes of evolution in animals, in man, and in the implements which man has used to fashion for himself a secure home on this planet; and a thousand and one other aspects of natural history.

I wonder how many readers of this article have viewed this panorama of the face of living things as pictured in that inspiring museum. Many, of course, have not had the opportunity, but I am sure that many who *have* had the opportunity have not made use of it. There, indeed, is a place to use your eyes. You who see can spend many fruitful days there, but I, with my imaginary three days of sight, could only take a hasty glimpse, and pass on.

My next stop would be the Metropolitan Museum of Art, for just as the Museum of Natural History reveals the material aspects of the world, so does the Metropolitan show the myriad facets of the human spirit. Throughout the history of humanity the urge to artistic expression has been almost as powerful as the urge for food, shelter, and procreation. And here, in the vast chambers of the Metropolitan Museum, is unfolded before me the spirit of Egypt, Greece, and Rome, as expressed in their art. I know well through my hands the sculptured gods and goddesses of the ancient Nile-land. I have felt copies of Parthenon friezes, and I have sensed the rhythmic beauty of charging Athenian warriors. Apollos and Venuses and the Wingèd Victory of Samothrace are friends of my finger tips. The gnarled, bearded features of Homer are dear to me, for he, too, knew blindness.

My hands have lingered upon the living marble of Roman sculpture as well as that of later generations. I have passed my hands over a plaster cast of Michelangelo's inspiring and heroic Moses; I have sensed the power of Rodin; I have been awed by the devoted spirit of Gothic wood carving. These arts which can be touched have meaning for me, but even they were meant to be seen rather than felt, and I can only guess at the beauty which remains hidden from me. I can admire the simple lines of a Greek vase, but its figured decorations are lost to me.

So on this, my second day of sight, I should try to probe into the soul of man through his art. The things I knew through touch I should now see. More splendid still, the whole magnificent world of painting would be opened to me, from the Italian Primitives, with their serene religious devotion, to the Moderns, with their feverish visions. I should look deep into the canvases of Raphael, Leonardo da Vinci, Titian, Rembrandt. I should want to feast my eyes upon the warm colors of Veronese, study the mysteries of El Greco, catch a new vision of Nature from Corot. Oh, there is so much rich meaning and beauty in the art of the ages for you who have eyes to see!

Upon my short visit to this temple of art I should not be able to review a fraction of that great world of art which is open to you. I should be able to get only a superficial impression. Artists tell me that for a deep and true appreciation of art one must educate the eye. One must learn through experience to weigh the merits of line, of composition, of form and color. If I had eyes, how happily would I embark upon so fascinating a study! Yet I am told that, to many of you who have eyes to see, the world of art is a dark night, unexplored and unilluminated.

It would be with extreme reluctance that I should leave the Metropolitan Museum, which contains the key to beauty — a beauty so neglected. Seeing persons, however, do not need a Metropolitan to find this key to beauty. The same key lies waiting in smaller museums, and in books on the shelves of even small libraries. But naturally, in my limited time of imaginary sight, I should choose the place where the key unlocks the greatest treasures in the shortest time.

The evening of my second day of sight I should spend at a theater or at the movies. Even now I often attend theatrical performances of all sorts, but the action of the play must be spelled into my hand by a companion. But how I should like to see with my own eyes the fascinating figure of Hamlet, or the gusty Falstaff amid colorful Elizabethan trappings! How I should like to follow each movement of the graceful Hamlet, each strut of the hearty Falstaff! And since I could see only one play, I should be confronted by a many-horned dilemma, for there are scores of plays I should want to see. You who have eyes can see any you like. How many of you, I wonder, when you gaze at a play, a movie, or any spectacle, realize and give thanks for the miracle of sight which enables you to enjoy its color, grace, and movement?

I cannot enjoy the beauty of rhythmic movement except in a sphere restricted to the touch of my hands. I can vision only dimly the grace of a Pavlowa, although I know something of the delight of rhythm, for often I can sense the beat of music as it vibrates through the floor. I can well imagine that cadenced motion must be one of the most pleasing sights in the world. I have been able to gather something of this by tracing with my fingers the lines in sculptured marble; if this static grace can be so lovely, how much more acute must be the thrill of seeing grace in motion.

One of my dearest memories is of the time when Joseph Jefferson allowed me to touch his face and hands as he went through some of the gestures and speeches of his beloved Rip Van Winkle. I was able to catch thus a meager glimpse of the world of drama, and I shall never forget the delight of that moment. But, oh, how much I must miss, and how much pleasure you seeing ones can derive from watching and hearing the interplay of speech and movement in the unfolding of a dramatic performance! If I could see only one play, I should know how to picture in my mind the action of a hundred plays which I have read or had transferred to me through the medium of the manual alphabet.

So, through the evening of my second imaginary day of sight, the great figures of dramatic literature would crowd sleep from my eyes.

The following morning, I should again greet the dawn, anxious to discover new delights, for I am sure that, for those who have eyes which really see, the dawn of each day must be a perpetually new revelation of beauty.

This, according to the terms of my imagined miracle, is to be my third and last day of sight. I shall have no time to waste in regrets or longings; there is too much to see. The first day

I devoted to my friends, animate and inanimate. The second revealed to me the history of man and Nature. Today I shall spend in the workaday world of the present, amid the haunts of men going about the business of life. And where can one find so many activities and conditions of men as in New York? So the city becomes my destination.

I start from my home in the quiet little suburb of Forest Hills, Long Island. Here, surrounded by green lawns, trees, and flowers, are neat little houses, happy with the voices and movements of wives and children, havens of peaceful rest for men who toil in the city. I drive across the lacy structure of steel which spans the East River, and I get a new and startling vision of the power and ingenuity of the mind of man. Busy boats chug and scurry about the river — racy speed boats, stolid, snorting tugs. If I had long days of sight ahead, I should spend many of them watching the delightful activity upon the river.

I look ahead, and before me rise the fantastic towers of New York, a city that seems to have stepped from the pages of a fairy story. What an awe-inspiring sight, these glittering spires, these vast banks of stone and steel — structures such as the gods might build for themselves! This animated picture is a part of the lives of millions of people every day. How many, I wonder, give it so much as a second glance? Very few, I fear. Their eyes are blind to this magnificent sight because it is so familiar to them.

I hurry to the top of one of those gigantic structures, the Empire State Building, for there, a short time ago, I " saw " the city below through the eyes of my secretary. I am anxious to compare my fancy with reality. I am sure I should not be disappointed in the panorama spread out before me, for to me it would be a vision of another world.

Now I begin my rounds of the city. First, I stand at a busy corner, merely looking at people, trying by sight of them to understand something of their lives. I see smiles, and I am happy. I see serious determination, and I am proud. I see suffering, and I am compassionate.

I stroll down Fifth Avenue. I throw my eyes out of focus so that I see no particular object but only a seething kaleidoscope of color. I am certain that the colors of women's dresses moving in a throng must be a gorgeous spectacle of which I should never tire. But perhaps if I had sight I should be like most other women — too interested in styles and the cut of individual dresses to give much attention to the splendor of color in the mass. And I am convinced, too, that I should become an inveterate window shopper, for it must be a delight to the eye to view the myriad articles of beauty on display.

From Fifth Avenue I make a tour of the city — to Park Avenue, to the slums, to factories, to parks where children play. I take a stay-at-home trip abroad by visiting the foreign quarters. Always my eyes are open wide to all the sights of both happiness and misery so that I may probe deep and add to my understanding of how people work and live. My heart is full of the images of people and things. My eye passes lightly over no single trifle; it strives to touch and hold closely each thing its gaze rests upon. Some sights are pleasant, filling the heart with happiness; but some are miserably pathetic. To these latter I do not shut my eyes, for they, too, are part of life. To close the eye on them is to close the heart and mind.

My third day of sight is drawing to an end. Perhaps there are many serious pursuits to which I should devote the few remaining hours, but I am afraid that on the evening of that last day I should again run away to the theater, to a hilariously funny play, so that I might appreciate the overtones of comedy in the human spirit.

At midnight my temporary respite from blindness would cease, and permanent night would close in on me again. Naturally in those three short days I should not have seen all I wanted to see. Only when darkness had again descended upon me should I realize how much I had left unseen. But my mind would be so crowded with glorious memories that I should have little time for regrets. Thereafter the touch of every object would bring a glowing memory of how that object looked.

Perhaps this short outline of how I should spend three days of sight does not agree with the program you would set for yourself if you knew that you were about to be stricken blind. I am, however, sure that if you actually faced that fate your eyes would open to things you had never seen before, storing up memories for the long night ahead. You would use your eyes as never before. Everything you saw would become dear to you. Your eyes would touch and embrace every object that came within your range of vision. Then, at last, you would really see, and a new world of beauty would open itself before you.

I who am blind can give one hint to those who see — one admonition to those who would make full use of the gift of sight: Use your eyes as if tomorrow you would be stricken blind. And the same method can be applied to the other senses. Hear the music of voices, the song of a bird, the mighty strains of an orchestra, as if you would be stricken deaf tomorrow. Touch each object you want to touch as if tomorrow your tactile sense would fail. Smell the perfume of flowers, taste with relish each morsel, as if tomorrow you could never smell and taste again. Make the most of every sense; glory in all the facets of pleasure and beauty which the world reveals to you through the several means of contact which Nature provides. But of all the senses, I am sure that sight must be the most delightful.

APPRECIATION HELPS

1. Show that the title is a challenge to your imagination. If you knew that you had only three days of sight, or three days of hearing, how would you spend them?
2. What stories have you read in which the hero had only a limited time to live?
3. Stevenson shows in " Aes Triplex " that men who think and prepare constantly for death do not really live. Some student might report this essay to the class and explain Stevenson's distinction between life and living.

4. When have you shifted your sense of values within the last four years on friends, music, books, sports?
5. Study your own power of observation to learn if you see and hear as much as those about you. Are your senses of taste and smell keen?
6. Would you like Miss Keller to test your sight and hearing? Why?
7. Discuss the knowledge Miss Keller gains through touch.
8. Comment on the author's plan for using three days of sight. What does she include that you would never think of?
9. How does this essay make you regard the author? Your own self?

COMPOSITION HINTS

1. The Seeing See Little
2. Discuss the author's contention that of all the senses, sight must be the most delightful.
3. Foreign Quarters I Have Visited
4. To Parks where Children Play
5. My City's Busiest Corner
6. Inveterate Window-Shoppers
7. Bridges — Lacy Structures of Steel

SIMEON STRUNSKY

Simeon Strunsky is one of the best-known newspaper men in the country. He is one of the "old crowd" of the New York *Evening Post,* which he left when Mr. Villard sold the paper, going to the editorial staff of the New York *Times.* He has done much work for the *Times* in other countries, notably at the Versailles Peace Conference.

Born at Vitebsk, Russia, in 1879, Simeon Strunsky came early to America, and was educated at Horace Mann High School, and at Columbia University, where he graduated in 1900. His first six years of editorial work were with the New International Encyclopedia. His books of essays are genial and humorous, and attract many readers. *Post-Impressions* (1914), *Belshazzar Court* (1914), *Sinbad and His Friends* (1921), and *The Rediscovery of Jones* (1931) are packed with fun.

ROMANCE[1]

AT 5:15 in the afternoon of an exceptionally sultry day in August, John P. Wesley, forty-seven years old, in business at No. 634 East Twenty-sixth Street as a jobber in tools and hardware, was descending the stairs to the downtown platform of the Subway at Twenty-eighth Street, when it occurred to him suddenly how odd it was that he should be going home. His grip tightened on the hand rail and he stopped short in his tracks, his eyes fixed on the ground in pained perplexity. The crowd behind him, thrown back upon itself by this abrupt action, halted only for a moment and flowed on. Cheerful office-boys looked back at him and asked what

[1] From *Post-Impressions,* published by Dodd Mead and Company, 1914.

was the answer. Stout citizens elbowed him aside without apology. But Wesley did not mind. He was asking himself why it was that the end of the day's work should invariably find him descending the stairs to the downtown platform of the Subway. Was there any reason for doing that, other than habit? He wondered why it would not be just as reasonable to cross the avenue and take an uptown train instead.

Wesley had been taking the downtown train at Twenty-eighth Street at 5:15 in the afternoon ever since there was a Subway. At Brooklyn Bridge he changed to an express and went to the end of the line. At the end of the line there was a boat which took him across the harbor. At the end of the boat ride there was a trolley car which wound its way up the hill and through streets lined with yellow-bricked, easy-payment, two-family houses, out into the open country, where it dropped him at a cross road. At the end of a ten minutes' walk there was a new house of stucco and timber, standing away from the road, its angular lines revealing mingled as-pirations toward the Californian bungalow and the English Tudor. In the house lived a tall, slender, grey-haired woman who was Wesley's wife, and two young girls who were his daughters. They always came to the door when his footsteps grated on the garden path, and kissed him welcome. After dinner he went out and watered the lawn, which, after his wife and the girls, he loved most. He plied the hose deliber-ately, his eye alert for bald patches. Of late the lawn had not been coming on well, because of a scorching sun and the lack of rain. A quiet chat with his wife on matters of domestic economy ushered in the end of a busy day. At the end of the day there was another day just like it.

And now, motionless in the crowd, Wesley was asking whether right to the end of life this succession of days would continue. Why always the southbound train? He was aware that there were good reasons why. One was the tall grey-haired woman and the two young girls at home who were in the habit of waiting for the sound of his footsteps on the garden path. They were his life. But apparently, too, there must be life along the uptown route of the Interborough. He wanted to run amuck, to board a northbound train without any destination in mind, and to keep on as far as his heart desired, to the very end perhaps, to Van Cortlandt Park, where they played polo, or the Bronx, where there was a botanical museum and a zoo. Even if he went only as far as Grand Central Station, it would be an act of magnificent daring.

Wesley climbed to the street, crossed Fourth Avenue, descended to the uptown platform, and entered a train without stopping to see whether it was Broadway or Lenox Avenue. Already he was thinking of the three women at home in a remote, objective mood. They would be waiting for him, no doubt, and he was sorry, but what else could he do? He was not his own master. Under the circumstances it was a comfort to know that all three of them were women of poise, not given to making the worst of things, and with enough work on their hands to keep them from worrying overmuch.

Having broken the great habit of his life by taking an uptown train at 5:15, Wesley found it quite natural that his minor habits should fall from him automatically. He did not relax into his seat and lose himself in the evening paper after his usual fashion. He did not look at his paper at all, but at the people about him. He had never seen such men and women before, so fresh-tinted, so outstanding, so electric. He seemed to have opened his eyes on a mass of vivid colors and sharp contours. It was the same sensation he experienced when he used to break his gold-rimmed spectacles, and after he had groped for a day in the mists of myopia, a new, bright world would leap out at him through the new lenses.

Wesley did not make friends easily. In a crowd he was peculiarly shy. Now he grew garrulous. At first his innate timidity rose up and choked him, but he fought it down. He turned to his neighbor on the right, a thick-set, clean-shaven youth who was painfully studying the comic pictures in his evening newspaper, and remarked, in a style utterly strange to him:

" Looks very much like the Giants had the rag cinched? "

The thick-set young man, whom Wesley imagined to be a butcher's assistant or something of the sort, looked up from his paper and said, " It certainly does seem as if the New York team had established its title to the championship."

Wesley cleared his throat again.

" When it comes to slugging the ball you've got to hand it to them," he said.

" Assuredly," said the young man, folding up his paper with the evident design of continuing the conversation.

Wesley was pleased and frightened. He had tasted another new sensation. He had broken through the frosty reserve of twenty years and had spoken to a stranger after the free and easy manner of men who make friends in Pullman cars and at lunch counters. And the stranger, instead of repulsing him, had admitted him, at the very first attempt, into the fraternity of ordinary people. It was pleasant to be one of the great democracy of the crowd, something which Wesley had never had time to be. But on the other hand, he found the strain of conversation telling upon him. He did not know how to go on.

The stranger went out, but Wesley did not care. He was lost in a delicious reverie, conscious only of being carried forward on free-beating wings into a wonderful, unknown land. The grinding of wheels and brakes as the train halted at a station and pulled out again made a languorous, soothing music. The train clattered out of the tunnel into the open air, and Wesley was but dimly aware of the change from dark to twilight. The way now ran through a region of vague apartment houses. There were trees, stretches of green field waiting for the builder, and here or there a colonial manor house with sheltered windows, resigned to its fate. Then came cottages with gardens. And in one of these Wesley, shocked into acute consciousness, saw a man with a rubber hose watering a lawn. Wesley leaped to his feet.

The train was at a standstill when he awoke to the extraordinary fact that he was twelve miles away from South

Ferry, and going in the wrong direction. The imperative need of getting home as soon as he could overwhelmed him. He dashed for the door, but it slid shut in his face and the train pulled out. His fellow passengers grinned. One of the most amusing things in the world is a tardy passenger who tries to fling himself through a car door and flattens his nose against the glass. It is hard to say why the thing is amusing, but it is. Wesley did not know he was being laughed at. He merely knew that he must go home. He got out at the next station, and when he was seated in a corner of the southbound train, he sighed with unutterable relief. He was once more in a normal world where trains ran to South Ferry instead of away from it. He dropped off at his road crossing, just two hours late, and found his wife waiting.

They walked on side by side without speaking, but once or twice she turned and caught him staring at her with a peculiar mixture of wonder and unaccustomed tenderness.

Finally he broke out.

" It's good to see you again! "

She laughed and was happy. His voice stirred in her memories of long ago.

" It's good to have you back, dear," she said.

" But you really look remarkably well," he insisted.

" I rested this afternoon."

" That's what you should do every day," he said. " Look at that old maple tree! It hasn't changed a bit! "

" No," she said, and began to wonder.

" And the girls are well? "

" Oh, yes."

" I can hardly wait till I see them," he said; and then, to save himself, " I guess I am getting old, Alice."

" You are younger tonight than you have been for a long time," she said.

Jennie and her sister were waiting for them on the porch. They wondered why father's kiss fell so warmly on their cheeks. He kissed them twice, which was very unusual; but being discreet young women they asked no questions. After dinner Wesley went out to look at the lawn.

APPRECIATION HELPS

1. What details emphasize the fact that John P. Wesley is a suburbanite?
2. Tell the class of times when you became bored with school, home, or social routine.
3. Describe the trip from your home to your favorite shopping-center. What on the way would especially interest a stranger seeing it for the first time?
4. Do you know families whose routine is as deadly regular as it is in John's family?
5. Are daughters in a modern household always at home to greet the returning father? the mothers?
6. What routine chores do the neighborhood men do in the mornings and evenings? the women?
7. What interesting glimpses of life may one find along the " uptown routes " in your city? (For example, foreign life; markets; crowded parks.)
8. Why did the strange faces in the city street-cars seem to John " outstanding, electric "?
9. Describe some garrulous strangers you have enjoyed visiting with on trains.
10. Why does one sometimes tell strangers so many confidences withheld from intimate friends?
11. Illustrate: " the fraternity of ordinary people."
12. Is the essay properly named? Was it romance to travel, or to arrive home?
13. Why is John so happy to get home?

COMPOSITION HINTS

1. The Five-Forty Express
2. Seen on the Subway Train
3. The Monotony of Routine
4. Routine — a Blessing
5. My Chores
6. Friends Made in Pullman Cars and at Lunch Counters
7. Traveling and Arriving

LIZETTE WOODWORTH REESE

Perhaps the most interesting fact in the life of Lizette Wood-worth Reese to a youthful reader is that she found time, during forty-five years of teaching, to write many widely recognized volumes of poetry and of prose. She has demonstrated, as did Charles Lamb, that creative work can be done along with the routine of a job. For those who find difficulty in writing easily, in making words fitly express thoughts, it is comforting to know that Miss Reese found composition a difficult task. She had mental pictures and she thought quickly, but expression was slow in coming. She was always writing. Her poems she sent as " far north as Cambridge in Massachusetts, and as far west as Chicago and St. Louis." Miss Reese began to write in an age when ornate writing was popular, but she learned to write simple and direct prose and poetry shorn of verbal tricks.

Miss Reese was born in Maryland, 1856. Her mother, a German, was " as sure of God as she was of the sun." On fine summer or winter days she would quote, " This is the day which the Lord hath made." Her father, a soldier in the Confederate Army, was a silent man, " with the tense and stern characteristics of his Welsh ancestry."

At seventeen she began her teaching, " raw, eager, dreamy, fond of young people, and having the gift of authority." In Baltimore, in an English-German school, she taught English half the day, and German the other half. Four years were spent in a high school for Negroes, and twenty years she taught English in Western High School, Baltimore. Two years after she resigned at Western, the school unveiled a bronze tablet on which was inscribed her most famous poem, " Tears." (The check for " Tears " arrived the day Miss Reese's father died.) Concerning this honor Miss Reese said: " Whenever I think of this tribute, of this tablet made fast in a place familiar to so many young people, it warms the very cockles of my heart."

Poetry lovers will read *Spicewood* (1920); *Wild Cherry* (1923); *White April* (1930). Both *A Victorian Village* (1929) and *The York Road* (1931) are prose autobiographies.

MY MOTHER[1]

WHENEVER I think of my mother, I think of gardens and of daffodils. She loved gardens; she loved daffodils. If she stuck a root or a bulb into the ground, up it came, and blew, and grew, and prospered. Her neighbors' roots and bulbs might come to nothing, rot in the dark clods, or straggle into a few spindling, plaintive leaves, but hers with their punctual white, or scarlet, or purple, flouted this sterility on the other side of the hedge. This was of much satisfaction to her. Was it magic, or love, or divination as to the proper course to follow which brought this ancient business to such a lovely conclusion?

Once a friend of mine sent me a lavender bush, a short, withered thing, from down Cambridge way, on the Eastern Shore, and my mother planted it deep in the grass plot in front of the house. It became at last almost as tall as a tall lilac bush, and at the end of every June broke out into hundreds of pale violet flowers, whose fragrance was blown through the whole house, and to which the bees came from the corners of the neighborhood, butterflies, too, like bits of white or dim yellow lace swaying over the spear-like bloom. This lavender was one of the delicate triumphs of her life. She used to sit out on the side porch, and listen to the admiring ejaculations of the passers-by, on their way from church, or to the shops, and retail it afterwards as though it were part of some ecstatic state affair or a matter of great and intricate national concern. Alas, the bush was tried too hard one perishingly bitter winter, and in spite of its cover of dead leaves and rich ruck, died down to a sad bundle of dried, chocolate-

[1] From *A Victorian Village,* copyright, 1929, and reprinted by permission of Farrar & Rinehart, Inc.

colored sticks! It was one of her few failures in gardening, and it affected her as though it were the loss of something out of herself, or some wreck done to her lively heritage. She never afterward tried to raise another lavender bush.

She loved daffodils. There was always the twist and turn of spring weather within and about her, expectancy, eagerness, an airy moodiness; she moved in a mist of adventure. She was gay. Many frets, and hurts, and anxieties had been hers; she had lost her sons; it was not until middle life that the exigencies of a fine poverty were lightened, and circumstances became so easy that she need not measure each dollar against dollar. And some of these experiences had been of a bitterness which would have trampled down to the clods a more trivial, less opulent creature. But her gayety survived, being bone of her bone and nothing else. Almost until the very hour of her death, a certain half-dozen light-hearted stories in the family, worn lean at the edges, which she had a passion for telling, made her, in the telling, go off into billowy laughter, the tears running down her cheeks, and the rest of us swept along with her, as though upon a surge of mirth and abandon. She had no especial sense of humor beyond this; at times her moods were such that a small matter stretched into a very great one, and a trifle towered to such a height that it practically overpowered her. We used to remember her billowy laughter, and wonder at this imaginative revulsion. If we left the house, and failed to return within the time we had specified, she would see us, with a scared eye, the victims of some swift and barbarous accident, already sheeted, tolled for, prayed over, put to bed. When we reached our doors at last we would find her pacing the rooms, in a whirl of dread and foreboding. Such a reasonable thing as the difference in clocks or the delays in trains was entirely and absolutely incomprehensible to her. We acquired the habit, therefore, of not setting any particular hour for our reappearing after visits, or marketing expeditions, or the various junketings down the bay or out into the parks.

A brightly tinted platter or dish of any kind would make

her happy for hours. She rarely went shopping without bring, ing home some piece of crockery, either imported or otherwise, to which she had taken a swift and settled fancy; her friends knew this and often came like the Greeks with gifts. A diminutive square table in her bedroom was filled with odd cups and saucers and the like, of delicate greens, or blues, or whites, or a dash of scarlet.

As she grew older no other lady of her age in the neighborhood was ever allowed to wear more expensive or more fashionable raiment than did she herself. If occasionally this happened, up would go her fine nose. In the near future, something new was purchased or something old made over into a dazzling new. A heavily ribbed silk coat of hers down to her heels, and embellished with flat crochet buttons, was like a challenge, the throwing down of a glove, to her contemporaries in the intimate, half-country streets where she lived for the last twenty years of her life. This was not envy or jealousy on her part — or very little at that — but an exaggerated sense of beauty made over into a personal one. She loved beautiful things, and she loved to possess them for herself, and to be the primal possessor of them.

Detective and all other stories containing mysteries and headlong adventures were the type of literature which she best appreciated. She considered these the most interesting, and her measurement of every scrap of literary effort was by its interest, a theory sound enough to commend itself to the critics. She was not invariably in love with the heroes and heroines, but she always whole-heartedly hated the villains. Any punishment, from boiling in oil, drowning in sacks, to hanging on a gallows, meted out to the latter, was a circumstance of most profound satisfaction to her; she not only believed that people should reap what they sow, but was anxious to be on the exact territory at the moment of that grim harvesting. She was neither a narrow nor a severe woman, but as concrete justice in her experiences in life had often been a failure, so she expected it all the more in books, as the authors had it in their power to dispense it. The happy ending never dismayed her; artistically it might be all to the wrong, but spiritually it was all to the right. It will be gathered from this that my mother's idea of literature was moral, and not intellectual; I do not think that she could have been called intellectual according to any strict acceptance of the word. And yet she had a distinct and certain sense for language. Sometimes, when in doubt about the rendering of a worrying line in a poem that I was writing, I would ask her to tell me which she considered the best combination of words for my purpose; she would immediately respond with the most artistic selection; and the reasons for this selection were the significant ones. Her judgment in some other matters was almost infallible. We went to her as the last resort. Her intuition also was as trustworthy as her judgment; what she said about a person was true in the saying. We might modify it on occasion, but the essentials of the truth remained. There was something almost unearthly about these faculties of hers. To my father in particular they were of much moment.

She seldom read a book herself; it was our privilege to read to her. Once in a while she would let loose memories of her early childhood in a small German town, and these were more pictorial than anything in any book. They were like the most delicate of etchings, so clear in their black and white that they gave you the impression of a warmer color. A street, a grey stone house, a spreading orchard; this was where she had lived. A little bonnet, pink and blue, with crimped and artificial flowers: this was a gift of an affectionate godmother. A great church, filled with children, each holding a lighted candle in the hand. This was Christmas Eve in Saxony. A lumbering, obese, tight-hatted gentleman; this was a tyrannical, hated, unsavory Grand-Duke.

Her impatience was perhaps her besetting offense. The peach must drop down at once off the wall into her mouth. Any delay, and the flavor was gone. If you told her of something pretty, or useful, or unusual which you had seen in a shop window, she desired it avidly and at once for her especial possession. If you had any errand on which to go, or any engagement for dinner or the theater to fill, she would hurry you out of the house as though otherwise disaster would overtake you. If an engagement came her way, she was ready an hour beforehand. She hated to wait for people or conveyances. But all this is only another way of saying that she was excessively nervous; she had never been more than fairly well or vigorous all her life, and this impatience was largely a manifestation of that.

Of her religious beliefs she rarely spoke; it would have abashed her to do so. She had a deep sense of the dignity of life, and religion she considered a part of that dignity. Would it not be a shabby and belittling thing to discuss — as you would the chops for your supper — the most secret secret of your experience? She was cheerfully dubious about some ancient matters in the catechism, or connected with the hard orthodoxies of her youth; she had little feeling for the priest, but a most affectionate one for the church. She was as sure of God as she was of the sun. There never came a fine day, winter or summer — and she loved fine weather, as she loved every beautiful thing — that she did not quote: " This is the day which the Lord hath made."

And in what other ways was she herself, and separate from her neighbors? She had a superb soprano voice, untrained, but true, smooth, soaring. When she sang, the music poured like a flood into every corner of the house. She came of a family of singers; her brothers had been enrolled among the choristers in the parish church of a Saxon country town, an older sister enriched with a voice even more beautiful than her own. Music was a portion of her heredity, which she had fallen heir to as she had to her gayety and her fine-fingered, short, efficient hands. She took her possession very simply, as one does the fact of good birth, or the set of black pearls handed down by a stately grandmother.

I am confident that her soaring soprano was something to talk and dream about. I know that people halted in the quiet street outside to listen to her singing; when it was finished, they did not forget it. It came back to them as does the sound of running water at twilight, when one star pushes out of the rich-colored sky.

She sang snatches of florid hymns as she went about her household tasks, and later, romantic songs, full of trills and high, sorrowful notes, stanza by stanza, learned at singing classes, or out of well-thumbed, longbacked, mellow old books. The rooms shook with that music.

She sang, almost with her youthful volume and sweetness, until she was eighty. Then the end came. One day she could sing, the next day she could not.

And was she a handsome, or a pretty, woman? She had soft grey eyes, fair hair, which turned white as she grew older, and lay like a gentle crown about her face, and a good country complexion. I think that people in general would have said that she was nice-looking. She should have worn smokeblue frocks, or blue of that color which paints the petaled wheel of the succory flower, or else the brisk green of the unfolding apple leaf. She wore, instead, black, grey, purple, and last of all shades from that of a hill's peak down to the mistiest tinge of lilac or violet, and she had done so, except for a brief interval of a few months, ever since the end of the Civil War. Her brother, her sisters, her parents all went. By the time that the mourning period, with its swathing veil and gloom of garments, was over for each, she considered herself too far removed from youth to deck herself in its cheerful colors, so kept to the long-familiar black, or grey, or purple. These gave her an age which did not belong to her, or lessened that look of April which was hers by every right of her gusty spirit. The interval of a few months in which she had dressed otherwise, happened when I was a child. She had bought herself a new bonnet, trimmed with bands of ribbon; the ribbon was a striped black and white, with an edge of clear corn-color. The next thing I remember, was that she was tall and unsmiling, sober-frocked again, a long crêpe veil floating down her back.

We used to beg her to wear white, and she compromised as far as to put on waists of that color, but somehow objected —

due perhaps to some Victorian rant about vanity and the sins of the flesh — to wear an entire gown of the same.

I wish that she had not been so inflexible in regard to the matter. I would love to recall her in thin white, or the blue of succory blossoms. As it is, I can see her very plainly in her palest lavender, standing quite still, with a smile on her lips, a slow, faintly knowing smile, as provocative as that of Mona Lisa.

She died very early one August morning in 1917, having lived nearly eighty-seven years. It was hard for us to pass the house which had been hers for nearly a score of Augusts. It had gone into the hands of strangers. It had a solemn look. April had abandoned it. It was given over — or so we saw it — to uses and to mortals that were far from spring, and the tricks and quips of tender, blowing, and growing things.

APPRECIATION HINTS

1. Suggest certain flowers, odors, colors, music, or food that you always associate with certain people. Explain the memory connection.
2. Describe a charming garden you enjoy, and tell the group about the person who had the art of making things grow.
3. What have you been especially proud of in your own garden? Do things grow for you?
4. Can you understand why the mother didn't grow a second lavender bush?
5. What troubles might have killed the " gay spirit " in another?
6. Point out intimate glimpses of family life revealed in the essay.
7. Do you recall old jokes told in your family which do not grow stale with age or with repetition?
8. Compare your own attitude towards the villain and the hero in fiction with that of the author's mother.
9. What vivid details bring the Germany of her childhood clear to us?
10. Find examples of happy phrasing such as " gusty spirit," " exigencies of a fine poverty."
11. Why are we glad to find some very human faults in the mother's character?

12. Observe how the author makes her mother live for the reader by her loves — flowers, china, clothes, reading, music, religion.

13. Why not find some volumes of the author's poems, and bring to the class ones you like?

14. Compare and contrast this tribute to a mother with " Mary White," the tribute of a father to his daughter (p. 214).

COMPOSITION HINTS

1. Whenever I Think of _____, I Think of _____ and of _____
2. Hardy Perennial Jokes in Our Family
3. When I Failed to Return Home at the Hour Set
4. My Hobbies
5. The Amazing Hobbies of My Friends
6. Twists and Turns of Spring Weather
7. Towering Trifles
8. Efficient Hands
9. In What Ways John Is Different from Other People

WILLIAM BEEBE

Few writers of today appeal so vividly to youth as does William Beebe, trained scientist, observer, and master of a charming and happy style. Under his guidance science becomes for us a thrilling and moving story. We share his enthusiasms and his zest for living things. A wit once remarked that the trait called curiosity in women has been capitalized by men and labeled " scientific research." We profit from Mr. Beebe's lively and insatiable curiosity as well as from his technical knowledge, and are glad that it has driven him to scientific study, for when he answers the questions raised by his own unquenchable curiosity, exact science speaks with charm, and the reader is promised hours of pleasure. He has given us knowledge of jungles and of the exotic plant and animal life there. We share with him the sights, smells, and sounds of the woods. Through his pages we catch the witchery of the underworld of water " where great whales come sailing by, Sail and sail with unshut eye," and where " seahorses are stabled in great green caves." Poetry and science unite on his pages. He is helpful to those who have not learned how to enjoy poetry and imaginative prose, for they know that if William Beebe says a thing is true, it is true. Sometimes the lure of fiction pales beside his literature of scientific observation.

Perhaps the potency of his charm lies in Mr. Beebe's own enthusiasms and in his zest for work. No dry-as-dust scientist would say: " Don't die without having borrowed, stolen, or purchased, or made a helmet, to glimpse for yourself this new world." The dullest stay-at-home catches a glimpse of his joy in the wonders of nature as he reads. In our " search for the otherwhere " we are carried away to far lands by the opening sentences of his essays: " Within gun-reach of me trudged my little Akawai Indian hunter." " The edges and rims of things are much more exciting than the things themselves." " On September twelfth I met a Great Blue Shark in the prime of life." " There are three things of the sea which have been delineated by man more than any others — dolphins, mermaids, and seahorses — and there are three things about which we know almost less than any others — seahorses, mermaids, and dolphins."

Mr. Beebe considers his scientific labors the most enchanting in the world, and he cannot imagine a more dreadful punishment than to be without work. To deprive him of work would bring a dreadful punishment to his readers. " The *Isness* of facts is boring and futile, the *Whyness* is the chief reason for going on living," says Mr. Beebe. No wonder that his favorite book of fiction is *Alice in Wonderland,* that his favorite author is Lord Dunsany, that he enjoys Kipling, John Buchan, and A. A. Milne.

Mr. Beebe was born in Brooklyn in 1877. In 1898 he graduated from Columbia University. He holds offices in many learned societies, such as Director of Tropical Research of the New York Zoölogical Society. He is our foremost American authority on tropical birds. He brings far places near: British Guiana, Galapagos, Sargasso, Hudson Gorge, Nonsuch, Pearl Island. Books for the interested reader are *Jungle Peace* (1918); *The Edge of the Jungle* (1921); *Jungle Days* (1925); *The Arcturus Adventure* (1926); *Pheasant Jungles* (1927); *Beneath Tropic Seas* (1928); *Nonsuch: Land of Water* (1932).

THE JUNGLE SLUGGARD[1]

SLOTHS have no right to be living on the earth today; they would be fitting inhabitants of Mars, where a year is over six hundred days long. In fact they would exist more appropriately on a still more distant planet where time — as we know it — creeps and crawls instead of flies from dawn to dusk. Years ago I wrote that sloths reminded me of nothing so much as the wonderful Rath Brother athletes or of a slowed-up moving picture, and I can still think of no better similes.

Sloths live altogether in trees, but so do monkeys, and the chief difference between them would seem to be that the lat-

[1] From *Jungle Days,* published by G. P. Putnam's Sons, 1925, and reprinted by permission of the author.

ter spend their time pushing against gravitation while the
sloths pull against it. Botanically the two groups of animals
are comparable to the flower which holds its head up to the
sun, swaying on its long stem, and, on the other hand, the
overripe fruit dangling heavily from its base. We ourselves
are physically far removed from sloths — for while we can
point with pride to the daily achievement of those ambulatory
athletes, floorwalkers and policemen, yet no human being can
cling with his hands to a branch for more than a comparatively
short time.

Like a rainbow before breakfast, a sloth is a surprise, an
unexpected fellow breather of the air of our planet. No one
could prophesy a sloth. If you have an imaginative friend who
has never seen a sloth and ask him to describe what he thinks
it ought to be like, his uncontrolled phrases will fall far short
of reality. If there were no sloths, Dunsany would hesitate to
put such a creature in the forests of Mluna, Marco Polo would
deny having seen one, and Munchausen would whistle as he
listened to a friend's description.

A scientist — even a taxonomist himself — falters when he
mentions the group to which a sloth belongs. A taxonomist
is the most terribly accurate person in the world, dealing with
unvarying facts, and his names and descriptions of animals
defy discretion, murder imagination. Nevertheless, when next
you see a taxonomist disengaged, approach him boldly and ask
in a tone of quarrelsome interest to what order of Mammalia
sloths belong. If an honest conservative he will say, " Eden-
tata," which, as any ancient Greek will tell you, means a tooth-
less one. Then if you wish to enrage and nonplus the taxonomist, which I think no one should, as I am one myself, then
ask him " Why? " or, if he has ever been bitten by any of the
eighteen teeth of a sloth.

The great savant Buffon, in spite of all his genius, fell into
most grievous error in his estimation of a sloth. He says, " The
inertia of this animal is not so much due to laziness as to
wretchedness; it is the consequence of its faulty structure. In-
activity, stupidity, and even habitual suffering result from its

strange and ill-constructed conformation. Having no weapons for attack or defense, no mode of refuge even by burrowing, its only safety is in flight. . . . Everything about it shows its wretchedness and proclaims it to be one of those defective monsters, those imperfect sketches, which Nature has sometimes formed, and which, having scarcely the faculty of existence, could only continue for a short time and have since been removed from the catalogue of living beings. They are the last possible term amongst creatures of flesh and blood, and any further defect would have made their existence impossible."

If we imagine the dignified French savant himself naked, and dangling from a lofty jungle branch in the full heat of the tropic sun, without water and with the prospect of nothing but coarse leaves for breakfast, dinner, and all future meals, an impartial onlooker who was ignorant of man's normal haunts and life could very truthfully apply to the unhappy scientist, Buffon's own comments. All of his terms of opprobrium would come home to roost with him.

A bridge out of place would be an absolutely inexplicable thing, as would a sloth in Paris, or a Buffon in the trees. As a matter of fact it was only when I became a temporary cripple myself that I began to appreciate the astonishing lives which sloths lead. With one of my feet injured and out of commission I found an abundance of time in six weeks to study the individuals which we caught in the jungle near by. Not until we invent a superlative of which the word *deliberate* is the positive can we define a sloth with sufficient adequateness and briefness. I dimly remember certain volumes by an authoress whose style pictured the hero walking from the door to the front gate, placing first the right, then the left foot before him as he went. With such detail and speed of action might one write the biography of a sloth.

Ever since man has ventured into this wilderness, sloths have aroused astonishment and comment. Four hundred years ago Gonzalo de Oviedo sat him down and penned a most delectable account of these creatures. He says, in part: " There is another strange beast the Spaniards call the Light Dogge, which is one of the slowest beasts, and so heavie and dull in mooving that it can scarsely goe fiftie pases in a whole day. Their neckes are high and streight, and all equall like the pestle of a mortar, without making any proportion of similitude of a head, or any difference except in the noddle, and in the tops of their neckes. They have little mouthes, and moove their neckes from one side to another, as though they were astonished; their chiefe desire and delight is to cleave and sticke fast unto trees, whereunto cleaving fast, they mount up little by little, staying themselves by their long claws. Their voice is much differing from other beasts, for they sing only in the night, and that continually from time to time, singing ever six notes one higher than another. Sometimes the Christian men find these beasts and bring them home to their houses, where also they creepe all about with their natural slownesse. I could never perceive other but that they love onely of Aire; because they ever turne their heads and mouthes toward that part where the wind bloweth most, whereby may be considered that they take most pleasure in the Aire. They bite not, nor yet can bite, having very little mouthes; they are not venemous or noyous any way, but altogether brutish, and utterly unprofitable and without commoditie yet known to men."

It is difficult to find adequate comparisons for a topsy-turvy creature like a sloth, but if I had already had synthetic experience with a Golem, I would take for a formula the general appearance of an English sheep dog, giving it a face with barely distinguishable features and no expression, an inexhaustible appetite for a single kind of coarse leaf, a gamut of emotions well below the animal kingdom, and an enthusiasm for life excelled by a healthy sunflower. Suspend this from a jungle limb by a dozen strong hooks, and — you would still have to see a live sloth to appreciate its appearance.

At rest, curled up into an arboreal ball, a sloth is indistinguishable from a cluster of leaves; in action, the second hand of a watch often covers more distance. At first sight of the shapeless ball of hay, moving with hopeless inadequacy, astonishment shifts to pity, then to impatience, and finally, as we sense a life of years spent thus, we feel almost disgust. At which moment the sloth reaches blindly in our direction, thinking us a barren, leafless, but perhaps climbable tree, and our emotions change again, this time to sheer delight as a tiny infant sloth raises its indescribably funny face from its mother's breast and sends forth the single tone, the high, whistling squeak, which in sloth intercourse is song, shout, converse, whisper, argument, and chant. Separating him from his mother is like plucking a bur from one's hair, but when freed, he contentedly hooks his small self to our clothing and creeps slowly about.

Instead of reviewing all the observations and experiments which I perpetrated upon sloths, I will touch at once the heart of their mysterious psychology, giving in a few words a conception of their strange, uncanny minds. A bird will give up its life in defending its young; an alligator will not often desert its nest in the face of danger; a male stickleback fish will intrepidly face any intruder that threatens its eggs. In fact, at the time when the young of all animals are at the age of helplessness, the senses of the parents are doubly keen, their activities and weapons are at greatest efficiency for the guarding of the young and the consequent certainty of the continuance of their race.

The resistance made by a mother sloth to the abstraction of its offspring is chiefly the mechanical tangling of the young animal's tiny claws in the long maternal fur. I have taken away a young sloth and hooked it to a branch five feet away. Being hungry it began at once to utter its high, penetrating penny whistle. To no other sound, high or low, with even a half-tone's difference does the sloth pay any heed, but its dim hearing is attuned to just this vibration. Slowly the mother starts off in what she thinks is the direction of the sound. It is the moment of moments in the life of the young animal. Yet I have seen her again and again on different occasions pass within two feet of the little chap, and never look to right or left, but keep straight on, stolidly and unvaryingly to the high jungle, while her baby, a few inches out of her path, called in vain. No kidnaped child hidden in mountain fastness or urban underworld was ever more completely lost to its parent than this infant, in full view and separated by only a sloth's length of space.

A gun fired close to the ear of a sloth will usually arouse not the slightest tremor; no scent of flower or acid or carrion causes any reaction; a sleeping sloth may be shaken violently without awakening; the waving of a scarlet rag, or a climbing serpent a few feet away brings no gleam of curiosity or fear to the dull eyes; an astonishingly long immersion in water produces discomfort but not death. When we think what a constant struggle life is to most creatures, even when they are equipped with the keenest of senses and powerful means of offense, it seems incredible that a sloth can hold its own in this overcrowded tropical jungle.

From birth to death it climbs slowly about the great trees, leisurely feeding, languidly loving, and almost mechanically caring for its young. On the ground a host of enemies await it, but among the higher branches it fears chiefly occasional great boas, climbing jaguars and, worst of all, the mighty talons of harpy eagles. Its means of offense is a joke — a slow, ineffective reaching forward with open jaws, a lethargic stroke of arm and claws which anything but another sloth can avoid. Yet the race of sloths persists and thrives, and in past years I have had as many as eighteen under observation at one time.

A sloth makes no nest or shelter; it even disdains the protection of dense foliage. But for all its apparent helplessness it has a *cheval-de-frise* of protection which many animals far above it in intelligence might well envy. Its outer line of defense is invisibility — and there is none better, for until you have seen your intended prey you can neither attack nor devour him. No hedgehog or armadillo ever rolled a more perfect ball of itself than does a sloth, sitting in a lofty, swaying crotch with head and feet and legs all gathered close together inside. This posture, to an onlooker, destroys all thought of a living animal, but presents a very satisfactory white ants' nest or bunch of dead leaves. If we look at the hair of a sloth we shall see small, grey patches along the length of the hairs — at first sight bits of bark and débris of wood. But these minute, scattered particles are of the utmost aid to this invisibility. They are a peculiar species of alga or lichen-like growth, which is found only in this peculiar haunt, and when the rain begins and all the jungle turns a deep, glowing emerald, these tiny plants also react to the welcome moisture and become verdant — thus growing over the sloth a protecting, misty veil of green.

Even we dull-sensed humans require neither sight nor hearing to detect the presence of an animal like the skunk; in the absolute quiet and blackness of midnight we can tell when a porcupine has crossed our path, or when there are mice in the bureau drawers. But a dozen sloths may be hanging to the trees near at hand and never the slightest whiff of odor comes from them. A baby sloth has not even a baby smell, and all this is part of the cloak of invisibility. The voice, raised so very seldom, is so ventriloquial, and possesses such a strange, un-animal-like quality, that it can never be a guide to the location, much less to the identity of the author. Here we have three senses — sight, hearing, smell — all operating at a distance, two of them by vibrations, and all leagued together to shelter the sloth from attack.

But in spite of this dramatic guard of invisibility the keen eyes of an eagle, the lapping tongue of a giant boa, and the amazing delicacy of a jaguar's sense of smell break through at times. The jaguar scents sign under the tree of the sloth, climbs eagerly as far as he dares, and finds ready to his paw the ball of animal unconsciousness; a harpy eagle half a mile above the jungle sees a bunch of leaves reach out a sleepy arm and scratch itself — something clumps of leaves should not do. Down spirals the great bird, slowly, majestically, knowing there is no need of haste, and alights close by the mammalian sphere. Still the sloth does not move, apparently waiting for what fate may bring — waiting with that patience and resignation which comes only to those of our fellow creatures who cannot say, "I am I!" It seems as if Nature had deserted her jungle changeling, stripped now of its protecting cloak.

The sloth, however, has never been given credit for its powers of passive resistance, and now, with its enemy within striking distance, its death or even injury is far from a certainty. The crotch which the sloth chooses for its favorite outdoor sport, sleep, is unusually high up or far out among the lesser branches, where the eight claws of the eagle or the eighteen of a jaguar find but precarious hold. If the victim were a feathery bush turkey or a soft-bodied squirrel, one stroke would be sufficient, but this strange creature is something far different. In the first place, it is only to be plucked from its perch by the exertion of enormous strength. No man can seize a sloth by the long hair of the back and pull it off. So strong are its muscles, so vise-like the grip of its dozen talons, that either the crotch must be cut or broken off or the long claws unfastened one by one. Neither of these alternatives is possible to the attacking cat or eagle. They must depend upon crushing or penetrating power of stroke or grasp.

Here is where the sloth's second line of defense becomes operative. First, as I have mentioned, the swaying branch and dizzy height are in his favor, as well as his immovable grip. To begin with the innermost defenses, while his jungle fellows, the ring-tailed and red howling monkeys, have thirteen ribs, the sloth may have as many as twenty; in the latter animal they are, in addition, unusually broad and flat, slats rather than rods. Next comes the skin, which is so thick and tough that many an Indian's arrow falls back without even scratching the hide. The skin of the unborn sloth is as tough and strong as that of a full-grown monkey. Finally we have the fur — two distinct coats, the under one fine, short, and matted, the outer long, harsh, and coarse. Is it any wonder that, teetering on a swaying branch, many a jaguar has had to give up, after frantic attempts to strike his claws through the felted hair, the tough skin, and the bony latticework which protect the vitals of this edentate bur!

Having rescued our sloth from his most immediate peril, let us watch him solve some of the very few problems which life presents to him. Although the Cecropia tree, on the leaves of which he feeds, is scattered far and wide through the jungle, yet sloths are found almost exclusively along river banks, and, most amazingly, they not infrequently take to the water. I have caught a dozen sloths swimming rivers a mile or more in width. Judging from the speed of short distances, a sloth can swim a mile in three hours and twenty minutes. Their thick skin and fur must be a protection against crocodiles, electric eels, and perai fish as well as jaguars. Why they should ever wish to swim across these wide expanses of water is as inexplicable as the migration of butterflies. One side of the river has as many comfortable crotches, as many millions of Cecropia leaves, and as many eligible lady sloths as the other! In this unreasonable desire for anything which is out of reach, sloths come very close to a characteristic of human beings.

Even in the jungle, sloths are not always the static creatures which their vegetable-like life would lead us to believe, as I was able to prove many years ago. A young male was brought in by Indians, and after keeping it a few days I shaved off two patches of hair from the center of the back, and labeling it with a metal tag I turned it loose. Forty-eight days later it was captured near a small settlement of Bovianders several miles farther up and across the river. During this time it must have traversed four miles of jungle and one of river.

The principal difference between the male and the female three-toed sloths is the presence on the back of the male of a large, oval spot of orange-colored fur. To any creature of more active mentality such a minor distinction must often be embarrassing. In an approaching sloth, walking upside down as usual, this mark is quite invisible, and hence every meeting of two sloths must contain much of delightful uncertainty, of ignorance whether the encounter presages courtship or merely gossip. But color or markings have no meaning in the dull eyes of these animals. Until they have sniffed and almost touched noses they show no recognition or reaction whatever.

I once invented a sloth island — a large circle of ground surrounded by a deep ditch, where sloths climbed about some saplings and ate, but principally slept, and lived for months at a time. This was within sight of my laboratory table; so I could watch what was taking place by merely raising my head. Some of the occurrences were almost too strange for creatures of this earth. I watched two courtships, each resulting in nothing more serious than my own amusement. A female was asleep in a low crotch, curled up into a perfect ball deep within which was ensconced a month-old baby. Two yards overhead was a male who had slept for nine hours without interruption. Moved by what, to a sloth, must have been a burst of uncontrollable emotion, he slowly unwound himself and clambered downward. When close to the sleeping beauty, he reached out a claw and tentatively touched a shoulder. Ever more deliberately she excavated her head and long neck and peered in every direction but the right one. At last she perceived her suitor and looked away as if the sight was too much for her. Again he touched her post-like neck, and now there arose all the flaming fury of a mother at the flirtatious advances of this stranger. With incredible slowness and effort she freed an arm, deliberately drew it back, and then began a slow forward stroke with arm and claws. Meanwhile her gentleman friend had changed his position; so the blow swept or, more correctly, passed, through empty air, the lack of impact almost throwing her out of the crotch. The disdained one left with slowness and dignity — or had he already forgotten why he had descended? — and returned to his perch and slumber, where, I am sure, not even such active things as dreams came to disturb his peace.

The second courtship advanced to the stage where the Gallant actually got his claws tangled in the lady's back hair before she awoke. When she grasped the situation, she left at once and clambered to the highest branch tip followed by the male. Then she turned and climbed down and across her annoyer, leaving him stranded on the lofty branch looking eagerly about and reaching out hopefully toward a big green iguana asleep on the next limb in mistake for his fair companion. For an hour he wandered languidly after her, then gave it up and went to sleep. Throughout these and other emotional crises no sound is ever uttered, no feature altered from its stolid repose. The head moves mechanically and the dull eyes blink slowly, as if striving to pierce the opaque veil which ever hangs between the brain of a sloth and the sights, sounds, and odors of this tropical world. If the orange back-spot was ever of any use in courtship, in arousing any emotion, aesthetic or otherwise, it must have been in ages long past when the ancestors of sloths, contemporaries of their gigantic relatives, the Mylodons, had better eyesight for escaping from saber-toothed tigers than there is need today.

The climax of a sloth's emotion has nothing to do with the opposite sex or with the young, but is exhibited when two females are confined in a cage together. The result is wholly unexpected. After sniffing at one another for a moment, they engage in a slowed-up moving-picture battle. Before any harm is done, one or the other gives utterance to the usual piercing whistle and surrenders. She lies flat on the cage floor and offers no defense while the second female proceeds to claw her, now and then attempting, usually vainly, to bite. It is so unpleasant that I have always separated them at this stage, but there is no doubt that in every case the unnatural affray would go on until the victim was killed. In fact I have heard of several instances where this actually took place.

A far pleasanter sight is the young sloth, one of the most adorable balls of fuzzy fur imaginable. While the sense of play is all but lacking, his trustfulness and helplessness are most infantile. Every person who takes him up is an accepted substitute for his mother, and he will clamber slowly about one's clothing for hours in supreme contentment. One thing I can never explain is that on the ground the baby is even more helpless than his parents. While they can hitch themselves along, body dragging, limbs outspread, until they reach the nearest tree, a young sloth is wholly without power to move. Placed on a flat bit of ground it rolls and tumbles about, occasionally greatly encouraged by seizing hold of its own foot or leg under the impression that at last it has encountered a branch.

Sloths sleep about twice as much as other mammals, and a

baby sloth often gets tired of being confined in the heart of its mother's sleeping sphere, and creeping out under her arm will go on an exploring expedition around and around her. When over two weeks old it has strength to rise on its hind legs and sway back and forth like nothing else in the world. Its eyes are only a little keener than those of the parent, and it peers up at the foliage overhead with the most pitiful interest. It is slowly weaned from a milk diet to the leaves of the Cecropia, which the mother at first chews up for her offspring.

I once watched a young sloth about a month old and saw it leave its mother for the first time. As the old one moved slowly back and forth, pulling down Cecropia leaves and feeding on them, the youngster took firm grip on a leaf stem, mumbling at it with no success whatever. When finally it stretched around and found no soft fur within reach it set up a wail which drew the attention of the mother at once. Still clinging to her perch, she reached out a forearm to an unbelievable distance and gently hooked the great claws about the huddled infant, which at once climbed down the long bridge and tumbled headlong in the hollow awaiting it.

When a very young sloth is gently disentangled from its mother and hooked on to a branch something of the greatest interest happens. Instead of walking forward, one foot after the other, and upside down as all adult sloths do, it reaches up and tries to get first one arm then the other *over* the support, and to pull itself into an upright position. This would seem to be a reversion to a time — perhaps millions of years ago — when the ancestors of sloths had not yet begun to hang inverted from the branches. After an interval of clumsy reaching and wriggling about, the baby by accident grasps its own body or limb, and, in this case, convinced that it is at last anchored safely again to its mother, it confidently lets go with all its other claws and tumbles ignominiously to the ground.

The moment a baby sloth dies and slips from its grip on the mother's fur, it ceases to exist for her. If it could call out she would reach down an arm and hook it toward her, but simply dropping silently means no more than if a disentangled bur had fallen from her coat. I have watched such a sloth carefully and have never seen any search of her own body or of the surrounding branches, or a moment's distraction from sleep or food. An imitation of the cry of the dead baby will attract her attention, but if not repeated she forgets it at once.

It is interesting to know of the lives of such beings as this — chronic pacifists, normal morons, the superlative of negative natures, yet holding their own amidst the struggle for existence. Nothing else desires to feed on such coarse fodder, no other creature disputes with it the domain of the under side of branches, hence there is no competition. From our human point of view sloths are degenerate; from another angle they are among the most exquisitely adapted of living beings. If we humans, together with our brains, fitted as well into the possibilities of our own lives we should be infinitely finer and happier — and, besides, I should then be able to interpret more intelligently the life and the philosophy of sloths!

APPRECIATION HELPS

1. Explain: " No one could prophesy a sloth."
2. Observe the interesting details given by Beebe which aid in giving the character of this sluggard.
3. Does the author's formula for a sloth, given in familiar images, give you a vivid picture?
4. Find places where you feel Beebe's eager enthusiasm for the facts of science.
5. What defenses against enemies has the sloth?
6. Describe the " cloaks of invisibility " of other animals.
7. Point out the way in which the senses — sight, hearing, and smell — all help to protect the sloth.
8. Note Beebe's constant awareness to both the plant and the animal world — " A bunch of leaves reaches out a sleepy arm to scratch itself."
9. Point out scientific *facts* which interested you in this essay.
10. Where do you find evidence in this essay of the author's belief in evolution?
11. In *Nonsuch*, by Beebe, read Chapter VI, " Flounders Are

Wonderful," for a charming study in adaptation to environment.

12. How does the author convince you that the sloth can hold its own in the struggle for existence?

13. If you are interested in the author's reference to the migration of butterflies, read " Migration," Chapter VII of *Nonsuch,* to learn of the strange migrations of birds and lemmings and butterflies.

COMPOSITION HINTS

1. " Time flies?   No!   Time stays.   We fly "
2. Time Flies and — Time Crawls
3. What I Would Do in a Cloak of Invisibility
4. I Desire Things out of Reach
5. Sluggards in School
6. Seen under the Microscope
7. " Animals I Have Known "

JONATHAN SWIFT

Among the names of the great writers of English prose you will always find that of Jonathan Swift (1667–1745). Swift was born in Ireland, though of English stock. He was poor but proud and shy, and it angered him to be cast on the charity of an uncle. Sir William Temple, a distant relative, offered him a place as secretary, and he was forced to accept the offer in spite of his recognition that Sir William Temple was his inferior in ability. Swift lived always conscious of his great but thwarted and baffled powers. In Sir William Temple's home he worked and studied and wrote books, or in the garden taught the charming young girl, a ward of Sir William, who later inspired his *Journal to Stella*. Englishmen of the eighteenth century loved these trim, formal gardens. Sir William Temple says of them: "In every Garden four things are necessary to be provided for, Flowers, Fruit, Shade and Water, and whoever lays out a Garden without all these must not pretend it any perfection."

Swift was trained for the church, but preferment was slow. At one time he was given a living at Larocar, so small that the congregation averaged fifteen. On a day when there was one person for his audience he began, "Dearly beloved Roger, the Scripture moveth us in sundry places . . ."

London, where the literary men of the day lounged in the taverns and coffee houses, drew him like a magnet, but most of his years he was forced — by poverty — to spend in Ireland. *Gulliver's Travels,* issued anonymously in 1726, has delighted the world since its publication. In the *Battle of the Books* Swift presents the rival claims of classic and modern learning. His keen and biting satire shows the strength of his intellectual ability. His literary style is so direct and clear that few writers equal him in power.

These "Epigrams" are taken from *Thoughts on Various Subjects.*

EPIGRAMS

WE have just religion enough to make us hate, but not enough to make us love one another.

No preacher is listened to but Time, which gives us the same train and turn of thought that elder people have in vain tried to put into our heads before.

When we desire or solicit any thing, our minds run wholly on the good side or circumstances of it; when it is obtained, our minds run wholly on the bad ones.

The latter part of a wise man's life is taken up in curing the follies, prejudices, and false opinions he had contracted in the former.

Whatever the poets pretend, it is plain they give immortality to none but themselves; 'tis Homer and Virgil we reverence and admire, not Achilles or Aeneas. With historians it is quite the contrary; our thoughts are taken up with the actions, persons, and events we read, and we little regard the authors.

When a true genius appears in the world, you may know him by this sign, that the dunces are all in confederacy against him.

Men who possess all the advantages of life, are in a state where there are many accidents to disorder and discompose, but few to please them.

The greatest inventions were produced in the times of ignorance; as the use of the compass, gunpowder, and printing; and by the dullest nation, as the Germans.

I am apt to think that in the day of judgment there will be small allowance given to the wise for their want of morals, and to the ignorant for their want of faith, because both are without excuse. This renders the advantages equal of ignorance and knowledge. But some scruples in the wise, and some vices in the ignorant will perhaps be forgiven, upon the strength of temptation to each.

Some men, under the notion of weeding out prejudices, eradicate virtue, honesty, and religion.

In all well-instituted commonwealths care has been taken to limit men's possessions; which is done for many reasons, and, among the rest, for one which, perhaps, is not often considered; that when bounds are set to men's desires, after they have acquired as much as the laws will permit them, their private interest is at an end, and they have nothing to do but to take care of the public.

There are but three ways for a man to revenge himself of the censure of the world: to despise it, to return the like, or to endeavor to live so as to avoid it. The first of these is usually pretended, the last is almost impossible, the universal practice is for the second.

I have known some men possessed of good qualities which were very serviceable to others but useless to themselves — like a sun-dial on the front of a house, to inform the neighbors and passengers, but not the owner within.

The stoical scheme of supplying our wants by lopping off our desires is like cutting off our feet when we want shoes.

The power of fortune is confessed only by the miserable; for the happy impute all their success to prudence or merit.

Ill company is like a dog, who dirts those most whom he loves best.

Satire is reckoned the easiest of all wit; but I take it to be otherwise in very bad times: for it is as hard to satirize well a man of distinguished vices as to praise well a man of distinguished virtues. It is easy enough to do either to people of moderate characters.

No wise man ever wished to be younger.

Some people take more care to hide their wisdom than their folly.

The humor of exploding many things under the name of trifles, fopperies, and only imaginary goods is a very false proof either of wisdom or magnanimity, and a great check to virtuous actions. For instance, with regard to fame: there is in most people a reluctance and unwillingness to be forgotten. We observe even among the vulgar how fond they are to have an inscription over their grave. It requires but little philosophy to discover and observe that there is no intrinsic value in all this; however, if it be founded in our nature, as an incitement to virtue it ought not to be ridiculed.

The common fluency of speech in many men, and most women, is owing to a scarcity of matter and a scarcity of words; for whoever is a master of language and has a mind full of ideas will be apt, in speaking, to hesitate upon the choice of both; whereas common speakers have only one set of ideas and one set of words to clothe them in, and these are always ready at mouth. So people come faster out of the church when it is almost empty than when a crowd is at the door.

To be vain, is rather a mark of humility than pride. Vain men delight in telling what honors have been done them, what great company they have kept, and the like, by which they plainly confess that these honors were more than their due, and such as their friends would not believe if they had not been told; whereas a man truly proud thinks the greatest honors below his merit and consequently scorns to boast. I therefore deliver it as a maxim, that whoever desires the character of a proud man ought to conceal his vanity.

A " nice " man is a man of nasty ideas.

Old men and comets have been reverenced for the same reason; their long beards, and pretenses to foretell events.

Most sorts of diversion in men, children, and other animals, are an imitation of fighting.

As universal a practice as lying is, and as easy a one as it seems, I do not remember to have heard three good lies in all my conversation, even from those who were most celebrated in that faculty.

Imaginary evils soon become real ones by indulging our reflections on them; as he who in a melancholy fancy sees something like a face on the wall or the wainscot, can, by two or three touches with a lead pencil, make it look visible, and agreeing with what he fancied.

Men of great parts are often unfortunate in the management of public business, because they are apt to go out of the common road by the quickness of their imagination. This I once said to my Lord Bolingbroke, and desired he would observe that the clerks in his office used a sort of ivory knife with a blunt edge to divide a sheet of paper, which never failed to cut it even, only requiring a steady hand: whereas if they should make use of a sharp pen-knife the sharpness would make it go often out of the crease and disfigure the paper.

I must complain the cards are ill shuffled, till I have a good hand.

Elephants are always drawn smaller than life, but a flea always larger.

APPRECIATION HELPS

1. Which of these epigrams, witty thoughts with shrewd contrasts, please you especially?
2. What proverbs do you know that express tersely some of Swift's epigrams? (For example, "Experience is a dear school, but fools learn in no other.")
3. Do you recall examples from history showing that men may have just religion enough to hate, but not enough to love?
4. Describe some older people who spend their age in curing the follies of their youth; some prejudices and false opinions you have outgrown.
5. Why does the creation of a great character in literature give immortality to the creator? Illustrate.
6. Name from history some men of true genius who have been opposed by the dunces of the world.
7. Discuss the advantages of having a government limit the wealth of its citizens, and compare this with Roosevelt's *The Strenuous Life* (p. 27), which stresses the obligations rich men have to society.
8. Describe some people you know who hide their wisdom; some who hide their folly.
9. Discuss the apparent contradiction that fluency in speech may come because of a scarcity both in matter and in words.
10. Are the games and sports you enjoy an imitation of fighting?
11. Point out the epigrams that seem modern in idea.

COMPOSITION HINTS

1. " No Wise Man Ever Wished to Be Younger "
2. False Opinions I Have Outgrown
3. " Fools Will Learn in No Other "
4. Some Advantages of Ignorance
5. Some American Men of Wealth Who Have Contributed to American Progress
6. Some Things I Can Do Without
7. List some of our immortal characters in literature, together with their creators.

LINCOLN STEFFENS

Lincoln Steffens has given a lifetime to journalism and he has earned the rewards of a great journalist. He has lived in far corners of the world when momentous things were happening; he has learned to tell tersely and with power what he has observed. What he says is important, for he is an authority on national problems.

California claims him. Born in San Francisco April 6, 1866, his youth was spent near there, and he graduated from the University of California in 1889. As a student of philosophy, he studied in the universities of Berlin, Heidelberg, Leipzig, and the Sorbonne. A letter from his father was waiting for him at quarantine in New York Harbor when he returned to the United States in 1892. It said: " My dear son: When you finished school you wanted to go to college. I sent you to Berkeley. When you got through there, you did not care to go into my business; so I sold out. You preferred to continue your studies in Berlin. I let you. After Berlin it was Heidelberg; after that Leipzig. And after the German universities you wanted to study at the French universities in Paris. I consented, and after a year with the French, you had to have half a year of the British Museum in London. All right. You had that too. By now you must know about all there is to know of the theory of life, but there's a practical side as well. It's worth knowing. I suggest that you learn it, and the way to study it, I think, is to stay in New York and hustle. Enclosed please find one hundred dollars, which should keep you till you can find a job and support yourself." At once young Steffens found work on the *Evening Post,* and later he was city editor of the *Commercial Advertiser.* *McClure's Magazine* and the *American Magazine* printed his penetrating criticisms of American politics. As a political interpreter he is recognized widely. *The Shame of the Cities* (1904) and *The Least of These* (1910) are vigorous books. Perhaps his *Autobiography* (1931) is one of the great

418

books of the last ten years. " I Get a Colt to Break In " is Chapter XI of this absorbing life-story. If you enjoy this moving and vigorous sketch, you will find in the remaining hundred and seven chapters of this extraordinary book much to your taste. Merely to read the table of contents is an adventure. It has been called the " vivid diary of a bold and humane pilgrim who so loved his fellowmen that he has never been able to condemn them."

I GET A COLT TO BREAK IN[1]

COLONEL CARTER gave me a colt. I had my pony, and my father meanwhile had bought a pair of black carriage horses and a cow, all of which I had to attend to when we had no " man." And servants were hard to get and to keep in those days; the women married, and the men soon quit service to seize opportunities always opening. My hands were pretty full, and so was the stable. But Colonel Carter seemed to think that he had promised me a horse. He had not; I would have known it if he had. No matter. He thought he had, and maybe he did promise himself to give me one. That was enough. The kind of man that led immigrant trains across the continent and delivered them safe, sound, and together where he promised would keep his word. One day he drove over from Stockton, leading a two-year-old which he brought to our front door and turned over to me as mine. Such a horse!

She was a cream-colored mare with a black forelock, mane, and tail and a black stripe along the middle of her back. Tall, slender, high-spirited, I thought then — I think now that she was the most beautiful of horses. Colonel Carter had bred and reared her with me and my uses in mind. She was a careful cross of a mustang mare and a thoroughbred stallion, with the stamina of the wild horse and the speed and grace of the racer. And she had a sense of fun. As Colonel Carter got

[1] From *The Autobiography of Lincoln Steffens*, published by Harcourt, Brace and Company, 1931.

down out of his buggy and went up to her, she snorted, reared, flung her head high in the air, and, coming down beside him, tucked her nose affectionately under his arm.

"I have handled her a lot," he said. "She is as kind as a kitten, but she is as sensitive as a lady. You can spoil her by one mistake. If you ever lose your temper, if you ever abuse her, she will be ruined forever. And she is unbroken. I might have had her broken to ride for you, but I didn't want to. I want you to do it. I have taught her to lead, as you see; had to, to get her over here. But here she is, an unbroken colt; yours. You take and you break her. You're only a boy, but if you break this colt right, you'll be a man — a young man, but a man. And I'll tell you how."

Now, out west, as everyone knows, they break in a horse by riding out to him in his wild state, lassoing, throwing, and saddling him; then they let him up, frightened and shocked, with a yelling broncho-buster astride of him. The wild beast bucks, the cowboy drives his spurs into him, and off they go, jumping, kicking, rearing, falling, till by the weight of the man, the lash, and the rowels, the horse is broken — in body and spirit. This was not the way I was to break my colt.

"You must break her to ride without her ever knowing it," Colonel Carter said. "You feed and you clean her — you; not the stable man. You lead her out to water and to walk. You put her on a long rope and let her play, calling her to you and gently pulling on the rope. Then you turn her loose in the grass lot there and, when she has romped till tired, call her. If she won't come, leave her. When she wants water or food, she will run to your call, and you will pet and feed and care for her." He went on for half an hour, advising me in great detail how to proceed. I wanted to begin right away. He laughed. He let me lead her around to the stable, water her, and put her in the stable and feed her.

There I saw my pony. My father, sisters, and Colonel Carter saw me stop and look at my pony.

"What'll you do with him?" one of my sisters asked. I was

bewildered for a moment. What should I do with the little red horse? I decided at once.

"You can have him," I said to my sisters.

"No," said Colonel Carter, "not yet. You can give your sisters the pony by and by, but you'll need him till you have taught the colt to carry you and a saddle — months; and you must not hurry. You must learn patience, and you will if you give the colt time to learn it, too. Patience and control. You can't control a young horse unless you can control yourself. Can you shoot?" he asked suddenly.

I couldn't. I had a gun and I had used it some, but it was a rifle, and I could not bring down with it such game as there was around Sacramento — birds and hares. Colonel Carter looked at my father, and I caught the look. So did my father. I soon had a shotgun. But at the time Colonel Carter turned to me and said:

"Can't shoot straight, eh? Do you know what that means? That means that you can't control a gun, and that means that you can't control yourself, your eye, your hands, your nerves. You are wriggling now. I tell you that a good shot is always a good man. He may be a 'bad man' too, but he is quiet, strong, steady in speech, gait, and mind. No matter, though. If you break in this colt right, if you teach her her paces, she will teach you to shoot and be quiet."

He went off downtown with my father, and I started away with my colt. I fed, I led, I cleaned her, gently, as if she were made of glass; she was playful and willing, a delight. When Colonel Carter came home with my father for supper, he questioned me.

"You should not have worked her today," he said. "She has come all the way from Stockton and must be tired. Yes, yes, she would not show her fatigue; too fine for that, and too young to be wise. You have got to think for her, consider her as you would your sisters."

Sisters! I thought; I had never considered my sisters. I did not say that, but Colonel Carter laughed and nodded to my sisters. It was just as if he had read my thought. But he went on to draw on my imagination a centaur; the colt as a horse's body — me, a boy, as the head and brains of one united creature. I liked that. I would be that. I and the colt: a centaur.

After Colonel Carter was gone home I went to work on my new horse. The old one, the pony, I used only for business: to go to fires, to see my friends, run errands, and go hunting with my new shotgun. But the game that had all my attention was the breaking in of the colt, the beautiful cream-colored mare, who soon knew me — and my pockets. I carried sugar to reward her when she did right, and she discovered where I carried it; so did the pony, and when I was busy they would push their noses into my pockets, both of which were torn down a good deal of the time. But the colt learned. I taught her to run around a circle, turn and go the other way at a signal. My sisters helped me. I held the long rope and the whip (for signaling), while one of the girls led the colt; it was hard work for them, but they took it in turns. One would lead the colt round and round till I snapped the whip; then she would turn, turning the colt, till the colt did it all by herself. And she was very quick. She shook hands with each of her four feet. She let us run under her, back and forth. She was slow only to carry me. Following Colonel Carter's instructions, I began by laying my arm or a surcingle over her back. If she trembled, I drew it slowly off. When she could abide it, I tried buckling it, tighter and tighter. I laid over her, too, a blanket, folded at first, then open, and, at last, I slipped up on her myself, sat there a second, and as she trembled, slid off. My sisters held her for me, and when I could get up and sit there a moment or two, I tied her at a block, and we, my sisters and I, made a procession of mounting and dismounting. She soon got used to this and would let us slide off over her rump, but it was a long, long time before she would carry me.

That we practiced by leading her along a high curb where I could get on as she walked, ride a few steps, and then, as she felt me and crouched, slip off. She never did learn to carry a girl on her back; my sisters had to lead her while I rode. This was not purposeful. I don't know just how it happened, but

I do remember the first time I rode on my colt all the way round the lot and how, when I put one of the girls up, she refused to repeat. She shuddered, shook and frightened them off.

While we were breaking in the colt a circus came to town. The ring was across the street from our house. Wonderful! I lived in that circus for a week. I saw the show but once, but I marked the horse-trainers, and in the mornings when they were not too busy I told them about my colt, showed her to them, and asked them how to train her to do circus tricks. With their hints I taught the colt to stand up on her hind legs, kneel, lie down, and balance on a small box. This last was easier than it looked. I put her first on a low big box and taught her to turn on it; then got a little smaller box upon which she repeated what she did on the big one. By and by we had her so that she would step on a high box so small that her four feet were almost touching, and there also she would turn.

The circus man gave me one hint that was worth all the other tricks put together. "You catch her doing something of herself that looks good," he said, "and then you keep her at it." It was thus that I taught her to bow to people. The first day I rode her out on the streets was a proud one for me and for the colt, too, apparently. She did not walk, she danced; perhaps she was excited, nervous; anyhow I liked the way she threw up her head, champed at the bit, and went dancing, prancing down the street. Everybody stopped to watch us, and so, when she began to sober down, I picked her up again with heel and rein, saying, "Here's people, Lady," and she would show off to my delight. By constant repetition I had her so trained that she would single-foot, head down, along a country road till we came to a house or a group of people. Then I'd say, "People, Lady," and up would go her head, and her feet would dance.

But the trick that set the town talking was her bowing to anyone I spoke to. "Lennie Steffens' horse bows to you," people said, and she did. I never told how it was done; by accident. Dogs used to run out at us and the colt enjoyed it;

she kicked at them sometimes with both hind hoofs. I joined her in the game, and being able to look behind more conveniently than she could, I watched the dogs until they were in range, then gave the colt a signal to kick. "Kick, gal," I'd say, and tap her ribs with my heel. We used to get dogs together that way: the colt would kick them over and over and leave them yelping in the road. Well, one day when I met a girl I knew I lifted my hat, probably muttered a "Good day," and I must have touched the colt with my heel. Anyway, she dropped her head and kicked — not much; there was no dog near, so she had responded to my unexpected signal by what looked like a bow. I caught the idea and kept her at it. Whenever I wanted to bow to a girl or anybody else, instead of saying "Good day," I muttered "Kick, gal," spurred her lightly, and — the whole centaur bowed and was covered with glory and conceit.

Yes, conceit. I was full of it, and the colt was quite as bad. One day my chum Hjalmar came into town on his Black Bess, blanketed. She had had a great fistule cut out of her shoulder and had to be kept warm. I expected to see her weak and dull, but no, the good old mare was champing and dancing, like my colt.

"What is it makes her so?" I asked, and Hjalmar said he didn't know, but he thought she was proud of the blanket. A great idea. I had a gaudy horse blanket. I put it on the colt and I could hardly hold her. We rode down the main street together, both horses and both boys, so full of vanity that everybody stopped to smile. We thought they admired, and maybe they did. But some boys on the street gave us another angle. They, too, stopped and looked, and as we passed, one of them said, " Think you're hell, don't you? "

Spoilsport!

We did, as a matter of fact; we thought we were hell. The recognition of it dashed us for a moment; not for long, and the horses paid no heed. We pranced, the black and the yellow, all the way down J Street, up K Street, and agreed that we'd do it again, often. Only, I said, we wouldn't use blankets. If the horses were proud of a blanket, they'd be proud of any-thing unusually conspicuous. We tried a flower next time. I fixed a big rose on my colt's bridle just under her ear and it was great — she pranced downtown with her head turned, literally, to show off her flower. We had to change the decoration from time to time, put on a ribbon, or a bell, or a feather, but, really, it was not necessary for my horse. Old Black Bess needed an incentive to act up, but all I had to do to my horse was to pick up the reins, touch her with my heel, and say, " People "; she would dance from one side of the street to the other, asking to be admired. As she was. As we were.

I would ride down to my father's store, jump off my prancing colt in the middle of the street, and run up into the shop. The colt, free, would stop short, turn, and follow me right up on the sidewalk, unless I bade her wait. If anyone approached her while I was gone, she would snort, rear, and strike. No stranger could get near her. She became a frightened, fright-ening animal, and yet when I came into sight she would run to me, put her head down, and as I straddled her neck, she would throw up her head and pitch me into my seat, facing backwards, of course. I whirled around right, and off we'd go, the vainest boy and the proudest horse in the State.

" Hey, give me a ride, will you? " some boy would ask.

" Sure," I'd say, and jump down and watch that boy try to catch and mount my colt. He couldn't. Once a cowboy wanted to try her, and he caught her; he dodged her forefeet, grabbed the reins, and in one spring was on her back. I never did that again. My colt reared, then bucked, and, as the cow-boy kept his seat, she shuddered, sank to the ground, and rolled over. He slipped aside and would have risen with her, but I was alarmed and begged him not to. She got up at my touch and followed me so close that she stepped on my heel and hurt me. The cowboy saw the point.

" If I were you, kid," he said, " I'd never let anybody mount that colt. She's too good."

That, I think, was the only mistake I made in the rearing of Colonel Carter's gift-horse. My father differed from me. He discovered another error or sin, and thrashed me for it. My practice was to work hard on a trick, privately, and when it was perfect, let him see it. I would have the horse out in our vacant lot doing it as he came home to supper. One evening, as he approached the house, I was standing, whip in hand, while the colt, quite free, was stepping carefully over the bodies of a lot of girls, all my sisters and all their girl friends. (Grace Gallatin, later Mrs. Thompson-Seton, was among them.) My father did not express the admiration I expected; he was frightened and furious. "Stop that," he called, and he came running around into the lot, took the whip, and lashed me with it. I tried to explain; the girls tried to help me explain.

I had seen in the circus a horse that stepped thus over a row of prostrate clowns. It looked dangerous for the clowns, but the trainer had told me how to do it. You begin with logs, laid out a certain distance apart; the horse walks over them under your lead, and whenever he touches one you rebuke him. By and by you substitute clowns. I had no clowns, but I did get logs, and with the girls helping, we taught the colt to step over the obstacles even at a trot. Walking, she touched nothing. All ready thus with the logs, I had my sisters lie down in the grass, and again and again the colt stepped over them. None was ever touched. My father would not listen to any of this; he just walloped me, and when he was tired or satisfied and I was in tears, I blubbered a short excuse: "They were only girls." And he whipped me some more.

My father was not given to whipping; he did it very seldom, but he did it hard when he did it at all. My mother was just the opposite. She did not whip me, but she often smacked me, and she had a most annoying habit of thumping me on the head with her thimbled finger. This I resented more than my father's thoroughgoing thrashings, and I can tell why now. I would be playing Napoleon and as I was reviewing my Old Guard, she would crack my skull with that thimble. No doubt I was in the way; it took a lot of furniture and sisters to represent properly a victorious army; and you might think as my mother did that a thimble is a small weapon. But imagine

Napoleon at the height of his power, the ruler of the world on parade, getting a sharp rap on his crown from a woman's thimble. No. My father's way was more appropriate. It was hard. "I'll attend to you in the morning," he would say, and I lay awake wondering which of my crimes he had discovered. I know what it is to be sentenced to be shot at sunrise. And it hurt, in the morning, when he was not angry but very fresh and strong. But you see, he walloped me in my own person; he never humiliated Napoleon or my knighthood, as my mother did. And I learned something from his discipline, something useful.

I learned what tyranny is and the pain of being misunderstood and wronged, or, if you please, understood and set right; they are pretty much the same. He and most parents and teachers do not break in their boys as carefully as I broke in my colt. They haven't the time that I had, and they have not some other incentives I had. I saw this that day when I rubbed my sore legs. He had to explain to my indignant mother what had happened. When he told it his way, I gave my version: how long and cautiously I had been teaching my horse to walk over logs and girls. And having shown how sure I was of myself and the colt, while my mother was boring into his silence with one of her reproachful looks, I said something that hit my father hard.

"I taught the colt that trick, I have taught her all that you see she knows, without whipping her. I have never struck her; not once. Colonel Carter said I mustn't, and I haven't."

And my mother, backing me up, gave him a rap: "There," she said, "I told you so." He walked off, looking like a thimble-rapped Napoleon.

APPRECIATION HELPS

1. Read the entire selection rapidly to get the fast-moving style. Notice the number of short sentences; the number of words of one syllable.
2. What are the admirable qualities of Colonel Carter?

3. Discover words and phrases which show that both Colonel Carter and the author knew horses.
4. Have you known horses that had a sense of fun? other animals?
5. What manly qualities must a boy develop before he is capable of breaking a horse wisely?
6. After reading the vivid description of the common way of breaking both the body and the spirit of a colt, you will like to read Vachel Lindsay's " The Broncho That Would Not Be Broken."
7. Discuss the value of patience and self-control in other jobs than breaking a colt — teaching a dog tricks, for example, or learning to sail a boat.
8. Explain: " A good shot is always a good man. He may be a ' bad man ' too."
9. Have you met in books horses and their masters that almost made centaurs? Tell the class about them.
10. What interests you in the long training of the colt necessary before her master rode her?
11. Discuss the things the author learned from the circus trainers.
12. Which of the tricks interested you most?
13. Do you see the author's distinction between the thimble-rapping his mother gave him and the hard punishment administered by his father?
14. What is your opinion of whipping in the bringing up of children?
15. If you like this selection you will enjoy reading *The Autobiography of Lincoln Steffens.*

COMPOSITION HINTS

1. Horses I Have Known
2. Chores Pleasant and Unpleasant
3. Teaching My Pet New Tricks
4. Learning to Shoot Straight
5. Tell some early incident that happened when you were too young to be wise.
6. Find some articles on the training of animals and summarize what you have read.
7. What I Have Learned from Discipline
8. A Punishment I Did Not Deserve
9. " I Told You So "

GEORGE SANTAYANA

In this topsy-turvy world of the year of our Lord 1934, Young America is likely to be confused by the contradictory opinions he hears and reads on war — its cost, its futility, its effects both immediate and remote, world peace, the relation of the World War to our present economic muddle, the prospect of future wars. Young America needs guidance.

Few men are better equipped to write sanely and wisely and impartially on war than George Santayana. His careful and liberal education and his philosophic mind have prepared him to discover the truth. " On War " is a clear and penetrating discussion of this vital subject.

Mr. Santayana was born in 1863 at Madrid, Spain, of Spanish parents. In 1872, at the age of nine, he came to America. His formal education was gained at Harvard, at Berlin, at King's College, Cambridge, and at the Sorbonne, Paris. He taught philosophy at Harvard for twenty years. In 1914 he went to Europe, but found it impossible to work in the atmosphere of the World War found everywhere in Europe. As he wandered from country to country he had a chance to observe the effects of war upon a world. Never at heart has Mr. Santayana been an American. He finds England " preëminently the home of decent happiness and a quiet pleasure in being oneself," and he now lives there.

Because of their subject matter, his books are not easy to read. One has to " weigh and consider " constantly. The effort required is worth while, however, for one finds in his well-turned phrases a tolerant and sane master. This full-blooded Spaniard is one of the greatest living artists in the use of the English language.

Lovers of Dickens like to remember that he has written possibly the finest essay on Dickens that has ever appeared. William Lyon Phelps, in *What I Like,* states that Mr. Santayana told him, in answer to a question, that when he took up Dickens during the war he discovered that he not only could read him but could not help reading him.

ON WAR[1]

To fight is a radical instinct; if men have nothing else to fight over they will fight over words, fancies, or women, or they will fight because they dislike each other's looks, or because they have met walking in opposite directions. To knock a thing down, especially if it is cocked at an arrogant angle, is a deep delight to the blood. To fight for a reason and in a calculating spirit is something your true warrior despises; even a coward might screw his courage up to such a reasonable conflict. The joy and glory of fighting lie in its pure spontaneity and consequent generosity; you are not fighting for gain, but for sport and for victory. Victory, no doubt, has its fruits for the victor. If fighting were not a possible means of livelihood the bellicose instinct could never have established itself in any long-lived race. A few men can live on plunder, just as there is room in the world for some beasts of prey; other men are reduced to living on industry, just as there are diligent bees, ants, and herbivorous kine. But victory need have no good fruits for the people whose army is victorious. That it sometimes does so is an ulterior and blessed circumstance hardly to be reckoned upon.

Since barbarism has its pleasures it naturally has its apologists. There are panegyrists of war who say that without a periodical bleeding a race decays and loses its manhood. Experience is directly opposed to this shameless assertion. It is war that wastes a nation's wealth, chokes its industries, kills its flower, narrows its sympathies, condemns it to be governed by adventurers, and leaves the puny, deformed, and unmanly to breed the next generation. Internecine war, foreign and civil, brought about the greatest set-back which the life of reason has ever suffered; it exterminated the Greek and Italian aristocracies. Instead of being descended from heroes, modern nations are descended from slaves; and it is not their bodies only that show it. After a long peace, if the conditions of life

[1] From *Soliloquies in England and Later Soliloquies,* published by Charles Scribner's Sons, 1922.

are propitious, we observe a people's energies bursting their barriers; they become aggressive on the strength they have stored up in their remote and unchecked development. It is the unmutilated race, fresh from the struggle with nature (in which the best survive, while in war it is often the best that perish), that descends victoriously into the arena of nations and conquers disciplined armies at the first blow, becomes the military aristocracy of the next epoch and is itself ultimately sapped and decimated by luxury and battle, and merged at last into the ignoble conglomerate beneath. Then, perhaps, in some other virgin country a genuine humanity is again found, capable of victory because unbled by war. To call war the soil of courage and virtue is like calling debauchery the soil of love.

Blind courage is an animal virtue indispensable in a world full of dangers and evils where a certain insensibility and dash are requisite to skirt the precipice without vertigo. Such animal courage seems therefore beautiful rather than desperate or cruel, and being the lowest and most instinctive of virtues it is the one most widely and sincerely admired. In the form of steadiness under risks rationally taken, and perseverance so long as there is a chance of success, courage is a true virtue; but it ceases to be one when the love of danger, a useful passion when danger is unavoidable, begins to lead men into evils which it was unnecessary to face. Bravado, provocativeness, and a gambler's instinct, with a love of hitting hard for the sake of exercise, is a temper which ought already to be counted among the vices rather than the virtues of man. To delight in war is a merit in the soldier, a dangerous quality in the captain, and a positive crime in the statesman.

The panegyrist of war places himself on the lowest level on which a moralist or patriot can stand and shows as great a want of refined feeling as of right reason. For the glories of war are all blood-stained, delirious, and infected with crime; the combative instinct is a savage prompting by which one man's good is found in another's evil. The existence of such a contradiction in the moral world is the original sin of nature, whence flows every other wrong. He is a willing accom-

plice of that perversity in things who delights in another's
discomfiture or in his own, and craves the blind tension of
plunging into danger without reason, or the idiot's pleasure in
facing a pure chance. To find joy in another's trouble is, as
man is constituted, not unnatural, though it is wicked; and
to find joy in one's own trouble, though it be madness, is not
yet impossible for man. These are the chaotic depths of that
dreaming nature out of which humanity has to grow.

APPRECIATION HELPS

1. Discuss: " Fighting is an instinct, and civilization means simply the conquest of instincts."
2. Why has war continued in spite of its waste and barbarity?
3. How do wars between men and fights between beasts differ?
4. For what various reasons do men fight?
5. Why is the true warrior unable to fight " for a reason and in a
   calculating spirit "?
6. Discuss: " To knock a thing down . . . is a deep delight to
   the blood."
7. What distinction is made between fighting for a reason and
   fighting from instinct?
8. Discuss: " Without a periodical bleeding, a race decays and
   loses its manhood."
9. Discuss some chief evils of war.
10. Explain: " Instead of being descended from heroes, modern
    nations are descended from slaves."
11. Discuss with an intelligent older person the statement that war
    wastes a nation's wealth and chokes its industries.
12. When does courage cease to be a virtue?
13. Why is it criminal for the statesman to delight in war?

COMPOSITION HINTS

1. A Generous Victor
2. When I Showed Blind Courage
3. Show the error in the statement that one man's good is found
   in another's evil.
4. Can War Be Outlawed?
5. International-Mindedness through Books
6. Discuss several articles you have read on war, and give your
   opinion of them to the class.

STUART CHASE

Never has there been a period in the United States when it has seemed so important to be intelligently informed on national and economic affairs. "Read or perish" and "Think or perish" are good slogans today. Both because of his training and because of his work, Stuart Chase is admirably prepared to guide our thinking on economic problems. Born in 1888, in New Hampshire, Mr. Chase was trained at the Massachusetts Institute of Technology, and later studied at Harvard, graduating in 1910. For seven years he was a certified public accountant, work which develops a passion for accurate figures. (He is still well known as an accountant.) Under the Federal Trade Commission, from 1917 to 1922 he investigated the meat industry and the packers. He knows thoroughly business and industrial organization. He sees the relation between the characteristics of national life to standard human values. Because in his opinion liberal leaders did not seem to know where they were going, he became critical of them. He felt that most of those engaged in liberal movements knew little of the "springs of human conduct," and that they failed to consider a scientific technique for establishing their ideas. The wastefulness of modern business accounts for many imperfections in modern life, he believes. *Men and Machines* (1929) has been widely discussed. It is a study of living-conditions as influenced by machines. *The Tragedy of Waste* (1925), *Your Money's Worth* (1927), and *Mexico — A Study of Two Americas* (1931) will stimulate the good reader.

COLUMN LEFT[1]

UTOPIA-MAKING is good fun, and so is sand sculpture at low tide. I know what path I should like to see my country take, but I can hardly expect her to take it. No prophecy is quite devoid of wish fulfillment, but let us try as honestly as may be to trace the curve of America's immediate economic future as it springs from the curve of her economic past. Thus we leap into space from firm ground. If I read the past aright, the course in the years before us veers to the left, in the direction of an increasing social control of industry. The extent of wish fulfillment in this conclusion I must perforce leave to your appraisal.

The American frontier, according to James Truslow Adams, ceased to exist about 1890. In that year the Bureau of the Census reported: " The unsettled area has been so broken by isolated bodies of settlement that there can hardly be said to be a frontier line." The mental habits engendered by the frontier have continued to this day, however, exhibiting a cultural lag of more than four decades. Mr. Adams describes some of these habits and I have added a few more. They include:

An unlimited optimism as to the economic future. " The United States cannot be sold short." We still feel sure of an infinite frontier of land, minerals, forests, potential population.

The gospel of hard work and getting things done in a hurry. The compulsion of speed.

Engineering ingenuity and mechanical ability.

The worship of financial success. A toleration for the means provided the end of money-getting is achieved. The cloaking of business with moral sanctions (*vide* Bruce Barton), and the seating of the business man at the pinnacle of the Republic.

[1] Reprinted from *Scribner's Magazine* by special permission of the editors, copyright, 1932, Charles Scribner's Sons.

The gospel of getting by, and of getting away with it.

A gross callousness toward the waste of land and natural resources, and toward the esthetics of land use. Stream pollution, litter, roadside slums.

A sturdy repugnance to all "foreign entanglements." There was more than enough work to be done at home.

The cheerful, nay, determined shoving of government into the hands of third-rate, easily manipulated men. It was assumed in a general way that a country of such unlimited resources did not need a government.

And, finally, a certain cowardice in facing economic realities. The pioneer was essentially a man so overborne with troubles at home that he preferred to take an ax and a covered wagon rather than remain and make a fight on the home front. This is particularly true of the great immigrant population. It chose escape as the easiest way out. The American frontier was the safety valve of popular economic unrest not only for the Eastern states but for Europe as well.

Meanwhile economic facts have been moving relentlessly onward in a direction increasingly at variance with this typical American outlook and ideology. The most explosive fact of all is that the frontier ended forty years ago, leaving us without a safety valve for more than a generation. As Charles A. Beard says: "We are living on the husks of the nineteenth century." Almost as shattering is the fact that the curve of population is rapidly heading into a plateau, and Dublin tells us that along about 1960 we shall probably come to a dead level of one hundred and sixty millions or thereabouts. What with birth control and the restriction of immigration, the ever expanding domestic market is doomed — certainly on the old gorgeous, automatic basis.

In the third place, the machine has bored so deeply into our economic structure that today a man can hardly do the simplest act — turn a faucet, go for a ride, smoke a cigarette, give a present to his sweetheart, listen to a song — without sending out economic waves which reverberate around the seven seas.

We are at last locked into a structure so complicated, inter-related, far-flung, and tenuous, that untold millions of delicate cog-wheels must join if Sam Smith is to eat tonight or Mary Robinson to have a new dress upon her back tomorrow. While Americans still view foreign entanglements with a malevolent eye, and while, theoretically, we could be a nation largely self-contained, the cold facts are that we have loaned some twenty billions abroad in recent years, and come increasingly to depend on exports to keep our wheels turning and our wheat waving. Without a number of key products not procurable at home — such as rubber, nitrates, coffee, sugar — we should promptly be most seriously embarrassed. We could be far more self-sufficient than we are, but the point is that we have never taken the effort, beyond flag-flapping and speech-making, and are now, whether we like it or not, clamped into a world economy.

The collapse of the frontier was a serious business, but its effects were slow in making themselves felt so long as population increased rapidly, markets were maintained, business opportunities continued abundant, and mechanization was not too cataclysmically complicated. These mitigating factors were in evidence until well into the nineteen-twenties, aided by a wide-open immigration policy, by the fillip to business given by the war, and by the phenomenal passion of Americans to own and operate a motorcar.

But at last the day of reckoning has come. Added to the usual downswing of the business cycle — a phenomenon we have known since the depresssion of 1819 — we find ourselves with no frontier to which to escape. (Nor can we even eat on our highly specialized, one-crop farms.) The war fillip has faded out, indeed reversed itself, as the sad realization dawns that we have loaned the money to foreigners with which foreigners have paid for our industrial activity during the past decade. Now the loans are marked frozen, and our mile-high tariff iceberg has helped to freeze them. Our population growth is sluggish and promises to be more so, which brings real-estate values to a full stop if not to a back somersault.

The whole theory of such values throughout the history of America has been to tie them to a mounting population curve. The future has already been capitalized and that future, according to Mr. Dublin, will probably not materialize.

We have oversold ourselves on gadgets pumped by the installment plan, enormously extending an industrial plant for the production of luxuries and semi-luxuries which, in a crisis, people do not need to buy and frequently, in the teeth of the advertiser's psychologist, will not buy. A recent commentator has estimated that the margin of " consumer capriciousness " in the present domestic market is at least twenty-five per cent. No former depression has known such a margin, and the current slump is rendered the more severe by virtue of a huge new element of overproduction in the sense of excess-plant capacity in the luxury trades. Where, for instance, are the Tom Thumb golf courses of yesteryear?

We have oversold ourselves on securities, an ominous percentage of the offerings of the past decade coming under the head of beautifully engraved cats and dogs and foxes. Loans — tremendous loans — have been duly advanced on this menagerie. The whole credit structure has become involved, and sways dizzily, wracked with an alarming internal pain.

Lastly — the technological process having marched to the tune of rugged individualism, no man seeking to guide it or ever to understand it — we find that the railroads have become technologically antiquated without our knowing it, and can never take their proud place again; and that the motorcar, which gave us such a mighty impetus in the twenties, is destined for a *replacement* rather than a *new* market, never again to furnish a spearhead for prosperity. A day's study would have been sufficient to provide any intelligent person with the railroad curve. He need only have cast up the tonnage being torn away by the motor truck, the high-power transmission line, the oil-pipe line, the natural-gas long-distance line, the hydro and central-power station. The handwriting has been on the wall for a dozen years, but it is a script which neither Wall Street nor American ideology can read. In 1925

I foretold the end of the motorcar new market (I placed it a little too soon, not counting on the dying gasp of the two-cars-per-family campaign), but I was obviously a crabbed knocker, untrustworthy and un-American.

How, gentlemen, do you propose to circumvent this bill of particulars? Even if I have erred in one or two of them, enough remain to bring us to a halt. And to a full stop we have indeed come. The business and political captains have tried holding the right thought for two and a half years and the results of their efforts may be found deftly documented in *Oh, Yeah?*

Ruin, disaster, the end of the world? Not at all. At least not necessarily. We have come to the end of the classic American formula, nourished on the frontier, the population curve, the luck of our natural resources, of a profitable world war (for us), of a four-wheeled gadget carrying immense psychological appeal. Our basic physical plant was never in better shape, our fields never more fertile. Our natural resources are growing a bit ragged, but vast quantities remain; our population is still reasonably healthy, ingenious, and adaptable. All that has happened — to be sure it is enough — is that the credit structure has jammed, the guiding formula has collapsed, and we are face to face with reorganizing the nation on the basis of economic stability rather than zooming speculation. For all I know, the Florida boom and the Big Bull Market were the last two great joy rides of an epoch which has ended.

For the first time in our national history since the opening of the West, we have to deal with a roughly static rather than an ever expanding structure, and, most painful of all, to discard frontier habits, ideologies, and slogans, and begin to think. There is no prairie, no mountain, no forest, to which we can escape; there are no bounding real-estate values to cushion our industrial mistakes; we have at last to face real things in a real world, stand our ground and fight. Our luck has run out. Thinking is good once in a while for men and for nations. We might even get used to it, alien as the process is, and enjoy thinking our way out. We might, for all I know, become enormously stimulated and thrilled — like the Russians — in liquidating a bankrupt economic epoch and building a new and better one. All the raw materials are ready to hand. We have to deal with a slower tempo of economic expansion; with a closed frontier and a closed safety-valve; with a world in which rugged individualism is — and has been for forty years — an anachronism; with the possibility of another orgy of speculation — such as the Big Bull Market — completely outside the picture; with the stark necessity of national and regional economic planning.

I do not happen to belong to the " plan or perish " school — except in a very general way. We shall probably have to do some radical emergency planning immediately to get us through the depression, but a long-swing program inaugurated in the next few months is not, in my opinion, the alternative to a general smash. We can probably muddle on for a few more years with temporary shots of adrenalin and temporary crutches. Planning is not a patent medicine which we must swallow or die, it is the inevitable answer to a chain of economic circumstances. The proponents of planning are under no compulsion to work out a complete blueprint, and, waving it at a recalcitrant business community, cry: Take this or expire! The logic of the circumstances which I have sought to recite above will force the business community, the government, the trade union, the public generally, to accept a new weapon for a new battle-front. Planning will probably make equal, if not greater, progress if its convinced advocates do no more than ask industrialist, banker, politician, merchant: Here are the conditions, what are you going to do? What are you going to do? What are you going to do? Conscious economic control rather than irresponsible drift is the only answer to these conditions. Sooner or later the fact will register in every intelligent brain. We are not necessarily doomed if we allow the registration process a reasonable time limit. Social habits have ever changed slowly.

If we do not plan constructively we shall not necessarily

perish — just yet, as Veblen used to say. But we must certainly plan, and that soon, if American civilization is to go *forward*. The goals are already outlined with some clarity. They include:

The creation of national minimum living standards, below which no family, able and willing to work, shall be permitted to fall. The liquidation of economic insecurity on the basis of plain food, shelter, clothing, and education.

The conservation of natural resources.

The use of land for human living rather than for profitable speculation, entailing the end of Megalopolis with its compulsion of speed, noise, dirt, ugliness, and overcrowding. A wide extension of those areas devoted to natural beauty, sunshine, and first-hand recreation. Though the frontier has gone, we have plenty of land.

The education of the consumer to buy *goods* rather than jumping-jacks, gadgets, and junk.

To achieve these goals, we shall probably have to experiment with such technics and methods as:

A managed currency. The end of King Gold.

The strict supervision of new investment in order that it may be at once genuinely productive and reasonably safe. In return for safety, the rate must be modest.

A drastic revision in the distribution of the national income to maintain an adequate volume of mass purchasing power. Income and inheritance taxes are the most obvious agents in this connection.

An enormous increase in the endowment for medical, agricultural, and industrial research.

A drastic decline in high-pressure salesmanship.

The declaration that all basic and essential industries are affected with a public interest, subject to public regularization, stabilization, and control. This implies the Interstate Commerce Commission technic extended to power, coal, oil, lumber, wheat, cotton, textiles, steel, copper, chemicals, and other groups.

National and regional planning boards to coördinate these activities, and above all to prevent the crystallization of industrial progress.

Who is to grasp these goals and work out these technics? We hear today a great hue and cry over the lack of leadership. Our business men and statesmen have failed us in this crisis. As for our scientists and professional men, nobody has ever expected anything from them. Their only function in the American saga has been to grease the wheels. Well, what does one expect, a psychological miracle? Nature does not act that way; she is not in the habit of producing stars from a vacuum. We have no leadership, because, forsooth, after the opening of the West, we never needed any. We were a self-generating perpetual-motion machine. There was no function for overhead economic leadership; no school in which such leaders could be trained. For about fifteen months in 1917 and 1918 we started a school, and called it the War Industries Board. But the emergency over, that academy was promptly sunk in a sea of normalcy. (Oddly enough, if we are to survive 1932 without a major lesion, it will probably be some of these old pupils who will pull us through.)

New conditions will create leaders. The times will call forth the man. Where the leaders are I do not know — though I could, if pressed, perhaps remove a bushel or two. Nobody knows. But they will come. You, my friend, may be hiding a marshal's baton under your coat at this moment. And the path along which they shall lead us can bear only to the left. No more excursions into the petrified forests of rugged individualism. No more attempts — save perhaps by job-hunting executive secretaries — to keep government and business single and celibate. No more jogging placidly in the middle of the road. No more mass movements to the good old days when the easiest thing to do with an overmortgaged house was to leave it to the mortgage-holder and take the sunset trail.

Right trails, center trails, are also posted No Thoroughfare. The left road is the only road, and willy-nilly we must take it. Why? Because we cannot ride out this depression without taking it. We cannot cope with the complexities of a machine civilization, we cannot conserve our irreplaceable natural resources, we cannot build up popular purchasing power to buy back the commodities we can so readily make, we cannot get rid of unemployment and overproduction, we cannot keep our banks from freezing periodically, we cannot meet the challenge of Russia, which hour by hour climbs up the eastern sky, we cannot hold a people, some day overborne with misery and disillusion, from turning to the barricades — unless we take it.

APPRECIATION HELPS

1. What is Utopia-making? What becomes of sand sculpture done at low tide?
2. Read the article through and then discuss its admirable opening and closing sentences.
3. Explain the significance of the title; of the expression, " social control of industry."
4. Discuss several of the mental habits of American people that have been born of the frontier and point out some in which danger lurks.
5. What evidences do you find of hurry in our modern life? of worship of financial success? of the gospel of getting by? of a distrust of " foreign alliances "?
6. Show that " escape from reality " may have helped to push back the frontier.
7. What relation is there between the vanishing of the frontier and our economic muddle?
8. Discuss: " The machine has bored deeply into our economic structure."
9. Is the passion to own a car more evident in Americans than in other nationalities?
10. Discuss the dangers of overspecialization — one-crop farms, for example.
11. Discuss the author's statement that we are oversold on gadgets, not *goods;* illustrate.

12. What are the merits of " social control of industry " as opposed to " rugged individualism "?
13. Discuss the author's solution for America's future. How much of his plan has been attempted since it was published (March, 1932)?
14. Does this vigorous article challenge you to help think your way out of the national muddle?

COMPOSITION HINTS

1. Childhood Utopias
2. Getting by in School
3. Haste Makes Waste
4. Intellectual Frontiers
5. Buying on the Installment Plan
6. Two Cars in Every Family

WALTER LIPPMANN

For any one man during these troubled times to judge and appraise adequately such perplexing questions as the causes and the nature of the depression, Mr. Hoover's task and how he dealt with it, war debts, the European depression, Congress, the Far East, Tammany, the two national party conventions, the problem of inflation, the New Deal in almost every aspect, seems impossible. Yet Walter Lippmann has treated all these questions and others as well in his editorial writings for 1931, 1932, and 1933. And thinking people read his opinions with respect. Some of them have been brought together in a single volume, *Interpretations* (1932). They challenge our interest and help to clarify and form our judgment.

Walter Lippmann, editor and writer, was born in New York in 1889. His undergraduate as well as his graduate work was done in Harvard. Philosophy was a chief interest there for him. Mr. Lippmann has been associate editor of the *New Republic,* and editor of the New York *World* until 1931. Now he is a special writer for the New York *Herald-Tribune* and his articles are widely syndicated, so that it is said that no other man in America reaches so large an audience. In 1917, from June to October, he was an assistant to the Secretary of War, and has later served the government on special assignments. That so young a man should have his opinions respected and sought for is a tribute to his ability and judgment.

A Preface to Politics (1913); *Liberty and the News* (1920); *Public Opinion* (1922); *A Preface to Morals* (1929) — these are books for the student interested in contemporary American life. Mr. Lippmann believes: " Liberty is not so much permission as it is the construction of a system of information independent of opinion." One can hardly afford not to read his opinions on current affairs, for his discussions are provocative. The essay here is from *Interpretations*.

DWIGHT W. MORROW[1]

Dwight Morrow entered American public life at a time when all political values were inflated and unreal. The war propaganda had dislocated the sense of truth and had brought into being marvelously effective devices for selling things at more than they were worth. It was the appearance, not the reality, that counted, and the politician, ambitious to succeed, surrounded himself not with the wisest counselors but with the smartest press agents. It was the function of these press agents to create a fictitious public character for the multitude to gape at, and the utmost care was taken by the politician never under any circumstances to let his private and real thoughts disturb the carefully built-up fiction.

This radical insincerity was regarded in the postwar years as the only practical politics. The effects were devastating. The public man himself became so preoccupied with maintaining his public personality that he tended to lose what personality and what personal conviction he may have had. He became so interested in the " reaction " to what he was doing that he lost sight of what he was doing. Plain speaking and honest thinking being at a discount, the public was fooled and yet knew it was being fooled. The younger generation who first encountered public life in this period turned from it in cynical disgust, and among the people generally there was less faith in the character of the government than at any time within memory.

The historic achievement of Dwight Morrow was that he broke through these conventions of insincerity in public life and raised a standard of intrinsic worth to which men could repair. Like the greatest teachers, he taught by example. When the demonstration had been made, as in Mexico and in his campaign for Senator, the artificial and synthetic careers which had looked so important seemed inexpressibly tawdry. Morrow did nothing to promote his popularity; it gathered

[1] From *Interpretations,* published by the Macmillan Company, 1933.

about him from all quarters and from every station in a kind of deep murmur of implicit confidence and deeply felt need. For the rise of Morrow in the esteem of the American people was like an awakening out of a daze of appearances and a rediscovery of the solid, honest substance of real things.

No man of our time has had the complete trust of so many different kinds of people. What were the qualities which made this man trusted in Wall Street and in Moscow, at the Vatican and among the Mexican revolutionists, among hard-boiled politicians and among star-eyed reformers? Was it because he succeeded in being all things to all men? On the contrary, it was because he based his whole public life on the deep principle that the one common thing to which all the warring sects of man must in the end submit is the truth itself. From this principle he derived the working hypothesis of his career, which was to assume that every man was interested in the truth.

He knew quite as well as the most sophisticated among us how often men, when left to their own devices, will deceive themselves and others. Nevertheless, he proceeded on the assumption that they intended to be honest, and by the very force of the assumption made them justify him. That was, I believe, the inner secret of his marvelous successes as a negotiator. By divesting himself of all weapons but these which could promote understanding, his adversary had either to disarm too or feel wretchedly uncomfortable at having to be a deliberate villain. Here, at the heart of his power, Dwight Morrow had possession of an ancient, mystical insight into human character which the merely worldly can never know. Thus because he touched the deeper chords of their natures all sorts of men trusted him. They loved him because he had the essential human wisdom which remembers always all the octaves of the human spirit. It is a kind of wisdom which is almost submerged by the raw efficiency of our machine-made ways. He had it, and with it he turned not away from the world to a contemplative religious life, but to the management of the most immediate and practical affairs.

The peculiar genius of Dwight Morrow lay in the fact that

he kept a mystical faith in men without losing his own intellectual standards. The commonest outcome of mysticism is muddle-headedness; the visionary can see nothing but the white light of the mystery, and for the rest his speech runs out into rhetoric and his actions into eccentricity. Dwight Morrow kept his mind by using it incessantly, so incessantly that it was sometimes exhausting to others and to himself. He lived at a pitch of mental activity many stages above that of the normal actively-minded man. His brain never stopped going and it never was aimless. It fed voraciously on anything and everything that came within the range of his attention, everlastingly purposeful, endlessly raising questions, forever finding explanations and solutions. He had the incandescence of genius and he never rested.

The acquired character of his mind, as distinguished from its native energies, was formed in the great tradition of English empirical thinking. Dwight Morrow was a genuinely learned man in the field of history, and had circumstances been different he might readily have been as eminent a scholar as he was a statesman. The history which he knew best was English and American history from the time of Cromwell. This meant that he knew intimately where were the roots of American institutions. Unlike most Americans of the present time, his mind was not severed from the past out of which this nation has come. He carried with him, as something known and understood, the central political tradition of American life, and in his own person he came to exemplify it. Those who have marveled that a successful banker should so quickly prove himself a successful statesman and an excellent practical politician will, I think, find a large part of the explanation there. Dwight Morrow did not come unprepared into public life. He came greatly prepared by the intimate acquaintance of a lifetime with the classic models of statecraft and politics. Thus the things which would have seemed new to an unread novice were through many precedents quite familiar to him.

Because of his loyalty to the Anglo-American tradition, it is impossible in our present intellectual confusion to classify him under such conventional labels as conservative or progressive. In a time when conservatives are for the most part high protectionists he was a free-trader by deepest conviction; in a time when progressivism is enchanted with the prospect of regulating mankind from central places, he was a resolute believer in decentralization, preferring the evils of liberty to those of authority. But though the pattern of his thought was the classic liberal view of human affairs, he had no disposition to impose his ideas.

This is, perhaps, the aspect of the man which was most inscrutable to many who watched him. Although he had enormous prestige, it did not interest him to use his influence to promote causes and instigate political movements. Some ascribed this diffidence to his alleged political inexperience. It should really be ascribed to his ultimate wisdom about human affairs. It was this wisdom which made him put relatively small value upon specific laws, arrangements, policies, and the greatest store upon weaving thread by thread the fabric of common understanding. For he was of those who believe that men make institutions, and that all depends at last, not on the forms of things, but on the intrinsic quality of men's dealing with each other.

Thus it was in the art of honest dealing that he was a master, and an example to his country.

APPRECIATION HINTS

1. How have the last five years influenced your attitude towards men in public life?
2. Name some public figures you greatly admire; some who have lost your respect.
3. What qualities should statesmen possess?
4. Have our public idols with " feet of clay " any qualities of character in common?
5. What qualities in Morrow are admirable?
6. Discuss the importance of sincerity in human relationships.
7. Show that human relationships are of prime importance in managing human institutions.

8. Discuss some fictitious public characters of politics; of the theater; of the screen; of sports — all created by the press agent.
9. What have press agents done for Babe Ruth? For Lindbergh? For Tunney?
10. Show that it is a particularly fine tribute to a man that all sorts of men respect him.
11. Why is it wise to assume that men intend to be honest?
12. Show that Morrow was neither a conservative nor a progressive.

COMPOSITION HINTS

1. Good Brains Raise Questions and Find Explanations
2. What Are Some *Acquired* Characteristics of the Mind?
3. Discuss several national figures eminent in more than one field. (For example, Theodore Roosevelt; Woodrow Wilson.)
4. The Art of Honest Dealing
5. Select any public man you choose and write an editorial on him, showing either his admirable qualities or those deserving of criticism.

BOOKS OF ESSAYS FOR WIDER
READING

It is hoped that this generous list for further reading will not frighten the young reader but will lure him on to more adventures and enthusiasms in this type of literature. Not only essayists represented in the book have been included, but other writers of this popular form are listed for the interested reader. No narrow interpretation of the word " essay " has been followed in compiling this bibliography. Books classified under another head, such as biography or travel, are found here. The search has been for books appropriate to be read during this study. It is hoped that the wide choice offered will encourage extensive reading, as well as provide books attractive to every taste. There is much easy reading here, but the critical taste of the mature and seasoned reader is also cared for. Essayists who are recognized masters in this field, who may well be read by students planning to enter college, are here: Bacon, Stevenson, Emerson. The familiar essay is more than generously represented, for young readers frequently become interested in nonfiction through this intimate and friendly form, as they may become interested in writing through reading the personal essay. A very definite effort has been made to include a good many writers on national, political, economic, and world relationships. Perhaps these essays in contemporary civilization are the most vital in the list. Read the titles and select some provocative and attractive ones, talk with your English or history teacher, and the librarian, and decide on the book you wish to read Enjoy the book, and share your enjoyment with the class.

Abbott, Lyman, *The Spirit of Democracy,* Houghton, 1910
Adams, James Truslow, *The Epic of America,* Little, 1931
Atlantic Classics; Ser. 1 and 2, Atlantic Monthly. 2 vols.
Bacon, Francis, Viscount St. Albans, *Essays,* Scribner, 1918

Baker, Ray Stannard (David Grayson), *Adventures in Content-
    ment,* Doubleday, 1907
    Adventures in Friendship, Doubleday, 1910
    Great Possessions, Doubleday, 1917
Barrie, Sir James Matthew, *Courage,* Scribner, 1922
    Margaret Ogilvy, Scribner, 1896
Beebe, William, *Edge of the Jungle,* Holt, 1921
    Jungle Days, Putnam, 1925
    Jungle Peace, Holt, 1918
    Nonsuch, Harcourt, 1932
Beerbohm, Max, *And Even Now,* Dutton, 1921
    Observations, Doubleday, 1925
Belloc, Hilaire, *On Nothing and Kindred Subjects,* Dutton, 1925
    On Something, Dutton, 1931
Benchley, Robert Charles, *Of All Things,* Garden City, 1926
    The Early Worm, Holt, 1927
Bennett, Arnold, *How to Live on Twenty-Fours Hours a Day,*
    Doran, 1910
    The Human Machine, Doran, 1911
    Things That Have Interested Me, Doran, 1921–26. 3 vols.
    Your United States, Doran
Benson, Arthur Christopher, *Escape, and Other Essays,* Century,
    1915
    From a College Window, Putnam, 1906
Bergengren, Ralph Wilhelm, *Comforts of Home,* Little, 1918
    Perfect Gentleman, Little, 1919
Briggs, LeBarón Russell, *School, College, and Character,* Hough-
    ton, 1901
    To College Girls, and Other Essays, Houghton, 1914
Brooks, Charles Stephen, *Chimney-Pot Papers,* Yale University
    Press, 1919
    Hints to Pilgrims, Yale University Press, 1921
    Roundabout to Canterbury, Harcourt, 1926
    There's Pippins and Cheese to Come, Yale University Press,
    1917
Broun, Heywood Campbell, *Pieces of Hate and Other Enthusi-
    asms,* Doran, 1922
    Seeing Things at Night, Harcourt, 1921
Bryce, James Bryce, Viscount, *Hindrances to Good Citizenship,*
    Yale University Press, 1909
Burroughs, John, *Birds and Bees,* Houghton, 1926

Canby, Henry Seidel, *Definitions; Essays in Contemporary Criticism; Second Series,* Harcourt, 1924

Center, Stella Stewart, ed., *Selected Letters,* Merrill, 1924

Chamberlain, Essie, ed., *Mirror for Americans,* Heath, 1930

Chesterton, Gilbert Keith, *Tremendous Trifles,* Dodd, 1909

    The Uses of Diversity, Dodd, 1921

Clemens, Samuel Langhorne, *In Defense of Harriet Shelley and Other Essays,* Harper, 1918

Cockayne, Charles Alexander, ed., *Modern Essays of Various Types,* Merrill, 1927

Conrad, Joseph, *Last Essays,* Doubleday, 1926

    The Mirror of the Sea, Doubleday

    Notes on Life and Letters, Doubleday, 1921

Crothers, Samuel McChord, *Among Friends,* Houghton, 1910

    The Cheerful Giver, Houghton, 1923

    Humanly Speaking, Houghton, 1912

    The Gentle Reader, Houghton, 1903

Dunne, Finley Peter, *Mr. Dooley in the Hearts of His Countrymen,* Small, 1899

    Mr. Dooley on Making a Will and Other Necessary Evils, Scribner, 1919

Eaton, Walter Prichard, *Green Trails and Upland Pastures,* Doubleday, 1917

    Penguin Persons and Peppermints, Wilde, 1922

Emerson, Ralph Waldo, *Essays,* Macmillan, 1926. (Also Houghton.)

Erskine, John, *The Moral Obligation to Be Intelligent,* Bobbs, 1921

Galsworthy, John, *A Motley,* Scribner, 1910

    A Sheaf, Scribner, 1916

    Another Sheaf, Scribner, 1919

    Tatterdemalion, Scribner, 1920

    The Inn of Tranquillity, Scribner, 1912

Gerould, Katharine (Fullerton), *Modes and Morals,* Scribner, 1920

Grahame, Kenneth, *The Wind in the Willows,* Scribner, 1923

Grayson, David. *See* Baker, Ray Stannard

Hagedorn, Hermann, ed., *The Americanism of Theodore Roosevelt,* Houghton, 1923

    You Are the Hope of the World, Macmillan, 1917

Hastings, William Thomson, ed., *Contemporary Essays,* Houghton, 1928

Hearn, Lafcadio, *Glimpses of Unfamiliar Japan,* Houghton. 2 vols.
 Out of the East, Houghton, 1895
Holliday, Robert Cortes, *Broome Street Straws,* Doran, 1918
 Turns about Town, Doran, 1921
 The Walking-Stick Papers, Doran, 1918
Holmes, Oliver Wendell, *The Autocrat of the Breakfast Table,*
 Houghton
Hudson, William Henry, *A Traveller in Little Things,* Dutton,
 1921
 The Book of a Naturalist, Dutton, 1919
 Far Away and Long Ago, Dutton, 1924
Irving, Washington, *Alhambra,* Macmillan
 The Sketch Book, Dutton, 1908
Johnson, Burges, *As I Was Saying,* Macmillan, 1923
 Essaying the Essay, Little, 1927
Keller, Helen Adams, *My Key of Life,* Crowell, 1926
 My Religion, Doubleday, 1927
 Out of the Dark, Doubleday, 1913
 The World I Live In, Century, 1908
Kirkland, Winifred Margaretta, *The Joys of Being a Woman,*
 Houghton, 1918
Lamb, Charles, *Essays of Elia,* Burt. (There are many editions.)
Leacock, Stephen Butler, *Behind the Beyond,* Lane, 1931
 Literary Lapses, Lane, 1931
 Short Circuits, Dodd, 1928
Lippmann, Walter, *Interpretations,* Macmillan, 1932
Lucas, Edward Verrall, *Adventures and Enthusiasms,* Doran, 1920
 Giving and Receiving, Doran, 1922
Lynd, Robert, *The Blue Lion and Other Essays,* Doran, 1923
Macaulay, Thomas Babington, *Select Essays,* Allyn
McCord, David T. W., *Oddly Enough,* Washburn & Thomas,
 1927
McFee, William, *Harbours of Memory,* Doubleday, 1921
 Swallowing the Anchor, Doubleday, 1925
Macy, John Albert, *The Spirit of American Literature,* Modern
 Library
Marquis, Don, *Prefaces,* Appleton, 1919
Mencken, Henry Louis, *Prejudices,* Knopf, 1924–27. 5 vols.
Milne, Alan Alexander, *If I May,* Dutton, 1921
 Not That It Matters, Dutton, 1925

Morley, Christopher Darlington, *Forty-four Essays*, Harcourt, 1925
    Mince Pie, Doubleday, 1919
    Pipefuls, Doubleday, 1920
    Plum Pudding, Doubleday, 1921
    comp., *Modern Essays*, Harcourt, 1921–24. 2 vols.
Morris, Mrs. Elisabeth (Woodbridge), *Days Out and Other Papers*, Houghton, 1917
Nevinson, Henry Wood, *Essays in Freedom and Rebellion*, Yale University Press, 1921
    Farewell to America, Viking Press, 1922
Newton, Alfred Edward, *The Amenities of Book-Collecting*, Little, 1918
Nicholson, Meredith, *The Provincial American*, Houghton, 1912
    The Valley of Democracy, Scribner, 1918
Palmer, George Herbert, *Self-Cultivation in English*, Houghton, 1909
Pearson, Edmund Lester, *Books in Black or Red*, Macmillan, 1923
Perry, Bliss, *The American Mind*, Houghton, 1912
Phelps, William Lyon, *As I Like It*, Scribner, 1923–24. 2 vols.
    Essays on Modern Dramatists, 1920–21, Macmillan. 2 vols.
    ed., *Essays of Robert Louis Stevenson*, Scribner, 1910
    What I Like, Scribner, 1933
Powys, Llewelyn, *Black Laughter*, Harcourt, 1924
Reese, Lizette Woodworth, *A Victorian Village*, Farrar, 1929
    York Road, Farrar, 1931
Repplier, Agnes, *Americans and Others*, Houghton
    Essays in Idleness, Houghton, 1893
    Essays in Miniature, Houghton
    Points of Friction, Houghton, 1920
Roosevelt, Theodore, *American Ideals and other Essays*, Putnam, 1920
    The Strenuous Life, Century, 1900. (*See also* Hagedorn, Hermann.)
Ruskin, John, *Sesame and Lilies*, Burt. (There are many editions.)
Santayana, George, *Soliloquies in England and later Soliloquies*, Scribner, 1922
Sharp, Dallas Lore, *The Face of the Fields*, Houghton, 1911
    The Magical Chance, Houghton, 1923
    Sanctuary! Sanctuary! Harper, 1926
    Watcher in the Woods, Century, 1903

Sherman, Stuart Pratt, *Americans,* Scribner, 1922
    Genius of America, Scribner, 1923
Smith, Logan Pearsall, *More Trivia,* Harcourt, 1921
    Trivia, Doubleday, 1917
    All Trivia, Harcourt, 1934
Stevenson, Robert Louis, *An Inland Voyage,* Scribner, 1903
    Travels with a Donkey, Scribner, 1905
Strunsky, Simeon, *Belshazzar Court,* Holt, 1914
    Sinbad and His Friends, Holt, 1921
Taintor, Sarah Augusta, and Monro, K. M., eds., *The Book of Modern Letters,* Macmillan, 1933
Tanner, William Maddux, ed., *Essays and Essay-Writing,* Little, 1917
    and Tanner, Mrs. Daisie, eds., *Modern Familiar Essays,* Little, 1929
Thomas, Charles Wright, ed., *Essays in Contemporary Civilization,* Macmillan, 1931
Thoreau, Henry David, *Camping in the Maine Woods,* Houghton
    Walden, Houghton
Tomlinson, Henry Major, *Gifts of Fortune and Hints for Those about to Travel,* Harper, 1926
    Old Junk, Knopf, 1923
Van Doren, Carl Clinton, *Contemporary American Novelists,* Macmillan, 1922
Van Dyke, Henry, *Camp Fires and Guide Posts,* Scribner, 1921
    Companionable Books, Scribner, 1922
    Days Off, and Other Digressions, Scribner, 1907
Walter, Erich Albert, ed., *Essay Annual, 1933,* Scott, 1933
Warner, Charles Dudley, *In the Wilderness,* Houghton, 1906
    My Summer in a Garden, Houghton, 1898
Warner, Frances Lester (Mrs. Mayo Dyer-Hersey), *Endicott and I,* Houghton, 1919
    Groups and Couples, Houghton, 1923
    Surprising the Family and Other Peradventures, Houghton, 1926
    The Unintentional Charm of Men, Houghton, 1928
White, Stewart Edward, *The Cabin,* Doubleday, 1911
    The Forest, Doubleday
Wilson, Woodrow, *Mere Literature,* Houghton, 1913
    When a Man Comes to Himself, Harper, 1915
Yeomans, Edward, *Shackled Youth,* Little, 1921

READING LISTS ACCORDING TO TYPES

NOTE. — Here are some essays classified as to type. The list may be helpful to the teacher or the student who wishes to emphasize a study by types. It is obvious, of course, that some of these essays might be included under more than one type.

PERSONAL OR FAMILIAR

A Young Desperado, T. B. Aldrich
Like Summer's Cloud, C. S. Brooks
The Furrows, G. K. Chesterton
My Chateaux, G. W. Curtis
Of Good and Evil Odours, David Grayson
My Last Walk with the Schoolmistress, O. W. Holmes
The Death of an Old Dog, W. H. Hudson
Three Days to See, Helen Adams Keller
Mackery End in Hertfordshire, Charles Lamb
Old China, Charles Lamb
Fires, E. V. Lucas
Which Class? Mary C. Robinson
A College Magazine, R. L. Stevenson
Ordered South, R. L. Stevenson
In Belshazzar Court, Simeon Strunsky
Romance, Simeon Strunsky
I Get a Colt to Break in, Lincoln Steffens
Who Owns the Mountains? Henry Van Dyke
Christmas, C. D. Warner
Juvuntus Mundi, C. D. Warner
Giving as a Luxury, C. D. Warner
Love's Minor Frictions, F. L. Warner

REFLECTIVE

Of Superstition, Francis Bacon
Of Suspicion, Francis Bacon
Of Great Place, Francis Bacon
Of Travel, Francis Bacon
Courage, J. M. Barrie
The Transition from School to College, LeB. R. Briggs
The Man Who Thinks Backwards, G. K. Chesterton

The Evolution of the Gentleman, S. M. Crothers
Compensation, R. W. Emerson
Manners, R. W. Emerson
The Art of Procuring Pleasant Dreams, Benjamin Franklin
The Art of Book-Making, Washington Irving
The Student Life, William Osler
The Mission of Humour, Agnes Repplier
Woman Enthroned, Agnes Repplier
On War, George Santayana
Epigrams, Jonathan Swift
Fair Play and Democracy, Henry Van Dyke
The Soul of a People, Henry Van Dyke
Is the World Growing Better? Henry Van Dyke
What Is a College For? Woodrow Wilson

DESCRIPTIVE

The Jungle Sluggard, William Beebe
The Wit of a Duck, John Burroughs
Animal Communication, John Burroughs
A Beaver's Reason, John Burroughs
April Odors, John Burroughs
Nature Lore, John Burroughs
The Plains of Patagonia, W. H. Hudson
Geese, W. H. Hudson
Follow Your Nose, David Grayson
The Hall of the Ambassadors, Washington Irving
Silverspot, the Story of a Crow, Ernest T. Seton
The Springfield Fox, Ernest T. Seton
Turtle Eggs for Agassiz, D. L. Sharp
The Scarcity of Skunks, D. L. Sharp
Hunting the Snow, D. L. Sharp
The Face of the Fields, D. L. Sharp
The Wild Mother, D. L. Sharp
The Sea Fogs, R. L. Stevenson
The Battle of the Ants, H. D. Thoreau
Brute Neighbors, H. D. Thoreau
Walden Pond, H. D. Thoreau

CHARACTER SKETCH

The Heroic Age, Joseph Conrad
Joan of Arc, Thomas De Quincey

The Man in Black, Oliver Goldsmith
My Mother, Lizette Woodworth Reese
The Spirit of Theodore Roosevelt, Julian Street
The Hunter's Family, R. L. Stevenson
An Adventurer in a Velvet Jacket, Henry Van Dyke
Abraham Lincoln, Woodrow Wilson

CRITICAL

Books, A. C. Benson
Coddling in Education, H. S. Canby
Poetry for the Unpoetical, H. S. Canby
On the Knocking at the Gate in " Macbeth,"
Thomas De Quincey
Oliver Wendell Holmes, W. D. Howells
Studies of Lowell, W. D. Howells
Defense of Poetry, H. W. Longfellow
Bunyan's " Pilgrim's Progress," T. B. Macaulay
American Literature, John Macy
Mark Twain, John Macy
The Philosophy of Composition, E. A. Poe
What and How to Read, John Ruskin
Sterne and Goldsmith, W. M. Thackeray

EDITORIAL

Female Orators, Joseph Addison
Living in a Pair of Scales, Joseph Addison
America and the English Tradition, Harry Morgan Ayres
Column Left, Stuart Chase
Why Do so Many Men Never Amount to Anything,
T. A. Edison
Dwight W. Morrow, Walter Lippmann
Our Responsibilities as a Nation, Theodore Roosevelt
The Stage Coach, Richard Steele
To an Anxious Friend, W. A. White

HUMOROUS

A Young Desperado, Thomas Bailey Aldrich
On Drawing, A. P. Herbert
Table Talk, Oliver Wendell Holmes

A, B, and C — The Human Element in Mathematics,
Stephen Leacock
The Decline of the Drama, Stephen Leacock
Which Class? Mary C. Robinson
What Do Boys Know? Alfred G. Rolfe
Fenimore Cooper's Literary Offenses, Mark Twain
Traveling with a Reformer, Mark Twain
Love's Minor Frictions, Frances Lester Warner

ACKNOWLEDGMENTS

In addition to the assistance given by one hundred teachers who answered the questionnaire on essayists to be studied in high schools, I want to express my appreciation of the aid given me by the following teachers who tried out in 1926 a special trial edition of *Essays Old and New* in their classes:

Miss Mabel Goddard, Technical High School, Indianapolis, Indiana.

Miss Mary Hargrave, Central High School, Madison, Wisconsin.

Miss Jeannette Marsh, Central High School, Madison, Wisconsin.

Miss J. Grace Walker, J. Sterling Morton High School, Cicero, Illinois.

Mr. William N. Otto, Shortridge High School, Indianapolis, Indiana.

Miss Agnes A. Cawley, High School, Bayonne, New Jersey.

Miss Mellie John, High School, Rockford, Illinois.

Miss Katharine E. Moog and Members of the English Department, Eastern High School, Baltimore, Maryland.

Mr. Merrill P. Paine, Director of English, Elizabeth, New Jersey.

Miss Amy L. Weeks, High School, New Haven, Connecticut.

Dr. Ella Warner, High School, New Haven, Connecticut.

Miss Marion Sheridan, High School, New Haven, Connecticut.

Miss Minnie Farrer, High School, Sheboygan, Wisconsin.

Miss M. P. Eaton and Members of the English Department, Wadleigh High School, New York City.

Miss Margaret Dixon, Lindblom High School, Chicago, Illinois.

Miss E. B. Rogers, High School, South Manchester, Connecticut.

Miss J. S. Taylor, Girls Commercial High School, Brooklyn, New York.